PLUNDERED

ALSO BY BERNADETTE ATUAHENE

*We Want What's Ours: Learning from South Africa's
Land Restitution Program*

PLUNDERED

HOW RACIST POLICIES UNDERMINE
BLACK HOMEOWNERSHIP IN AMERICA

Bernadette Atuahene

LITTLE, BROWN AND COMPANY
New York   Boston   London

Little, Brown and Company
Hachette Book Group
1290 Avenue of the Americas, New York, NY 10104
littlebrown.com

First Edition: January 2025

Little, Brown and Company is a division of Hachette Book Group, Inc.
The Little, Brown name and logo are trademarks of Hachette Book Group, Inc.

The publisher is not responsible for websites (or their content) that are not owned by the publisher.

The Hachette Speakers Bureau provides a wide range of authors for speaking events. To find out more, go to hachettespeakersbureau.com or email HachetteSpeakers@hbgusa.com.

Little, Brown and Company books may be purchased in bulk for business, educational, or promotional use. For information, please contact your local bookseller or the Hachette Book Group Special Markets Department at special.markets@hbgusa.com.

Print book interior designed by Bart Dawson.

ISBN 9780316572217
Library of Congress Control Number: 2024946949

Printing 2, 2025

LSC-C

Printed in the United States of America

For my parents, Beatrice Achampong and Kofi Kwarteng Atuahene.
I thank you for your fierce love and protection.
May your souls continue to rest in perfect peace and power.

CONTENTS

CONTENTS

PART IV:
GOVERNMENT ENTITIES THAT PROFIT FROM RACIST POLICIES:
THE GRANDSON'S PLAN

THIS HOUSE MEANS EVERYTHING TO ME

Ms. Mae, born in 1945 as Anna Mae Jackson, has lived in Detroit her entire life. Distinguished by her soft silver Afro, dark sun-kissed skin, paisley walking stick, and radiant smile, she says she never allows her troubles to steal her joy, and loves "talking spicy" in order to make folks laugh. Ms. Mae most looks forward to the summertime, when she can be out on her spacious porch, chatting with her neighbors for hours on end.

"I've been in this house for fifty years," Ms. Mae explained from her customary seat on the porch. "At one time I didn't feel safe 'cause somebody climbed in my bedroom window. It was morning time, in broad open daylight. I was sitting up here in the front room and when I looked up and seen this man standing in my hallway, I started shooting at him. He left the sole of his shoe in my bed, and he went out through the alley." In 1970, when Ms. Mae first moved in, there was an icehouse behind her property that attracted significant foot traffic and all manner of people from outside the area, including the intruder. Ms. Mae continued, "But since then, I've had no problems and feel safe in my house."

Despite the slow decline of the American auto industry and the economic chaos that this brought to Detroit's doorstep, Ms. Mae's community has remained vibrant for much of the fifty-plus years she has resided there. Today, however, her neighborhood — once full of conversation partners, warmth, and verve — has become desolate. There are now twice as many vacant lots overgrown with brush as occupied homes. An outside observer might reasonably come to the conclusion that a devastating fire visited the block, or a capricious tornado tore away some homes and left others standing. But the blight that has eviscerated Ms. Mae's neighborhood, and indeed much of Detroit, is a man-made disaster, one with a surprising cause: illegally inflated property taxes.

One study found that between 2009 and 2015, the City of Detroit inflated the market value of 53 to 84 percent of its homes, violating the Michigan Constitution's rules on how to properly calculate property taxes.[1] Additionally, a *Detroit News* investigation found that between 2010 and 2016, the City of Detroit overtaxed homeowners by at least $600 million. And of the 63,000 Detroit homes with delinquent tax debt in 2019, the City overtaxed about 90 percent of them. Systematic overtaxation has caused an enormous transfer of wealth from homeowners in this majority-Black city to government coffers.[2]

Though the City of Detroit overvalued Ms. Mae's home for years and her low income qualified her for an exemption from paying property taxes altogether, she had no way of knowing this. Nowhere on the official property tax notice mailed to homeowners does it tell them how to determine the market value the City has assigned to their home. The City also did not advertise the exemption, and even when low-income homeowners did find out about it, the City blocked access by erecting unnecessary barriers.

It is then no surprise that Ms. Mae and thousands of other cash-strapped residents could not pay their property taxes. Three years after a homeowner fails to pay off all the property taxes, fines, fees, and interest for any particular year, the County places the dreaded yellow bag on their door, announcing the home's impending tax foreclosure to all passersby. Ms. Mae had not paid her 2018 property tax debt, so she had a yellow bag attached to her door in

2020, warning that she was in danger of tax foreclosure in 2021. Seeing it, she prayed, "Lord, don't make me lose my house." Ms. Mae then said, "I hurried up and snatched it off so didn't nobody see it because I didn't want them to know I hadn't paid my taxes. Then, as I looked down the street, everybody had them on their houses. It made me feel a little relieved, but I still had to pay my taxes some kind of way."

Since unfairly calculated property taxes disproportionately affect Detroit's most depressed neighborhoods, yellow bags dangling on these doors in October have become as common as Christmas lights hanging from roofs in December. Even worse, Detroit has had more property tax foreclosures than any other American city since the Great Depression. As of 2009, the local government has confiscated one in three homes, robbing over a hundred thousand families of wealth, stability, and the relationships they have developed with neighbors over decades. While Detroit's number of Black homeowners in 1970 was 41 percent above the national rate,[3] today the local government is robbing residents of the wealth their predecessors fought hard to acquire and pass down, exacerbating the racial wealth gap, which is already severe: in 2022, the median white family held $285,000 in wealth, and this number was $61,600 for Hispanic families, and only $44,900 for Black families.[4]

Ms. Mae's experience exemplifies this trend. To become homeowners, her parents, Sam and Ida Jackson, had to sidestep several pitfalls that commonly prevented Blacks from purchasing homes in the twentieth century. Now, in the twenty-first century, property tax injustice threatens to rob Ms. Mae of her shingled legacy.

The Jackson family's homeownership journey began when Sam and Ida, childhood sweethearts from rural Georgia, wed as teenagers in 1930. Because Sam's uncle and granduncle had both education and land, white vigilantes murdered them for being uppity and not knowing their place, hanging them in their front yard to send a ruthless message to other Blacks. With the compliance of religious, political, and other societal leaders, whites lynched about thirty-five hundred Blacks in the United States between 1895 and 1968.[5] Because Southern whites routinely lynched Blacks for defying their subordinate position in society, and afterward sat down for dinner with their families, praying over their food, in 1937, Sam gathered his bride; his only brother, Johnny; and his family and drove to Detroit, never looking back. The Jackson family joined millions of other African Americans escaping the South's racial terrorism to head North, hoping to secure dignity and lucrative jobs in Detroit's auto industry.

Sam and Johnny eventually obtained jobs at Ford Motor Company's foundry, where workers poured molten metal into molds to cast engines and other car parts. It was dangerous work. But it was far more profitable than sharecropping, allowing the brothers to build their families. Johnny and his wife had seven children, and Sam and his wife had a daughter, Mae, and adopted their orphaned nephew, Jasper.

Sam and Ida were, however, homesick and eager to reconnect with the family they had left behind. In the early 1950s, when factory workers went on strike, Sam and Ida used this opportunity to take their daughter and nephew back home to Georgia for the very first time. Ms. Mae was only about eight years old, and what she remembers best was a terrifying run-in with her aunt's chickens.

"I was just sitting there, looking at them feed the chickens," Ms. Mae began, her face suffused with a mischievous smile. "And a chicken came after me. The chicken was trying to get me! So I ran up the steps, I crawled up my mother's body, and I was on top of my mama's shoulder." Shifting into full body-rocking laughter, Ms. Mae continued, "I can still remember her telling me, 'Get off me, you damn fool!' 'cause I had torn the front of her dress off of her." Ms. Mae did not have to tolerate those spiteful chickens for too long, because just a few days after they arrived, Uncle Johnny called her dad to let him know that the strike was over and he needed to return to work.

Although they sorely missed their families, Sam and Ida happily traded Georgia's red-clay dirt and spacious fields for Detroit's black pavement and congested housing.

To accommodate their thirteen-person extended family, the brothers rented a three-bedroom house on Brewster Street in a bustling Black community known as the Hastings Street neighborhood. "That's where all the happening was at. The prostitutes, the pimps, the shows," Ms. Mae said. "You had the colored grocery store, the Dave and Ms. Queen grocery store. You had Louie's grocery store. You had a shoeshine shop on the corner. Then Victor's had the clothing store. We had the movie theater. We had the bars. We had a skating rink up over the grocery store. We had Brewster Recreation Center there with a swimming pool and the best women basketball champions that came out of it." As the memories overtook her, Ms. Mae paused for a long moment. "It was nice."

Despite the fact that Hastings Street was a neighborhood rich in social cohesion, a place where people looked out for one another and neighbors became chosen family, outsiders viewed it as a slum. This was because both the federal government and financial institutions designated these Black communities as high credit risks, drawing red lines around them on their official maps. This process, later known as redlining, prevented the inflow of financial services like mortgages, insurance, and home improvement loans. Without the funds to invest in upkeep, dilapidated buildings and other squalid conditions were the inevitable result.

But for Ms. Mae, Hastings Street was not a slum. It was home. It was the place where she grew up, attended school, found her first love, and experienced her first heartbreak when he left her for another woman. While Ms. Mae was nursing her broken heart, Walter, the next-door neighbor with two grown children, began courting her. They fell in love. After six months of dating, they married, and because Walter was forty-five years old and Ms. Mae was only nineteen, Sam and Ida were furious when they found out.

"They didn't like him cause he was nasty talking. He ain't have no respect for nobody. What come up, come out," Ms. Mae described. "They knew him from years back, from on the streets. He called himself being half pimp." After a long pause, she continued, "Yeah, he was a humdinger."

Before the nuptials, local authorities announced their urban renewal program, which would bulldoze the Hastings Street community to construct the Interstate 75 Chrysler Expressway. By the time construction finished in 1964, the Hastings Street neighborhood — with all its valuable, time-worn relationships, social capital, and dynamic businesses — had vanished. Blacks relocated to homes and apartments in the inner-city neighborhoods that whites were fleeing. Suburban communities were off-limits due to racial covenants: legal agreements created by homeowners and developers that prohibited Blacks from occupying certain homes.

"Everybody had to move, and so they found this house I am in now out here on Devine Street in 1965 and paid nine thousand five hundred dollars for it," Ms. Mae explained. "My father always had a new car, but this was the first time they bought a house." The house, built in 1923 on the City's east side, was a one-and-a-half-story bungalow covered in white wood shingles, with four bedrooms, two full bathrooms, and one half bathroom. The home's most prized features were its capacious porch, which extended the entire length of the home, and the enclosed garage, where Sam parked his treasured Buick Wildcat, a two-door gray beauty.

Like Sam, most of the breadwinners on his new street worked in the auto industry. Although Blacks and whites worked side by side on assembly lines, it was not common for them to live next door to each other, so Ida and Sam were only the second Black family on the block. "Mr. Fred and Ms. Fanny, they were the Italians next door. Mary and Bill across the street, they was hillbillies. Mr. Summa and them, they was Italian," Ms. Mae remembered. "They were all white, but they were different denominations of countries." There was never racial tension between the Black newcomers and white old-timers on the block. Everyone got along swimmingly.

Nevertheless, when more Black homeowners started buying in the neighborhood, in a phenomenon called blockbusting, real estate agents and other intermediaries began convincing white homeowners that the arrival of their Black neighbors would tank their home values. This prompted the white families to sell quickly and at fire-sale prices. The intermediaries then sold those homes to Blacks at a significant markup, securing morally questionable profits. As a result, although the Jacksons were only the second Black family on the block, within five years, there was only one white family left.

Detroit's 1967 Uprising — one of twentieth-century America's largest civil disturbances — caused many remaining white homeowners and white business owners to desert the city, further depleting the tax base and economically crippling neighborhoods. "Me and my husband were living on Parker when the riot started. They was tearing up everything," Ms. Mae said. "We went home and we was there for about four, five days 'cause we couldn't get out 'cause of the national guard and everybody was riding through the streets with their guns and on the army trucks."

Although whites decamped to the suburbs, Ida and Sam stayed. "They stayed because, at the time, they didn't have no place to go," Ms. Mae said. Blacks had very limited housing mobility, so Devine Street became Ms. Mae and her family's permanent home. "That house means everything to me 'cause my parents bought it for me. They bought it for them, but it was for me because they knew I had to have somewhere to live because my husband wasn't nothing," Ms. Mae said. "He was one of them husbands didn't want to work. He wasn't paying no bills. He wanted the woman to work to take care of him."

Five years after purchasing the Devine Street home, Sam died in a car crash. Ms. Mae and her husband left their apartment and moved into the home to care for Ida, whose grief over her husband's recent death was exacerbating her existing heart condition. Since

Ida's health was quickly deteriorating, she began to worry about how her children would fare if she died. To give them added security, she tried to pay off the home loan, giving the lender, Auer Mortgage, $5,000 in cash, about half of what they had paid for it five years earlier. Surprisingly, the company told Ida that her bulk payment covered only the mortgage interest and not the principal. Even though Ida knew that this did not make sense, she did not have the resources or specialized knowledge to fight the mortgage company.

Four short months after Ms. Mae and Walter moved in, Ida literally died of a broken heart. Ms. Mae and her cousin Jasper inherited the home on Devine Street. After paying $97 per month, in 1974, they finished paying off the mortgage. Ms. Mae and Jasper did not know that in 1976, the National Bank of Royal Oak filed suit against David Auer, the owner of Auer Mortgage, for mismanaging mortgages that the bank had contracted his company to service.[6] Then, in 1983, Michigan's attorney general, Frank Kelley, filed a consumer protection lawsuit against Auer Mortgage and a group of other firms.[7] Months later, Auer was found stuffed in the trunk of his Mercedes-Benz, forcing Kelley to drop the investigation. Word on the street was that Auer's shady dealings had finally caught up with him.[8] Since Auer's victims never had their day in court, Ms. Mae never even knew about any of this.

Although they were forced to pay off a predatory mortgage loan, Ms. Mae and Jasper owned their inheritance free and clear. But with Walter in the house, they did not feel free. He beat Ms. Mae relentlessly, drew a gun on Jasper, and threatened to burn down the house with both Ms. Mae and Jasper inside. Of all the abuse, Ms. Mae most vividly remembered how Walter humiliated her the night he took her to an Emanuel Laskey concert on the city's west side.

Laskey, who like Ms. Mae was born in 1945, was an African American soul singer known for his 1977 song whose plaintive chorus declared: "I'd rather leave on my feet than live on my knees, darling. I'd rather leave on my feet than continue to live on my knees."

The lyrics struck a chord with Ms. Mae, describing her bitter marriage better than she could with her own words. Basking in the moment, she began swaying, laughing, and singing along. "I said, 'Sing Emanuel, sing.' Next thing I know I got hit upside the head. I couldn't even enjoy a concert. He said, 'You don't be laughing and telling no other goddamn nigga to sing and dance in front of me.'" Walter did not allow Ms. Mae to have even simple joys. She was living in hell.

In 1986, after twenty-four years of marriage, Walter was shot to death. "I did it," Ms. Mae soberly explained. "He came home and tried to jump on me. I was sitting there watching TV, and he pulled his shotgun to shoot me, and so I got it, and I shot him." Deflated, she added, "It was either him or me." In the following weeks, Ms. Mae stood trial for the murder of her husband.

Ms. Mae could only afford a neophyte lawyer, with her case being just the second of his entire career. To finance her defense, she took a $10,000 lien on her home. After a short trial, the jury acquitted her of all charges. It was not, however, until ten years later that she was able to pay off her legal debt and remove the lien.

Walter's death gave Ms. Mae a new lease on life. But lurking around the corner, waiting to pounce on her, were new tragedies. In 1994, she injured her shoulder while lifting a patient at the nursing home where she worked. Even after the doctors completed major surgery, Ms. Mae still did not have full use of her shoulder. To make matters worse, the following year, when her shoulder was still in a sling, Ms. Mae went down to drain her flooded basement, slipped, and injured her spine. She would never work again.

With scant income, there was no money for the home repairs that the Devine Street home sorely needed. "My roof got holes. My kitchen and bathroom ceiling is leaking. It's coming down in there. The ceiling fell in the basement from the roof leaking," she explained. "When the flood came, it messed up my basement, my washer and dryer, and the furnace, and the hot water tank. Now I don't have hot water. I have to boil it."

This type of structural deterioration was not affecting Ms. Mae alone. It was happening to homes up and down Devine Street because, for decades, redlining deprived homeowners of access to home repair loans and other capital. Then, during the Great Recession, predatory mortgage loans and the accompanying mortgage foreclosure crisis decreased home values in these same redlined areas even further. Consequently, the cost of home repairs often exceeded the home's value, leaving these homeowners' children and grandchildren to inherit money pits instead of assets, further undermining intergenerational wealth. After a cost-benefit analysis, many walked away from their ramshackle patrimonies.

As Devine Street has declined, there has been a dramatic rise in the number of vacant, unmowed lots with grass as tall as trees. Although Ms. Mae lives in the middle of the city, it feels more like a forest, and the wild rooster patrolling the neighborhood is proof positive. Several neighbors had complained that this feathered stud was gallivanting through the streets, crowing at full volume in the early-morning hours, climbing and scratching cars with its sharp claws, running through their yards, and wreaking general havoc.

"I was home and he was sitting on top of my neighbor's car. And when I seen that rooster, it took me back to my first trip to Georgia," Ms. Mae remarked, smiling. "The rooster had done got off the car and was lying in front of the car at the side door, like he was talking to the car. Just standing talking, and I'm peeking out the door. I was scared to come out, but had to go to the doctor, so I had to get out. I got my crooked butt on down the step with my stick in my hand. He sat there and he looked at me and I looked at him. And I said, 'Please, Lord, don't let this chicken come over here 'cause he's gonna die. He gonna die this morning.'" Her body rocking with laughter, Ms. Mae continued, "He didn't mess with me and I ain't seen him no more. I don't know if he dead and gone or somebody done cooked him. If they done cooked him, they got one tough meal."

Although Devine Street has transitioned from a bustling area full of people to a desolate place where roosters roam, in 2023 the City of Detroit taxed Ms. Mae's home as if it were worth $31,200, an amount far higher than it could ever sell for on the open market. What's worse is that Ms. Mae's parents purchased the home in 1965 for $9,500, which, adjusted for inflation, is about $92,500 in 2023 dollars. Instead of increasing, her home's value decreased. Under normal circumstances, over time, ownership creates wealth because the market value of a home rises and the equity also rises as homeowners pay off their mortgage. Homeowners can pass this wealth to subsequent generations, who gain an advantage when they combine these inheritances with money they are able to generate on their own. This is not how it turned out for Ms. Mae and her neighbors, however.

This is in stark contrast to the suburban communities where Mr. Fred, Ms. Fannie, Mr. Summa, and the other whites who once lived on Devine Street fled in the 1960s. In 2020, the median home value in Grosse Pointe was between $300,000 and $399,999; in Livonia it was between $200,000 and $249,999; in Dearborn it was between $150,000 and $174,999; and in Warren it was between $125,000 and $149,999. Detroit's median home value, however, was only between $50,000 and $59,999.[9] Racial covenants tucked into the deeds of suburban homes kept Blacks out, denying them the opportunity to live in homes that increased in value over the years instead of decreasing.

Ms. Mae's story is plagued by several overlapping *racist policies* — more imprecisely known as structural or systemic racism — *which are any written and unwritten laws and processes that produce or sustain racial inequity.*[10] While racist policies such as racial covenants, urban renewal, redlining, blockbusting, predatory mortgage lending, and, most recently, illegally inflated property tax assessments undermined Ms. Mae's ability to accumulate assets, blame falls on the things that are most visible: the homeowners themselves. That is, due to their own "irresponsibility" or "ignorance," homeowners are presumed culpable and thus deserving of their hardships. Therefore, the State's role is to fix the people by providing services like financial management classes or soft-skills training. Meanwhile, racist policies, the true culprit, vanish into the background.

Using data from over eight years of research on the property tax foreclosure crisis in Detroit—including over two hundred interviews with homeowners, real estate investors, and policymakers, as well as participation in a grassroots movement for property tax justice—this book reveals and gives a name to an overlooked but widespread phenomenon: predatory governance, which is when local governments intentionally or unintentionally raise public dollars through racist policies.

Our national conversations about racism accelerated when cell phone footage captured violent images of police officers murdering Trayvon Martin, Sandra Bland, George Floyd, and other Black people. *Plundered* seeks to shift the focus of our nation's racial justice conversation from the *physical violence* that state agents exert to the less conspicuous but intensely damaging *bureaucratic violence* that they routinely inflict through racist policies like those that have harmed Ms. Mae and her neighbors. The story of Devine Street, the story of Detroit, and indeed the stories of many other cities across the U.S. are, in fact, tales of predatory governance.

To understand why and how public officials replenished public accounts through laws and processes that produce racial inequity, and how these racist policies arose, flourished, and devastated individuals and families, this book begins with a tale of two grandfathers: Grandpa Bucci, who is white, and Grandpa Brown, who is Black. From the time these sharecroppers arrived in Detroit in the early 1900s to look for work at Ford, a series of overlapping racist policies, beginning with racial covenants and ending with illegally inflated property taxes, dramatically altered their family trajectories. Although both grandfathers came from poverty and worked hard to acquire the homes they passed down to their respective grandchildren, Robert Ficano, Grandpa Bucci's grandson, inherited a valuable asset, while Myrisha Brown, Grandpa Brown's granddaughter, inherited a money pit that the local government put on the auction block because she failed to pay her illegally inflated property taxes. Through the lives of these two Detroit families, readers will come to understand both the architecture of predatory governance and its consequences.

Though this book is focused on the specific laws of one city, predatory governance is a national problem that plays out through a variety of public policies and private practices, affecting many other U.S. cities with a large African American presence, including Ferguson, Missouri; Washington D.C.; New Orleans; and Chicago.

In Ferguson, for example, the U.S. Department of Justice's 2015 report showed that the police department violated the U.S. Constitution's First, Fourth, and Fourteenth Amendments by targeting African Americans, unfairly subjecting them to excessive fines and fees for traffic and parking tickets, as well as housing code violations. In 2013 alone, Ferguson courts issued over nine thousand arrest warrants when victims failed to pay their accumulated debts, although the relevant legislation did not contemplate jail time for the underlying infractions.[11] In doing so, the Ferguson police and courts prioritized raising city revenues over securing public safety.

Civil forfeiture laws allow police to seize property that they suspect was involved in a crime without charging owners for violating any laws. The Washington D.C. police department abused this law by requiring property owners to post bonds of up to $2,500 to get their property back. When impoverished property owners, who were overwhelmingly racial minorities, did not have the required funds, D.C. officials, in a gross violation of due process, took title to their property, profiting around $4.8 million between 2010 and 2012 alone.[12] When, in *Brown v. District of Columbia*, the D.C. Public

Defender Service filed suit on behalf of 375 car owners, the court ruled in favor of the plaintiffs, and local politicians agreed to reform D.C.'s wayward practices.

Since the Orleans Parish Criminal District Court used court debts to fund itself, it aggressively collected them. In the process, the court frequently failed to examine defendants' ability to pay court debts prior to jailing them for nonpayment. In 2018, a U.S. federal district court ruled that this practice, which disproportionately affected racial minorities, violated the Fourteenth Amendment because it revived the very debtors' prisons that our nation outlawed long ago.[13]

A Pulitzer Prize–nominated *Chicago Tribune* series found that homes in minority neighborhoods on the south and west sides of Chicago were paying effective tax rates twice as high as those in wealthier, predominantly white neighborhoods on the north side.[14] This inequity violated the law, which since 2011 has required the assessed value of all residential properties in Cook County to be 10 percent of their market values.[15] Additionally, a national study by Professors Avenancio-León and Howard used panel data covering 118 million U.S. homes and found that Black and Hispanic homeowners pay, on average, a 10 to 13 percent higher property tax rate than whites, and for the median Black or Hispanic homeowner, this translates into an extra $300 to $400 annually.[16]

Whether it is targeted tickets and fines in Ferguson, abuses of civil forfeiture in Washington D.C., jailing defendants for court debts in New Orleans, or inequitable property taxation in Chicago and a slew of other cities, American cities routinely replenish public accounts by bleeding Black and brown citizens, further widening the racial wealth gap. To bring this national phenomenon to light and give voice to those affected, like Ms. Mae, *Plundered* unearths and dissects the racist policies undergirding Detroit's property tax foreclosure crisis.

PART I:

THE ORIGIN OF RACIST POLICIES

A Tale of Two Grandfathers

1

THE RISE OF TWO SHARECROPPERS

Tommie Brown Jr., affectionately known in his later years as Grandpa Brown, was born on a North Carolina farm in 1901. A mere thirty-six years earlier, the American Civil War concluded, legally ending chattel slavery and destroying the chains that bound his grandparents, who were both born enslaved. The former slaveholders nevertheless forced most Blacks to continue working the land under exploitative sharecropping arrangements, the South's primary mode of agricultural production after slavery.[1]

Tommie Sr. and Louella, Grandpa Brown's parents, were share-croppers who lived in Newton Grove, forty-five miles from North Carolina's capital. With their twelve children, the couple worked the former slave master's land. As it had been in the antebellum era, the former slave owner did not pay Tommie and Louella a salary for their labor. Instead, he loaned them money to pay for land rents and farming implements that they were obligated to purchase from him. They were also required to sell their harvest to him at the price he determined.

In slavery's new iteration, indebtedness replaced brute violence. Exploitation persisted. When sharecroppers could not escape debilitating cycles of debt, they were portrayed as stupid, lazy, and criminal. Their accumulated debts and abject poverty were depicted as a product of their moral shortcomings rather than the inherent unfairness of the sharecropping arrangements.[2] The comments made by a distinguished colonel in 1871 well illustrate this point. "Even these systems (the laborer receiving a portion of the crop)," the colonel said. "Do not afford sufficient incentive to the negroes to be industrious and as a consequence the result often proves unprofitable to the planter and to the laborer." He continued, "The negroes are, as a class, lazy and thriftless, working only when driven to it by necessity."[3] This narrative of personal irresponsibility would play on repeat for generations to come, drowning out discussions about structural injustice.

For Blacks who challenged the legal, political, and social inequalities of the day, castigation was swift and savage. A common punishment was lynching, a form of public torture and murder often deployed when Blacks dared to resist their subordinate station in society. Grandpa Brown drew his very first breath in a society where lynchings were rampant. Between 1880 and 1900, North Carolina recorded fifty-eight lynching victims, forty-five of whom were African American.[4] North Carolina, however, was not alone. Throughout the nation, whites lynched nearly eight hundred Blacks between 1900 and 1909, but only ninety-five whites in the same ten-year period.[5] Racial violence upheld America's caste system.

Even the president of the United States could not escape the racial caste system's entangling web. In 1901, the year Grandpa Brown was born, President Theodore Roosevelt invited a former slave, Booker T. Washington, to the White House for a meal to discuss the Republican Party's Southern strategy.[6] This simple act, viewed as a seditious suggestion of social equality, provoked immediate Southern backlash. The *Memphis Scimitar* reported that when Roosevelt "invited a nigger to dine with him at the White House" he committed the "most damnable outrage which has ever been perpetrated by any citizen of the United States." The *New Orleans Picayune* wrote that the president was "the worst enemy to his race of any white man who has ever occupied so high a place in this republic." The *Macon Telegraph* in Georgia asserted that God erected the barrier between the races and "no President of this or any country can break it down."[7] Adding to the frenzy, Ben Tillman, a former governor of South Carolina, then serving as one of the state's U.S. senators, declared that "the action of President Roosevelt in entertaining that nigger will necessitate our killing a thousand niggers in the South before they will learn their place again."[8] President Roosevelt had unintentionally fanned the flame of equality, and outraged Southern whites enthusiastically extinguished it.

Racial subjugation was not, however, exclusively a Southern problem. No city in America went untouched by the racial caste system. Northern cities preferred to keep African Americans in their place by relying primarily (but not exclusively) on legal violence such as racial covenants found in deeds, rather than lynchings in the public square. In search of reprieve from the South and its physical violence, Jim Crow laws, and exploitative sharecropping arrangements, between 1910 and 1940, 1.5 million African Americans migrated to Northeastern, Midwestern, and Western cities such as New York, Detroit, and Los Angeles, with another five million migrating by 1970.[9]

Many refugees from racial terrorism came to Detroit because on January 5, 1914, industrialist Henry Ford announced that his Detroit-based company would double its workers' wages to $5 a day.[10] Management used generous wages to counter the high employee turnover that was slowing production and hindering profits. News of the handsome wages reached Southern Blacks through Pullman porters, Black newspapers, the Urban League, and other cultural conduits.[11] Exploitative sharecropping arrangements could not compete with Ford's unparalleled salaries, ergo a tidal wave of African Americans from Southern cities flooded Detroit in search of opportunity.

When word of Ford's living wage reached Newton Grove in the 1920s, Grandpa Brown's eldest sibling promptly migrated to Detroit with her new husband. Grandpa Brown was not far behind. These voyagers left all they knew and loved for a fresh start, only to discover that, like city and country cousins, the civilized racism of the North and the uncivilized racism of the South were very closely related. Segregation was God in both regions.

Although the racial caste system followed Grandpa Brown to Detroit, the employment opportunities were far better. By 1920, 79 percent of Detroit's Black men worked manufacturing and mechanical jobs.[12] Then restrictive federal immigration legislation passed in 1921 and 1924 drastically reduced European immigration, further expanding opportunities for Black workers.[13] Grandpa Brown benefited from these conditions when, in 1925, he got a highly sought-after job at Ford's River Rouge facility.

Three years prior, in 1922, an Italian immigrant named Paris Bucci, too, officially secured a job at Ford's River Rouge factory. He, however, had started working unofficially years earlier because Ford, in desperate need of laborers, knowingly hired him and other undocumented European immigrants who did not have the required work permits. "The immigration officers would come into the shop and they would hide all the immigrants that jumped over into a separate room," Robert Ficano, Paris's grandson, said, recalling the stories his grandfather told. "The guys would do the inspections and then they would let them back out once the immigration officers left."

Paris Bucci, later known by his most treasured title, Grandpa Bucci, was born in 1905 in Italy; more specifically, in the town of Galliano, just outside Florence. The gem of Galliano is the Basilica di San Vincenzo, a circular church built of rugged cobblestones, miraculously standing tall and intact since AD 1007. Like most of their neighbors, generations of whom lived beside the basilica over the centuries, the Buccis were devout Catholics. Indeed, when Paris's mother died unexpectedly in his childhood, his father married a former nun who renounced her sacred vows for love.

The Buccis worked in Italy's agricultural economy as sharecroppers, relying upon livestock and the land's bounties to support their family. Italy's sharecropping system, prevalent from the early nineteenth century until World War II, was called *mezzadria*.[14] Typically, landlords divided land into plots, gave each family one to farm, and divided the crops grown equally between themselves and their tenants.[15] *Mezzadria* left tenants economically vulnerable because while they could not work outside the landlord's farm, landlords could terminate their contracts at any time.

When Grandpa Bucci was about nine, World War I began, exacerbating the vulnerabilities of sharecropping families like his own. In fact, the Great War turned Grandpa Bucci's life upside down, stole his older brother's life, and left his country's economy in tatters. After the war, Italy's currency was one-fifth its prewar value,[16] and Italy sank into a vortex of debt, leading the famous English economist John Maynard Keynes to advise Britain not to grant new loans to Rome because Italy was a "hopeless case."[17]

Like many Italians, Grandpa Bucci's older sister could not find work after the Great War, and when tensions with her strict and sanctimonious stepmother became unbearable, she emigrated to France in search of a better life. She was not alone. In response to France's increased demand for labor, millions of Italians, who were willing to work in harsher conditions for less pay, immigrated there,[18] becoming France's largest immigrant group between 1901 and 1968.[19] Although he was only a teenager with a third-grade education, Grandpa Bucci followed his sister to France.

Low on book learning but loaded with street smarts, he found work in a coal mine where working conditions were dangerous and dirty, shifts were long, and wages were low.[20] Grandpa Bucci spent his days hunched in a shaft, worlds away from the fine food, clothes, and shops characteristic of Paris, the city for which he was named. Instead, Paris Bucci came home each day covered in soot, lungs blackening.

Grandpa Bucci abhorred the mines. Consequently, within a few years, he packed his few belongings and left for Canada. "He joined his other sister, who immigrated to Canada (Hamilton, around that area), and this is when he heard that Henry Ford had this new experiment that they're going to pay people five dollars a day," Robert recounted. "So he jumped over." Grandpa Bucci would work at the Ford Motor Company for more than thirty years, starting in its River Rouge foundry.

Opened in 1918, the Rouge plant was a titanic complex, sprawling over two square miles with nineteen buildings, a man-made harbor, electricity plants, a foundry, and ninety-two miles of railroad tracks.[21] Thousands of workers, using a series of conveyors and tracks, seamlessly and at breakneck speeds, pumped out Ford's most prized car, the Model T. Henry Ford's son, Edsel B. Ford, commissioned Mexican muralist Diego Rivera to capture the intricacies of this industrial marvel. Rivera's mural features workers of all colors, laboring together on factory lines, sinewy tan, black, and brown forearms straining against impenetrable stainless steel.

Working at River Rouge's foundry was, without doubt, one of the Ford Motor company's most hazardous jobs. Blazing-hot furnaces smelted iron ore, and workers poured this scalding liquid iron into molds to fashion car parts. Even Grandpa Bucci's stint in France's coal mines could not fully prepare him for the foundry's exacting physicality and peril. In fact, nothing could have prepared Grandpa Bucci for the work accident that sliced his right thumb off. The smooth black nub that remained served as a permanent reminder of the risks he assumed daily.

In a detailed journal entry, one man employed at the foundry described the dreadful conditions workers endured. He said that when a man would pass out from the intense heat, the foreman would have two men take him to the side on a stretcher, give him fifteen minutes to revive, and then send the felled man back to work. If a machine broke down, the plant subtracted the idle time from the workers' pay even though it was not their fault, making their earnings erratic. Men would be so dirty that, at the lunch hour, they could not recognize their friends by clothes or looks.[22]

During Grandpa Bucci's time at the foundry, he was primarily working alongside African American men like Grandpa Brown. Two of every three Blacks hired at River Rouge between 1918 and 1927 worked in the foundry, compared to one in four whites,[23] and this was the trend at all auto plants, not just Ford. At the Graham-Paige auto plant, for instance, management told a Black worker that the only jobs available were in the foundry, although whites hired at the same time received polishing and carpentry positions.

"As I looked around, all the men were dirty and greasy and smoked up. They were beyond recognition. There were only three or four whites," a Black foundry worker observed. "Their faces looked exactly like Negro faces. They were so matted and covered with oil and dirt that no skin showed." He continued, "My friend and I went home discussing how it was that they could say everyone was free with equal rights up North. There was no one in the foundry but Negroes."[24]

Because of workplace discrimination, lower-paying janitorial work or dirty and dangerous jobs such as positions in the paint room and foundry overwhelmingly went to African American men.[25] Justifying these racist employment policies, one automotive official explained that they were forced to hire "niggers" because the harmful work "soon kills a white man." And when asked about the work's effect on Blacks, he replied, "it shortens their lives, it cuts them down, but they're just niggers."[26] Racism rendered Black lives disposable, their humanity invisible.

With the dawn of the Great Depression, the auto industry severely contracted, taking all city residents, Black and white, in a downward economic spiral. In 1929, Detroit was producing 5.34 million vehicles; by 1930 this number dropped to 3.36 million, and further declined to 1.33 million by 1931.[27] By 1932, Ford had laid off two-thirds of its workers.[28] Both Grandpa Brown and Grandpa Bucci lost their full-time employment at Ford, but the Depression hit Blacks particularly hard: In 1930, the unemployment rate in Michigan for whites was 3.8 percent, but it was 10.1 percent for Blacks.[29]

Desperate for jobs, workers would stand outside the Ford factory, praying they would be chosen for a day's labor. But there was a selection hierarchy, with whites on the top and Blacks on the bottom. Robert recalled the stories his grandfather told him about the Depression days at Ford. "He'd seen so much abuse and struggles. He would go and stand in line and you're outside the plant, and that day it's you, you, you, or you." Robert gestured, as if picking people from a crowd. "And that's who gets the work. And people are trying to curry favors and all sorts of stuff that was going on with it." He continued, "It changed over eventually with the formation of the UAW and organized labor." The United Auto Workers (UAW) union helped working men, like Grandpa Bucci, demand job security, fair wages, and safe working conditions from Detroit's automobile tycoons because workers had few rights.

Henry Ford was unequivocally against unionizing workers at his plants, and his opposition continued even after Congress secured workers' right to unionize by passing the 1935 National Labor Relations Act. The 1937 Battle of the Overpass, the infamous Depression-era showdown between the UAW and Henry Ford, proved that the union was the proverbial David, willing to take on seemingly invincible giants in defense of working people. The clash happened during the daily shift change when thousands of workers crossed the pedestrian overpass going from Miller Road to gate four of the River Rouge plant. On this busy overpass, the UAW launched a leaflet campaign, demanding that Ford convert his standard compensation package of eight-hour days paid then at $6 per day to six-hour days paid at $8 per day.[30]

In an attempt to stop the campaign, Ford's internal security force, led by Harry Bennett, beat down several UAW union organizers.[31] Grandpa Bucci witnessed this historic clash firsthand and told his grandson that he and his coworkers fled. "He said it was frightening. He didn't anticipate it would turn violent like it did. The big thing that he always, always brought up was how he hated Bennett." Robert chuckled as he remembered his grandfather's long-standing, unrepentant grudge against Bennett. Despite Ford's efforts to destroy the photographic evidence, snapshots of the savage beatings appeared on the front pages of newspapers across the nation. As the story spread, Bennett unwittingly created a swell of UAW supporters, Grandpa Bucci among the most enthusiastic.

In the early months of 1941, the new National Labor Relations Board ordered Ford to stop undermining its workers' right to organize. Then, on April 1, workers went on strike to protest the firing of several union members, closing down the River Rouge plant. On June 20, 1941, Ford signed its first contract with the UAW.[32] The unions won the fight. Grandpa Bucci immediately became an active member of the UAW branch organized for workers at the River Rouge plant, Local 600. Even though he still came home dirt-caked just as when he worked in France's coal mines, Grandpa Bucci took great pride in his job at Ford because the changes secured by the UAW ensured that his work was dignified.

Grandpa Brown's early experiences with organized labor stand in sharp contrast to those of Grandpa Bucci. Because various written policies and unwritten practices subordinated Blacks in the workplace, Grandpa Bucci and other European immigrants were able to obtain the more desirable jobs, secure employment and promotions first, and make more money for comparable work.[33] In its infancy, the UAW unabashedly protected this white privilege. It is thus not surprising that when the union called a strike, Blacks unashamedly crossed the picket line to secure jobs and provide for their families. This is exactly how Grandpa Brown got rehired at Ford after the Great Depression. But crossing the picket line was no easy feat because there were so many Black men trying to do it.

Frederick Brown, Grandpa Brown's youngest son — who inherited his brown skin, thick black eyebrows, and full lips — recalled the stories his father told. "My father crossed the picket line and went in to apply for the job. There was a line of folks, and there was a Black guy at the gate that was letting people in. If you didn't know nobody or you didn't have a hookup, well, you were out of luck. That guy, he was like honorary white folk. He was very selective." One labor scholar writes that, by allying with antiunion Black ministers and other community leaders and using them as employment agents, Ford used the Black community to weaken unions. For example, a letter from a certain pastor would ensure employment, which increased the pastors' power within the Black community, and in exchange, Ford gave their churches generous donations as they preached against the union from the pulpit.[34] Since Grandpa Brown did not have a relationship with one of these community power brokers, he had to rely on his own wits.

"My daddy said he just went there four or five days in a row and the man wouldn't let him in," Frederick remembered. "So he said he went around to the back and climbed over the fence. He come around and snuck in the building and got a job." Frederick chuckled, delighting in his father's resourcefulness.

Although there was fierce competition for work in the Depression era, the start of World War II returned jobs and prosperity to Detroit. Between 1940 and 1947, manufacturing employment increased by 40 percent as factories worked overtime to produce war machines.[35] Because industrialists needed laborers to keep pace with surging demand, Black laborers were in high demand, though they still occupied the bottom rung of the hiring ladder.

World War II also brought America's racial inequalities into stark relief. Though forced to serve in segregated units, more than one million Blacks fought for the United States. They eventually brought their fight from the battlefields of Europe back to their own cities and towns as they combated entrenched discrimination in all avenues of life, including the workplace. Blacks walked off the job to protest employment discrimination, and then when they received the promotions they sought, whites walked out, contending reverse discrimination. From 1941 to 1944, a merry-go-round of these so-called wildcat strikes turned Detroit's automotive factories into hotbeds of racial tension.[36]

One of these wildcat strikes triggered the largest occurrence of racial violence during World War II—Detroit's 1943 race riot. It began after the Packard Motor Company, attempting to address historically unequal employment practices, hired three Black machinists to work on its assembly line.[37] In protest, twenty thousand white workers walked out. The racial tension eventually exploded into physical violence severe enough that President Roosevelt approved the deployment of United States Army troops armed with tanks and automatic weapons.[38] The violence subsided quickly, but not before thirty-four people died, twenty-five of whom were Black.[39]

Since the wartime and postwar economic boom created labor shortages, it was in the interest of unions and industrialists to ensure that Blacks and whites labored side by side peacefully. Because protecting white privilege now came at too high a cost, unions began to oppose strikes protesting Black equality and even expelled strike leaders. With the changing tide, the Black community became a staunch ally of the unions, nullifying divide-and-conquer tactics employed by industrialists. By the early 1940s, the Rouge plant employed 99 percent of the Ford Motor Company's Black workers,[40] so by the 1950s, its UAW branch, Local 600, became one of the UAW's most radical units, joining forces with the National

Negro Labor Council, a Detroit-based advocacy group protecting the civil rights of Black workers.[41]

Most importantly, because of the union, Grandpa Brown and Detroit's other Black autoworkers had access to the nation's most lucrative blue-collar jobs.[42] At the beginning of the Second World War, Black autoworkers made almost double the average yearly salary of all Black manufacturing workers. Their average yearly earnings of $1,092 were even higher than the nationwide average of white manufacturing employees, which was $1,002.[43] As a result, by 1950, Detroit's Black community had the highest earnings of any Black community in the nation,[44] with the median Black household income reaching $2,298, whereas the national median was $952.[45]

With their union jobs at Ford's River Rouge plant, both grandfathers seemed poised for successful futures after World War II. Both Grandpa Brown and Grandpa Bucci had sizable salaries and respectable working conditions that should have unlocked the dignity and opportunity they both dreamed of when they were humble sharecroppers. But this is not what happened. Because of the racial caste system, their families had access to drastically different opportunities, and this, over time, led to drastically different outcomes.

2

THE AMERICAN NIGHTMARE

Dr. Ossian Sweet, like Grandpa Brown, was the grandson of enslaved people. In the 1920s, the two men both arrived in Detroit full of hope. Initially, Sweet, a medical doctor, took up residence in Black Bottom, which, along with Paradise Valley, was one of the neighborhoods where authorities permitted Blacks to live. Although Black Bottom had a vibrant cultural milieu, including theaters, nightclubs, restaurants, and about 350 black-owned businesses,[1] it was also over-populated and flush with homes decaying from disinvestment.

Dr. Sweet, wanting to provide his family with the best he could afford, left Black Bottom and purchased a home in a white neighborhood where the houses were newer, bigger, and cheaper. Dr. Sweet knew that whites would perceive this flagrant disruption of the city's racial geography as heresy, but he was intent on erasing the color lines. He would soon discover that confronting racism comes at a great cost.

Upon moving into their new home at 2905 Garland Street in the fall of 1925, mob violence greeted Dr. Sweet and his family. Their new white neighbors surrounded the home and threw rocks while police stood idly by. In imminent danger and determined to protect his family, Dr. Sweet's brother fired shots into the crowd. One of those shots killed a white man, leading authorities to charge everyone inside Dr. Sweet's house with murder. After several tempestuous months, a jury of twelve white men acquitted everyone charged, but Dr. Sweet never fully recovered from this traumatic experience. He committed suicide at age sixty-four. Through stories like Dr. Sweet's, Grandpa Brown and other newly arrived Blacks learned a bitter lesson: if they did not remain in their appointed ghettos, whites — in partnership with law enforcement — would put them back in their place by any means necessary.

In the same year when Dr. Sweet attempted to move into a white suburb, Grandpa Brown returned to Newton Grove determined to marry his childhood sweetheart, Betty, and bring her back to Detroit. Betty's parents were sharecroppers, and since her mother's death when she was a girl, Betty had been in charge of cooking, cleaning, and caring for her younger siblings while her father and the older children worked in the fields. Like many Blacks faced with the decision to leave the South, Betty was torn. On one hand, she did not want to abandon her father, who relied upon her heavily, but on the other hand, she was madly in love and wanted to build a life with Brown. "My daddy said, 'Either you go now or I won't be back,'" Frederick recalled. "I don't think he was being mean, but he was serious."

With the begrudging blessing of Betty's father, in January 1926, the couple married. Immediately following their nuptials, the lovebirds left Newton Grove to begin their brave new life in Detroit. Since Grandpa Brown's sister and her husband were already settled in Detroit, the newlyweds moved into their subdivided apartment, and eleven months later, conceived their first child, Jessa. Even though the apartment was uncomfortably crowded, the extended family was fortunate to have a roof over their heads, as de facto segregation left Blacks with very few housing options. A 1919 survey reports that there was not a single vacancy in several "Negro areas" in Detroit, and finding three or four families crammed into one apartment was not exceptional.[2]

Between 1909 and 1917, numerous American cities relied upon zoning ordinances to segregate the races,[3] but in a 1917 case, *Buchanan v. Warley,* the Supreme Court outlawed this.[4] In response, to uphold segregation, neighborhood associations formed with the explicit purpose of organizing residents to create and enforce what are known as racial covenants or racially restrictive covenants. Developers of new subdivisions also routinely adopted these covenants. One such covenant found in the deed of a Detroit home read: "Said lots shall not be sold or leased to or occupied by any person or persons other than of the Caucasian race, but this shall not be interpreted to exclude occupancy by persons other than of the Caucasian race when such occupancy is incidental to their employment on the premises."[5]

Legal covenants, usually found in deeds, are private agreements between landowners that impose duties on subsequent owners, even though they were not parties to the original contract. Today, covenants are most commonly used to ensure that homeowners in gated communities maintain their landscaping and facades. Racial covenants, prevalent in the twentieth century, were private agreements that specifically prohibited racial groups from occupying and owning homes. Throughout the U.S., the majority forbid Black ownership and occupancy, but on the West Coast, they commonly extended to both Blacks and Asians.[6]

Racial covenants allowed Northern cities to politely use contract law the way Southern cities impolitely used lynchings, Jim Crow laws, and cross burnings — to maintain American apartheid. In a 1922 case, *Parmalee v. Morris,* the Michigan Supreme Court upheld these racial covenants as legally valid, arguing that "the law is powerless to eradicate racial instincts or to abolish distinctions which some citizens do draw on account of racial differences" because they are matters of "purely private concern."[7] Racial covenants were not, however, a purely private matter.

As a condition of dispersing federally backed mortgage loans, the Federal Housing Administration (FHA) regularly directed developers to insert racial covenants in residential deeds, thereby using state power to perpetuate exclusion.[8] Taking its cue from the FHA, after World War II, the Veterans Administration (VA) also advised developers and homeowners to place racial covenants in their deeds in order to increase their chances of receiving a VA mortgage.[9] As a consequence, even though Detroit's Black population grew by almost 3,000 percent in a thirty-year period, from approximately 4,000 in 1900 to 120,000 in 1930,[10] there were still only a few designated ghettos where Blacks could reside.

In the 1920s, when Grandpa Brown arrived in Detroit, builders inserted racial covenants in the deeds of most new housing in the city.[11] By the 1940s, 80 percent of properties outside Detroit's inner city had these covenants,[12] and residential subdividers, real estate boards, and neighborhood associations originated about 90 percent of them.[13] As a result, only one in four Blacks lived outside the city's lower east side.[14]

Once racial covenants corralled Blacks into a few neighborhoods, the federal Fair Housing Administration (FHA) drew a red line around these communities, declaring them a hazardous credit risk and excluding them from its government-insured mortgages created by the New Deal to spark the economy and exit the Great Depression. By 1939, lending maps marked 26 percent of Detroit red or "hazardous" because these areas were majority Black; the maps labeled 51 percent yellow or "definitely declining" because these areas were mixed race; and the maps classified only 23 percent green or blue, which meant "best" or "still desirable," indicating a majority white community.[15] Redlining marked Black people as deviants, transforming them into a plague, their mere presence becoming enough to weaken home values and initiate neighborhood decline.

While redlining ensured that there was no capital to upgrade the inner city's old, decaying homes, racial covenants confined Grandpa Brown and other Blacks to these areas, artificially creating congestion, fragility, and blight. As a result, the only option most Blacks had was to live in ghettos where most of the residences needed major repairs and often lacked a toilet, a bath, running water, heating, or lighting. For instance, federal officials classified two-thirds of Paradise Valley's housing as substandard in 1940.[16] The unsanitary conditions invited rodents, with area residents reporting 123 rat bites in 1951 and 83 in 1952.[17] Although Detroit had rat control regulations in place, rather than hire exterminators, landlords paid the resulting fines, ranging from $25 to $150.[18] Unmitigated rat infestations proved fatal when they germinated illnesses such as tuberculosis, which was prevalent in Black areas.[19]

During the wartime and postwar economic boom, Black men like Grandpa Brown were making record wages, but could not translate this triumph into better housing for their families. Blacks needed at least 10,000 units of housing during World War II, but only 1,895 units of public housing and 200 units of private housing were available for them.[20] While developers built roughly 186,000 single-family houses in metro Detroit during the 1940s, only 1,500 were available to Blacks.[21]

Since there was very high demand for housing and low supply, Blacks paid a premium. In the 1940s and 1950s, for example, they paid 20 to 40 percent more in rent than whites for equivalent apartments.[22] Overpriced, inadequate housing reminded Black migrants that just because they had escaped the Jim Crow South did not mean that old Jim would not haunt them in their workplaces and neighborhoods up North.

Unwilling or unable to see that these segregated, blighted neighborhoods were the consequence of racial covenants, redlining, and other racist policies, society viewed the people living in them as the core problem, branding Black people as lazy, criminal, dirty, and

uneducated. In a study exploring the reasons for residential segregation, one white respondent said, "I think blacks, a lot of them,
don't keep up their homes. They tend to hang out on street corners
instead of in school where they belong. More drugs, alcohol problems. Whites don't want to be around them." Another said, "A 'black
neighborhood' vs. a 'white neighborhood' is dirtier, less maintained,
more inclined to be abused by the residents."[23] Given that the disease
and blight prevalent in Black communities supposedly resulted from
Black people's moral shortcomings and their irresponsible behavior, the "logical" remedies were more education, interventions to
improve moral behavior, and promotion of hard work. Abolishing
racist policies was not a prominent part of the betterment agenda.

And, like Dr. Ossian Sweet in the 1920s, when Blacks tried to
leave the redlined communities where racial covenants sequestered
them, violence greeted them. One of the most notable instances
happened in 1942, when white suburban parents-turned-vigilantes
fought tenaciously to prevent Blacks from moving into the Sojourner
Truth Homes — a housing project built for Blacks that was next to
white neighborhoods.[24] White protesters threw rocks at Black families, and they responded, in turn, with violence. The police arrested
217 Blacks but only 3 whites, which was not unusual. Immediately
after World War II, whites perpetrated more than two hundred violent acts against Blacks who sought to move into their neighborhoods,[25] and police most often defended the perpetrators of racial
violence rather than its victims.

The whites held their ground for several months, successfully
blocking Blacks from moving into the Sojourner Truth Homes.
The standoff dominated headlines. Consequently, the UAW, trying
to deal with racism within its own ranks, voiced its support for the
Black families, calling for integration of all facilities.[26] When the first
six families finally moved into the Sojourner Truth Homes, it was
only possible with the help of 1,100 city and state police officers and
1,600 members of Michigan's National Guard.[27] Although they won

this particular battle, Blacks were unequivocally unwanted and thus losing the war against segregation.

In 1948, there was a ray of hope. The U.S. Supreme Court outlawed racial covenants, ruling unanimously that their enforcement violated the U.S. Constitution's Fourteenth Amendment. Interestingly, three of the Supreme Court's nine justices — Robert Jackson, Stanley Reed, and Wiley Rutledge — recused themselves because they owned property subject to racial covenants. This historic decision caused whites to panic. Profiting from this fear, in 1949, Albert Cobo won Detroit's mayoral race — defeating the prolabor candidate George Edwards — by vowing to oppose racially integrated housing, which he referred to as "Negro invasions."[28]

The exodus of whites from the city of Detroit accelerated in the 1940s, as they moved to larger and cheaper housing in the suburbs. Blacks, in turn, moved into the homes whites had left behind, expanding beyond the limited inner-city areas where racism had once confined them.[29] The Browns left their shared apartment for a single-family house on the city's east side near Highland Park, which Grandpa Brown rented from an Italian coworker. This is where the Browns grew their family to seven children.

Grandma Brown, a full-time homemaker, spent her days caring for her household just as she did back in Newton Grove. When anyone ate her chicken and dumplings, mashed potatoes, or turkey with dressing, it was like they ingested a potion, making them dizzy with delight, and by all reports, her pineapple upside-down cake and sweet potato pie cast a spell that made hard men tender. "[My mother] made sure Daddy had breakfast, lunch, and dinner every day," Frederick said. "In the mornings, as I got older, she would get up maybe a half an hour before Pops's alarm would go off and go in the kitchen. Man, I could smell the bacon and eggs. It would wake me up out of my sleep."

Through scrumptious family meals and bonds built with neighbors, the rented house became a home, holding invaluable memories.

Nevertheless, without giving Grandpa Brown adequate notice, his Italian co-worker suddenly sold the house. The Browns had to move abruptly, and could only secure replacement housing in a Black woman's dingy basement. Frederick was a toddler at the time, but he remembered his mother recounting the abuse inflicted by their former landlady. "My mother would pay the woman, and the woman would keep coming back talking about, 'You didn't pay me.' Like my mother was stupid. The woman was overcharging my folks," Frederick recollected. The Browns tolerated this because they had exceptionally few housing options.

In 1950, after spending a few years in the dreary, overpriced basement apartment, the Browns moved to an area on the city's west side where racial covenants and racial violence had once prohibited Blacks from residing. Together with their oldest daughter, Jessa, and her young family, Grandma and Grandpa Brown purchased a duplex at Fifteenth Street and Buchanan. "My brother-in-law had a job in the factory, and together, they got up enough money to get up in there," Frederick said. They "stayed upstairs with their family, and we stayed downstairs."

The Browns' new home was more than bricks and mortar — it gave them an asset to grow their wealth. It also provided physical security, stability, increased privacy, and supplied a canvas to express their identity. For Blacks, acquiring a home also provided psychological refuge from a profoundly racist society.

Even though Grandpa Brown worked his entire career at the Ford Rouge plant, which is in the suburb of Dearborn, virulent racism prevented him from ever purchasing a home there. Orville Hubbard, mayor of Dearborn from 1942 to 1978, adopted policies unapologetically designed to keep Blacks out.[30] "I am for complete segregation, one million percent," Hubbard declared. "Quit pushing the whites around. We've been pretty good to you. We've nursed you along, we've kept you here since the Civil War, put shoes on your feet."[31]

Because Hubbard was exceptionally brazen in his efforts to maintain Dearborn's racial purity, in 1965 a grand jury indicted him for violation of a federal civil rights statute, claiming he ordered Dearborn police to stand by as a violent crowd stoned a house whose owner had purportedly sold it to a Black family. After he was acquitted of all charges, the *New York Times* reported that Hubbard took the jury out for a steak dinner.[32] Hubbard had no incentive to clean up his act and embrace civil rights because race baiting helped him get elected fifteen times, often winning more than 70 percent of the vote.[33]

In the neighborhoods where Blacks could reside, redlining cut their access to traditional bank financing, leaving land contracts as their only means to purchase a home. A land contract is a form of lending that combines the responsibilities of homeownership with the disadvantages of renting, thereby denying homebuyers the benefits of both. While bank financing offers lower interest rates, standard terms, mandated disclosure, and thus more security, sellers finance land contracts, which typically have larger down payments, higher interest rates, less favorable terms, and thus more insecurity. With a land contract, for instance, if buyers miss one payment, the seller can evict them and they can lose all of their prior payments. Contrast this with a traditional mortgage, in which late payments do not result in buyers losing all accumulated equity. Due to redlining, Black people could only secure inferior housing on inferior terms.

Racist policies led not only to inferior housing but also to substandard schools. Frederick Brown was eight in 1954 when the U.S. Supreme Court decided *Brown v. Board of Education,* which prohibited racially segregated public schools, declaring "separate educational facilities are inherently unequal." But even with de jure segregation outlawed, Black children still did not sit in the same classrooms as white children. By 1972, 70 percent of Black students in Detroit attended schools where at least 90 percent of the student population was also Black, while about three-quarters of the suburban white students went to schools that had no Blacks enrolled, and the other one-quarter went to schools that were 90 percent white.[34]

Since Blacks and whites did not live in the same neighborhoods, busing was one tool used to overcome this de facto school segregation, but white authorities nonetheless found ways to undermine this policy and maintain racial separation. "When we got to the fourth or fifth grade, they bused us to Kennedy Elementary, a school over there farther south and west, a predominantly white area," Frederick said, running his hand through his gray hair. "The students were white, and they didn't put us in class with the students from that area. They kept us all separated from those kids." Instead of integrating the school, authorities created a school-within-the-school for Black students in order to keep them apart from white children.

After school, when Frederick returned to his home on Fifteenth Street, along with his mother, segregation greeted him daily. Even though both Black and white Southerners responded to the automotive industry's siren song by migrating to Detroit, they did not live side by side. "From Buchanan to Grand River, on Fifteenth, was mostly Black folks," Frederick said. "But from Buchanan going back south of Fifteenth, it was hillbillies. A lot of hillbillies. White folks from the South."

Like a tired old dog, segregation was stubborn and unmoving. But it also produced Detroit's famed music scene, which saturated Frederick's neighborhood with both melodies and opportunities. As a self-taught, naturally gifted musician, Jimmy Brown — Frederick's older brother — played bass, drums, sang, and even eventually assembled his own children into a musical group similar to the Jackson 5. Both Grandpa Brown and Jimmy encouraged Frederick's musical interests.

"When I got to be about twelve, I kept bugging my daddy about a guitar. He said, 'Oh, you don't want to play.' I kept bugging him and bugging him. Finally, he went to the store and got me a guitar." Every week, the Browns spent $2 on Frederick's lessons, and as his guitar skills blossomed, Grandpa Brown witnessed firsthand how music lifted his son to a celestial place.

"His friends would come by and he'd say, 'Get your guitar. Play them a song.' I said, 'Oh, Daddy, I don't want to.' I was shy, but he insisted. They'd give me a little change, a dollar or two. I said, 'Oh, looky here.'" These living room performances made young Frederick realize he could make money doing what he most loved. He made up his mind then and there—he was going to be a professional musician.

In 1959, when Frederick was thirteen years old, Berry Gordy founded his iconic music label, Motown. Gordy worked in an automotive factory, and it was there, at the Lincoln-Mercury plant, that he had an idea that would flourish into the most successful African American–owned business of the era. He would make music using an assembly line.[35] Gordy hired choreographers, voice coaches, stylists, session musicians, makeup artists, hairdressers, producers, and writers, who were each responsible for a distinct part of an artist's development as they went down Gordy's assembly line. A young person could come in Motown's door with nothing but raw talent and exit a fully assembled star, ready to cruise straight to the top of the *Billboard* charts. This was true for soul music legends such as Diana Ross, Stevie Wonder, Smokey Robinson and the Miracles, Marvin Gaye, Gladys Knight and the Pips, the Jackson 5, the Temptations, the Supremes, and the Four Tops.

One day, Frederick's neighbor James Jamerson—who in 2020 *Rolling Stone* magazine named number one among the "Greatest Bassists of All Time"—took Frederick down the street to Motown's headquarters. "We went around to the boulevard and went up in Hitsville. He said, 'Sit in that chair and don't move.' Then they started to record." After a long, rapturous inhale, Frederick continued, "I saw that and died and went to heaven. I was so excited."

At just fifteen years old, Frederick began playing bass at nightclubs with Detroit blues artist Washboard Willie. As Frederick's reputation as a talented bass player took root, several opportunities to play for Motown sprouted. "I had to play behind all the acts that didn't have their own guitars. Smokey had his own, Temptations had their own, but the other acts did not," Frederick explained. "This is how I first got to play behind Stevie."

Frederick played with Little Stevie Wonder — an eleven-year old blind prodigy — as well as many other Motown luminaries, but his big break came when he got the opportunity to play behind the architect of rock 'n' roll music: Little Richard. With his signature song, "Tutti Frutti," and other hit songs like "Good Golly Miss Molly" and "Long Tall Sally," Little Richard successfully melded the bad-boy blues tradition with the sacred shouts of gospel music to become one of the most celebrated musicians of his time.

Little Richard called on Frederick to play with his band several times. Frederick played bass while Little Richard danced, sang, and thumped his piano in a performance style best described as deliciously flamboyant. But before long, Frederick's sweet opportunity turned sour. "Richard asked me to go on the road with him, so I tried it for a while," Frederick recalled. "He made a couple of passes. I said, 'Oh, no. That ain't my bag.' I had to give that up."

Around the same time, Frederick went to go see Stevie perform at an Atlanta show. When he was backstage chatting with Stevie and his producer, Clarence, he told them he needed to leave his gig with Little Richard. "Clarence Paul said, 'When you get back to Detroit, you've got a job with Stevie.' So he got me switched from bass with Little Richard to guitar with Stevie. That worked out quite well."

When Frederick returned from touring with Stevie Wonder, he met his future wife, Mona, a preacher's daughter from Indianapolis who became a professional dancer. "My dad was a minister and so he disapproved," Mona said. "But my mom saw my talent, so she allowed me to get involved in a lot of little contests. I would go to auditions, and that's how I ended up being what you call a backup dancer." Before long, Mona got her big break, appearing on a nationally aired show called *Swingin' Time* with host Robin Seymour.

Frederick will never forget the day he met Mona. "I was with Stevie. I was home from the road and went over there to a recording studio on Warren and she comes in," Frederick said, momentarily becoming the shy and dazzled young man who first laid eyes on Mona. As soon as Mona saw Frederick, she, too, was enamored. The two quickly became a couple, working for Motown and regularly attending barbecues with its famed artists. They were having the time of their lives.

While Motown employed Frederick and many other young Detroiters, the automobile industry provided respectable union wages for Grandma and Grandpa Brown, four of their seven children, and many other African American families. That is, despite all the obstacles that the racial caste system placed in their paths, Black families in Detroit found a way to flourish. By 1970, 53 percent of African Americans in the metro Detroit area owned their homes, which was higher than Chicago (26 percent), Washington D.C. (30 percent), and Los Angeles (38 percent).[36] Maya Angelou aptly described the miracle of Black resilience in the face of relentless racial subordination when she so eloquently wrote:

You may shoot me with your words,
You may cut me with your eyes,
You may kill me with your hatefulness,
But still, like air, I'll rise.

3

THE AMERICAN DREAM

Soon after arriving in Detroit, Grandpa Bucci became captivated by a beautiful olive-skinned brunette named Mafalda, whose petite frame belied her impressive physical strength. Mafalda was likewise smitten because, with a physique hardened by manual labor, Paris Bucci was an attractive man who also had steady employment. They were, coincidentally, both from the same small town in Italy called Galliano. While Grandpa Bucci did not remember Mafalda, she certainly remembered him, because the priests forced the children who misbehaved in school to serve as altar boys during Sunday Mass.

"My grandmother always commented that she remembered seeing my grandfather as the altar boy quite a bit in church," Robert Ficano said, chuckling. While sitting in the church pews, trying not to fidget during the service, Robert's grandparents could not have imagined that one day scarce economic opportunities in Italy would push them out of Galliano and into Detroit — and each other's arms.

Initially, Mafalda's father had left her and her mother behind while he went to the U.S. to search for work. Once he found employment and a suitable husband for his daughter, he sent for her. Mafalda's suitor had been working on the assembly line at Ford for several years and was hence considered well-off. He, however, was also very old and very ugly. Mafalda did not want anything to do with the "*ingrugnato*," or "pig face."

"There's no way! I'm not going to marry this guy. Send me back to my mom," Mafalda cried out at one Sunday dinner. Enraged by her rebuff, Mafalda's father said he would do just that. He did not, however, follow through on his threat. Instead, when Mafalda's mother arrived in the U.S., she supported Mafalda's quest to marry for love, or at least to marry a man who did not resemble a farm animal. Hot on the heels of this epic family showdown, Mafalda met Paris Bucci, the naughty altar boy from her childhood. They fell in love and got married in 1927.

Soon thereafter the couple rented a house on Mound Road between Seven Mile and Eight Mile, which was not far from the home that Grandpa Brown's Italian co-worker rented to his family. The Buccis' new home was located on the near east side, which is where Italians from all over Italy settled when they first arrived in the 1880s.[1] As employment opportunities in Detroit's automobile industry grew, so did its Italian population, surging from 900 in 1900 to 42,000 in 1925.[2] Because racial covenants did not prohibit them from moving to any part of the city or the suburbs, over time, the growing Italian population left the near east side.

In 1929, the Great Depression struck Michigan like a wrecking ball, and the prosperity that had drawn droves of Italian immigrants to Detroit halted. Between 1930 and 1933, Michigan's unemployment rate was 34 percent, while the national rate was only 26 percent.[3] Food was scarce, leaving soup kitchens as the only institution standing between thousands of Detroiters and starvation. The Buccis and other families rarely had three meals a day, and meat became a luxury item. Although there were over a hundred evictions per day, forcing families to sleep in parks, pool houses, or wherever they could find space, the newlyweds managed to stay in their home. In 1932, during these insecure times, Paris and Mafalda had their first and only child, Lena.

When the Depression ended, in addition to regaining his full-time job at Ford, Grandpa Bucci also had a thriving side gig, screening Italian films for Detroit's Italian community. Authorities even allowed him to hold screenings for Italian prisoners of war during World War II, when Michigan held about six thousand German and Italian prisoners in thirty-two small camps throughout the state.[4] It was because of this side job that, as a teenager, Lena met her future husband, Anthony Ficano.

To ensure that his film screenings were well attended and turned a sizable profit, Grandpa Bucci purchased ads from Carl Ficano, a printer by day who ran a local radio station's Italian hour in the evening. Like many other immigrants, Carl Ficano came to America before his wife and child in order to establish himself. But before he could send for them, World War II broke out, and when Italy joined the Axis powers, the U.S. stopped giving visas to Italians. Carl's wife died when a war plane accidentally bombed the Sicilian hospital where she was receiving care for a kidney infection, and their young son, Anthony, was stranded in Italy without parents until U.S. immigration restrictions eventually eased.

In 1946, Anthony Ficano, age fourteen, came to America on a Red Cross boat. A few years later, while helping his father at the radio station, he met Lena Bucci, who had accompanied her father to purchase ad time. Anthony and Lena were instantly enamored with each other, and they became a couple while Lena was still attending St. Rita, a Catholic high school on the city's northeast side.

St. Rita School opened in 1926, with students in six grades, and by 1954, it had over a thousand students enrolled across all grades. The Sisters of St. Joseph, who ran the school, also had a rapidly growing congregation known for its commitment to eradicating segregation. The parish was particularly known for its antiblockbusting stance,[5] as it combated real estate agents and other housing intermediaries who coaxed white owners into selling their property rapidly and hence at a cheap price in order to resell the properties to Blacks at a higher price, making a handsome profit.

Soon after Lena graduated from St. Rita in 1950, she got engaged to Anthony, and family and friends gathered at the Buccis' east side home for the engagement party. Upon entering, guests placed their coats and purses in the upstairs bedroom and then joined the festivities underway in the basement. While Italian wine and food flowed freely and jubilation abounded, a burglary was afoot. "Somebody came in and they stole a lot of the women's purses and the money out of it," Robert said, retelling an incident that has since become family lore. "So my grandfather actually found out how much was stolen and he repaid everybody."

Lena and Anthony married on October 22, 1950, and the newlyweds lived with Paris and Mafalda in their rented home. Two years later, Lena gave birth to their first and only child, Robert (Bobby) Ficano, at Holy Cross, a nearby Catholic hospital. This momentous event transformed Paris and Mafalda into Grandpa and Grandma Bucci, the titles and roles they most treasured.

The Buccis finally saved up enough money to purchase their first home in 1954, and they moved in, together with Lena and her new husband and child. Like most whites, they chose to move out of Detroit to the suburbs, where the houses were newer and cheaper and the neighborhoods were almost completely white. The Buccis purchased a home for about $6,000 in a western suburb adjacent to Detroit called Redford Charter Township.

Located on Winston Street, the home was a modest brick structure with two bedrooms, one bathroom, and a basement. "I didn't realize how small it was until I went back as an adult," Robert mused, noting how even humble homes can seem like mansions through a child's eyes. "Some of my favorite memories in the Redford home were of playing baseball with the neighborhood kids. I loved baseball."

Most of little Bobby's baseball buddies came from families who had recently immigrated from Europe, including the German family next door and the Polish family with eight children who lived a few houses down. In 1950, Redford had a population of about 19,000 people, 99.87 percent of whom were white.[6] This was not a fluke. Racial covenants prohibited families like the Browns from occupying or purchasing these suburban homes. At the same time, white working-class families, like the Buccis, used government-insured loans with low down payments and affordable monthly mortgage payments to buy suburban homes and take part in the American Dream. In contrast, between 1945 and 1959, African Americans received less than 2 percent of federally insured home loans.[7]

Unlike newly arrived European immigrants, Blacks, whose families had been living in America for centuries, were living the American nightmare. Orsel and Minnie McGhee's experience is illustrative. In 1944, the McGhees — fed up with paying higher prices for the lower-quality housing in congested, redlined neighborhoods — moved with their two sons into 4626 Seebaldt Street, in a majority-white community on Detroit's west side. Even though the McGhees could afford the rent, they were legally barred from living there by a racially restrictive covenant in the subdivision, which stated: "This property shall not be used or occupied by any person or persons except those of the Caucasian race."[8]

To push the McGhees out of their new home, white neighbors assailed them with threats and racial abuse. But the family did not budge. The neighbors, undeterred, turned to the courts, filing a case called *Sipes v. McGhee*. Twenty-four neighborhood organizations, joined by the North Redford Association and the Northwest Redford Improvement Association — the active neighborhood associations in the Buccis' new suburban community — filed a brief, encouraging the court to uphold the racial covenant.

The brief, which is baldly discriminatory yet couched in the language of freedom, reads as follows:

In certain of the briefs which have been filed, which we have examined, it appears that various contentions have been made having to do with discrimination in relation to the negro. In order to consider the status of the negro, it is fundamental that he exists in this country as a free member of a free society. The greatest right which a free member of a free society possesses is his free right to contract. This free right to contract has been exercised by an overwhelming majority of the owners of homes in a subdivision area entirely white, which the negro now seeks to destroy. If the argument of the negro is to be considered, then it would appear that in order for the negro to exist as a free member of the free society, he must destroy the freedom of contract of other members of the same free society. This obviously cannot be the case, and consequently, those of the Caucasian race who have exercised their free right to contract work no discrimination upon the negro.[9]

The brief concludes by saying, "The court well knows that if violations are permitted that soon the general character of the entire area will change and those who have acquired their homes in reliance upon use and occupancy restrictions will be forced to seek other locations and will suffer irreparable, economic loss."[10]

The case traveled to the Michigan Supreme Court, which in 1947 affirmed the lower court decision, mandating that the McGhees evacuate their home within ninety days.[11] With the NAACP's valiant lawyer, Thurgood Marshall, on their side, the McGhees appealed to the U.S. Supreme Court, which bundled their case with one from St. Louis called *Shelley v. Kraemer.* In 1948, *Shelley* outlawed racially restrictive covenants, declaring that the Constitution prohibited states from enforcing these discriminatory private contracts. Despite this landmark decision, real estate professionals and others continued to insert racial covenants in residential deeds for decades more because, although they were not legally actionable, the covenants still sent a powerful signal, letting Blacks know they were not welcome.

Adding to the register of racist policies, two federal programs systematically destroyed the communities where racial covenants sequestered Blacks. First was the Housing Act of 1949, which facilitated urban renewal programs already underway. Through the 1950s and 1960s, local governments used the powers granted by this act to designate certain communities as blighted. Then, using their eminent domain powers, they transferred the properties they seized to private companies at heavily subsidized prices in exchange for the promise of redevelopment. The evicted Black families received meager relocation assistance.[12] By 1970, urban renewal had uprooted over 5,500 Black families in Detroit.[13] This racist policy also uprooted Black families in many other cities, including 14,600 in Chicago, 9,700 in Philadelphia, 6,400 in Baltimore, 5,800 in St. Louis, 3,600 in Atlanta, 1,800 in Birmingham, and 1,400 in Memphis.[14]

The federal government has never taken responsibility for the fact that, by cutting off investment in Black neighborhoods through redlining, it manufactured the blight that its urban renewal programs sought to erase.[15] This seemingly righteous work of eradicating blight had unholy consequences because razed alongside the "blight" were also long-accumulated social capital and "unblighted" residences. Gone, too, were the productive enterprises and vibrant cultural spaces — such as the jazz and blues clubs, barbershops, and grocery stores.

Additionally, the Highway Act of 1956 worked in conjunction with urban renewal to further raze "blighted" Black communities. This time, however, in the name of progress, authorities built freeways, which often ran right through Black communities, destroying them while also facilitating white suburban exodus. For example, in Detroit, by 1958, construction of the John C. Lodge Freeway (M-10) destroyed approximately 2,200 buildings in an overwhelmingly Black neighborhood. By the end of the 1950s, construction of the Edsel B. Ford Expressway (I-94) leveled about 2,800 buildings in another mostly Black community.[16] The Highway Act also affected Black communities in cities across the country, including New York, Miami, Chicago, Minneapolis, Pittsburgh, Oakland, Nashville, Baltimore, and Atlanta.[17]

The demolition of Black communities through the Highway Act and urban renewal further restricted the already limited housing supply for Blacks, leading to even higher prices for even more substandard housing. Displaced families could only relocate from one distressed and segregated neighborhood to another. The newly reconfigured communities were vulnerable to crime and physical decay because the anchoring social networks and social trust necessary to counter these ills vanished along with the old neighborhood. Social psychiatrist Mindy Fullilove found that these uprooted populations often suffered from what she calls root shock: "the traumatic stress reaction to the destruction of all or part of one's emotional ecosystem."[18] The intergenerational consequences of root shock include anxiety, psychological trauma, enfeebled communities more vulnerable to negative forces, chronic illness, and even death.[19]

Unencumbered by racial covenants, redlining, or mass displacement and its accompanying root shock, the Buccis and other poor European immigrants were free to move to the suburbs and live the American Dream. The Buccis did not, however, forsake their Italian culture. The Italian language was king in the Bucci home, so even little Bobby was fluent. And inside their single-car garage was Grandpa Bucci's Ford automobile as well as his traditional Italian wine-making operation. "He would prune the grapes and he had me help. He'd have both the green ones and the red ones," Robert remembered. "And then inside, he'd have the huge barrel. I'd help crush them and stomp on them. He would make a batch every year."

The Redford home was where the extended family came together for the holidays and for Sunday dinners. While Grandma Bucci cooked on the weekdays, Sunday was Grandpa Bucci's time to shine.

He would go downstairs to a separate kitchen he had constructed in his basement and, from scratch, prepare a pasta appetizer and a hearty main dish. Alongside the food, Grandpa Bucci would serve his homemade wine to everyone at the table, even little Bobby. Since food had been scarce during the Depression, the Buccis lavished money, time, and energy on their Sunday dinners, splurging because they now could.

Robert's most poignant memory of the Redford home was not the annual wine-making, the family meals, or the baseball games with his little buddies, but rather a specific conversation he had with his grandfather.

"My grandfather, he was working in the plant. He came home. The shifts used to end around three o'clock, three thirty, so he'd come home and I was real excited to see him," Robert said. Before Grandpa Bucci had a chance to settle in and change out of his oil-stained work clothes, Robert darted into his lap and wrapped his grandfather in a welcoming embrace. "Grandpa, I want to do what you do when I grow up," Robert announced.

Robert's words hit Grandpa Bucci like a punch, knocking the adoring smile off his face. Grandpa Bucci paused. Then, in a tone as serious as it was gentle, he explained: "There's nothing wrong with what I do. Because of the union, there is food on the table, we have a house now, and I have benefits."

He spread his weathered hands out taut before him. There was a black rounded nub where his thumb had been. "Look at my hands," he told his grandson. As Robert shifted his gaze, Grandpa Bucci continued, "My hands are this color so that yours don't have to be."

Until that moment, Robert had never noticed Grandpa Bucci's permanently discolored skin. As Robert moved his gaze from his grandpa's stained hands back to his face, Grandpa Bucci said, "I came to America for work, but also so you can go to college and get an education. You," he said, looking Robert straight in the eye. "You're gonna go to college."

"Okay," Robert obediently replied.

Overhearing their conversation, Grandma Bucci joined her husband and grandson.

"Well," she asked. "What do you want to do?"

"I want to be a lawyer," Robert replied.

Even though Robert's family members were manual laborers, because they lived in the suburbs where the schools were superior, Robert's dream was not out of reach. Between 1948 and 1963, the South Redford School District built six new state-of-the-art schools,[20] where aspiring lawyers could take courses like business law and economics, debate, speech, communication skills, Latin, American history, sociology, and American government.[21] With resources like this at his disposal, if Robert studied hard, it was likely that he would, indeed, one day become a lawyer.

Because there were no limits on where they could live, Robert's parents could move to a community where he would have even better educational opportunities than in Redford. This led them, in 1959, to Livonia. Lena and Anthony had saved up enough money to move out of Grandma and Grandpa Bucci's Redford home and purchase one of their own. For about $8,000, the couple bought a newly constructed two-bedroom, one-and-a-half-bath redbrick bungalow with wood-framed windows on Pinetree Street. Although the home was only about a thousand square feet, it sat on a large lot and had a spacious, neatly manicured front lawn. Most importantly, the house was located in a resource-rich suburb.

A once-bucolic area dominated by dairy farms and fruit orchards, Livonia became a city in 1950 in order to capture tax revenues from a racetrack built in 1949.[22] After General Motors built a transmission plant there in 1949 and Ford did the same in 1952, the suburb began attracting feeder businesses and developing a dynamic economy. In 1959, the suburb's desirability increased even more when it became home to the largest regional shopping mall in western Wayne County, Wonderland Shopping Center, which was a fifty-six-acre open-air development that housed popular stores like Woolworth's and Montgomery Ward. All of this development produced a strong tax base to support Livonia's extensive public amenities. [23]

Lena and Anthony valued the suburb's schools as well as its employment opportunities. Lena transitioned from a secretarial job at Ford Motor Company to a secretarial job in the Livonia school district. Anthony was a qualified carpenter who struggled to find work in the Eisenhower recession of the late 1950s. "I remember standing in the unemployment office lines with him," Robert said. "It seemed like the cycles for carpenters were boom or bust, and I think he'd had enough." Anthony decided to leave carpentry to work as a school custodian, like Grandma Bucci, and found work in the school district. To bring in extra money, after his morning shift at the school, Anthony also worked in the afternoon as a janitor at a funeral home.

With their humble jobs, the Ficanos could only afford a home on the less affluent side of the suburb. "The Ninety-Six runs through Livonia," Robert explained. "South of it, it doesn't have as much wealth. You get up into the Seven Mile, Eight Mile area, there are just more Ford executives, and people like that live there. We lived south of Ninety-Six."

Before authorities constructed the I-96 freeway in the 1970s, a railroad track divided the affluent and working-class sections of Livonia. Even though they resided on the wrong side of the tracks, the Ficanos had access to all of the suburb's amenities, including the excellent schools, well-resourced public libraries, abundant retail and grocery shopping options, and extensive outdoor recreation spread over eighteen hundred acres of parkland. When they lived in Redford, the children played baseball in the streets as parents vigilantly watched for stray balls from their porches, but in Livonia, Robert and his new neighborhood friends had an array of safe, well-maintained parks in which to play. So they roamed free and played baseball night and day.

With their relocation from Detroit's east side to Redford and then Livonia, Lena and Anthony became part of a larger exodus of whites out of Detroit, where the houses were older, but more expensive than in the suburbs. In 1950, the median price of a home was about $9,357 in Detroit and $8,988, or about 4 percent lower, in Livonia.[24] Since suburban houses were cheaper and larger, whites fled: in 1950, whites composed 83 percent of Detroit's population, and this number fell to 71 percent in 1960, 56 percent in 1970, 34 percent in 1980, 22 percent in 1990, and 12 percent in 2000.[25] Even Lena's Catholic high school, St. Rita, closed in 1972 because its membership dwindled as the church's progressive white parishioners moved to the suburbs.[26]

Since racist policies prevented African Americans like Grandpa Brown from living beside their white co-workers in Livonia and other resource-rich suburbs, white and Black children did not have substantial contact with each other. Robert's Cub Scout troop, which had no Black boys, was a perfect example. One of Robert's dearest memories was when his scrappy troop of eight- and nine-year-old boys — led by den mother Sylvia Scarelle — set out to earn the badge for knotting a necktie. "My father and grandpa were blue-collar, so they would wear suits to a wedding or special occasion, but they didn't dress in suits," Robert said. The badge was important, not simply for his role as a Cub Scout, but as a marker of the white-collar future to which he aspired.

Unlike Lena and Anthony, blue-collar Blacks could not work hard and enroll their children in Livonia's Cub Scout troop to participate in the same rituals of middle-class life. As new subdivisions supplanted farmlands, Livonia's population exploded — growing from about 17,500 in 1950 to 66,700 in 1960 and 110,100 in 1970 — but its Black population did not. Racist policies relegated Blacks to inner-city communities starved of investment.

Since Robert did not live in the same neighborhood as African Americans, they did not attend the same schools, nor were they part of his Cub Scout troop. Baseball became one of the only interracial spaces in Robert's childhood. He and his white suburban friends idolized African Americans playing for the Detroit Tigers, like Willie Horton, Gates Brown, and Earl Wilson. "Baseball was a great equalizer, it really was," Robert insisted. "My dad loved Colavito because he was Italian, but you'd pull for Horton because he won games. You're always pulling for him to hit a home run." The Detroit Tigers' players were interracial, as were its fans. Blacks and whites, cheering the team to victory, found common cause.

Robert played baseball during both the school and summer seasons. While his neighborhood baseball crew and school team were all white, in the summers he played on more diverse teams. Because team managers were concerned with one thing, winning, they traversed racial lines to scout the best talent possible. "We were fortunate enough to be good enough that we'd go to Grand Rapids for playoffs," Robert said proudly. "So you're living a week with the team." For the boys in the summer league who traveled and lived together, this was the first time many of them were able to foster genuine friendships with people who did not look like them.

Robert specifically remembers one exceptional first baseman, "Lenny I wanna say his name was." Lenny was an African American boy from Detroit. After a lifetime of living racially segregated lives, Lenny and Robert were suddenly on the same baseball team, where their "smack talking" skills were almost as important as their technical acumen. "The umpire sometimes didn't care if the hitter is saying some smack to the catcher, or the catcher's saying some smack to him. They'd do it from the bench as well," Robert recollected. "Lenny was real good at it. He was constantly bantering back and forth, using terms like 'cracker' and all that kind of stuff among all of us on the team, on the bench, and on the other team." Robert paused, released a nervous laugh, and then continued.

"There were no holds barred. He said what he wanted. Everybody was comfortable with it. The camaraderie is that we're on the same team and we're all fighting for the same thing." On the looming question — what did the white boys on the team call Lenny in response to his racial banter — Robert was silent. Baseball placed white and Black boys in the same space for the first time, and they awkwardly used racial humor to bridge the chasm as they made the very difficult transition from complete strangers to teammates.

While Robert insists that he did not "see color" as a child, he did see several disadvantages Lenny and his other Black teammates endured that he did not. "I remember we used to play in Detroit, and the outfield would have holes and the chance of twisting your ankle was a lot greater," Robert recalled. "Then in the suburbs, the grass in the outfield was level and Parks and Recreation groomed the fields." It was not just lumpy baseball fields that Lenny and other Black children in Detroit suffered — they also had inferior schools, housing, health care services, and retail options. These and other blatant inequalities kindled the explosive 1967 Uprising that would surface right in the Browns' front yard, but far from the tranquil white suburbs like Livonia.

4

THE COLOR OF SUBURBIA

Four years prior to Detroit's 1967 Uprising, Martin Luther King Jr. led a 125,000-person march in the city called the Detroit Walk to Freedom. In his speech at the end of the march — a test run of his fabled "I Have a Dream" speech, which he would deliver a few months later at the March on Washington — King railed against segregation, acknowledging its pervasiveness in the North as well as the South. "I have a dream," King intoned, "that one day right here in Detroit, Negroes will be able to buy a house or rent a house anywhere that their money will carry them and they will be able to get a job."[1] King inspired many, both Black and white, with his prophetic, soul-stirring words. But while people waited for "one day" to arrive, America's unyielding racial caste system continued to elevate whites and subordinate Blacks, forcing them to endure dehumanizing conditions.

At that time, the Detroit Walk to Freedom was the largest civil rights demonstration in the nation's history,[2] a sign of how much Detroit's Black community respected King and his unwavering commitment to nonviolence. But people can only tolerate so much injustice before they snap. And on July 23, 1967, Detroit's Black community had had enough, igniting one of the largest civil disturbances of the twentieth century. Just as rotten meat begets maggots, racial subjugation and racist policies breed racial violence, so the 1967 Uprising (also known as the Rebellion) was, in fact, the fourth time authorities called in federal troops to stop racial bloodshed.[3]

A police raid of the Blind Pig, a Detroit bar, started the 1967 Rebellion. While police brutality was the match igniting the insurrection, poverty, racial discrimination, entrenched segregation, poor housing, underfunded schools, employment discrimination, and industrial decline were the fire's tinder. "I'd never seen nothing like it before. It lasted only a couple of weeks, but it was so scary," Frederick Brown said, his voice thick with emotion, as if the Uprising had transpired five weeks ago rather than over fifty years ago.

"I will tell you where I was at, sitting on the porch looking at the people across the street. There was a furniture store on the opposite corner of Fourteenth, and people were bringing TVs out, and furniture, and rolling it down the street. Someone said, 'Can we leave this in your yard?' My daddy said, 'No, take that stuff along with you. You can't leave nothing here.'" The Rebellion rudely and abruptly showed up on the Brown family's front porch.

The Detroit police and firefighters, the Michigan State Police, the Michigan National Guard, and the U.S. Army came to quash the revolt and put out the fires, but law enforcement's overwhelming presence made Frederick and other African Americans feel preyed upon rather than protected. "A lot of folks, innocent folks, got killed," Frederick said. "They wasn't doing nothing to deserve getting killed."

Over the course of five days, law enforcement eventually restored order, but not before hundreds were injured, over a thousand fires were sparked, thousands were arrested, and forty-three people were killed, thirty-three of whom were Black. Those murdered included Nathaniel Edmonds, twenty-three, shot by a white man who accused him of breaking into a nearby store; Roy Banks, forty-six, a deaf man who was en route to catch the bus to work when he was shot by a National Guardsman, who claimed that Mr. Banks was spotted looting a bar at Mack and Rohns; and Tanya Blanding, four, killed when a National Guard tank commander ordered machine-gun fire directed against her apartment building because he believed sniper fire originated from it.[4]

In response to the eruption of racial violence in Detroit and other U.S. cities, President Lyndon B. Johnson commissioned the Kerner Report, which concluded that "our nation is moving toward two societies, one black, one white — separate and unequal." Excluded from white neighborhoods stockpiled with privilege, Blacks knew this truth better than anyone else. In the aftermath of the Uprising, Black communities became even more separate and unequal as white flight accelerated.

Prior to the Uprising, between 1950 and 1960, white flight had already begun, eliminating 20 percent of Detroit's population. But after the Uprising, white flight went from a leak to a flood, with over forty thousand residents fleeing Detroit in 1967, and in the following year, this number doubled.[5] Detroit became increasingly Black and increasingly impoverished. Although Detroit's total population declined by about 20 percent between 1970 and 1980, the African American population increased from about 44 percent to 63 percent, and the number of residents whose earnings fell below the poverty line increased from 15 percent to 22 percent.[6]

Over time, Detroit's racial divide transitioned from white and Black enclaves within the city to a majority-Black city with majority-white suburbs. Segregation shifted but stayed the same. In 1960, Detroit's level of Black and white segregation was 87 percent, and three decades later, in 1990, it was still about 87 percent despite the passage of landmark federal legislation such as the 1968 Fair Housing Act, which prohibited discrimination in the sale, rental, and financing of housing.[7] In 1990, the mean level of residential racial segregation of the forty-five largest metropolitan areas was 66 percent, but Detroit's stood at 88 percent.[8] According to the 1990 census, Detroit was the most segregated large city (with a population of one million or more) in the nation and the only one where, during the 1980s, Black-white segregation did not drop.[9]

The 1967 Rebellion not only permanently transformed Detroit's racial and socioeconomic composition, but it also decimated the services available in the city's neighborhoods. "The white businesses that got burnt had insurance. They got their money, and they hauled you-know-what to the suburbs, away from here," Frederick noted. "Before the riots, in my area, you had the drugstore. You had the cleaners. You had a bank. You had a five-and-dime store. You had a meat market. All right in a four- or five block area. All that changed. The riots wiped out the best parts of the city." After a short pause, he continued, "People didn't realize that all the burning and the looting was self-annihilation to a certain extent."

Since the deep frustration African Americans in Detroit felt was foreign to most suburbanites, they most often viewed the violence as a senseless riot instead of an uprising against injustice. "How can people who rightly demand to be treated as human beings (and there shouldn't be any question — we are all human beings) act like enraged maniacal beasts?" one suburbanite asked in a letter to the editor published days after the Uprising. "Even an animal kills only for food or preservation — not for the sheer sake of killing. How in the name of God can anyone say they want a better life for their children and then burn cities and people and homes and hope for their children? Your children's dreams and future are going up in smoke — your smoke from your fires."[10]

Though Robert Ficano's home in Livonia was less than twenty miles from the city, the Uprising did not turn his or his grandparents' suburban neighborhood into a food and commerce desert, subject them to physical violence by the very law enforcement officials who were supposed to protect them, or burn down their homes, businesses, and opportunities. Like most suburbanites, Robert and his family were merely curious bystanders of the Uprising, watching while unaffected. "The only thing I remember is I was playing baseball, and all these U.S. military helicopters flew over the field, and they were heading for Detroit," Robert said.

After the Uprising, Robert and his family never visited the city of Detroit. There was, however, one exception. "We still went to Tigers games," Robert said. "We went all the time. So I can't say it stopped us from going down there or anything." Like fish swimming in a bowl of water, whites lived in racial isolation, ignoring the consequences for Blacks, who were not allowed into their suburban communities, left outside gasping for air.

Although the Rebellion dramatically altered things for the Brown family and other Blacks in Detroit, after it was over, they moved forward. As life went on, Mona had some important news for Frederick. She was pregnant. Frederick was young, scared, and taken aback. His world was already changing faster than he could keep up with even without a newborn. "I kept fumbling around and fumbling around," Frederick recalled. "She says, 'Well, if you don't marry me, I'm going to get rid of it.' I said, 'Oh, no, don't you do that.' She was about eighteen or nineteen. I married her." Their first child, Myrisha, was born in January 1968, and their second child, Nancy, was born prematurely just eight months later. Mona and Frederick went from frolicking at Motown barbecues to sleepless nights, caring for two infants in a city convalescing from the Rebellion but ensnared in a downward economic spiral.

Mona and Frederick's untried marriage suffered. Money was one of many stressors. "I still was doing different shows at Motown and he was traveling," Mona recalled. "But it was a strain because the work wasn't coming in, but now you got a family." In an attempt to keep his young family together, Frederick went to work at a car factory. It seemed like the right thing to do because, like many African American families in Detroit, the entire Brown clan was deeply embedded within the auto industry. But Frederick was not like them. He simply detested working on the assembly line.

Being a musician required creativity and improvisation, but the assembly line mandated its antithesis: rote physical labor. Frederick knew that if he gave up his music, the repetitive and physically taxing work of the assembly line would cause his spirit to slowly wither, so he worked on Chrysler's assembly line during the day while still playing music five nights a week. The situation was untenable. Frederick, however, would have given up both kidneys before he gave up his music. Music gave him life. After ninety days, Frederick quit the Chrysler job, and he also quit trying to fit into a mold that was not his. The marriage ended, and Frederick returned to his first love — music.

After the divorce, Frederick was not the primary breadwinner for his daughters. This duty fell upon Mona. "I didn't even know he had worked for Chrysler until I found an old check stub. And I'm like, 'Wow,' because I never knew him to hold a job," Myrisha reflected. "There wasn't huge child support because he never worked a full-time job, so we would get a few gifts for Christmas. He'd take us out for ice cream. Little stuff like that." While Frederick did not provide for his daughters in the traditional sense, he did provide music. "All I can remember is it was always music," Myrisha said fondly. "He even bought me a guitar that he used to hang on the wall and they let me play whenever he and his group were rehearsing. And most of the places we went together were when he was going to work musically."

After his attempt to start his own nuclear family failed, Frederick moved back in with his parents and would live with them until they both died. "My dad never did anything other than music," Myrisha lamented. "That was all I ever knew him to produce. He never purchased his own car. Never had aspirations to purchase a home." In many ways, Frederick was the complete opposite of his father, Grandpa Brown, who was a factory worker, homeowner, and family man.

After a couple decades toiling in Ford's River Rouge factory, Grandpa Brown eventually moved up to a less onerous job in the plant. Ford elevated him from the foundry to the position of press operator, monitoring the plant's aging machinery and providing much-needed quality control. Around the same time, Grandpa Bucci left the Rouge plant and moved to its new transmission plant in Livonia, a hulking facility that occupied 182 acres. Pleased as he was with his promotion to a parts inspector at the new plant, Grandpa Bucci was not thrilled to leave his beloved Local 600 at the old Rouge plant. He was, however, happy to join Local 182 in Livonia and return home each evening with his hands less black.

Because many of Ford's existing plants were becoming outdated, the company spent $2.5 billion between 1945 and 1957 building new plants, all of which were located in the suburbs.[11] In fact, Detroit's Big Three (Ford, Chrysler, and General Motors) built twenty-five new plants between 1947 and 1958, all of them in the suburbs.[12] While most white workers, like Grandpa Bucci, moved to these modernized suburban plants with greatly improved working conditions, workplace and housing segregation marooned African Americans at River Rouge and other antiquated plants. As a consequence, employment at the Rouge factory fell from 85,000 in 1945 to 54,000 in 1954, and to 30,000 in 1960.[13] Although the plant had been drastically downsized, Grandpa Brown stayed at River Rouge until his retirement in 1969, laboring over thirty years for the automotive giant.

By the time Grandpa Brown retired, Ford and other industrial titans were already in decline. The U.S. automotive industry's year of reckoning, however, came in 1973, when the Organization of Petroleum Exporting Countries (OPEC) implemented an embargo, preventing oil sales to the U.S. and other states antagonistic to Arab interests in the fourth Arab-Israeli War. As a consequence, gasoline prices soared. From 1972 to 1979, gas prices tripled, rising from $0.37 per gallon to $0.90,[14] creating an outsized demand for smaller, fuel-efficient cars. Asian and European car manufacturers were well positioned to respond to this sharply reconfigured consumer demand, but Detroit's Big Three could not pivot quickly enough. After this, the Big Three never regained market dominance.

It was not just America's car industry that was in decline, but rather its entire manufacturing sector. While the number of Black men who worked in factories increased from 29 percent in 1940 to 45 percent in 1950,[15] the years following presented a very different picture. From 1947 to 2012, the number of manufacturing firms in Detroit declined by 88 percent, and the number of workers in Detroit's manufacturing sector plummeted by 95 percent.[16] The decline hit African Americans especially hard because, in 1970, the manufacturing sector employed about one-third of Detroit-area Blacks, which was double the proportion of whites.[17] Lucrative blue-collar jobs had allowed Grandpa Brown and his contemporaries to flourish, but their children and grandchildren floundered when deindustrialization snatched these jobs away.

Nothing and no one, however, could snatch away Grandpa Brown's much-desired reward for years of hard labor — a bigger home in a better neighborhood. Although nestled between downtown and the Wayne State University area, the Browns' well-located neighborhood was becoming increasingly dangerous. "It had been better in the earlier years, but declined by the time that my folks decided to buy another house," Frederick recalled. In their retirement, Grandma and Grandpa Brown sought tranquility, but their neighborhood dispensed chaos, so they sold their house on Fifteenth Street and moved.

Because the area had deteriorated, Myrisha estimated that her grandparents received only between $10,000 and $20,000 for their home, money they used in 1973 to purchase a new two-story, six-thousand-square-foot home on Baylis Street. Built in 1923, the spacious home had two full baths, three bedrooms, and a detached garage. Detroit is best known for its small bungalows, so the Browns' home stood as a redwood in a field of daisies.

"It was beautiful when we moved over there," Frederick recalled. "It was a nice house and it was a nice neighborhood." With his voice in playful falsetto, he added, "There were even a few white folks there." While most white neighborhoods in Detroit fought to maintain racial purity and its accompanying economic benefits, there were a few islands of integration in the city's segregated landscape where prosperous Blacks and whites coexisted then and now: Palmer Woods, Indian Village, Sherwood Forest, and Boston-Edison.[18] The Brown family decided to purchase a home near Palmer Woods.

"If you were a mobile Black person and you were interested in moving out of the inner city, you moved on the Eight Mile stretch," Frederick explained. "And my parents moved on Seven Mile and Livernois area. That area has University of Detroit there. There is also what they call the Avenue of Fashion, where you had a lot of mobile upscale Black people opening small businesses."

It may seem strange that the Browns and other African American families did not move in large numbers to the suburbs, given that these areas had faster-rising home equity, more highly rated schools, and other first-class amenities. In previous decades, of course, they could not: Between 1940 and 1947, deeds in every new subdivision in Detroit's suburbs specifically excluded Black people from moving in. [19] But after *Shelley v. Kraemer* made racially restrictive covenants null and void in 1948,[20] Black families still did not migrate to the suburbs in large numbers. Although segregation in Detroit's suburbs declined somewhat in the late 1980s and 1990s, they remain largely segregated to this day.[21]

When asked why his parents did not move to the suburbs, Frederick replied, "Well, during that time, the suburbs weren't really big here in Detroit." Scholars have identified *three* primary reasons why the suburbs "weren't really big" among Detroit's African American population: housing market discrimination, racial policing of space, and neighborhood preferences.

First, while the Fair Housing Act of 1968 outlawed housing discrimination, it has persisted nevertheless, serving as an indestructible yet invisible barrier to entering the suburbs. Both the actual and the expected experience of discrimination prevent Blacks from seeking housing in white suburbs. A 1992 survey found that 89 percent of Blacks in the Detroit metro area expected or experienced lenders who employed discriminatory policies against them, whereas only 56 percent of whites answered similarly.[22] The problem, however, is not just lenders.

One of the most enduring yet clandestine forms of discrimination is racial steering, which is when real estate intermediaries cater to the racial prejudice of their customers.[23] Historically, this entailed real estate agents who would blatantly refuse to show Black homebuyers houses in white neighborhoods, but contemporary examples are often far less overt. In 2019, for instance, the federal Department of Housing and Urban Development charged Facebook with a Fair Housing Act violation, claiming that the company used an algorithm that allowed advertisers to exclude certain individuals from viewing housing ads based on their race and other protected characteristics.[24] In 2022, Facebook settled the lawsuit, agreeing to change its advertising algorithm and end its outsized role in housing discrimination.[25]

Second, like an electric fence, racially discriminatory policing, including racial profiling and arbitrary stops, jolts African Americans with a current of fear, making them hesitant to enter white suburbs.[26] A study conducted in Eastpointe, a predominantly white suburb at Detroit's northern border, is illuminating. Within the Eastpointe police department's jurisdiction, Eight Mile Road was the location where African American motorists traveled most because it is the dividing boundary between Detroit and Eastpointe. Conversely, Black motorists rarely drove on Eastpointe's inner streets, but it was on these streets and not on Eight Mile Road where Eastpointe police were most likely to search and arrest Black motorists.[27]

For example, on the border road (Eight Mile Road) where Black motorists were most present, the Eastpointe police searched whites and Blacks in equal measure. But on two specific interior roads (Nine and Ten Mile Roads), Eastpointe police searched 34 percent of Black motorists, although they constituted only 5.3 percent of drivers.[28] These racialized surveillance practices were not, however, about stopping crime because — measured by contraband found and contraband arrests made — Blacks stopped had less criminality than whites. Through racially discriminatory policing, Eastpointe and other suburban communities tell African Americans, with resounding clarity, that they do not belong. Keep out.

Third, neighborhood preferences prevent African Americans from taking up residence in white suburban communities. Both African Americans and whites desire to live in integrated communities, but conceptions of what constitutes integration vary wildly. A 2004 opinion study found that the vast majority of Detroit-area whites, 78 percent, were willing to live in a neighborhood where African Americans constituted no more than 20 percent of the population. When African Americans comprised one-third of the population, only 51 percent of whites said they were willing to live in the neighborhood, and when the number of Blacks rose to slightly over 50 percent, the number of whites willing to live there dropped to 34 percent.[29] In contrast — according to studies conducted in 1976, 1992, and 2004 — African Americans consistently preferred neighborhoods where the population was equal parts Black and white.[30] So as more African Americans move into any neighborhood, it becomes more desirable for African Americans, prompting an influx of Black families that makes the community increasingly less desirable for whites. Detroit-area Blacks and whites are trapped in a destructive game of Whac-A-Mole that ends only one way, with Black and white segregation.

These three factors — housing market discrimination, racial policing of space, and neighborhood preferences — have led to Black erasure from Detroit's suburbs, which has had dire consequences for wealth accumulation, education, and employment. In 2023, the median home value in predominantly white suburbs like Bloomfield Hills and Royal Oak was $833,100 and $236,600, respectively, while the median value in Detroit was only $52,700.[31] Lower home values are not, however, just a Detroit problem. Nationally, the value of an African American home is about 21 to 23 percent lower than it would be in a non-Black neighborhood.

Schools suffer, as they receive almost half their funding from local property taxes. One scholar found that "with fewer funds from lower property taxes, schools in majority Black or Latino neighborhoods end up receiving $5,000 less per student than do schools in majority White neighborhoods."[32] Funding differentials have had a devastating impact on the quality of education in Detroit public schools, which by the 1970s were over two-thirds Black.[33] But when officials created a plan to fix this, the U.S. Supreme Court undermined it.

More specifically, in a 1974 case called *Milliken v. Bradley*, the court struck down a plan to bus students across fifty-three school districts in the Detroit metro area, ruling that segregation was permissible so long as it was not an explicit policy of the school district. After this landmark decision, resource-starved Detroit public schools continued to flounder, prompting state authorities to wrest control from elected school board officials several times. But despite repeated interventions, Detroit public schools continue to woefully underperform, with only 6 percent and 11 percent of third through eighth graders testing at the "proficient" level for math and English in the 2017–18 school year.[34] Without access to the suburbs, Black children in Detroit have no gateway to well-funded public schools that prepare them for college and middle-class employment.

Without access to the suburbs, African American employment rates also suffer. African Americans cannot easily obtain the blue-collar manufacturing jobs through which Grandpa Brown and his contemporaries ascended to the middle class because from 1972 to 1992, these jobs declined by 75 percent,[35] and to the extent that these jobs still exist, they have relocated to the suburbs along with other low-skill jobs.[36] During the 1980s, the number of Detroit jobs within a ten-mile radius of the average African American worker's home declined by 18 percent,[37] and the lion's share of jobs that remain in Detroit require college degrees,[38] which most Blacks in Detroit do not have: in 2021, only 18 percent of Detroit residents had a bachelor's degree or higher, compared to 34 percent in Michigan overall.[39] Consequently, the employment opportunities accessible to most African Americans are located far from where they live, creating what is known as a spatial mismatch.

Several factors that impede driving—low car ownership rates, high car insurance rates, racialized police stops, and warrants for unpaid fines—worsen the spatial mismatch's adverse impact, as do discriminatory regional policies that render suburban and city bus systems separate and uncoordinated. For instance, for a Costco worker to get from downtown Detroit to her job in Livonia, it would take about twenty minutes in a car, but on public transportation, she would need two bus transfers and about two hours in transit time. Not only does the uncoordinated transit system squander time, but it also depletes much-needed capital. One study reports that in 2021 African Americans in metro Detroit spent, on average, 23 percent of their wages on public transit, while their white counterparts spent just 12 percent.[40] Most detrimentally, these racist transportation policies have hindered African Americans from accessing gainful suburban employment.

It is against this backdrop that Grandma and Grandpa Brown bought their new dream house in Detroit instead of the suburbs. For a time, they lived a good life there. Like clockwork, every Thanksgiving, Christmas, Easter, and Mother's Day, the entire Brown clan assembled to feast on Grandma Brown's scrumptious Southern cooking, creating delicious lifelong memories. To cultivate color and vitality in their new home, Grandpa Brown sowed a small garden and Grandma Brown planted flowers in their yard.

At the center of the yard stood something venerable and timeless — an apple tree. It was imposing, branches naked in the winter and speckled with green fruit come spring. "Because he was so tall, he could just pick the apples down," Myrisha said, fondly remembering her grandfather. "And then, once the tree started shedding apples, we'd clean them up off the grass so he could cut the grass." Against all odds, Grandma and Grandpa Brown had successfully raised their family and, in their retirement, finally moved into their dream home. Just as the tree bore fruit over the years, so did they.

Like the Browns, the Buccis also acquired their dream home in retirement. Grandma Bucci was insistent that, in their golden years, she and her husband move closer to their only child, Lena. While other grandparents were downsizing, the Buccis upsized with a brand-new house. For Grandma Bucci, a "used" home would not do. In 1976, they sold the Redford home and built a larger home in Livonia worth around $28,000. Their new one-story brick home was on Fitzgerald Street and had three bedrooms, two and a half bathrooms, just over two thousand square feet of living space, and a large yard.

Unfortunately, soon thereafter, Grandpa Bucci suffered a stroke and could no longer walk. Even though she was also old and frail, Grandma Bucci took good care of him, hauling his wheelchair in and out of the car and making sure his needs were met. Because they were nearby, Lena and her family also helped out significantly, making Grandma Bucci glad that she'd insisted on moving to Livonia.

Livonia was about 99 percent white in the 1950s when Lena and Anthony first moved there; it was 99 percent white in the 1970s when Grandpa and Grandma Bucci moved there; and it was 86 percent white in 2023.[41] While its racial makeup has barely budged, the mechanisms keeping Blacks out have changed. Livonia and other suburban communities no longer use racially restrictive covenants and racial violence. Today, there is no elected official who will at full volume declare, "Goddammit, I don't hate niggers. Christ, I don't even dislike them. But if whites don't want to live with niggers, they sure as hell don't have to. Dammit, this is a free country. This is America," as Hubbard, Dearborn's mayor, did in 1969.[42] This type of overt racism offends the sensibilities of most suburban whites.

Today, suburban communities keep African Americans out through exclusionary zoning, tacitly allowing the market to do the dirty work once done by explicitly discriminatory policies. Exclusionary zoning is when local governments use lot size or density requirements to prohibit low-income apartments and similar land uses. The restrictions limit the supply of housing and thus increase its price, barring poorer individuals and families from residing in these suburban communities. On their face, these policies are race neutral because, so long as they can afford it, any African American can move to these suburban communities. But in reality, affordability is a choice rather than a variable outside local lawmakers' control. That is, if suburban communities provided affordable housing, this would yield racial and income diversity.

In the 1970s, President Jimmy Carter's Housing and Urban Development secretary, Patricia Harris, launched a frontal attack on exclusionary zoning by threatening to withhold federal aid from communities that refused to provide housing options for low- and moderate-income families. With its 99.6 percent white population and nearly nonexistent rental housing stock, HUD made Livonia a target for transformation.[43] But Edward McNamara — Livonia's Democratic mayor from 1970 to 1986 and a former member of its city council — was fully prepared to decline $1 million in annual federal funding in order to uphold its exclusionary zoning practices.[44]

"What they are really saying is, 'Livonia, you share in the social problems of the world by creating a ghetto in your community,'" Mayor McNamara said, referring to HUD's crackdown. "This is a single-family type community. That is what the people who live here want. Our community has been well planned."[45] The plan was to keep poor people out, and with them, Black people. Mayor McNamara and his slightly veiled rhetoric of racial exclusion stand in stark contrast to Livonia's Democratic mayor Maureen Brosnan, who when elected in 2020 became the first woman to hold the job.

Mayor Brosnan proudly declared, "We will not tolerate racism in Livonia." She continued, "In response to the George Floyd murder, I recommissioned the Livonia Human Relations Commission, providing them with a new vision and new appointees dedicated to improving diversity, equity, and inclusion in our community."[46] Despite Mayor Brosnan's bold antiracist stance, since she and other Livonia Democrats have failed to rescind exclusionary zoning laws, which are a primary driver of racial segregation, Livonia remains just as lily white as the overtly racist officials of yesteryear intended. Additionally, through racialized policing, Livonia's police department ensures that African Americans feel unwelcome. Even though African Americans accounted for only 4 percent of Livonia's population in 2019, African American men constituted about 39 percent of arrests, while African American women comprised 22 percent.[47]

While exclusionary zoning and discriminatory policing exclude Blacks from the suburbs, liberal policymakers ignore these racist policies, choosing instead to convene committees and commissions on racism. Conservative policymakers, in contrast, most often deploy narratives of personal irresponsibility to explain African American poverty and their resulting absence from resource-rich white suburbs: "Black people need to stop committing crimes"; "Black people need to stop having babies out of wedlock"; "Black people need to work hard and get off of welfare." For instance, in 2018, Republican congressman Jason Lewis said, "I happen to think actually that the modern welfare state has really devastated African-American communities, minority communities by making certain that young black males are raised by one parent, not holding fathers accountable. You've added sort of gasoline to the fire of poverty. Now you've got young men with no way to express themselves in a proper way, so violence begets violence and the cycle keeps going on and on and on. You simply can't say the same thing about other groups."[48]

In the end, African Americans have systematic disadvantages that society attributes to their personal shortcomings, while whites living in the suburbs have systemic advantages that society attributes to their hard work. Racist policies — which drive both systemic advantages and disadvantages — remain invisible.

5

BLACK WEALTH, WHITE WEALTH

Myrisha and her sister, two of Grandma and Grandpa Brown's beloved grandchildren, spent much of their childhood laughing and playing at their grandparents' dream home on Baylis Street. These memories, idyllic and untarnished, are true life treasures. Since their son Frederick was a lackluster father, Grandma and Grandpa Brown stood in the gap, spending quality time with their granddaughters . and encouraging them to get the best education possible. "My grandmother was five three, a little bitty lady," Myrisha said with deep affection. "She was like our second mother when my sister and I were away from our mom. My dad would just go about doing what he was doing."

By the time Myrisha was born, her grandparents were slowing down, so Grandpa Brown, then approaching his eighties, could not gallop through the house with his grandchildren on his back. But the love between them was nevertheless profound. Grandpa Brown, always a stoic man, became even more reserved as he aged, seeking refuge in things he loved, like baseball and fishing.

"He watched the Tigers," Myrisha said, a smile slowly lighting her face. "You had the Saturday games and he'd have his Miller beer, sit back, and that was his relaxation. He had a special chair that he would sit in and we'd sit in the chair with him and watch baseball. I didn't have no interest in baseball, but just the fact that we could sit on his lap, in his chair, was just relaxing. Not a whole lot of conversation. Just enjoying the time being in that space with one another."

Although Grandpa Brown rarely spoke, when he did it was always to stress the importance of education. These constant admonitions about getting a good education were how both Grandpa and Grandma Brown demonstrated their love for their grandchildren, planting seeds of wisdom to bloom their futures. Myrisha's lofty educational goals served as proof positive. She dreamed of attending Detroit's premier public high school, Cass Technical High School.

Founded in 1907, Cass Tech has remained Detroit's top high school even as the city has deteriorated economically. "There was no other high school that she wanted to go to. That was it for her," Mona, Myrisha's mom, said. Although Cass Tech is highly selective, Myrisha took the entrance exam and prayed for the best. Mona continued, "I remember the day when that acceptance letter came in the mail and I handed it to her. She was ecstatic."

Getting to Cass Tech by 8 a.m. each day, however, was not easy. Myrisha had to catch two buses, the first arriving at 6 a.m. Myrisha's father, Frederick, never paid child support, but his one and only financial duty was to provide bus fare for his daughters to get to school. "I can remember there would be times that I would call him because he didn't bring the bus fare over," Myrisha said. "I would be worried about if I was going to have money to get to school." Experience taught her that she could not rely on her father. Her mother was her rock and her provider.

One day, Myrisha asked her mom to buy her a Coach bag and Levi's jeans because, like most teenagers, she wanted to sport the hottest name brands. If the kids on popular TV shows like *The Facts of Life* and *Silver Spoons* could wear the latest trends, why couldn't she? Moreover, since Cass Tech is Detroit's premier high school, many of her classmates came from affluent families who could afford to buy their children designer clothes. "Well, I can't on my budget. I can't afford that," Mona explained to Myrisha. "But if you get your education, and you get yourself a good job, these are things that you can obtain on your own because you'll have your own money." Myrisha was disappointed but decided that she was going to work extra hard to become a doctor so she could one day buy fancy clothes and anything else her heart desired. "She would be up till three o'clock or four o'clock in the morning, her head down in her books in the dining room on the table studying," Mona said.

When Myrisha was a freshman at Cass Tech, Grandpa Brown fell ill. It was not until many years later that the family realized it was Alzheimer's disease. At the time, they only knew that a man whose energy and determination had once been boundless was declining. "He was doing the landscaping and keeping the yard up," Myrisha recalled. "After he got sick, I never saw him ever going into the backyard again. No one maintained it." As Grandpa Brown deteriorated, so did the home's cherished garden and majestic apple tree.

Before long, the family had to put him in a nursing home, where Grandma Brown visited her beloved husband daily, ensuring that he was fed, bathed, shaved, and dressed in clean clothes. Myrisha also visited her grandfather regularly at the nursing home, and in May 1984, she was there to celebrate his eighty-third birthday. When he died a month later, his funeral was not a somber occasion. Instead, the family was thankful that their patriarch had lived a good, long life and that he was no longer suffering. He was finally at peace. But after more than fifty years of marriage, his bride was devastated. Grandma Brown had lost her lifelong partner. She had lost her best friend. Afraid of also losing the precious memories held by the Baylis home, she was determined to remain there until her dying day.

After Grandpa Brown died, Myrisha visited her grandmother more regularly. But in 1986, she graduated from Cass Tech and left Detroit for Bradley University, a small liberal arts college in Peoria, Illinois. Myrisha was premed and enjoyed her classes quite a bit. She also loved the new sister friends she made at Bradley. Myrisha was having the time of her life and was even able to purchase the Coach purse she had begged her mother for years earlier. Although Myrisha was making decent grades, after three years at Bradley, she returned to Detroit to take care of her mother, Mona, who was expecting again.

"I was having a lot of difficulty with my eighth pregnancy, which was my son. I was older. I was in my forties and just a lot going on, and just not feeling good. I tried to keep this from her, but she wanted to come home and look after me until I had delivered," Mona said. "So she says, '[College] is something that I can do later on. I can always go back to it, but I got to see about my mom.' So that's what she did."

Being the eldest of her mother's eight children and female, Myrisha has always carried a heavy caretaking load. It felt, therefore, natural for her to put aside her aspirations to take care of her mother and siblings. Like a broken record, this trend has played on repeat throughout her life, unceasing. Myrisha left Bradley in 1989 and never made it back to finish her degree. Her dream to become a doctor died because her family needed her. When Myrisha returned to Detroit, she worked in retail while she cared for her mother and her newborn brother. Almost a decade later, after her grandmother fell and broke her hip in 1998, Myrisha helped her father, Frederick, who still lived with Grandma Brown, with these caretaking responsibilities as well.

Now that she was forced to use a walker, Grandma Brown's movements were labored, but her mind was razor-sharp. She made it abundantly clear that she was not going to a nursing home. So her oldest son and legal guardian, Uncle Bill, installed a hospital bed in the dining room. With time, Grandma Brown's muscles atrophied because she spent the bulk of her days lying in the hospital bed or sitting on a chair in the dining room next to the fireplace, venturing outside only when her eldest daughter picked her up for doctors' appointments. While she was confined to the house, TV was Grandma Brown's constant companion, beating back loneliness.

"Just lying in her bed, listening to the news, she would occupy herself with singing," Myrisha recollected, her voice smiling. "She always sang this song." Then, with perfect pitch, Myrisha began to sing, "You are my sunshine, my only sunshine. You make me happy when skies are gray."

Myrisha visited her grandmother at the Baylis home three or four times a month to help out. Without a car, it was difficult for Frederick to run errands. While he could do some shopping at Savon and Glory, two neighborhood grocery stores with limited selections and higher prices, Myrisha would drive him to a major supermarket chain for his more substantial grocery runs. "If I hadn't taken him, it would have been two bus rides or a bus ride about a half a mile and then walking a couple of blocks," Myrisha reported.

Myrisha would also regularly drive her father to the laundromat to wash clothes because flooding in the basement had destroyed the family's washer and dryer. Most often, Myrisha would pull up, honk the horn, take her father on his errand, and then drop him off. She did not always go inside to see her grandmother, and when she did, she could not stay long because her various caretaking responsibilities and job made intense demands on her time. As best she could, Myrisha supported her father as he tried to take care of his mother.

"Now, my dad was no housekeeper at all," Myrisha said, disapproving anger permeating every syllable. Because of Frederick's half-hearted efforts, the house was in cluttered disarray, a prime candidate for the TV show *Hoarders*. Her grandmother, now in her nineties, was no longer able to tidy up the house, and could only watch as her dream home fell further into disrepair. "She wanted to pedal around and do something, but she was just pretty much reduced to being in the living room or sitting on the edge of her bed probably like the last five years of her life." As these memories resurfaced, Myrisha began to weep.

The clutter, however, was the least of the worries. The shower and tub in the upstairs bathroom were inoperable. Frederick and his mom had just the downstairs half bathroom with only a sink and a toilet. This did not present a problem for Grandma Brown, who could not climb the stairs anyway and so relied on the weekly sitz bath that her daughter or a nurse gave her. With no other options available, Frederick washed up using a similar method. If ever state social workers had entered the home, Myrisha was certain they would have removed her grandmother.

"On the ceiling right up over my grandmother's head (I guess there had been some type of roof leak or some other plumbing issue in the bathroom), that ceiling had fallen in, the plaster, and that hadn't been repaired. And my initial thought was, 'You've got to be kidding me,' because at that point in time, her being home, she could've had different weatherization programs that I know of for a fact, through the City of Detroit, that would have paid for that." Voice now shaking, Myrisha continued, "I was angry, and I mentioned it to my dad, 'Why aren't we getting things repaired? Why is this house in such bad shape?' And he said, 'Well, that's your uncle Bill. He's the one who handles all the money.'"

Uncle Bill was, indeed, his mother's legal guardian, charged with managing her finances and ensuring her general well-being. Uncle Bill was, however, in his seventies and had recently emerged victorious from a battle with cancer. He did not have the capacity to fight for his life and also manage his mother's affairs. Grandma Brown's surviving daughters, who were in their seventies and eighties, were also unable to care for her. One had just lost her husband, and the other was caring for her ill husband and disabled child. On top of it all, Frederick's own health was failing. Under the circumstances, family members suggested that a nursing home could better accommodate Grandma Brown, and while Frederick agreed, his mother did not. Under no circumstances did she want to leave, even if the Baylis house was crumbling, the moribund home burying her and her son alive.

The standoff came to an end in February 2008 when Grandma Brown was not feeling well and the visiting nurse ordered Frederick to rush her to the hospital. Although it turned out to be a minor urinary tract infection, she stayed in the hospital for one week, the longest she had been away from her home in some time. Now that she was far from all that was familiar, depression set in, and Grandma Brown stopped eating. Myrisha, her aunt, and a few cousins took shifts visiting the hospital to feed her. During that time, the person sharing her hospital room said, "Well, you know, she calls out all night for Frederick." When Myrisha heard this, she said, her heart dropped to the floor and cracked a little.

Upon her release from the hospital, the family did not return Grandma Brown to the Baylis home to live with Frederick. Instead, Grandma Brown's children used the opportunity to settle her into a nursing home in Southfield, a nearby suburb, where her daughter lived. Myrisha did not agree with this decision because it was contrary to her grandmother's explicit wishes. "Her health rapidly declined after getting to the nursing home," Myrisha lamented. After about three weeks at the nursing home, Grandma Brown stopped living. Betty Brown died at the ripe old age of 102. In mourning, the one thing that consistently lifted Myrisha's spirits was singing her granny's favorite tune: "You are my sunshine, my only sunshine. You make me happy when skies are gray."

During the quick visits with her grandmother before she died, Myrisha did not get a full picture of just how badly the Baylis home had deteriorated. It was not until Grandma Brown died that she saw the decay with clear eyes. "At some point my aunt and I came over to box up a lot of her stuff and go through it. I just started thinking, 'This is crazy,'" Myrisha said. In addition to the ceiling damage above Grandma Brown's hospital bed and the unusable upstairs bathroom, the plumbing in the basement was also inoperable, which was what caused the flooding that had destroyed the washer and dryer. Lead paint abounded, as the Browns had never remediated the home. Nor had they upgraded the house's old windows, causing severe energy inefficiencies. "There were no repairs and no updates done on the house," Myrisha said. "My uncle just paid for taxes, utilities, and food."

Given that her husband had worked at Ford for over thirty years, Grandma Brown should have had a sizable pension, affording her a comfortable life. But she did not. According to Frederick, she only "got along" because when Grandpa Brown retired, he opted to collect his pension in a lump sum, which left Grandma Brown without much income. As a musician who could not travel to gigs because he was his mother's full-time caretaker, Frederick, too, had scant income. Both relied upon Uncle Bill, a senior vice president at Ford, who was a man of means.

While his mother was living in Detroit, Uncle Bill and his second wife were "living out their suburban dream in Bloomfield Hills," Myrisha said, with contempt for this 84 percent white Detroit suburb.[1] With 39 percent of owner-occupied homes having a value of more than $1 million, Bloomfield Hills is one of the wealthiest cities in the United States with a population over 1,000.[2] In 2020, the average income for married couples in Bloomfield Hills was close to a quarter of a million dollars, and the median household income was $177,614, almost three times the median of all Michigan households, which is $59,234.[3] With his world now centered in Bloomfield Hills, Myrisha felt that Uncle Bill had turned his back on Detroit and those he left behind. Myrisha would never do that. Never.

Uncle Bill dropped by the house monthly to bring his mother money for groceries and utilities, so "he had to have known, just visually looking, that that house was in disrepair," Myrisha said. "That was his choice." The house was crumbling and Uncle Bill, indeed, was partially to blame. But in holding Uncle Bill fully responsible for the home's deterioration, Myrisha ignored the reasons that made it difficult for her grandparents to take care of it in the first place. There was an invisible culprit responsible for the deterioration of the Brown family's home and other homes throughout the city — racist policies such as redlining and predatory land contracts.

While the Fair Housing Act of 1968 and the 1974 Equal Credit Opportunity Act made it illegal for banks to prohibit lending in minority neighborhoods, redlining still occurs in other forms. As an informal practice, banks do not typically lend to homes valued under $50,000. From 2011 to 2017, banks issued only 14 percent of mortgages to Detroit homes worth less than $50,000, but 79 percent of Detroit homes sold in this range.[4] Consequently, this informal practice is, in effect, redlining by a different name.

Since banks have not provided a substantial number of mortgages in Detroit, residents customarily have purchased homes through land contracts, a costlier form of financing. The extra costs rob homeowners of the funds necessary to maintain and renovate their homes, while various forms of redlining have deprived them of traditional home improvement loans. Bereft of investment, the city suffers pervasive blight.

With the Baylis home in ruins, Uncle Bill, like many others in his position, chose to walk away from it after his mother died. In 2008, he signed the home over to Myrisha. "When my grandparents moved over there, it was very stable," Myrisha said of the surrounding neighborhood. "But you had a lot of people who, like me, inherited homes from older people living in the homes, but the homes weren't being maintained and being upgraded. Just visually looking at them, a lot of them needed windows, siding, roofs." Like a deep-sea diver denied oxygen, once-vibrant homes and neighborhoods deprived of investment die an inescapable death.

This left Myrisha and many other Detroit residents in a bind: What exactly do you do with a dead or dying home? Families who walk away from their bequeathed blight make it a prime target for scavengers, who typically strip the home of all copper pipes and other valuable metals, rendering the building not only useless but also a public safety hazard that the City is eventually forced to demolish. Where dream homes once stood, there are now only empty lots. Myrisha knew that two important buildings in the family's history had already been demolished by the City of Detroit: the house near Highland Park that the Browns first rented from Grandpa Brown's Italian co-worker, and the first one they purchased, on Fifteenth Street. She could not bear the thought of another family home, which held so many of her precious childhood memories, being demolished. She was, therefore, determined to rescue the Baylis home.

"My grandparents worked hard for that home," Myrisha said. "They came from North Carolina, lived in Highland Park, and my grandfather was able to get a job from Ford. They bought a house (their first home), and this house was their upgrade. That's where my attachment to it comes from. I was there. I was a little girl. This is their legacy." She continued, "I'm looking at the fact that my younger family members, they never got to come over there and eat apples off the apple tree."

But the legacy that Myrisha inherited was a money pit rather than a wealth-producing asset. As the years passed, even the apple tree, once a majestic symbol of all that Grandpa and Grandma Brown had achieved, perished. "By the time that I inherited the house," Myrisha grieved, "the tree was dead."

Although Robert Ficano was also the grandchild of a sharecropper who immigrated to Detroit and worked at Ford's foundry, his experience was considerably different from Myrisha's. After Grandpa Bucci died in 1990 at Henry Ford Hospital from stroke complications, at age eighty-five, and Grandma Bucci, age ninety-four, joined him in the afterlife in 2004, Robert inherited the Livonia home that they had purchased and customized in 1976 for $28,000. Robert still lives in his legacy today. "I'm living in their house now because I don't have a note on it," Robert said, his voice jolly. "So that's the biggest reason." After Robert upgraded the home, it is currently worth about $250,000.

It was not at all easy for Grandpa and Grandma Bucci and other poor European immigrants to secure housing and establish themselves in a brand-new country. Racist policies, however, made the white housing experience different from the African American one. Racial covenants placed no restriction on where foreign-born whites could live, so they could rent or purchase a home anywhere in the city of Detroit, including the areas designated for Blacks. They could also do what Dr. Ossian Sweet could only dream of — safely move to the more spacious, newer, cheaper, and higher-quality housing with superior amenities that was popping up like dandelions in the city's outskirts. Also, the federal government did not redline the communities where European immigrants resided, cutting off investment, ensuring that their communities decayed, and transforming Italians or Germans or Poles into pariahs whose very presence threatened housing prices.

In contrast — because of redlining, racial covenants, predatory mortgage lending, and other policies of disinvestment that cement America's racial caste system — the Detroit home that Grandma and Grandpa Brown left their granddaughter was worth less than $10,000. Myrisha inherited a dead apple tree. The problem, however, is bigger than Myrisha's suffocated inheritance. All African American families confined to Detroit did not have the same opportunity as whites in the suburbs to build intergenerational wealth, which happens when valuable assets, such as cash, financial market investments, businesses, and homes are passed from one generation to another. While wealth transfer through stocks and business holdings is most common for upper-class families, housing is usually the largest financial asset passed down in middle- and working-class families.[5] But, as shown in the figure below, home values in Detroit have declined markedly since 1970, while the values in Livonia and other Detroit suburbs have increased or remained constant.

Figure 1: Median value of single-family home adjusted to 2020 dollars[6]

	DETROIT	LIVONIA	DEARBORN
1970	$104,052	$180,757	$152,076
1980	$133,450	$194,366	$154,174
1990	$50,688	$187,308	$137,412
2000	$95,400	$242,700	$193,950
2010	$95,676	$217,413	$172,907
2020	$52,700	$204,300	$154,100

These numbers are not just the result of historic policies, they are also caused by contemporary racist policies, such as unfair property tax practices, which continue to strip intergenerational wealth from Black communities. For instance, between 2010 and 2020, the effective property tax rate in Detroit's public school district was about 14.92 percent, while it was only 1.96 percent in Livonia's and 4.53 percent in Redford's.[7] Although for many years dominant discourses painted inner-city African Americans as welfare-dependent tax burdens, data show that they are, in fact, overtaxed. Even worse, because of persistent racial segregation, many have been unable to protest the high property tax rates by leaving the city.

Additionally, between 2013 and 2016, local property tax authorities illegally inflated the home values of about 70 percent of Detroit homes in violation of the Michigan Constitution, but only 32 percent in Livonia.[8] Then, because authorities failed to provide free and easy access to the poverty tax exemption — which partially or fully releases indigent homeowners from the obligation to pay property taxes — tens of thousands of Detroit homeowners completed the property tax foreclosure process for failure to pay property taxes that they should not have owed in the first place. Wayne County and the State of Michigan compounded these problems with their overly complicated property tax relief programs, and statutorily mandated an 18 percent interest penalty on delinquent amounts, in addition to other fines and fees.

Along with blockbusting, redlining, and urban renewal, the city, county, and state property tax policies, while racially neutral on their face, disproportionately impact African Americans, and hence are a quintessential example of racist policies, which operate silently in the background. Victims are left foregrounded and thus drawing all the blame. As a result, the public discourse becomes about Black people's poor individual choices. Myrisha, however, inherited a blighted home not because of her family's bad choices or moral failings, but because of racist policies. Without a clear understanding of how racist policies led to the unequal inheritances Grandpa Brown and Grandpa Bucci passed down to their grandchildren, it is easy to come to the incorrect conclusion that the primary reason Grandpa Bucci and his descendants have more wealth is because they worked harder. Grandpa Brown and his progeny, too, worked hard.

Racist policies are not a relic of the past, but instead have rigged the game board, causing the current racial wealth gap. But in discussions about racial inequality, most Americans are obsessed with identifying the racist because Hollywood has trained us all to look for the villain. That is, we want to locate the corrupt person or group of wicked people responsible. Talking about the damage done by an amalgam of racist policies does not fit the good-and-evil paradigm that Hollywood has drilled into our collective consciousness. Consequently, conversations about racist policies and their long shadow are not part of the dominant discourse. It is time for change.

PART II:

THE CONSEQUENCES OF RACIST POLICIES

The Granddaughter's Pain

6

BURDENS OF CARETAKING

Myrisha has a willowy frame, fine features, ageless caramel-colored skin, and a girlish pixie cut. Although slender, she has a weighty laugh that wraps her interlocutors in a warm, heavy embrace. Her delicate stature belies an indomitable spirit. As a woman in an economically fragile family, she has borne on her narrow shoulders a crushing caretaking load that would crumple most people. Myrisha, nevertheless, has found a way to thrive.

In addition to her father, mother, siblings, and children, Andricus, the father of Myrisha's two children, was among the long list of folks she cared for, despite the many ways he mistreated her. Myrisha first met Andricus, an attractive man dripping with confidence, at a nightclub in 2000. By 2002, they had a son together. Myrisha had no idea that eleven months before her son was born, when she and Andricus were ostensibly together, Andricus had married another woman and fathered another child.

Despite his infidelity, when Andricus was carjacked and shot multiple times in the back and chest in 2005, Myrisha took him in and nursed him back to health. "The oxygen was cut off from his brain for a few minutes," Myrisha reported. "So he had to learn how to walk and talk." Andricus would spend the rest of his life between a wheelchair and a walker.

Disabled and on a fixed income that was subject to automatic deductions for various child support payments, Andricus needed help. Myrisha answered the call, allowing him to remain in her house even after he recovered. Then, in 2008, Myrisha and Andricus had their second child—a girl. Their living arrangement got awkward when Andricus had other "secret relationships" and several more surprise children materialized. Although humiliated, Myrisha wanted to keep her family intact.

"Our relationship had ended after my daughter was born," Myrisha said. "But we decided he would live with me, so my kids could live in the house with their dad. We did parenting together, but the relationship with all the other mothers was very stressed." According to Myrisha, in exchange for tolerating Andricus's womanizing, she got "free" child care. While she readily offered help to others, Myrisha had to pay a high price to get the help she herself so desperately needed.

The birth of her beloved daughter in 2008 was a bright spot in what was one of the most difficult years of Myrisha's life. First her grandmother died. Then Myrisha was forced to close her car detailing business, a labor of love that she built from the ground up. She got started with this line of work in 1990 when she was "fumbling around," trying to figure out her next big move after leaving college. Mike, her childhood friend, invited her to manage one of his two car detail shops. After Myrisha abandoned her dreams of becoming a doctor, she decided to become a businesswoman, so the opportunity to run one of Mike's operations seemed like a step in the right direction. Over time, Myrisha had earned a bachelor's degree in business, stopped working for Mike, and started operating two of her own thriving car detailing locations, which employed about twenty people.

Myrisha, however, had to walk away from all of this in 2008 because a series of family medical crises brought her life to a screeching halt. Her sister Lisa fell mortally ill while seventeen weeks pregnant. Doctors found abscesses in her brain and conducted six brain surgeries in a span of five months. Lisa survived, but her brain damage was irreversible. Nevertheless, Myrisha and Lisa's mother, Mona, was unequivocally against aborting the baby, so Lisa delivered her baby boy through C-section. He was born in perfect health, and today he is an intelligent, rambunctious preteen. His mother, on the other hand, has remained medically fragile and mentally inert, suffering from severe depression, seizures, and a host of other maladies.

In addition to taking care of Lisa and her newborn, Myrisha and Mona also had to take care of Myrisha's two children: an infant daughter and a son in kindergarten. Additionally, since Myrisha's sister Bertie, who suffered from schizophrenia, had been in and out of mental institutions her entire life, the duo cared for her and her son as well. As if this were not overwhelming enough, Myrisha's sister Allie has an autoimmune disease that regularly lands her in the hospital, so Myrisha and Mona cared for both Allie and her young son.

More than ever, Mona and Myrisha depended on each other to keep their family afloat. This is why Myrisha had to make a very hard choice: she could either run her businesses or help her mother with all of their family's caretaking responsibilities. She could not do both. "I closed the businesses," Myrisha reported. Just as she had left university to take care of her mother when Mona was having complications with her pregnancy, Myrisha now shut down her businesses to care for her sisters and their children. As the eldest child and a woman, Myrisha carried a heavy burden of duty. She would never turn her back on her family even when it came at great cost to herself.

After shuttering her businesses, Myrisha was living on the meager income she earned through the foster care system for taking care of her nephew, but she was, nevertheless, determined to rehabilitate her inheritance. "I'm fixing it up one room at a time out of my own finances and trying to juggle paying taxes," she said. Even as Myrisha scraped money together to repaint the living room where she had spent many happy hours with her grandparents, Detroit's Office of the Assessor was illegally inflating her property tax bill. Unemployed, Myrisha fell behind on her property tax payments.

In 2008, the year she took ownership of the Baylis home, Detroit's Office of the Assessor taxed the home as if it were worth $82,684, despite its having no functioning shower, tub, or heating system, as well as countless other problems. Within a three-block radius of the Baylis home, nine homes sold in 2008, and the median sale value was $12,000, while the highest sale value was $34,000. The data also show that between 2011 and 2017, the City of Detroit inflated the values of more than half the neighboring homes in violation of the Michigan Constitution.[1]

When asked if she knew about the overtaxation, Myrisha responded, "Back then, I just did not know." Myrisha did not know that she had to examine the assessment notice that came every January, find the property's assessed value, then multiply that number by 2. If the amount equaled more than the market value of her home, this was a violation of the Michigan Constitution. Myrisha did not know this because the City does not print this constitutional standard, which all assessors must comply with, on any documents mailed to homeowners. Without access to accurate information, Myrisha blindly created her own metrics of fair taxation.

"I had no problem with the taxes because the home was paid for," Myrisha replied when asked whether she then believed that her annual property tax bill was fair. "What I was paying in rent would have been equivalent to paying the taxes. Well, at that point, what I'm thinking in my mind is I'm not paying a mortgage on the house. If you're somewhere paying rent of four hundred and fifty dollars or up, that is equivalent to what I was paying in taxes. For me, as a working person, it made sense." But the property taxes on a home that has been fully paid off should not be comparable to rent or mortgage payments. According to the law, her inflated property tax bill made no sense at all and was clearly illegal.

If the City overvalued a home, the owner had only fifteen days —

February 1 to February 15 — to file an appeal because Detroit was the only city in Michigan to legally mandate that homeowners go through an extra step in the appeal process called the Assessor Review. Myrisha, however, had no clue that a property tax appeal process even existed. Most low-income homeowners are in a similar situation: either they do not know about the appeals process or they submit ineffective appeals, which leaves them to pay their illegally inflated property tax bills. In contrast, flanked by lawyers or real estate specialists, affluent homeowners in Detroit and throughout the nation are more likely to file a protest and win substantial reductions.[2]

To achieve accurate and fair property tax bills, correct property valuations are necessary. But this can be difficult for local governments to accomplish because, while the sales tax is based on the *actual* sales price of an item, the property tax is based on an *estimate* of the home value, so there is significant room for error. Property tax appeals processes are in place in every locality throughout the U.S. because, as in any large administrative process, it is impossible for even the best-intentioned local government to reach 100 percent accuracy in property valuation estimates. Appeals are designed to correct the few inevitable errors.[3] But a study shows that between 2009 and 2015, Detroit's Office of the Assessor overvalued between 53 and 84 percent of Detroit homes in violation of the Michigan Constitution.[4] Since Detroit's entire system for valuing homes was in error, the appeals process could not possibly fix this type of systemic malfunction.

Nevertheless, at a town hall meeting, Detroit mayor Mike Duggan said that while the illegally inflated assessments were unfortunate, all homeowners had an opportunity to appeal, so the City was not liable for compensating them.[5] By relying on homeowners to file appeals to correct systematically inaccurate property tax assessments, the City forced homeowners to do its job, few of whom had the skills or resources to take on this sizable responsibility. When homeowners failed to appeal, City officials framed this failure as irresponsible behavior, declaring that the City, therefore, could not be expected to bear the consequences. Once again, the blame-shifting personal irresponsibility narrative masked the true story of systemic injustice.

It gets worse. Myrisha, and many other residents who were struggling to make their payments, shouldn't have been responsible for paying any property taxes at all. The poverty tax exemption ("the exemption") releases low-income homeowners from paying their property tax bill. As an unemployed person, Myrisha, like the 40 percent of Detroit residents living below the federal poverty line, qualified for the exemption. However, due to the lack of information and the City's unduly onerous application process, she and many other qualifying Detroit homeowners did not receive this entitlement. Adding insult to injury, Michigan law required them to pay an 18 percent interest penalty on delinquent amounts, as well as other fines and fees.[6]

As a consequence, Myrisha had considerable property tax debts in 2008 ($2,106), 2009 ($1,858), and 2010 ($1,768). The County allowed Myrisha to enter a payment plan that extended and reduced her payments, but she could not afford even this amount. Once a property tax debt is three years old, under Michigan law, the county can foreclose on the home and sell it at auction to collect the past-due amounts. So if Myrisha did not find a job and pay off her 2008 taxes by March 2011, the Baylis home would land on the auction block.

Fortunately, in February 2010, Myrisha secured employment at a Chevrolet dealership, doing what she loved most, detailing cars. Her starting salary at the dealership was $24,000, but after she turned their detailing service into a profitable department, she rose to a management position a few short months after she began the job. She was now not only receiving a salary but also a commission based on her new department's profits, earning between $50,000 and $60,000 annually. It was more money than she had ever made in her life. Most importantly, with this new job, she was able to pay part of her tax debt and save her inheritance from property tax foreclosure.

After saving the Baylis home, Myrisha turned her energy to rescuing Frederick Brown. Although he had not been much of a father, Myrisha took care of Frederick because along with her grandparents' house, she had also inherited its sole occupant. Only half jokingly, she referred to both as "the problem child." Myrisha quickly realized that, just as he had been unable to maintain the house, Frederick had done a poor job taking care of himself.

"One winter," Frederick said, "they cut the gas off, so I had these little electrical heaters in the room and closed the room off. It got cold at times." He continued, "One of them winters, with all the below-freezing temperatures, Arthur jumped on me." After a mischievous chuckle, Frederick disclosed that Arthur is the name he has given to his arthritis.

When Frederick began complaining about his inability to see, Myrisha paid out of pocket for him to have an eye exam and get glasses because, though he was eligible, he did not yet have Medicaid. With his teeth in terrible shape, Myrisha's sister scheduled a dental appointment for Frederick. Through the help of government programs, Frederick was eventually able to get some long-overdue extractions and a set of partial dentures. But Frederick's arthritis, poor vision, and rotten teeth paled in comparison to his most urgent problem — a flesh-eating disease, in which bacteria chomped his buttocks and back, leaving oozing blisters and open lesions in its wake.

One day Myrisha picked Frederick up for their monthly grocery run and he could barely walk, the back of his pants drenched in putrid liquid. Myrisha had had enough and decided to take charge of the situation. "I met with the doctor who was treating him, asking questions. By then it was just so severe where the flesh had been eaten. It devastated me to see that. It was like we were looking at raw hamburger, raw meat." Myrisha discovered that the doctor had been treating Frederick for some time, but after the flare-ups calmed, Frederick had not gone back to the hospital.

Because Frederick did not have health insurance, the doctor gave

Myrisha specific instructions to ensure that he received the help he sorely needed: "Take your dad to Detroit Receiving Hospital through emergency. They are going to admit him. They're going to call me and I'm going to say he has to have surgery. Do not let him out of the hospital." Despite the searing pain, Frederick did not want to go to the hospital for surgery, but Myrisha ignored his wishes and admitted him. Immediately, doctors intravenously administered potent antibiotics, and a surgeon deftly removed the decay. She then grafted skin from Frederick's thighs to replace the decomposed flesh.

After the surgery, Myrisha brought her dad home and "from that point, I was his caregiver," she said. "I had to go over every day after work to dress his wounds. He had to have his behind totally cleaned and I had to dress it." And so, in addition to all the other lives she had taken responsibility for, Myrisha cared for a father who throughout her life had rarely cared for her.

Frederick's situation is not unique. Many people in Detroit do not have access to the medical care they need. Just as redlining and other forms of systemic disinvestment have caused Detroit's housing stock to decay, associated resource deficits have caused the city's health care infrastructure to crumble as well. While Detroit had forty-two hospitals open in predominantly African American neighborhoods in 1960, by 2010 only four remained, and they were forced to serve larger populations without the increased resources required, leading to understaffing, inadequate maintenance of facilities and equipment, and substandard care.[7]

Once her father's health stabilized, Myrisha helped Frederick start the paperwork for Medicaid and Social Security, ensuring that he would finally have an income, health care, and hence some stability. Myrisha also knew she needed to get him out of the Baylis home, even though Frederick was dead set against leaving. "I put my foot down," Myrisha declared. "I'm like, 'Look, you can't be in this house, Dad. You cannot even bathe in here.'" She helped her dad apply for senior housing in Highland Park, which was less than two miles from the Baylis home and blocks from the home Grandpa Brown's Italian co-worker had allowed them to rent back in the day. Just as the Baylis home's decay pushed Frederick's mother out, it would also force him to evacuate.

In 2012, with his medical and dental issues resolved, a Social Security check, and a subsidized apartment, Frederick rejoined society. "Before, he was really apprehensive about getting out to do things because he didn't feel confident," Myrisha said, referring to his pungent sores and rotting teeth. "So now he's in a good place and he's able to handle himself." After years of sacrificing his musical career to care for his parents, Frederick now plays bass at several churches in town.

With Frederick relocated and the house empty, Myrisha allowed her younger sister Allie and her young son to live in the home. Due to her illness, Allie was unable to work consistently and desperately needed a place to stay, but because the Baylis home was in such poor condition, she stayed there only when she got tired of sleeping on other people's couches. As the upstairs was largely uninhabitable, Allie and her son set up camp in the living room where Grandma Brown had spent her last days.

Since the house was only intermittently occupied, it became bait for burglars, who took the security gates from the front and back doors and shattered the house's brittle windows. After entering, they stole the hot water tank and even Frederick's record collection, which was so extensive that he could not take it all with him. Myrisha could not afford to fix the damage, so she hammered boards over the window frames to keep the elements out. She believed that the thefts occurred because, after years of vacancy, the corner home adjacent to hers had become a dumping ground that attracted criminals. One study confirmed her intuitions, finding that after a property becomes vacant, the violent crime rate within a 250-foot radius of the property is 19 percent higher than the rate in the area between 250 and 353 feet from the property. Additionally, longer periods of vacancy have a greater effect on crime rates.[8] The corner home was, indeed, attracting crime, but a larger, less conspicuous illegality was also occurring.

As with all the other homes in the neighborhood, the City of Detroit had been overestimating this corner home's value for years, leading to illegally inflated property taxes that the owner could not afford to pay (see Figure 2). To calculate a home's property tax bill, Michigan officials need to know the assessed value, property tax rate, exemptions, and inflation rate. Calculating these factors is fairly straightforward, with the exception of the assessed value, which is the dollar value local authorities assign to a home. The Michigan State Constitution, along with supporting legislation and case law, says the assessed value can be no more than 50 percent of the property's market value. Therefore, if a property is worth $50,000, then its assessed value cannot exceed $25,000.

Figure 2:

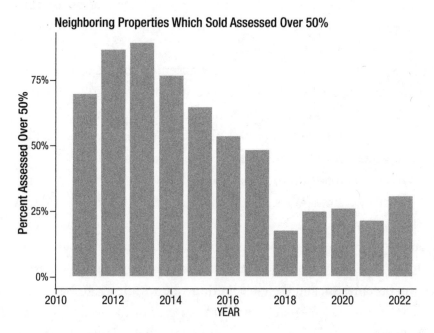

Neighboring Properties Which Sold Assessed Over 50%

Officials determine a home's market price through the sales comparison approach, which uses recent sales of comparable properties sold voluntarily on the open market.[9] If, for example, three properties in a neighborhood with similar features — such as square footage, building age, building material, improvements, and amenities — have recently sold for $100,000, $105,000, and $110,000, then the market value of the home is between $100,000 and $110,000.

In 2011 and 2012, the City of Detroit taxed the neighboring home as if it were worth $43,528 and $39,680, respectively. But at that time, sales of similar properties indicated that the true market value was closer to $7,407 and $4,337 in those years. Since the City taxed the corner home at six to nine times more than its true market value, the property tax bill was $2,002 in 2011 and $2,014 in 2012. When the owner could not keep up, in 2013, Wayne County foreclosed and sold the corner house for $3,600 at its property tax auction to a limited-liability company (LLC) registered in California. All auction buyers can only view the outside of any property for sale, so after purchase, when they finally have an opportunity to enter the property, many buyers abandon homes once they figure out that the repairs needed would cost more than the finished home would be worth.

While the corner home was vacant, two sets of squatters took up residence there. One was a woman in her thirties with two small children who told all the neighbors that she was trying to buy the house. Myrisha did not believe her, and her suspicions were confirmed when the woman asked if she could "borrow" some electricity by running an extension cord through the Baylis home. Myrisha refused. Like many vacant homes, the corner home was left without access to electricity and water when scrap metal thieves stripped the home of everything valuable, including metal pipes, copper wires, and the furnace. Left without utilities, after about a year, the woman and her family departed.

Within a few months, a man moved in, occupying the home intermittently for another year. Then, in 2015, Myrisha's worst fear came to pass—the corner home's garage caught on fire and the untamed flames quickly spread to the Baylis home's garage. This type of fire is tragically common in Detroit, with 2,256 fires damaging 1,653 structures in the city between January 1 and July 31 of 2015.[10] Additionally, of the 26,244 foreclosed properties in Wayne County in 2014 and the 28,200 in 2015, 665 caught fire.[11]

Like many LLCs that acquire homes through the tax foreclosure auction, the California company never paid property taxes. Consequently, after three years, the County again confiscated the corner home through tax foreclosure. But since the home, now fire-damaged, was so badly deteriorated, no one bid on it and the Detroit Land Bank Authority took possession. Like so many other Detroit homes, the corner house followed a familiar and tragic trajectory: overtaxation followed by tax foreclosure, vacancy, and blight.

With property tax foreclosure affecting eleven of the twenty homes on her block alone, Myrisha's neighborhood was rotting away. Nevertheless, she intended to rehabilitate her grandparents' home, investing in her inheritance instead of abandoning it. Since her new job at the Chevrolet dealership came with a sizable salary, Myrisha was more determined than ever to complete the renovations.

Her mother, however, gently questioned the wisdom of her resolve. "Do you really want to do this?" Mona wondered. "You are working, but you don't have a huge income. Trying to save the house and take care of the kids, it is a lot." Myrisha took her mother's words to heart, but she had to keep moving forward. Renovating the Baylis home was not something she wanted to do, it was something she *had* to do.

Beaming with pride, Mona described her daughter's undertaking. "Myrisha just started by cleaning everything out and sending stuff out; all the old stuff that didn't need to be there," Mona said. "She had a lot of friends that she had gone to school with and everybody chipped in as much as they could, putting their time in to help her get the house together. One of her classmates painted the house. Another did the electrical work. So it was like inch by inch." For the tasks her friends could not complete, Myrisha hired contractors, who required constant monitoring and became an endless source of frustration.

Notwithstanding her limited budget and substantial caretaking obligations, Myrisha was able to make significant progress with the renovation. "And over time, I was just shocked. I'm like, 'Wow, I can't believe looking from how it was to where you've brought it up,'" Mona confessed. Myrisha estimated that she spent a total of $15,000 on home improvements, which included painting, new sinks and toilets, roof repair, water damage rectification, hot water tank installation, and tearing down the charred garage. Despite Myrisha's herculean efforts, the house was not yet in compliance with the local housing code because it lacked heat. Also, new siding, plumbing, and windows were needed, which Myrisha estimated would cost at least another $25,000.

These sums could have been used for a down payment on a newer home in the suburbs, where her family would find better public schools and amenities, so why didn't Myrisha simply choose to leave? "I believe in the city of Detroit," Myrisha responded. "I live here. I want to see the rebirth of the city. And if we keep walking away from homes and moving to the suburbs, our neighborhoods are going to continue to deteriorate."

7

THE YELLOW BAG

Since Myrisha was determined to resurrect her legacy, in 2013, she applied for a $6,000 home improvement loan from the Fifth Third Bank to fix the furnace so that it would be in compliance with Detroit's housing code. But the bank denied her application, stating that her credit was not up to par. As a result, Myrisha continued using her earnings to renovate her legacy one room at a time, even as she rented an apartment with her children and their father. The situation, however, was not sustainable. By 2013, she was back in property tax trouble.

Unlike most other Detroit homeowners with property tax debt, Myrisha had the good fortune of discovering the Michigan State Housing Development Authority (MSHDA) Step Forward Program, a loan assistance plan operating from 2010 to 2020 that used federal Hardest Hit Fund monies to stop foreclosures and revitalize neighborhoods. These federal funds were born of outrage over the Obama administration's failure to help homeowners during the Great Recession, even as the government bailed out the banks that had engaged in the predatory mortgage lending practices that caused the 2008 housing market crash in the first place. To ease voter resentment, the federal program initially awarded $1.5 billion to the five states — Michigan, Arizona, California, Florida, and Nevada — with the steepest home price declines so that they could create local foreclosure prevention programs for people struggling to meet their mortgage payments.[1] It eventually grew to a $9.6 billion program, involving eighteen states and the District of Columbia.

In 2010, Michigan created Step Forward (also known as Michigan's Hardest Hit Fund loan program) to expend $761 million in federal monies it received.[2] Initially, Michigan authorities focused on mortgage foreclosure prevention, but then they expanded Step Forward's ambit to include property tax foreclosure prevention in 2010 and blight removal through demolition in 2013. From July 2010 to December 2017, the Step Forward program spent $66,970,735 across the state, disbursing 73 percent of the funding for property tax debt assistance and only 27 percent for mortgage debt assistance.

This demonstrates that inequitable and unaffordable property taxes were a statewide problem. In fact, research shows that in Michigan, the lower-valued properties systematically pay a higher property tax rate than the higher-valued properties, meaning property taxes are regressive. From 2007 to 2017, Michigan was the second most regressive state in America.[3] Beat only by Alabama.

By the time Myrisha discovered Step Forward in 2013, her past-due principal, interest, and fees amounted to $5,925 for her 2010 property tax bill, $2,015 for the 2011 bill, and $1,430 for the 2012 bill. Compounding her troubles, the Wayne County treasurer hung a yellow bag on the Baylis home's front porch — the shameful mark of foreclosure. If Myrisha did not pay her 2010 debt by March 2013, the yellow bag made it clear that the treasurer would foreclose on her home and sell it at auction. Myrisha was on a payment plan that would stave off tax foreclosure so long as she paid her current property taxes, along with $615 per month on her past debt, but the required payments were still unaffordable. Caught in an avalanche of indebtedness that was suffocating her, Myrisha hoped that the Step Forward program was the rescue team.

In theory, Step Forward provided a zero percent forgivable loan of up to $30,000 so owner-occupants could pay their delinquent mortgage and property tax bills. For Detroiters mired in property tax debt, this should have been a deliverance. In reality, however, the program provided, on average, only $4,000 to each applicant, and the State structured the program so it primarily benefited middle-class homeowners who experienced momentary financial struggles rather than low-income homeowners who endured chronic poverty. In other words, the hardest hit did not qualify for Michigan's Hardest Hit Fund loan program. How did this happen?

The program required that prior to the onset of the delinquency, the homeowner must have experienced a "qualifying involuntary hardship," which authorities defined as "an unexpected event beyond your control that caused the delinquency or has impacted your ability to maintain payments." Chronic poverty did not qualify as hardship, which the program narrowly defined as a medical event, job loss, underemployment, receipt of unemployment benefits, death, divorce, or a one-time critical out-of-pocket expense.[4] Homeowners were out of luck if they experienced a series of cascading hardships that did not fit neatly into one of these predetermined boxes. In addition, since applicants had to prove that the qualifying hardship occurred in the same year that they fell behind on their property taxes, if families cut other expenses or spent down reserves in that year to keep up with payments, they would not qualify.

MSHDA also required applicants to prove that they had sufficient income to avoid future property tax delinquency. This disadvantaged people who were self-employed or worked in the informal economy, where there are no pay stubs or other documentation that the program required. This requirement also disadvantaged low-income people who qualified for the poverty tax exemption. When Detroit activists requested that MSHDA cancel this income requirement for homeowners who qualified for the exemption — which would ensure that there were no future delinquencies — authorities refused.

There was another major reason that those who most desperately needed Step Forward funds couldn't access them: Michigan's rules concerning land contracts. In 2020, the mortgage denial rate for African Americans was 27 percent, but only 13 percent for white applicants.[5] Since it is especially difficult for low-income Black homeowners to get a mortgage in Detroit, they most often purchase homes via land contracts, which, as discussed in earlier chapters, involve unregulated seller financing that replaces the advantages of homeownership with the disadvantages of renting. As the number of owner-occupied homes in Detroit without a mortgage steadily increased, land contracts became more commonplace, and in 2008, land contracts exceeded mortgages in Detroit.[6] Despite these trends, payments due on land contracts were not eligible for Step Forward funds.

Step Forward required applicants for property tax debt relief to have recorded property titles, but buyers in a land contract typically do not receive the property title until they have completed all payments. Michigan authorities did not accept recorded land contracts. Additionally, the portion of the tax debt accumulated before purchasers paid off their land contracts and had title transferred into their names was not eligible for Step Forward monies. Since the program's rules regarding land contracts sorely disadvantaged low-income homeowners unable to access mortgages, activists requested that MSHDA revoke them. Although MSHDA successfully petitioned the Treasury Department to make over a dozen other amendments to Step Forward, authorities did not make any of the amendments Detroit activists requested.

As a result, Detroit homeowners who were drowning in property tax debt most often could not access Step Forward. From July 2010 to December 2017, MSHDA received only 16,831 applications from Detroit homeowners, although between 2014 and 2017 alone, 97,913 Detroit homes had property tax debt.[7] MSHDA approved 44 percent of the applications it received, declined 37 percent, and withdrew 19 percent. For those approved, it was as if they had won the lottery.

Myrisha won the lottery. She was among the few Detroiters who discovered the program, applied, traversed the labyrinthine rules, and emerged triumphant, rewarded with funds. To accomplish this feat, Myrisha first had to fit her idiosyncratic situation into one of the predetermined "involuntary hardships." Luckily, she fit into two existing categories. Myrisha was "unemployed," starting in December 2008 and ending in February 2010, when she secured her job at the Chevrolet dealership. She also had a "one-time critical out-of-pocket expense" because the IRS had withheld her tax refund from 2009 to 2011 to pay a federal income tax debt. Most importantly, she had specific paperwork to document these authorized hardships, circumventing a common obstacle. Because her involuntary hardships corresponded with the year of her oldest property debt, which was 2010, Myrisha was also able to evade this snare, which eliminated many others.

The next challenge that most low-income homeowners could not overcome was the income requirements, but now that Myrisha had a full-time job, she successfully sidestepped this problem. Also, since she had inherited a fully paid home, Myrisha did not have a land contract and skirted around this hurdle, which tripped up many others. Myrisha's prize for successfully making her way through the labyrinth came in April 2013: $9,400 to pay her 2010, 2011, and 2012 property tax debts. She was finally free of all property tax debts. "It was a great relief," Myrisha said with a sigh. "I focused from that point on actually starting to put money into the house to try to get it up to some type of standard where it just didn't look like a vacant house, unattended."

Even though the erasure of Myrisha's property tax debt removed a great weight, heavy caretaking responsibilities still threatened to squash her. She was taking care of the Baylis home. Taking care of her father. Taking care of her own children and their father. Taking care of her sisters' children. Then, just as Myrisha was taking care of so much, holding so much emotional and economic weight, the car dealership fired her. "I'm working sixty-plus hours to try and take care of all these different households," Myrisha said, frowning. "And in the midst of that, in 2014, out of nowhere, my boss just comes to me and says that they're eliminating my position. My health care, all my benefits, everything just gone."

Myrisha is a fighter who does not understand defeat, so she was down, but not for long. She soon found another detailing job at a company called Metro Cars. "So now I go from a position where you're salaried and commissioned to just an hourly, forty-hours-a-week situation. I took a thirty-thousand-dollar pay cut," Myrisha said. Unsurprisingly, she again fell behind on her property tax payments.

The 2013 property taxes for the Baylis home were due in 2014, and Myrisha did not have the $1,470. Likewise, in 2015, Myrisha did not have the $1,050 to pay the 2014 taxes. "Trying to make the house livable and paying bills, it became a situation where I know I need to be paying on the taxes, but I've got to be doing this, that, and the other to keep the utilities on and that kind of thing," Myrisha said. "So I got behind."

Myrisha was only able to make sporadic payments, which did not make even a dent in the mountain of accumulating property tax debt. It was now the tax debt from 2013 that threatened to place Myrisha's inheritance on the auction block in 2016. She, however, believed she had to pay the entire $11,000 due for all years rather than just the $1,800 for 2013. Records show that she made payments on the 2013, 2014, and 2015 taxes when, to save the Baylis home, she should have used all the money to pay off the 2013 debt. "I don't recall being told that," Myrisha said. "I also did not have any understanding of property tax."

Consequently, in October 2015, the Wayne County treasurer again placed the reviled yellow plastic bag on her door. *Wayne County Treasurer Tax Foreclosure NOTICE* are the words printed on one side of the flimsy yellow bag filled with papers. Because the City of Detroit systematically inflated property tax assessments in violation of the Michigan Constitution, like the yellow plastic tape that cordons off a crime scene, the yellow plastic bag gave notice that a misdeed had occurred.

By law, the treasurer is required to physically attach notice of a home's impending property tax foreclosure on the property, providing public notice that the government is on the verge of confiscating a citizen's home, an act of legal violence with intergenerational resonance. Like a light switch, the "notice" documents in the yellow bag have the potential to illuminate homeowners' options, bringing clarity on how to save their homes. But instead, the documents confuse homeowners with impenetrable legalese. In a 2016 letter to Detroit homeowners about how to avoid property tax foreclosure, Mayor Mike Duggan admitted, "Many homeowners are often confused by the notices and may not understand the seriousness of the situation."[8]

The yellow bag contains several items, including a paper detailing the seven conditions homeowners can use to contest the property tax foreclosure. Promising as it sounds, it is dense with confusing language like "No law authorizes the tax" and "The owner of property subject to foreclosure is a minor heir." "Nothing there was self-explanatory," Myrisha remarked after reading the listed conditions. Without professional help, Detroit homeowners had no chance of contesting their foreclosure. They could only pay the amount due.

The bag also contains a formal legal notice, in an eye-stretching font, informing the homeowner that their property has been forfeited to the Wayne County treasurer as of March 1 of the current year and that the court will enter a final foreclosure judgment if all forfeited taxes, interest, penalties, and fees are not paid by March 31 of the coming year. This document lists the property address and legal description, the total amount required to redeem the property, and information about the two hearings that will occur before the judgment becomes final. There is also text written in eighteen languages saying, "Attention: If you do not understand this notice, you are urged to have this translated immediately," without information about where to get translation services. The contents of the yellow bag also explain the remote and in-person methods homeowners can use to pay the property tax bill as well as a short announcement that payment plan enrollment and reinstatement are possible. The most helpful enclosure is the extensive list of community partners who can provide homeowners with some of the assistance they will sorely need.

For homes where tenants resided, rather than owner-occupants, the yellow plastic bags were often the first notice they received that their landlords were at risk of property tax foreclosure and that, although timely in paying rent, they could lose their home. The yellow bag left renters with questions such as: Do I need to move? How soon? How will I find housing that I can afford? Should I continue paying rent? Can I buy the home?

For many owners, the yellow plastic bag was a signpost of shame, loudly notifying neighbors of their personal and financial failures. "This is not an attempt to embarrass or humiliate anyone," Eric Sabree, the Wayne County treasurer, said in a video posted on his website, discussing the yellow bag. "It is simply the law to make a personal visit to each property."[9] Despite Sabree's stated intentions, the yellow bag is humiliating, evoking a cocktail of emotions, including shame, worry, and fear, which work together to induce panic. At the bottom of the yellow bag, in tiny letters, it says, "Warning: Keep this plastic bag away from children; Misuse may cause suffocation." But it is the adults — shuffling bills and eliminating necessities to pay delinquent taxes and save their homes from foreclosure — whom the yellow bags threaten to suffocate.

Stigmatizing as the bag can feel to a home's occupants, it also serves as a reliable distress signal. Tax foreclosure is an invisible process, and the yellow bag is the only visible sign of difficulty prior to the appearance of a dumpster on eviction day. Although embarrassing, the yellow bag can prompt a neighbor to put the homeowner in touch with a nonprofit or alert family members that their loved one is suffering in silence.

Most important, the arrival of the yellow bag marks the first time many people realize the systemic nature of the tax foreclosure crisis. For instance, because the yellow bags were on almost every single door on her block, Myrisha assumed it was a Valpak advertising circular. "Once I saw what was in the yellow bag, then I was like, 'Okay, this is happening a lot on this block. Wow! This is what's going on?!'" Myrisha said, finally able to connect the dots. With one in three Detroit homes completing the property tax foreclosure process since 2009, the bags' ubiquity created space for homeowners to move past the shame of a personal failure toward the righteous rage engendered by systemic injustice.

For Myrisha, the yellow bag had delivered a painful punch. She, however, was not giving up. Myrisha had a job, but she kept looking for a better-paying one that could sustain her sizable caretaking responsibilities, and in December 2015, she caught a break. She found a more lucrative job at another dealership detailing cars. Now, with the disposable income she needed, she wanted to pay down the property taxes and continue renovating her grandparents' home.

"My intention was to always rehab the house and move in and keep the house, but I couldn't do so paying rent where I lived and utilities and all those things," Myrisha said. "So then I decided, well, I'll move in, that way I'm not necessarily paying rent, but I could use that money to actually work on the house." Myrisha got the upstairs bathroom functioning, and by January 2016, she was no longer straddling residences but was living in the Baylis home full-time. This move cemented her quest to rehabilitate her grandparents' home, and there was no turning back.

Because the home's antiquated heating system had completely collapsed, Myrisha's two children and their father did not move in immediately. "At one point in time there was a fireplace, so I was heating it that way or just turning on the stove during the winter months." When the fireplace and stove could not hold the cold at bay, Myrisha employed a costlier alternative, space heaters. With the Baylis home's boarded windows and aged infrastructure, Myrisha's electricity and gas bill averaged about $350, and her water bill about $150, bringing her total expenditure on utilities to around $500 monthly. Myrisha was energy insecure, which is a term Professor Diana Hernandez coined to describe low-income individuals and families who occupy older homes with extensive structural damage, energy inefficiencies, unhealthy home temperatures, dangerous coping strategies, and high utility bills.[10] Myrisha was in an impossible situation: she could not afford to be energy insecure, nor could she afford not to be because fixing the underlying problems was prohibitively expensive.

Even worse, Myrisha's exorbitant utility bills curtailed her ability to pay her inflated property tax bills. She began to lose faith and formed a plan B, hoping that even if she could not save her inheritance, someone else could. "At that point, I was thinking that someone would purchase the house, put the furnace in, and do the things that really needed to happen," she said. "I just did not want the house to be left totally vacant because it would really be totally destroyed and end up like some of the other houses."

Not yet ready to give up and move to her plan B, later in January, Myrisha took a day off work to follow the only clear set of instructions in the yellow bag, and attended the Wayne County treasurer's "show cause" hearings at her scheduled time: January 12, 2016, 11:30 a.m. When she arrived for her appointment, there were already so many people that the line to board the elevator to the treasurer's office on the fifth floor snaked outside the revolving door on the first floor. "It was like a maze," Myrisha remembered.

Myrisha's experience was not an anomaly. The Baylis home was among the 13,855 properties (about 7,173 owner-occupied) headed to tax foreclosure that year. The year prior, in 2015, *Detroit Free Press* columnist Nancy Kaffer described the fourth day of the show cause hearings, which the County held for the 75,000 homes it slated for tax foreclosure (25,000 of which were owner-occupied). That day, there were over 900 people trying to save their homes. Many had restless children in tow because a record-breaking snowstorm had closed Detroit's public schools.[11] The lines were so long that at 2 p.m. officials served customer number 300, who had drawn her number at 9 a.m. When their turn finally came to speak with a representative, homeowners at no point had any opportunity to tell their story or contest their impending foreclosure, as the event's name suggested. The treasurer only gave them an opportunity to pay their debts in full or, if unable, to get on a payment plan. A more apt name than a "show cause" hearing, therefore, would be a "pay now" hearing.

The show cause hearings, although misnamed, did have one excellent feature — as attendees waited for the treasurer's office to call their number, they could visit any one of the invited government and community organizations that offered distressed homeowners services and valuable information. "It was a one-stop-shop thing," Myrisha recalled. For instance, the City of Detroit's Office of the Assessor helped attendees with crucial paperwork. The Accounting Aid Society provided information about the earned income tax credit. Lakeshore Legal Aid supplied free civil law advice. The Michigan Department of Health and Human Services filled out state emergency relief applications.

With more than twenty tables chock-full of brochures, attendees could find Step Forward counseling, utility bill assistance, home repair resources, employment opportunities, job training resources, and specialized services for seniors and veterans. Attendees left the building with their arms bursting with pamphlets. Many were unable, however, to convert the relief promised by the flyers into anything tangible because they were paralyzed by their impending foreclosure or overwhelmed by the flood of information.

When the treasurer's office finally called her number, Myrisha discussed her overdue property taxes with the representative, who suggested that Myrisha walk across the hall to the United Community Housing Coalition's (UCHC) table for further assistance. Through one-on-one counseling, UCHC assists each client to enroll in the optimal payment plan, sign up for exemptions, and locate public funding to pay their tax debt and avoid foreclosure. Because she had to get back to work, Myrisha could not wait in yet another line to access UCHC's services, so her only option was to visit their offices for an intake appointment on Monday, Wednesday, or Friday between 9 a.m. and noon. UCHC's clients often have to miss work and wait for hours on end because everyone is seen on a first-come-first-served basis. No appointments are available.

On March 16, 2016, Myrisha walked into UCHC's offices and the scent of musty file cabinets and freshly brewed coffee greeted her. She took a number and waited alongside dozens of folks desperately trying to save their homes, children fidgeting and adults tightly clutching their paperwork. "It was very frustrating," Myrisha said, teeth clenched. "More so because I have the type of job that you're only making money if you're actually working. As a service technician, you get paid by what you do, not hourly." UCHC counselors called out numbers and retrieved clients, taking them one by one to an individualized counseling room. After several hours, one of the counselors, Michele Oberholtzer, called Myrisha, sat with her, and reviewed her available options.

"We advise people about the best payment plan, how to get caught up, the best place to spend their money, and where they could get financial help from other grants or other resources," Michele explained. That year, the Wayne County treasurer offered various payment plans for owner-occupants like Myrisha. There was the Interest Reduction Stipulated Payment Arrangement (IRSPA), which immediately removes owners from foreclosure and gives them five years to pay their debt, retroactively decreasing the interest penalty from 18 to 6 percent. The State Equalized Value Stipulated Payment Arrangement (SEVSPA) reduced a delinquent taxpayer's total property debt to one half the State Equalized Value (SEV). The Distressed Owner Occupant Extension (DOOE) mandated that owners have all tax debts older than three years paid in full, and it did not reduce the homeowner's debt or interest rate — it only bought the homeowner time to pay the foreclosable debt. Additionally, the State of Michigan offered cash assistance to pay property debts through its State Emergency Relief (SER) Program, which provided up to $2,000 to pay property tax debts.

If the rules for IRSPA, SEVSPA, DOOE, and SER sound convoluted, it's because they are. In this alphabet soup of programs, it is almost impossible for owners to decipher which ones they qualify for without the assistance of a trained expert, like Michele. "I am a college graduate with a degree in business and I could not figure out what was going on without UCHC," Myrisha said with exasperation. "I cannot even imagine what it must have been like for Detroiters who do not have the same level of education. Most don't." While UCHC presents clients with their full range of options, it is still difficult to make sense of everything.

The payment plans are not only confusing, they are also ineffective. Analyzing 12,000 Wayne County properties on an IRSPA between 2016 and 2019, a *Detroit News* investigation found that the Wayne County treasurer foreclosed on 13 percent of these properties, with another 27 percent off their payment plans and at risk of foreclosure in 2020. Additionally, the investigation found that about one in four properties owed more property tax debt than they did three years earlier, and only 18 percent paid off all their delinquent property tax debts.[12]

Because people living below the poverty line are exempt from paying property taxes altogether, the payment plans are also unjust. If they were lucky enough to walk through the doors of a community organization like UCHC or come into contact with the organization at a resource fair, low-income homeowners received counseling on the most beneficial payment plan *and* the exemption. If homeowners did not work with a community organization and instead went, as instructed by the yellow bag documents, straight to the treasurer's office to pay their bill, they would not find out about the exemption or receive an application from the treasurer. These low-income homeowners would instead struggle to pay the current bill and delinquent debts — neither of which, again, they were supposed to be paying in the first place. While one might say that these homeowners "fell behind" on their payments, it's more accurate to say that the brutally broken system left them behind.

Michele advised Myrisha to sign up for the SEVSPA, which required Myrisha to secure two other documents: the Principal Residence Exemption (PRE), which is evidence that the owner uses the home as their primary residence, and the Property Transfer Affidavit (PTA), which all new owners must file in order for the local government to recognize the transfer. Since Myrisha came to UCHC on March 16 and the treasurer was set to enter his foreclosure judgment on March 31, Myrisha only had fifteen days to save her home. So, to buy time, Michele advised Myrisha to sign up for the DOOE while waiting for the State to process the PTA and PRE paperwork.

"I prepared a PRE with her and a PTA, she signed it, and I prepared a DOOE as well," Michele said. Pointing to her notes, she continued, "I said 'need deed and DTE bill to complete.'" While deeds are public records that UCHC can obtain if needed, DTE utility bills are not accessible, so UCHC could only rely upon Myrisha to deliver this document. To save her legacy, all Myrisha needed to do was bring in her utility bill to show proof of occupancy before March 31. That was it.

Myrisha, however, did not bring in the utility bill and UCHC did not call to remind her. It was not until June 28 that UCHC called Myrisha, but this was to pick up her PTA and PRE. She came the very next day. "I had never heard anything about bringing a utility bill because all the utilities were in my name, so I know that if somebody had told me that, I would have been able to produce that," Myrisha recalled. "What I was focusing on was getting my name put on the assessment. I recall going down to the city-county building and having that done in a little office."

During the counseling session, Michele inundated Myrisha with waves of detailed and complicated information, involving the alphabet soup of programs and requirements, all of which ultimately drowned out one important detail — Myrisha needed to produce the DTE bill. "Counseling now, remotely, we have all these ways of getting documents. You'll text it to me, we'll get it on the Google Voice and then we'll print it, so we're doing things differently," Michele said, describing the changes dictated by the coronavirus pandemic. "But, for Myrisha, she probably needed to come back to intake in our office with those supporting documents. I don't know if we even called her to remind her of what she was missing. I don't know how much capacity we had for that outreach."

Years later, when Myrisha discovered the consequences of this unfortunate miscommunication, she was devastated. She acknowledged UCHC's good intentions and attributed its failure to its huge number of clients, the resulting long waits, and hence the limited time counselors could spend coaching each client on how best to wade through the hodgepodge of programs and payment plans. "I'm like, 'I'm doing steps, whatever they tell me to do, I'm just gonna do it,' and you're leaning on that person to be dispensing the knowledge or the expertise that's gonna get you out of that situation," Myrisha explained. "But it's almost like when you go to an emergency walk-in clinic and it's really just a triage. I know what good customer service is: when people really go above and beyond to really try to resolve your issues. I didn't get that from Michele and I didn't really feel that way necessarily with the agency, from the receptionist all the way up because they were overwhelmed with so many people."

As the primary nonprofit organization providing property tax foreclosure and other housing-related assistance to low-income

Detroiters, UCHC carried a backbreaking load, serving 8,912 house-holds in 2016, 26,351 in 2017, 10,482 in 2018, and 10,057 in 2019.[13] "It is extremely exhausting. I and everyone on my team — right before we were forced not to come to work in March — we were all breaking down. Our office was a fire hazard before there was even a biohaz-ard from coronavirus. We had people lined up at the door. One hun-dred people," Michele explained. "Let's just be honest here, when I see these staff notes, my heart sinks. Like, I want to cry. I want to go back in time."

After taking a long pause, giving her tears time to recede, she continued, "I want to know what language did I use to explain what the DOOE was? What paperwork did I hand her to remind her that this is what you're missing and this is how to provide it, and this is why you need to do it? Did I fail to write clear enough notes? Like, what thing could have happened with just a little bit more eye con-tact and counseling that would have changed all of this?" Michele gave a nervous chuckle. "The bottom line is, the reason why we're able to be so effective is because we have such fragility. It shouldn't be possible that you could save someone's home by getting a copy of their DTE bill. Right?" Michele was correct. The fact that Myrisha was in imminent danger of losing her home because she did not sub-mit a utility bill is a glaring sign of an illegitimate system, one where precariousness has replaced fairness.

After the miscommunication at UCHC, Myrisha had one last shot to save her home. Although the legal deadline for tax foreclo-sure was March 31, the Wayne County treasurer, Eric Sabree, has the discretion to remove homes from the foreclosure list for sev-eral months after this date. In 2016, Sabree allowed owners to save their homes by getting into payment plans through the end of June.[14] Consequently, on June 30, the treasurer had the legal right to send about 37,000 properties, 28,000 of which were occupied homes, to the tax foreclosure auction. The treasurer's office was pure chaos. His team was understaffed, overwhelmed, and completely unprepared to handle the swarm of frantic owners that descended upon their offices that day.

At 9 a.m. that day, one Instagram post reported that the next customer service ticket number available was 300, and the screen indicated that customer 100 was next. A *Detroit Free Press* article reported that by noon, the customer service tickets had reached number 999, so the office had to start a new roll.[15] Another social media post noted that "By 4:30 PM, the building entrance is packed to the point that the revolving doors aren't turning because there is no space to walk into." Despairing homeowners waited hours to get a ticket and then hours more for their turn at the counter.

Myrisha was there in the chaos. Again, she had been forced to take off work so that she could navigate this bureaucratic nightmare, although she needed the hours to pay down her debts. When she arrived, she got in the line to get on the elevator, which stretched to the sidewalk outside the building and around the corner. After standing under the scorching sun for a long while, she finally reached the elevator and got into another line to obtain a customer service ticket number. Her number was in the six hundreds, and she remembers the room being packed from wall to wall, elderly people on oxygen tanks fainting from heat exhaustion.

"Now, I'm on the last day, and I go down to the tax office in the morning. It was definitely a last-last-ditch, eleventh-hour kinda thing," Myrisha admitted. But after waiting for about three or four hours, she gave up and left. "I had my kids to pick up from school and work to complete. It was just no way that I could continue to sit there."

If Myrisha had withstood the insufferable chaos, stayed in the line, and successfully reached the desk, she could have presented the representative with her paperwork (PTA and PRE) and enrolled in a payment plan. Myrisha had the money for the payment plan, but the impossible process Wayne County established for people to save their homes, again, tripped her up. This time she fell hard. In July, the Wayne County treasurer foreclosed on the Baylis home for fail-ure to pay an $1,800 tax debt, stripping legal title from Myrisha as well as 14,000 other property owners,[16] at least 7,170 of whom were owner-occupiers.

Myrisha could not scrounge up $1,800 to save her legacy, but oth-ers lost their homes for much less. "Before 2015, we had a policy not to foreclose anything under $1,500," Wayne County treasurer Eric Sabree noted. But now, "it doesn't matter what the amount is, if you haven't paid your taxes, you're still eligible for foreclosure. If you owe $50, you still can get foreclosed." In 2016, the County foreclosed on approximately 51,000 properties, about 2,700 of them for less than $1,000.[17]

Figure 3:

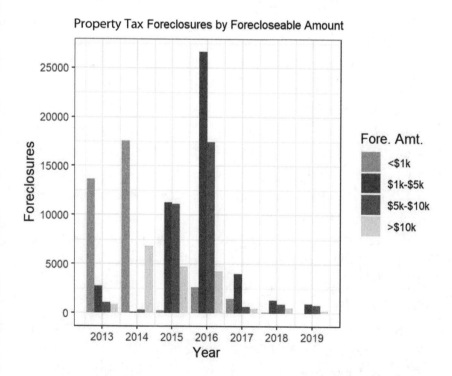

When reflecting on her grave loss, what came to Myrisha's mind was a scene from the 1996 movie *Set It Off,* a bank heist drama starring Jada Pinkett, Queen Latifah, and Vivica Fox. "What's the procedure when you are being robbed?" a police officer yells while placing a gun to the head of Fox, playing a bank teller who has just been robbed. Fox responds by rattling off the standard procedure. The bank, however, fires her on the spot because she did not follow it. In this scene, the victim was blamed for the crime, and Myrisha felt this was exactly what she was experiencing. "I felt like I had a gun to my head."

Myrisha's own personal heist drama had climaxed, but it was not yet over. While it wouldn't be easy, Myrisha learned that she and other owners could repurchase their properties in the property tax auction. Over the years, UCHC has supported at least three thousand homeowners in doing just this.[18] But by the time Myrisha tried to repurchase the home, the County had already sold it. She, again, came up short.

"I didn't understand the severity of it because I was caught up with so many other things," Myrisha concluded in her postmortem analysis of her loss. "With so many balls juggling, trying to be the breadwinner and trying to hold things together for others, that I didn't focus as much as I should have." Despite pervasive systemic inequalities — such as the City of Detroit illegally inflating property tax assessments and curbing access to the poverty tax exemption, banks' limited lending in the city, poor health care access, employment discrimination, and lack of investment in the social safety net, which leaves many women with unduly onerous care obligations — Myrisha's personal narrative nevertheless focused on her failings as an individual. Unjust, invisible, formless systems had no shoulders on which to carry blame. Only Myrisha did.

Since Myrisha's faith drives her to believe that everything happens for a reason, she tried to make sense of her stolen legacy. "I kind of felt a sense of relief. These are tears of joy," Myrisha, filled with emotion, explained. "I was just being used to stabilize the house, so somebody else could benefit from it. So it wasn't in vain. And I don't feel bad that I did what I could do. It's a legacy that that house is still standing. Even if you just drive by and you say, 'That house is still standing.'"

Since the houses on both sides of the Baylis home were vacant and there were many more vacant homes on this one block alone, Myrisha added, "People say, 'Well, why would you still want to live in that neighborhood?' It may be the only house on the block, but it means something to them. People see empty lots, but that used to be a neighborhood. That used to be a school where somebody attended." Where others saw emptiness, Myrisha saw what once was, as well as what could be. She saw her legacy.

Just as illness had struck several members of Myrisha's family, her city had contracted a carcinogenic property tax foreclosure crisis. The jaundice-yellow bag was the first public manifestation of the illness. The confusing payment plans were the incoherent treatments offered by the County and State, so it is no surprise that they did not cure the disease. With one in three homes completing the tax foreclosure process since 2009, the cancer was eating the city and its residents alive.

8

STOLEN LEGACY

On December 1, 2016, the Wayne County treasurer transferred the deed to Grandma and Grandpa Brown's home to Top Tier Ventures — a limited-liability company with its registered address in St. Clair Shores, a suburb near Detroit. Even though the company purchased the Baylis home for $7,200, its owners could not just kick Myrisha out. Instead, when investors acquire occupied homes in the property tax foreclosure auction and its occupants do not leave voluntarily, the investors must either negotiate a lease with occupants or take them through the formal court eviction process. Because she needed to stand guard over her legacy, ensuring that blight did not topple it, Myrisha hoped to negotiate a lease with the new owners.

With the lease on their apartment expiring in October, Myrisha moved her children and their father into the Baylis home with her that month, and then they all waited for the new owners to knock on the door. When the company's representative finally came in late December, nobody was home, so Myrisha called the phone number on the card he left in the mailbox. "I contacted them and, of course, they wanted me to stay in the home and wanted to immediately negotiate rent," Myrisha said with annoyance. "And I said, 'Well, wait a minute now, you're negotiating rent; however, this house is not up to code. Let's start from that point. What do you plan on repairing and what is the time frame that you plan to do it in? There's not an operable furnace. There's missing windows. There are a lot of things that are in desperate need of a repair.'"

To confirm Myrisha's assessment of the home's condition, a Top Tier representative came to do a walk-through. Although the company now owned the Baylis home, this was the first time anyone affiliated with Top Tier had viewed the home's interior, as auction buyers are not allowed to enter the homes before purchase. He found that the two most urgent repairs required were the home's windows, two of which were boarded up, and the furnace. Although Top Tier quickly fixed the windows, the company did not immediately install a code-compliant heating system, so as the January temperatures plummeted to freezing and below, the cold took its toll. Through her yearslong quest to renovate her inheritance, Myrisha had learned about the City of Detroit's housing code, and although not an expert, she knew one thing — without heat, Top Tier could not legally rent the house.

"They purchased a home sight unseen and did not have the capital to do what was needed," she said. "They were banking on the fact that they could just collect rent and not put anything really in." Myrisha, an unexpectedly well-informed resident, threw a wrench in the company's plans when she refused to pay rent until the home had heat. While waiting for the new heating system, Myrisha continued to rely on space heaters and the oven to combat the cold. On extremely frosty winter nights, when her heating hacks could not prevent the ravenous cold from eating through their gloves and blankets, she and her children had no choice but to leave. Myrisha's mom, Mona, offered them warm refuge, and when temperatures rose, they returned to the Baylis home. As they went back and forth, Myrisha and her children were dizzy with distress.

"Had my children been a lot younger, I would say that I would have made different choices," Myrisha assured. "The important thing was just to have a home set up. I painted their rooms. They both had new bedroom furniture. We had a new refrigerator and stove."

In the cold of February 2017, Andricus left the Baylis home to move in with one of his girlfriends, leaving Myrisha and his children to manage on their own. Soon thereafter, Myrisha learned he was dead. Andricus had suffered a long string of complications arising from the gunshot wounds he had received during the carjacking years earlier, the last of which was a hernia that made it difficult for him to breathe and bend over. Although hesitant, the doctors operated, and this led to fatal complications. Myrisha and her children were devastated. To add to their woes, at the funeral, they discovered that Andricus had fathered additional children they did not know about: in total, there were seven children by six different women. This news, combined with the freezing temperatures, made that February especially hard.

March brought warmer temperatures and the much-needed heating system. But Top Tier chose the cheapest and least energy-efficient option available, installing baseboard heaters in six rooms — including the kitchen, the dining room, the living room, and the three bedrooms — leaving the bathrooms and entrance hall without heat. The company also repaired the remaining windows, made the upstairs bathroom fully operable, and painted.

Although Myrisha remained suspicious of Top Tier's renovation practices, she was relieved that the company was making the Baylis home habitable. Consequently, she finally signed a lease, which began in April 2017 and ended in December 2018, mandating an $800 monthly rent payment and an $800 security deposit. Although she no longer owned it, she was living in her legacy. The situation was not ideal, but it was workable. That is, until Myrisha lost her job at the car dealership in September 2017 and was, again, unemployed.

"They wanted me to leave that department and transition into a position that was an hourly position of fifteen dollars an hour, which would cut out my salary and cut out my commission," Myrisha explained. "I would be getting less than half of what I had been earning." Myrisha believed management demoted her to give the position to a white man who had worked with the company for over thirty years. Instead of accepting the demotion, Myrisha walked out of the dealership, her last paycheck in hand and dignity in tow. For the next five months, she collected a weekly $362 unemployment check that was insufficient to cover her household expenses and utilities, which soared as fall approached and the air became increasingly chilly.

Thanks to the new baseboard heating system, the decaying Baylis home devoured electricity. "My average bill was about three hundred dollars, three fifty during April through September," Myrisha remembered. "I would say, like, October, the bill would creep up to maybe about five hundred to six hundred dollars, double. That became a problem." She continued, "It wasn't until they put up the heaters all around the house, the electric heaters in every room, that the bill got like that." To reduce the hefty heating costs, Myrisha and her children confined themselves to the second floor, and this strategy worked until the freezing temperatures hit.

December 14, 2017, registered historic cold temperatures as massive snowstorms delivered eight inches of snow, dropped temperatures to 14 degrees, and closed over seven hundred schools across metro Detroit.[1] With record-breaking cold, Michiganders were more worried about the pipes freezing than ever before. If Myrisha had been a regular renter, she would have worried only about keeping her children warm and left the landlord to worry about the pipes his bootleg heating system could not warm. But, of course, Myrisha was no regular renter. She ensured that the pipes did not freeze by cranking the heat up from January to March, which came at great personal cost.

"My electricity, gas, and water bill—those three definitely, on average—was about twelve hundred to fifteen hundred dollars per month December through March," Myrisha estimated. Although her utility bills rocketed to a faraway place her budget could not reach, she could not allow frost to bite her family and destroy her home.

As winter ended, March brought spring and a new season in Myrisha's life. Just as her unemployment benefits ran out, she found a new job at another dealership, which paid $16 per hour. She was back to detailing cars, but no longer in a managerial role. Nevertheless, she was happy to be back to work and earning more than Michigan's unemployment payments. Now that she was regaining her financial footing, the pressing question was: With the rent and utilities for the Baylis home exceeding $2,000 monthly in the winter, why did Myrisha not consider moving after her lease expired?

She had four primary reasons for staying. First, many Detroit homes, saturated with intergenerational memories, have met one consistent fate: demolition. Myrisha was committed to saving her legacy from this common yet unhappy ending. She wanted her experience to contribute to the burgeoning narrative about Detroit's revival rather than the dominant one about its demise.

Second, although Myrisha could have moved into a suburban neighborhood with much-improved public safety, education, home quality, and amenities, she believed that suburban rentals were unobtainable. "I was trying to find housing, but now they started looking at credit scores and these kind of things," she explained. "So you can't even get the type of house that you would like, nor can you live in an area outside of Detroit for less than probably twelve hundred dollars a month plus security deposit. So you're talking five thousand dollars (all moving-related expenses added) to move in somewhere."

The rental price difference between Detroit and its nearby suburban communities was not as much as Myrisha thought, however. Between 2018 and 2022, median rent in Detroit was $989, while it was $1,205 in Dearborn, $1,238 in Ferndale, and $1,235 in Livonia.[2] But based on her belief that rental housing in the suburbs was inaccessible, Myrisha did not even bother searching for housing there.

Myrisha's third reason for staying in the Baylis home was that living in Detroit provided a unique benefit for her children. Through the Detroit Promise program, students who live in Detroit, attend Detroit high schools for all four years, and earn at least a 3.0 cumulative GPA are eligible for free tuition to participating community colleges or four-year institutions.[3]

Myrisha's fourth and final reason for staying in the Baylis home was that, given her budget, she believed moving within Detroit would only take her from one slumlord to another. In May 2017, Detroit's city council tried to address its slumlord problem by passing a revised rental registry ordinance,[4] requiring landlords to provide habitable residences. Prior to the 2017 revision, the ordinance was ineffective and underenforced.

A *Detroit News* investigation reports that in 2016, landlords registered only 4,174 properties, although the census estimated there were 140,000 rental units in Detroit.[5] Failure to register rental properties was supposed to result in a ticket, but from 2014 to 2017, the City issued fewer than 5,000 tickets, 85 percent of which were unpaid, amounting to almost $2 million in lost revenue.[6] To put this in perspective, the City issued more tickets for improperly placed trash cans than for unregistered properties.[7]

Under the revamped rental ordinance, before receiving a Rental Certificate of Compliance, landlords must pay all existing blight tickets, be current on their property taxes, register their properties on the City's website, and pass a rental inspection.[8] For one- to two-unit homes, owners must complete a rental inspection every three years.[9] If the property does not pass the initial inspection, there may be a need for a subsequent inspection, costing an additional $300 to $500.[10] If the inspector finds lead, then the owner must get an additional lead inspection, ranging in cost from $500 to $700. Until owners remove the lead paint, they must get a new lead risk inspection every time a new tenant moves in. "Why do I have to get a new risk assessment so often?" one landlord quipped. This is because in

Michigan, if the owner knows that a residential housing unit contains a lead-based paint hazard, it is a criminal offense to rent the unit to a family with minor children who have elevated blood lead levels.[11]

To ensure that landlords complied with the revised rental ordinance, the City hired additional inspectors and increased the fine for noncompliance to $500 for the first offense, $1,000 for the second, and $1,500 for the third and subsequent offenses.[12] Critics, however, worried that landlords would pass on these increased costs to their tenants, depriving low-income renters of the opportunity to endure substandard housing in exchange for below-market rents. "I used to have a house set to rent for five hundred dollars because I had little repairs, very little upkeep, and I had an agreement between the tenant and I," one landlord remarked. "Now I come in and I have to pay a minimum of fifteen hundred dollars to register the property and I have to put those costs somewhere. They gotta go to the tenant, and in turn, what that's done is make housing unaffordable for most tenants."

According to another disgruntled landlord, "They don't hold the tenant accountable for anything, which is not fair. The tenant gets an opportunity to walk into the property, and if the tenant is happy with the conditions in which I gave them and we've agreed upon these conditions, I don't understand why the City comes in and wants to police what the agreement is between the tenant and the landlord."

Because landlords and tenants in Detroit most often do not have equal bargaining power, the ordinance seeks to balance the scales by ensuring that landlords provide a basic level of habitability to all tenants, regardless of their ability to demand these conditions themselves. To even the scales, the ordinance's most potent provision allows tenants in unregistered properties to withhold rent and place it in an escrow account. If a landlord fails to register their rental property in ninety days, they forfeit the right to collect the rent.

Before the updated ordinance took effect, unregistered landlords could evict tenants who did not pay rent, even in dwellings without heat during winter months, and with broken windows, vermin infestations, sewage-filled basements, and hazardous electrical systems. In fact, in 2015, before the revised ordinance took effect, landlords were unregistered in twelve of every thirteen eviction cases. Courts demanded that tenants comply with rental laws even when landlords did not.[13] The revamped ordinance aimed to end these hypocritical practices, correcting the asymmetry of power between vulnerable tenants and legally noncompliant landlords. Many other cities — like Baltimore, Los Angeles, Jersey City, Washington D.C., and San Francisco — have enacted similar ordinances for similar reasons.[14]

Despite the legal protections found in Detroit's revised rental ordinance, when tenants tried to protest substandard housing conditions by withholding rent, Detroit's 36th District Court initially ignored the law and allowed evictions to proceed.[15] For instance, Chastity Rodgers, a Detroit resident, entered into a one-year lease for $525 per month, and after moving in she learned that her landlord had not secured the required Rental Certificate of Compliance from the Detroit Buildings, Safety Engineering, and Environmental Department (BSEED). Following a City worker's advice, Chastity withheld her rent and placed it in a BSEED escrow account. Since the landlord failed to secure a Certificate of Compliance in the first ninety days of escrow, BSEED awarded Chastity the escrowed rent monies, as required by the ordinance. When the landlord registered the property during the following sixty days, BSEED gave him the rent accumulated in the escrow account for this period, as per the ordinance.

Although Chastity followed the letter of the law, the trial court ordered her eviction for nonpayment of rent during the initial ninety-day period, nullifying the ordinance's primary enforcement provision. With the help of Lakeshore Legal Aid, a nonprofit that provides free civil legal aid to indigent populations in the Detroit metro area, Chastity appealed the lower court decision and won, establishing the ordinance's rent-withholding provision as legal and enforceable.[16] The 36th District Court now has language on its website warning landlords that they will have to produce a Certificate of Compliance in eviction proceedings, and that failure to do so could negatively impact their case.[17]

Despite the court's turn, records show that as of February 2021, of the estimated 87,000 rental properties citywide, only 2,743 had secured a Certificate of Compliance.[18] Additionally, one lawyer — representing Detroit landlords in eviction cases for almost twenty years and completing, on average, one hundred eviction cases per month — reported that the 36th District Court has never stopped an eviction because his client failed to register the property. Likewise, a landlord who owns more than three thousand rental properties reported that the court has never halted an eviction because her property was not registered.

Another problem is that many tenants fail to put their withheld rent in the City's escrow account, exempting them from protections. A spokesperson for BSEED indicated that between 2018 and 2022, only 116 escrow accounts had been approved.[19] The rental registry ordinance — designed to even the scales and hold landlords accountable — strands tenants in Detroit's subpar housing in a sea of problems with no way to return to shore. Landlords, consequently, maintain the upper hand, forcing most tenants to pay rent for substandard dwellings because their only other option is to search for alternative accommodations in a tight housing market with few affordable choices.

While most Detroit tenants have never even heard of the rental registration ordinance, Myrisha, fortunately, had. "I've become knowledgeable in how things should work," she explained. Top Tier was collecting rent for a home that was not up to code and was unregistered, giving Myrisha an advantage. But Top Tier also had leverage because, given the scarcity of affordable housing, Myrisha had nowhere to go. "It's like a gunfight," she said. "Both people are holding guns to each other, but nobody's gonna shoot because we know we're in positions that we need one another for whatever. Theirs was I need to generate some revenue. And mine was I need to have housing."

Tensions between Myrisha and the company remained high throughout the 2017–2018 lease term because she kept demanding repairs and threatening to call the City. As a consequence, for Top Tier, the problems associated with the Baylis property quickly began to outweigh its worth, causing the company's investors to bicker. Myrisha established a working relationship with one of the investors — a gentleman with a thick accent reportedly from Sweden — who gave her insight into the squabbling.

"He was very frustrated with working with the partners. Then it came to a point that he had totally fallen out with the partners," Myrisha explained. Starting in April or May, "I could just send the money directly to him, and he was collecting the money." Although this arrangement seemed strange, Myrisha went along with it because the Swedish investor had become a reliable ally.

When he learned that Myrisha had run up her electricity bill, trying to prevent the pipes from freezing, he compensated her with two months of free rent. As their camaraderie grew, the Swedish investor confided in Myrisha. "At that point is when he divulged that they really wanted to dump that house. He appreciated what I was doing and how I was working with them, keeping the landscaping up, the home kept clean, all of those things." After assuring Myrisha that she could stay in the home through the end of her lease term in December 2018, the investor worked closely with her to schedule several showings throughout the summer.

During this time, there was an accident at the Baylis home. After a major storm, a tree from the adjacent problem corner property crashed down over the dividing fence, toppling the Browns' once-stately apple tree. In addition, the apple tree's sinewy roots, slowly expanding for decades, had reached and breached the sewage drain, causing flooding in the basement. The impending sale compelled Top Tier to promptly fix the sewage problem and repaint the basement to ensure that the house was in optimal condition during the showings. But the apple tree lay where it had fallen. "The tree was down for like months," Myrisha recalled with disgust. "I was like, 'Hey, can you guys come clean this up?'" The Baylis home had become a money pit that the company could not get rid of fast enough, so although Top Tier did not want to spend one more dime on the property, they eventually had the tree removed. The apple tree — the symbol of all that Grandma and Grandpa Brown had accomplished — was gone.

After four or five showings, in October 2018, Top Tier found a buyer, and they scheduled the closing for December. Records reveal that on December 28, 2018, Top Tier sold the Baylis home to another investment company called DERE for $36,000, and although this was $28,788 above the price Top Tier paid at the property tax auction, their profit margin was more modest, given the various repairs they had made to the windows, bathroom, heating, and basement.

In December 2018, while the Baylis home changed owners, Myrisha made a change of her own. "I left [the dealership] because there was a problem with the management trying to reduce the amount of work that I was doing," she explained. "A new manager came in and wants to say, 'Okay, you're going to do two cars a day because I'm going to spread it around.' I was the seasoned veteran and got paid the most, but I also had the highest productivity. But you were hiring other people and wanted me to train them, and then you'd give them the cars that I could do, which significantly impacts my ability to make twelve hundred dollars or more a week. So we just didn't agree."

Sick and tired of being sick and tired, Myrisha not only left the dealership, but left the detailing business altogether. Back in 2017, Myrisha had cofounded a nonprofit that provides assistance to struggling students at her alma mater, Cass Tech High School. In January 2019, she began driving for Uber so she could dedicate more time to her nonprofit.

Even though she changed jobs and the Baylis home changed owners, Myrisha remained steadfast. She refused to walk away from her legacy. The house's new owner, DERE, was a company created for the sole purpose of purchasing homes in Detroit. The company owners — three friends from Argentina and Puerto Rico who sell real estate and do property management in South Florida — created the company after their very first visit to Detroit in August 2018.

"We were hearing a lot of people were heading out to Detroit, so a couple of years ago me and a couple of my friends went out just to kinda check it out to see what the city was about, and see if all the rumors that you can buy houses for close to nothing and make money were real," Beatriz Hernandez, one of DERE's owners, said. Upon arrival, the friends were dazzled by the colorful murals that adorn building walls throughout the city. They were equally impressed by the growing number of deliciously chic restaurants in downtown and midtown that have turned Detroit into a premier foodie destination.

Most of all, Beatriz and her friends bought into Detroit's much-touted comeback narrative, which boldly advertises that the city has overcome bankruptcy and is now attracting multimillion-dollar investments, including projects like Google's Detroit headquarters and Ford's new innovation campus, which has renovated the old Michigan Central Station, once an icon of Detroit's demise. The narrative broadcasts a tantalizing promise — invest in Detroit real estate because you can buy low, sell high, and earn substantial profits flipping homes. Supporting this claim, a 2015 *Detroit Free Press* headline reads, "Detroit among top 5 metro regions for flipping houses."[20] When ranked by percent return on home price, the article reports that metro Detroit's average profits of 58.3 percent put it in fifth place nationwide.

Through a friend who purchased several commercial buildings downtown for "next to nothing" during Detroit's bankruptcy, Jerry Jones, a different Florida-based real estate investor, heard the same siren song as Beatriz. "So I took a trip up there and what I was expecting to see was panic zone properties. Every city has a place where the police and ambulances won't go," Jerry said. "I was totally blown away. I couldn't believe how nice the houses looked. I couldn't believe how nice the streets were. There's plenty of streets that are beyond repair, but it looked like the opportunity was there." He continued, "Not only is there a financial opportunity, but we could be part of the Detroit comeback. To put it bluntly, I get off if I can help other people and if we can create jobs and improve an economy."

After running the numbers, Jerry recruited other investors whom he regularly does business with, and they were all in. In 2017, the group initiated a real estate investment trust (REIT) and started purchasing homes to renovate and rent, hiring an in-house team to manage the local operation. As of 2021, Jerry and his partners owned three hundred properties, most of which are tax-foreclosed houses they purchased from the County's property tax foreclosure auction or the Detroit Land Bank Authority.

Jerry and his partners built a team of contractors that could deliver twelve to fifteen fully renovated units per month, but the pandemic put everything on pause, so the REIT began to focus exclusively on its rentals. Seventy percent of its tenants participate in the Housing Choice Voucher Program (also known as Section 8) — a federal housing program that subsidizes low-income individuals and families in the private rental market. This is the REIT's preference because Section 8 landlords receive a large portion of the rent payment directly from the government, providing a more reliable stream of income.

"We are providing high-quality affordable housing in Detroit," Jerry said proudly. "Some people think that you buy a house, you slap a coat of paint on it, you put a renter in it, and then if they have a problem, they can go screw themselves. But you have to protect your investments and you have to make sure that your tenants are taken care of. They're your clients."

Like Jerry, DERE's business model was to purchase homes and collect rent payments, providing cash flow while they waited for their properties to appreciate as Detroit's comeback took hold. DERE, however, was a typical low-capital investor, willing to invest only the bare minimum required to rent the homes, while Jerry and his REIT were high-capital investors that upgraded homes substantially. For instance, because Jerry's REIT has an in-house management team and significant investment dollars, their properties far exceed the standards set by Section 8, while Beatriz and her partners struggled to make their homes Section 8 compliant.

"We had to replace a floor because the floor was stained," Beatriz complained. "It wasn't like the tiles were coming up or anything like that, but Section 8 would not approve us for the second year until we replaced the floor. And so for people who have experience here in Florida, that never happens in Florida unless the floor is falling down or the tiles are coming up, or it's a danger, like a trip hazard, a fire hazard, a danger like that." With sarcasm filling her voice, she added, "They don't come in and tell us that we have to cosmetically make this house the most beautiful house on the street."

Prior to the pandemic, DERE acquired thirty-eight houses in Detroit, and while the company still owns many of these homes, it sold others to its wealthy clientele and transitioned from the role of owner to property manager. Many of DERE's wealthy clients are Argentina's elite, who are searching for a safe place to park their substantial assets because the Argentine peso has one of the highest inflation rates in South America. DERE is positioning Detroit as the newest, hottest investment destination for its Argentine clientele who have been priced out of places like Miami. Right now in Miami "it's very difficult to get anything for less than a hundred fifty thousand dollars. That's on the super low-end, and that's difficult," Beatriz said. "But in Detroit, I bought one of my houses for like thirteen thousand dollars, so there's a huge difference there."

But unlike Miami and other cities in South Florida where DERE has invested, Spanish is not Detroit's lingua franca, so the company serves as an intermediary, striving to be Latin America's gateway to Detroit. Since most of DERE's clients will never set foot in Detroit to see their properties, trust is central to the company's business model, and referrals are the company's lifeblood. We make "sure that we do things correctly the first time with the first person and that person goes and tells their friend," Beatriz said, explaining how DERE wins clients. "These are millionaires and their friends are millionaires, so if you get into the right pocket, you're pretty good. Birds of a feather flock together." To survive, DERE had to keep their existing clients happy by ensuring that they received a steady flow of income from rent payments. If not, the wealthy birds would no longer flock to the investment nest DERE was assembling in Detroit.

Soon after Beatriz and her two partners' inaugural trip to Detroit, they purchased their first batch of houses, which included Grandpa and Grandma Brown's home. The Baylis home stood out because of its large size and its proximity to one of Detroit's most affluent neighborhoods. "The street is beautiful!" Beatriz exclaimed. "The houses are not bungalows, they're colonials. The neighborhood is amazing." Like Myrisha, Beatriz was able to look past the vacant homes and lots that surrounded the Baylis home to see its true potential. DERE purchased the home for $36,000 and decided to flip the house to make an immediate profit. After holding the property for less than three weeks, records show that on January 14, 2019, DERE sold the Baylis home to a real estate investment company based in South Florida, which is owned by an Argentine couple who are their long-standing clients. DERE sold Myrisha's legacy for $59,000, raking in a swift $23,000 profit.

DERE contracts local Detroit companies to manage their properties and manages the management company on behalf of their clients, who, by and large, do not speak English. "I get a letter and it is from a property management company," Myrisha said, explaining her first interaction with DERE's agent. "The previous owners never did give me the name of whoever it was that was purchasing it, so I did my due diligence to say, 'Hey, you're going to have to produce some paperwork of ownership.' Immediately, this company was like, 'Well, hey, we're telling you.' I said, 'You're not getting any money until you produce those things.'" From the very first moment to the last, Myrisha's relationship with DERE was filled with acrimony.

Myrisha was no pushover and she knew her rights. She, therefore, insisted that they make essential repairs before she paid any rent. Because of the inefficient heating system installed by the prior owners, in the winter of 2019, Myrisha's electricity bill alone again reached $2,000 for that season. She was overwhelmed.

The new property management company that DERE hired demonstrated genuine sympathy for Myrisha's plight and tried to work with her because, on the coldest days, at great cost to herself, Myrisha kept the heat running even when her family was not in the home to ensure that the pipes did not freeze. "He did send various people out (heat and cooling, plumbing) and they put in repair orders to the new owners," Myrisha said, speaking kindly of the property manager. "But immediately the new owners were like, 'Oh, no, we're not spending this kind of money.'"

"Every month we were getting charges for two hundred dollars here, a hundred dollars here, a hundred and fifty dollars every single month," Beatriz said, complaining about their property management company. "Some of the houses are ours and some of them are our Argentine clients', so it was a hard call to tell someone in Argentina that you're not gonna get any money this month because it was spent fixing the porch." DERE had promised its clients that its

Detroit investment would generate money, not swallow it, and if this promise proved false, then word would begin to circulate among the company's rich Argentine investors, killing DERE's business before it could even launch.

It was not long before DERE's owners realized that it was not easy to make money in Detroit. Decades of redlining and other state-enabled disinvestment had ravaged the city's housing stock, leaving many homes in dire need of comprehensive repairs. "After you close, then all of a sudden the tenants are like, 'Oh my God, my house is falling apart,'" Beatriz complained. "And you think you're buying something for forty thousand dollars, and at the end of the day it's like sixty thousand dollars. It's not one house. It is just about every single house that that happens." Exasperated by all the pushback she received from Myrisha and other Detroit tenants, in a defeated tone Beatriz said, "Yeah, they're very smart over there."

Since Myrisha was no longer employed at the dealership, in March 2019 she finally qualified for assistance with her expensive DTE bills for electricity and gas through The Heat And Warmth (THAW) Fund, a nonprofit organization founded in 1985 to help Michigan families facing energy insecurity. After THAW wiped out about $1,300 in past-due debt, Myrisha's monthly DTE bill decreased to an average of $325 per month. Most importantly, the utility company was no longer threatening to shut off her service, which according to Myrisha "is the next scariest thing to being homeless outdoors." Although the assistance drastically improved her DTE bill, it was still unaffordable.

Unlike the property management company that was very sympathetic to Myrisha's plight, Beatriz and her partners did not care about the prohibitively expensive DTE bill. Since Myrisha was withholding the rent, the new owners wanted her out. Myrisha soon received an eviction notice, instructing her to appear on March 13, 2019, at Detroit's 36th District Court before Judge Donald Coleman. Many eviction cases result in default judgments because tenants cannot afford to take off work or even momentarily abandon their caretaking responsibilities and so do not attend their court hearings.[21] Myrisha, however, did show up.

But like so many other vulnerable tenants in her situation, she could only afford to represent herself, while DERE hired a lawyer. Myrisha's only advantage was that she knew that her landlord was unregistered and thus in violation of the new ordinance, giving her the right to withhold rent. She came to court prepared to argue her case with three $800 money orders in hand for the January, February, and March rent. However, she did not know that rent withholdings were allowed only if tenants deposited the money into a city escrow account. If not, they were delinquent, and the ordinance did not cover tenants who were behind on rent. Myrisha went to court assuming the law was on her side, but it was not.

When DERE's eviction lawyer met Myrisha outside the courtroom, she thought he was a court-appointed mediator. She, therefore, began telling him her version of what had transpired. The lawyer put the property management company on speakerphone to confirm Myrisha's story, and after thirty minutes of discussion, Myrisha agreed to turn over the money orders in exchange for the promised repairs. More specifically, in the consent judgment signed by the landlord, tenant, and judge, Myrisha agreed to pay $2,400 plus $150 in legal costs by March 25. And, in exchange, the judgment read, "Plaintiff will make reasonable repairs....If defendant is unhappy with repairs she can escrow judgment with the court and file a motion." Although she signed the agreement, Myrisha did not know what "escrow judgment" meant, and she certainly did not know how to "file a motion," so if DERE failed to complete the promised repairs, she had no chance of holding them legally accountable. "I signed it because I felt like I had a gun to my head. With no place to go," Myrisha confessed.

Additionally, the eviction hearing left Beatriz and her partners feeling bitter and resentful toward Myrisha, whose "entitled" behavior outraged them. "We thought it was going be a quick process. At the end of the day, she grabbed all the money and she paid the money when they were in court. She just withheld it for no reason, and then made a big hoopla!" Beatriz exclaimed. "The crazy thing is we were ready to fix the house. It was absolutely gorgeous, and we didn't want it to go to waste. I paid lawyers, and evictions run between nine hundred and twelve hundred dollars. But remember, these are rents of seven hundred fifty to a thousand dollars, so already we're out a month." Her tone bitter, she continued, "We don't want the tenant anymore, but in Detroit we have to stay with the tenant. With this bad, ill-mannered tenant. Would you want somebody that took you through hell to continue in your house?"

After the eviction hearing, DERE fired their property management company because they insisted on completing costly repairs requested by tenants. "There was a lot of fixes that they did that were not emergency things that needed to be done, like they replaced furnaces and hot water tanks in the summer," Beatriz groaned. "Just because I'm an investor doesn't mean I have all this extra money to spare. Instead of putting it into a 401(k), I'm putting it into real estate, so I don't have money just floating around for all these things."

It was the new property management company, under strict orders to minimize costs, that commenced the repairs mandated by the eviction court. They hired a plumber and made minor repairs to the windows, but they failed to address Myrisha's most acute concern — the missing furnace, which after years of neglect required expensive plumbing work to install. Nevertheless, Myrisha was happy that she had successfully evaded eviction. She did not know that tragedy was lurking around the corner.

Later in March, Andricus Jr., the half brother of Myrisha's children, died violently. During an altercation at a family member's home, someone shot him in the chest, killing him two months before his high school graduation. "They have not caught the person who did it," Myrisha said irately. "They know who did it, but there's the no-snitch policy. His mother even put out a ten-thousand-dollar reward, which didn't do anything. And she's left to bury her son." With only an eighteen-month age difference, Myrisha's son and Andricus Jr. were very close. So throughout the rest of the summer, the mood in the Baylis home was somber.

In October 2019, as temperatures fell, Myrisha again stopped paying her rent because the crude heating system started to greedily eat electricity, again spiking her DTE bill. "I said, 'I cannot pay you eight hundred dollars in rent and have these kind of heating bills. It is not happening.'" Like the old management company, the new management company was ready to make the repairs. But again, Beatriz and her partners did not want to pay for the furnace. The management company complained that DERE was a slumlord, and DERE complained that the management company's overly eager responsiveness to tenant complaints was curbing profits.

"Every tenant that they put in they repainted, they did new kitchens, new bath. I'm not lying, new kitchens, new bath, new! And then all of a sudden they would give us a quote, not even a quote, a bill, an invoice of like six thousand or seven thousand dollars," Beatriz said, outraged by the management company. "I'm not a slumlord, but before you know it the money is just kind of disappearing." DERE fired the property manager and was not certain who would replace them, but they were absolutely certain that they wanted Myrisha out.

As a result, on October 10, DERE took Myrisha back to eviction court for withholding that month's rent. Again, before Judge Coleman, Myrisha argued that the owners had not installed a furnace and she would happily stop withholding rent once they did so. The judge ruled in favor of the landlord because DERE had evidence of repairs, and the furnace was not specifically listed in the March consent decree. If Myrisha did not pay the back rent or vacate in ten days, then DERE's lawyer could file an order of eviction within the next thirty days. The entire experience left Myrisha feeling that Detroit's low-cost housing market was dominated by slumlords and the City's rental ordinance had altogether failed to rein them in, leaving only landlords with a pistol in the proverbial gunfight.

Myrisha received all the required eviction notices by mail but ignored them because she thought DERE would call it off like last time. "I'm still thinking I'm working with them and we're not going through with an eviction process," Myrisha said. "The management company was still sending the person out doing repairs. So I thought that they were planning to honor the agreement."

On November 1, DERE's lawyer filed the order of eviction, which became final on November 13. If tenants do not leave immediately and of their own accord after this order is final, owners can hire a court officer to forcibly enter the home and physically eject the tenant, tossing their belongings into a dumpster. This is exactly what happened on December 4, 2019.

Myrisha was at a Cass Tech High School girls' basketball game, volunteering at the concession stand. "I get a phone call from my son," Myrisha recalled. "He said, 'The neighbor said there's a dumpster outside our house, and they're bringing our furniture out.'" Myrisha was flabbergasted. Without saying a word to the other volunteers, she grabbed her car keys and ran out, accidentally leaving behind her purse. "When I got the call, I kind of thought, 'Is someone breaking in our house?'" Myrisha said, her cadence rising. "But then when my son said 'There is a dumpster outside,' I knew."

When Myrisha finally arrived home, she could not believe her eyes. Her belongings lay on the front lawn, smaller items clad in black trash bags while the bigger items sat naked, waiting for the movers to carry them to the dumpster. None of it felt real. Lost in her disbelief, Myrisha called her mom. "I got this call from her and the call was…[long pause]…it was chilling," Mona said. "I've never heard her voice sound like that. It sounded like she had been abducted and she got to a phone just to let me know what was going on. It was frightening." Mona continued, "And what she said was, 'Mom, can you get over here, they're evicting me. They're taking everything out of the house.'"

After getting off the phone with her mom, Myrisha turned to the man who appeared to be in charge. She did not know what to do or say, so in an instinctive attempt to form a connection and foster empathy, she told him her story. Dealing with discarded people was both physically exacting and emotionally laborious, and experience had taught the mover that, in order to help Myrisha maintain her dignity in the midst of the eviction, he had to hear her out.

After allowing Myrisha to tell her story, "the guy said, 'Listen, I really hate that this is happening to you. You seem like the nicest person, but we don't have a choice,'" Myrisha recalled. "He said, 'I'll tell you what, I can't stop the guys from working, but if you want to go and get a truck, I'll have them just set stuff out and you can load it into the truck.'"

Myrisha quickly realized that it would, indeed, be incredibly difficult to yank her possessions from the large dumpster. She appreciated the mover's advice and immediately got to work, ensuring that the things she wanted to preserve did not end up in the dumpster. Prior to 2002, movers in Detroit chucked an evicted tenant's possessions on the sidewalk or lawn, transforming their treasured personal effects into common litter, furthering the blight terrorizing many neighborhoods. In response, a 2006 Detroit ordinance mandated that landlords rent a dumpster and give tenants forty-eight hours to remove their belongings before the company must haul the dumpster away, taking ownership of whatever remains inside.[22]

Just as Myrisha began to instruct the movers what to set aside, her mom arrived with her daughter in tow. "I got over there and they had already halfway emptied everything out of the house," Mona explained. "She was standing there composed. And I said, 'What do you need me to do?' She said, 'Can you go get a trailer,' and I said, 'Absolutely!' So there was a U-Haul not too far from there.

I got the U-Haul, brought it back." Myrisha's teenage son and his young buddy from across the street, who had first alerted them to the eviction, began packing the modest-sized U-Haul trailer with the family's belongings. Knowing it was not big enough to salvage everything, Myrisha allowed the workers to load many of the home's bulky items, like her furniture and family relics such as her grandmother's antique stove, into the dumpster.

Myrisha sacrificed these items in order to preserve her children's belongings. As a mother, Myrisha's primary mission in the midst of the chaos was mitigating the eviction's impact on her children. "I immediately started grabbing the things that I knew that the kids were going to need — food, school clothes, electronics, their furniture, their birth certificates, and their things that meant the most to them — and loaded those in the truck," Myrisha remembered. She was not, however, able to save all of their things.

The movers had started upstairs, so before Myrisha arrived, they had already manhandled the brand-new bedroom sets Myrisha had purchased for her children when they first moved into the Baylis home. They were now ruined. Of all the things that had gone wrong that day, it was the destruction of her children's bedroom furniture that brought Myrisha to the brink of a breakdown. "I had tears, but I was holding them because if you break down, what happens?" she asked. "I needed to hold it together for my children. They lost their father abruptly in 2017, and then in 2019, in March, they lost their brother to a homicide, so it was a lot of stuff that they were dealing with." Through the entire eviction, Myrisha never shed a tear. Instead, she chose to focus on the specks of brightness in a very dark situation because any other path would have led to her complete collapse.

The eviction "just was something I didn't expect," Myrisha confessed. The eviction shocked her because she had received mixed messages from the management company, which was genuinely trying to find middle ground between her and the owners. "I think they had good intentions," Myrisha said. "I just think you had owners going, 'No, we want to evict.' It wasn't illegal, but it was something that they said that they weren't going to do."

Because of DERE's determination to cut expenses at all costs, in their first two years doing business in Detroit, they cycled through four different property management companies. What Myrisha did not know was that the current management company and the owners were feuding. Consequently, at the end of November, abruptly and without the contractually required notice, the management company quit, handing the owners the keys and paperwork to all the properties they managed. DERE did not find a new management company until mid-January, and in the interim, chaos reigned, so DERE did not even know about the eviction. The owners thought Myrisha had left willingly after the October eviction hearing, and the lawyer who represented DERE in the eviction case had not even been paid in full.

After DERE ejected her, Myrisha moved her family's belongings to her sister's garage, and then they moved in with her mom. This was an especially smooth transition for her young daughter, Leigh, who daily waited at her grandmother's home for Myrisha to finish work and pick her up. In fact, Leigh already had her own bed and TV at her grandmother's house, as well as many of her games. So after the eviction, Leigh was fine but not unscathed.

"The first day or two she went to school, she had her uniform, but she didn't have her uniform pants, so I bought her some other pants to wear," Myrisha recalled. When Leigh's sixth-grade teacher asked why she was not wearing her regular uniform, Leigh told her teacher her family was kicked out of their house. "I think they might have thought that we were totally homeless, outdoors," Myrisha explained. "So they had sent some T-shirts with the school name on it, and the principal called me and said, 'Hey, Ms. Brown, what can we do for you?'" Myrisha told the principal what had happened in painstaking detail, reliving the eviction to assure her that Leigh was okay. "That hurt me because here you have an eleven-year-old trying to explain what's going on," Myrisha said. "So there were tears with that." Myrisha, for the first time, finally allowed herself to cry.

In the end, despite her epic tenacity, Myrisha lost her legacy. Forever. Just as Myrisha did not know she had to bring her utility bill back to UCHC in order to halt the tax foreclosure process in 2016, in 2019 Myrisha was unaware that she had to put the October rent check in a city escrow account in order to halt the eviction and force the investors to install a furnace. No matter how superhuman Myrisha was — miraculously juggling several caretaking responsibilities while fighting for her home — she was doomed to fail. Individual efforts are no match for broken systems.

"The house is probably empty now," Myrisha conjectured. "If not already, they will be walking away from the house. What I wanted to do initially is try to make sure that the property was not left an eyesore; not left to just deteriorate and make the neighborhood worse. That's probably going to happen anyway." Expressing remorse woven with disgust, she added, "The thing that really hurt me the most is that I was trying to do everything right and do everything legally, but yet I still ended up being evicted. And I thought, how unfair was that? There were no laws holding these people accountable for what they should have been doing in terms of keeping up the property correctly. These owners don't want to fix anything. I just don't understand where they're coming from with that."

Although most of the properties they own and manage are unregistered, DERE estimated that it had evicted tenants for nonpayment of rent in approximately 25 percent of its homes. With a portfolio of thirty-eight properties, the company only received one fine for an unregistered property after two years of doing business in Detroit. One study finds that: "Roughly 9 in 10 pandemic-era eviction filings involved properties operated unlawfully by landlords in violation of the City of Detroit's rental ordinance, despite the law stating that landlords may not occupy rental units or collect rent without a Certificate of Compliance (CoC)."[23] The City of Detroit has created a situation where tenants must follow the rules but landlords' disobedience is most often unpunished.

"I'm listening to the mayor talk about, 'We need to have property that is acceptable to the City of Detroit,'" Myrisha said, voice shaking with outrage. "You're saying that, but you're not following through on it. It made me so angry and I was like, 'I'm going to start writing letters. I'm going to speak out about this!'" Then she confessed, "But because so many other things were happening, I just didn't have the time to follow up."

The eviction forced Myrisha to search for affordable, quality housing in the middle of winter. She searched and searched but could not find an adequate rental unit for her family, so she gave up for a time. "We get through winter, and I'm ready to start looking in March, then we have this COVID situation and the stay-at-home quarantine placed in Michigan, so I could not do anything," Myrisha recounted. "So now we just opened up, and now I'm looking for housing, which is still a problem because you have property that's tied up because other people haven't been paying rent. So it's just been a whole nightmare."

In June 2021, Myrisha finally caught a break. One of her long-standing detailing customers, with whom she has had a twenty-five-year friendship, is a contractor who purchases and renovates homes from Detroit's Land Bank Authority. Although he did not have any homes available, he was renovating a home for a client that he thought might be a good fit for Myrisha, so he showed it to her. "As soon I stepped into the home, I felt a connection. It was everything that I wanted. It was a corner house. A sturdy brick house," Myrisha said. "But the only thing is, there was no garage. The block has a lot of vacant houses, but it is in a pretty good area. And now that my kids are not going to neighborhood schools, that does not matter."

Because it was a three-bedroom, two-bathroom, immaculately renovated single-family home renting for the affordable price of $800 a month, once it came on the market, there would be substantial demand. With over a year of rent saved from living with her mom, Myrisha was able to secure the home by offering to pay one year of rent up front, an offer the owner could not refuse. Although a bit nervous because she had never lived on the city's east side, Myrisha was grateful to have found a new home. "My hope is to possibly buy the home through a land contract at the end of the year, or by that time I will have my credit together and can get a loan from a bank," she estimated. "But either way, I am set for the year."

Like so many properties in Detroit, Myrisha's new rental home had a troubling backstory. Since mortgage companies most commonly pay the property taxes, her new rental is a prime example of how inflated property taxes can lead not only to tax foreclosure but also to mortgage foreclosure. Between 2010 and 2016, the *Detroit News* estimates that the City overtaxed Myrisha's new rental by at least $3,580. Then, in 2019, the home went through mortgage foreclosure. On the deed, the bank listed the foreclosure amount as $13,300, meaning that overtaxation constituted about 25 percent of the mortgage debt. In 2020, the bank resold the home for $18,000.

Through a devastating game of musical chairs, property tax foreclosure unjustly ejects Detroit homeowners from their homes. These individuals and families must then scramble to find homes to rent, which stand empty because inflated property tax debt contributes to both mortgage and tax foreclosure. Consequently, Detroit transitioned from a city that has long been majority homeowners to one that is now majority renters. Between 2010 and 2019, there was a 5.4 percent decrease in the city's homeownership rate, even as the State of Michigan showed only a 1 percent decrease.[24]

Curious about how Detroit's destructive game of musical chairs played out for her legacy, on one cold day in February 2022, Myrisha returned to the Baylis home for the first time since she had been evicted three years earlier. Dressed in a puffy down jacket, she pulled up to the home in her 2020 Kia Soul and walked toward the house. Apprehensive about what was awaiting her, Myrisha felt her heart racing. It did not take her long to determine that her worst nightmare had occurred. The home was standing vacant. After chatting with some new neighbors, she discovered that it had long been uninhabited. Later she would discover that because their tenants were not paying rent during the coronavirus pandemic, DERE had collapsed and Beatriz and her partners had walked away from all their Detroit properties, including the Baylis home.

As Myrisha slowly walked around the home's perimeter, both memories and tears raced forward. She intentionally lingered on the spot where the home's majestic apple tree once bloomed, speckling the backyard with its green fruit. From that vantage point, she could see the spot where the garage had been before the fire that originated at the neighboring corner home burned it to the ground. As she ambled along, moving from the backyard to the side of the home, she stopped, leaned over, and peered through the side window. What she saw left her aghast. The pipes she had fought so hard to keep intact had finally frozen and burst, covering the living room, where Grandma Brown once resided, in at least a foot of ice. Myrisha wailed.

9

RIGGED GAME

Myrisha's story is a clear example of predatory governance, which is when public officials replenish public coffers through racist policies. Just like the flesh-eating bacteria gnawing away at Frederick Brown's buttocks, predatory governments implement policies that, without mentioning race, quietly injure racial minorities in their own body politic, sometimes with malice and other times without. The local government's usurpation of Myrisha's inheritance was predicated upon the following written and unwritten laws and processes that produced racial inequity.

First was the City of Detroit's systematic overvaluation of homes in violation of the Michigan Constitution, and the County's practice of foreclosing on and selling homes at its property tax foreclosure auction despite widespread evidence of illegality. Detroit is one of Wayne County's forty-three cities, villages, and townships, thirty-three of which have a population that is 70 percent or more white and three of which have a population that is 70 percent or more African American: Detroit, Inkster, and Highland Park. While cities in the County with a supermajority of African American residents experienced high rates of illegally inflated property tax assessments and tax foreclosure, the cities with a white supermajority did not.[1]

Second were the County's unclear payment instructions, which led homeowners with an impending property tax foreclosure to pay their current bill instead of the three-year-old tax debt, which was the only thing that could hold foreclosure at bay.

Third was the City of Detroit's unnecessarily complicated exemption process, which caused tens of thousands to lose their homes for nonpayment of property taxes they were not supposed to be paying in the first place.

Fourth was the County's statutorily mandated 18 percent interest rate on delinquent property tax debt, as well as its other fees, fines, and penalties, which made it almost impossible for poor people to get out of debt.

Fifth was the County and State's incomprehensible alphabet soup of payment plans for delinquent property taxes.

Sixth was the state and federal government's ineffective anti-discrimination employment regime, which did nothing to counter-balance the gross asymmetries of information and power between employers and workers, leaving the burden and risk of addressing discrimination on vulnerable workers.[2] Consequently, Myrisha, like so many others, could not successfully hold her employers accountable for their discriminatory actions, which left her in a revolving door of unemployment, despite her impeccable work ethic and abilities.

Seventh was the eroded social safety net, which has elevated costs for women who are left, with low or no pay, to do the caregiving work that the welfare state should — specifically, the lack of national health insurance, affordable child care, and accessible disability care.[3]

Eighth was MSHDA's hardest hit program, which was designed to assist middle-class homeowners having temporary problems and not low-income homeowners experiencing chronic poverty.

From the time when Grandpa and Grandma Brown and other Blacks began arriving in droves during the Great Migration, to the era of their grandchildren and great-grandchildren, racist policies have dogged African Americans in Detroit. But the mystery for many is: How did racist policies commence and survive in Detroit, a majority-Black city run, principally, by Black politicians and bureaucrats since the 1970s?

It surely was not because the problem was hidden. The property tax foreclosure crisis has caused such massive displacement of families and disassembling of neighborhoods that activists began calling it a hurricane with no water.[4] This dehydrated hurricane was on full display each fall when Wayne County placed yellow bags on the doors of every home at risk of tax foreclosure. "At first I thought it was just me," one Detroiter who lost his home to tax foreclosure recounted. "But when I seen yellow baggies on my entire block, I knew something wasn't right. I knew something was up."

While most Detroit residents could not recite statistics, they knew that tax foreclosure had become Detroit's yellow fever, infecting homes on every block and in every neighborhood. But even though the problem was clear for all to see, the causes of it were harder to identify. More precisely, both victim-blaming and corruption discourses have long obscured the true causes.

Victim-blaming discourses are best illustrated by the words of David Szymanski, Detroit's former treasurer, who said, "People decided to buy purses instead of pay their taxes." In this convenient and common framing, fault lies with the victims because of their poor personal choices, laziness, ignorance, or their membership in "cultures" bereft of strong moral values, respect for education, and hard work. The solution to the property tax foreclosure crisis, therefore, involves character-building, improved decision-making, and increased personal responsibility. Most importantly, when victim-blaming discourses are dominant, the solution is never a structural intervention designed to uproot racist policies.

Even worse, individual irresponsibility narratives not only place blame on victims, but they also cause victims, like Myrisha, to blame themselves, creating an environment of shame that prevents them from fighting back. In her postmortem on how she lost her legacy, Myrisha said, "With so many balls juggling, trying to be the breadwinner and trying to hold things together for others, that I didn't focus as much as I should have." She blamed herself. Overlapping racist policies got off scot-free.

The other dominant societal narrative—the "bad apples" theory—lays the blame for Detroit's property tax foreclosure crisis squarely at the feet of the City's corrupt leadership. "Detroit is known for having people in positions that don't do anything but step on the City to prop themselves up," one third-generation Detroiter said with deep conviction. For many, Kwame Kilpatrick, Detroit's mayor from 2002 to 2008, stands as the poster boy for what they believe is Detroit's primary problem—corruption. After a federal court convicted him of perjury and obstruction of justice in 2008, Kilpatrick resigned. Then, in 2013, a federal court convicted him of twenty-four offenses and sentenced him to twenty-eight years in prison. Kilpatrick's downfall coincided with the Great Recession, so political instability and scandal deluged the city at the very time when it instead needed stable, trustworthy leadership to navigate through turbulent economic waters.

While Kilpatrick's corruption was highly visible, it was not singular. In 1992, a federal jury convicted Detroit police chief William L. Hart of stealing $2.6 million in taxpayer money over seven years and sentenced him to ten years in prison.[5] In 2015, federal courts convicted at least six different public officials—including Jeffrey Beasley, Detroit's treasurer from 2006 to 2008—of looting funds from Detroit's pension system.[6] According to a *Detroit News* database on corruption in Detroit, within a ten-year period, federal prosecutors have charged 108 politicians, police officers, bureaucrats, and labor leaders with corruption-related crimes, including embezzlement, fraud, and money laundering.[7]

Additionally, authorities have charged several members of the Detroit City Council with criminal offenses. In 2004, federal

Figure 4: Detroit Public Officials Criminally Charged

Date Convicted	Name	Title	Charge	Amount of (alleged) illegal benefit	Sentence (months)
Sept 12, 2011	Derrick Miller	Detroit chief administrative officer	Corruption and tax offenses	$115,000	0
March 11, 2013	Kwame Kilpatrick	Detroit mayor	Twenty-four counts of extortion, mail fraud, tax violations, and racketeering	$1,000,000	336
August 05, 2013	Sandra Campbell	Detroit Public Schools accountant	Program fraud con-splracy, money laundering con-spiracy, and tax charges	$530,091	70
August 13, 2013	George Stanton	Chief of staff for Detroit Councilwoman Alberta Tinsley-Talabi	Accepting bribes	$100,000	0
April 15, 2014	Timothy Cromer	Detroit Public Library official	Bribery, conspiracy, and receiving bribes	$1,400,000	120
Dec 08, 2014	Ronald Zajac	General counsel, Detroit Pension Funds	Conspiracy to commit honest services mail and wire fraud	$150,000	Died while awaiting sentencing
Dec 08, 2014	Jeffrey Beasley	Detroit treasurer	Honest services fraud conspiracy, extortion, and bribery	$250,000	132
May 04, 2016	Clara Flowers	Detroit Public Schools assistant superin-tendent	Conspiracy to defraud the U.S. and tax evasion	$324,785	36
May 05, 2016	Nina Graves-Hicks	Detroit Public Schools principal	Bribery, Conspiracy	$27,385	12
June 29, 2016	Carolyn Starkey-Darden	Detroit Public Schools director	Federal program fraud	$1,275,000	18
July 11, 2016	Bryan Watson	Detroit police officer	Conspiracy to interfere with commerce by extortion and robbery	$916,000	108
July 11, 2016	David Hansberry	Detroit police lieutenant	Conspiracy to interfere with commerce by extortion and robbery	$960,000	151
August 18, 2017	John Hamilton	Operating Engineers Local 324 leader	Extortion, Conspiracy	$500,000	24
May 15, 2018	Masharn Franklin	Detroit Audit & Payroll employee	Embezzlement	$265,573	18
Dec 04, 2019	Joe Ashton	UAW vice president and GM director	Wire fraud and money laundering conspiracies	$250,000	30

prosecutors indicted Councilwoman Kay Everett on bribery charges, but she died of kidney disease before the courts resolved the case. After Councilman Lonnie Bates used city money to pay his mistress and her daughter for work they did not do, as well as cashing a former employee's checks and pocketing the money, federal courts convicted him of multiple charges in 2006, including public corruption. In 2009, Councilwoman Monica Conyers, wife of U.S. Congressman John Conyers Jr., who represented Michigan from 1965 to 2017, pleaded guilty to bribery and received a thirty-seven-month sentence In 2021, federal prosecutors charged and sentenced City Councilman Gabe Leland to 2.5 years of probation for a bribery scheme involving a felonious $7,500 cash campaign contribution, and charged City Councilman Andre Spivey with accepting $35,000 in bribes.

Since there is no question that corruption among Detroit's leaders is a significant problem, it is easy to point to unethical, law-breaking politicians as the primary cause of the city's property tax foreclosure crisis. But the truth is that the reason for the pervading property tax injustice in Detroit was not the actions of a few corrupt individuals. Instead, it was caused by several intersecting policies and practices that this chapter will explain in detail.

Corruption discourses are deceptively alluring because if the problem is a specific set of malicious individuals, then the solution is easy — remove them. So begins the hunt for the bad apples. Is it Detroit's chief assessor? Although it would make for a thrilling, made-for-Hollywood story, the leaders of Detroit's Office of the Assessor were neither corrupt nor wildly incompetent.

Corruption discourses are also problematic because they often lead Black communities to defend corrupt individuals with Black skin because they receive more scrutiny and punishment than corrupt individuals with white skin. As one Detroit public school teacher said, "I believe that Kwame Kilpatrick was guilty. But I also believe that his sentence was excessive. It was disproportionate." She continued, "There was a microscope over him more than others. More than white people." Cognizant of the bias against Black leaders, vulnerable people often end up protecting the very people who are victimizing them.

It is time to replace the misleading corruption and personal irresponsibility explanations for property tax injustice in Detroit with the truth, which is complex. The true culprit behind illegally inflated property taxes and the resulting foreclosures in Detroit is racist policies. When racist policies are at work, individual bad actors certainly exist, but removing them is not enough to achieve justice. Additionally, poor individual decision-making is also an inescapable reality, but changing individual choices alone cannot collapse the larger injustice.

While historians show that local governments have been overtaxing African American–owned property ever since the U.S. has allowed Blacks to own property,[8] the most immediate cause of Detroit's property tax injustice was the Great Recession, which lasted from December 2007 to June 2009. The Great Recession was the worst economic decline in U.S. history since the Great Depression. Subprime mortgages, low interest rates, excessive borrowing, and inadequate regulation caused the housing market to crash, precipitating a worldwide recession. Even though the entire nation and global community experienced economic decline, majority-Black communities, like Detroit, were hit especially hard because this was where U.S. banking institutions most actively issued predatory, subprime loans. Between 2004 and 2006, subprime loans accounted for 40 percent of all bank-issued loans in metro Detroit.[9] Consequently, Detroit's 2007 mortgage foreclosure rate of 5 percent was the nation's highest.[10]

It is, therefore, no surprise that Detroit's housing market collapsed. In 2008, Detroit's average home value was about $80,000. By 2010, this number had plummeted to $23,800.[11] Linda Bade, Detroit's chief assessor during the mortgage foreclosure crisis, tried to respond to the drastic market declines but lacked the staff required to change the valuation on thousands of homes. "It was impossible to target cuts neighborhood by neighborhood because the resources did not exist to do that," Alvin Horhn, Detroit's current chief assessor, who worked under Linda Bade, said. "The City was having serious financial troubles and it was just trying to keep firemen and police on the streets. There was no money for an army of appraisers, so Bade made cuts across the board."

Alvin continued, "When Bade started making cuts in 2007, the total SEV [State Equalized Value] was fourteen billion dollars."[12] This means that the Office of the Assessor estimated that the market value of all taxable property in Detroit was about $28 billion. Alvin explained that "by the time she left in June 2013, the total SEV dropped to six billion dollars,"[13] which meant that the estimated market value of all taxable property had dropped to $12 billion. He added, regretfully, "Since the cuts were substantial and uniform across the board, some property owners got cuts they did not deserve, and others did not get enough. Linda knew it was wrong and burned herself to the ground trying to deal with it all."

In spite of Linda Bade's best efforts, conservative estimates show that between 2009 and 2015, Detroit's Office of the Assessor illegally inflated the property tax assessments of 53 to 84 percent of homes.[14] Myrisha and other Detroit homeowners suffered from illegally inflated property tax assessments and bills despite the fact that they could not afford this. Making matters worse, when the Great Recession triggered the bankruptcy of General Motors and Chrysler, Detroit's unemployment rate skyrocketed to 24 percent in 2009, 2.4 times the national average.[15] As a consequence, by 2011, 47 percent of Detroit property owners did not pay their overinflated property tax bills,[16] leaving about $131 million in taxes and fees uncollected, which amounted to 12 percent of Detroit's general fund budget.

As the city's economic crisis snowballed, in December 2011, Michigan's treasurer announced that the State would conduct a formal review of its finances.[17] State authorities found that from 1960 to 2013, the number of city employees had contracted from 26,386 to 10,525, but the number of pensioners had increased from 10,629 to 21,113.[18] With revenues decreasing but pension obligations increasing, the City used capital market debt to finance the yawning gap, and its debt rose from $2.8 billion (measured in 2013 dollars) in 1990 to $8 billion in 2013.[19] As Detroit's debt became unmanageable, early in 2013, Michigan's governor, Rick Snyder, wrested control of Detroit's fiscal operations from its democratically elected leaders, asserting that the City was in "operational dysfunction."[20]

Governor Snyder transferred control to his appointed emergency manager, Kevyn Orr, who throughout his eighteen-month tenure had one overarching mandate: to drastically cut debt and expenditures to balance the City's books.[21] Orr cut monies for police, courts, transportation, water operations, and maintenance, despite the fact that the city had the highest violent crime rate of any American city with a population over two hundred thousand; police response time was, on average, about fifty-eight minutes, whereas the national average was about eleven minutes;[22] the City could not afford to fix tens of thousands of broken streetlights, leaving many neighborhoods blanketed in darkness at night; and the City could afford to keep only a small fraction of its municipal parks open.[23]

With the City's $18 billion debt and long-term liabilities far exceeding its assets, Orr decided to file for bankruptcy on July 18, 2013. This stands as the largest municipal bankruptcy in U.S. history—four times the size of the next largest, the $4.2 billion bankruptcy in 2011 of Jefferson County, Alabama.[24] Since most of the debt owed consisted of pension and health benefits due to retired workers, as well as municipal bonds, Detroit's pensioners suffered most of all. "I could have worked someplace else and made more money, but I was told if I worked here I'd have a steady job and in my old age not be in poverty," Michael Mulholland, who retired after almost thirty years in the Water Department, remarked. "It's morally indefensible."[25]

With Orr's decision to file for bankruptcy, it may seem like the State of Michigan came in to clean up the economic mess that Detroit's officials had made, but the truth was that the State of Michigan greatly contributed to Detroit's financial disorder. In 2012, one year prior to Detroit's bankruptcy, the governor covered the state's budget deficit by creating the Economic Vitality Incentive Program (EVIP). While the State of Michigan collects all sales taxes, it is supposed to give its cities and towns some portion, which are called statutory revenue-sharing payments. The EVIP drastically reduced these essential payments to Michigan cities. In the program's first year, for instance, Governor Snyder cut revenue-sharing payments by about one-third,[26] which resulted in a $70 million funding reduction for Detroit. That is, when property tax payments — the primary revenue source of most Michigan cities — were at an all-time low because of the Great Recession, through its EVIP, the State of Michigan exacerbated the financial vulnerability of its cities.

But even after the state eliminated its budget deficit and financially recovered from the Great Recession, revenue-sharing payments did not return to their pre-EVIP levels.[27] In fact, while sales tax revenues rose from $6.6 billion to $7.72 billion between 2003 and 2013, statutory revenue-sharing payments declined from over $900 million to about $250 million, resulting in a reduction of $732 million in Detroit, $54.9 million in Flint, $40 million in Pontiac, and $40 million in Lansing.[28]

Also, through driver responsibility fees instituted in 2003, the State of Michigan extracted additional monies directly from its citizens to cover earlier budget deficits. By significantly increasing fines and fees for routine automobile infractions — including driving without insurance, without a license, under the influence of alcohol, or recklessly[29] — from 2003 to 2017, Michigan's secretary of state raised between $99 million and $115 million a year.[30] Seventy thousand Detroit residents alone owed more than $100 million.[31] The fees were unjust for many reasons, including the fact that when poverty prevented drivers from making timely payments, the State suspended their license and instituted a hefty reinstatement fee, which prevented people from reaching the very jobs that would allow them to pay their debts. After considerable public outcry, the state repealed driver responsibility fees in 2018, but they had already done significant financial damage.

At the same time that the State of Michigan instituted extractive measures and decreased revenue-sharing payments to its cities and towns to cover its budget deficits, Detroit's federal funding was also declining. For example, the Community Development Block Grant (CDBG) program, created in 1974, provides flexible federal funding to states and localities to benefit low- and moderate-income people and aid in the elimination of blight and other conditions that threaten the health and safety of residents.[32] In 2003, the CDBG program provided $6.6 million to Wayne County and $46.5 million to Detroit, but fifteen years later, despite inflation, these numbers had declined to $5.5 million and $34.5 million, respectively.[33] Reduced federal and state funding caused financial desperation and greatly contributed to property tax injustice in Detroit.

Another factor contributing to property tax injustice in Detroit was a series of contradictions embedded within the Michigan Constitution. Article IX of that document states: (1) Michigan localities cannot assess any property at more than 50 percent of its market value; and (2) until sold, annual increases in a property's taxable value can be no more than the inflation rate or 5 percent, whichever is less (known as Proposal A). However well-intentioned, these two constitutional provisions put local authorities in a thorny bind. On one hand, in a booming housing market with rapidly increasing property values that far outpace inflation, local governments cannot fully tax these gains, depriving them of significant revenue. In fact, the Michigan Department of Treasury reports that between 1994 and 2003, Proposal A cut $63 billion in local property taxes.[34]

On the other hand, in a steep market downturn, like that prompted by the Great Recession, local taxing authorities had two bad choices. Option A was to abide by the Michigan Constitution and reduce assessed values to reflect the decline in market values. Although legally mandated, this option would lock in low values even if the real estate market recovered in the next year or two because until a property is sold, its taxable value can rise by no more than 5 percent. Thus, by following the law, local taxing authorities could impair their jurisdiction's ability to raise revenues and hence provide vital public services for a long stretch of time. "Proposal A does not allow jurisdictions to recapture value once the market recovers because no one ever imagined a sustained housing crash would occur," Alvin Horhn explained. "No one conceived of this."

Option B was to ignore the law by not adjusting assessed values to reflect the sharp decline in market values. But once the market recovered, assessed values would comply with the law and all would once again be well. So if a home's market value declined from $100,000 to $50,000, instead of reducing the property's assessed value from $50,000 to no more than $25,000, as required by the Michigan Constitution, the local assessor would continue to assess it at $50,000 or slightly reduce it to $40,000. If in a year or two the home's value bounced back, then local authorities would once again be legally compliant without taking a long-term hit to revenues.

In the meantime, the Office of the Assessor would effectively pass the burden of correcting assessed values to individual taxpayers, who would have to appeal the illegally inflated property tax assessments. Those who did not (or could not) appeal literally paid the price. Since studies consistently show that local authorities are more likely to illegally inflate the assessed value of the lowest-valued homes, it is most often the most vulnerable homeowners who have paid the price of this illegality.

When Detroit's Office of the Assessor failed to lower assessed values to reflect the steep drop in housing values after the Great Recession, it chose option B, breaking the law rather than jeopardizing revenues. But as shown in Figure 5, property values in Detroit did not quickly bounce back, so the illegality was not temporary. It persisted.

While the Great Recession and the legal contradictions embedded in Michigan's Constitution were outside Detroit leaders' control, there were other factors within their control — namely, their dysfunctional Office of the Assessor. In 2012, the City's auditor general published a report examining the Detroit Office of the Assessor's performance from July 2008 to June 2011, concluding that the division's property tax assessment and data management activities were "inefficient and ineffective."[35] The report divulged that the division's property data was highly inaccurate, and without accurate data, it could not produce correct property tax assessments.

The auditor general identified two primary problems. First, according to 75 percent of employees interviewed, the Office of the Assessor had inadequate staffing.[36] "In 1997, we had one hundred staff members," Alvin Horhn recounted. "Then Linda retired. When she came back in April of 2007, we had fifty-seven people. In 2013, Linda retired again, and at that point we were down to thirty-five people. When people left, they were not replaced." With a grimace, Alvin added, "We did not have manpower because the City was focused on public safety, but thirty-five people could not get the job done." This personnel shortage caused existing staff to work excessive overtime, burn out, and leave; and then, because of budget cuts, the division could not replace them.

The workforce shortage also meant that the division's existing staff did not have the capacity to perform legally required site visits.

Figure 5: Detroit Home Value Index, 2000-2024

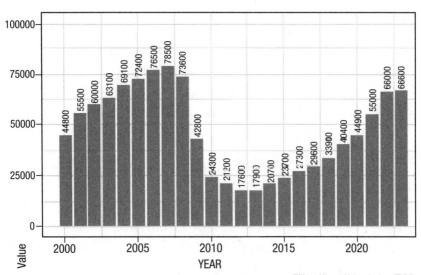

Zillow Home Value Index (ZHVI)
from https://www.zillow.com/research/data/
Data is shown for Detroit City as of January each year.

At that time, the State of Michigan required local assessors to visit 30 percent of all properties annually in order to update property values and descriptions. With one of the state's highest rates of arson, vacancy, mortgage foreclosure, and property tax foreclosure, site visits were especially important for Detroit and its swiftly changing housing stock. Nevertheless, according to the auditor general's report, on average, the last recorded site visit had been thirty years earlier for residential properties and 22.8 years earlier for commercial and industrial properties.[37]

"We could not get out of the office, so we used the property transfer affidavits and sales available to us," Horhn explained. "But you cannot confirm the value of a house if you are not out there to review sales. We didn't have staff to do what we needed to do." Throwing his hands up, he added, "We were in the middle of the storm trying to keep our heads above water while everything was crashing down all around us." Without the staff to complete routine site visits, the accuracy of the division's property records, and the assessments based upon them, were appallingly low.

Massive data loss caused by the Office of the Assessor's botched transition from its antiquated mainframe assessing software to its new operating system called Equalizer was the second fundamental problem that the auditor general's report highlighted.[38] Although the conversion occurred between 2002 and 2003, it "should have happened over several years with officials going into the field and verifying the information," Horhn remarked. "But in 2002, things began going south in Detroit and we did not have the manpower or funding to do the switch properly." Consequently, the Office of the Assessor's property descriptions and valuations were systematically inaccurate or incomplete. In fact, the auditor general reported that, for 23 percent of residential properties it audited, the record in Equalizer was incorrect.[39]

Without accurate data, Detroit's Office of the Assessor could not follow the property tax assessment calculation standards specified by the Michigan Constitution. Instead, the division used incremental, ad hoc adjustments to previously estimated property values to calculate property tax assessments. "We took statistical averages of what we could get our hands on. But with limited resources and limited access to data, you will come up with garbage," Alvin confessed. "In the best circumstances, this is not what we should have been doing." When property values fell in 2008, this already cracked system completely shattered.

As part of Detroit's Office of the Assessor's own internal quality control processes, after the division's appraisers inspect and value properties, they submit these valuations to their managers for intermediate approval, and the managers then submit all the valuations to a three-member Board of Assessors for final approval. But with no accurate data or documentation to serve as a benchmark, all these levels of review and approval were meaningless.

After the Office of the Assessor produces the tax assessment roll, the Board of Review is the entity charged with ensuring that it is accurate and equitable, but the faulty data also undermined its ability to do so. Although Willie Donwell, the Board of Review leader since 2004, knew about the data lost in the bungled conversion and the resulting systemic inaccuracies, the Board of Review did not have the capacity to fix this systemic problem.[40] It could only adjudicate appeals filed by a small percentage of Detroit homeowners, and instead of using market data to determine the value of each home before it, the board made informal estimations. Consequently, the board was working in tandem with the Office of the Assessor rather than holding it accountable for its systematic miscalculations.

In one case, for example, the Office of the Assessor argued that the market value of a property was $40,000, but when the homeowner's advocate presented a certified appraisal showing that the property's market value was closer to $10,000, the Board of Review president disregarded the appraisal altogether and just gave a "back-of-the-envelope" 3 percent reduction in the property's assessed value. The rest of the board rubber-stamped his decision, as was their custom. But when the homeowner took the case to the Michigan Tax Tribunal, its judges overturned the board's decision and reduced the property's value to around $10,000 in accordance with the certified appraisal.

According to Alvin Horhn, during the Great Recession and subsequent bankruptcy, the City lost 90 percent of its tribunal cases because its data were highly inaccurate. The City also did not have the manpower to even respond to tribunal complaints, so taxpayers regularly won default judgments. Without representation, however, most Detroit homeowners could not reach the tribunal.

The next step in the oversight process was county and state equalization. But bad data also prevented these processes from holding the Office of the Assessor accountable. Using its own sales and appraisal studies, the county annually verifies that the cumulative assessed value of each property category (i.e., residential, commercial, industrial) does not exceed 50 percent of the category's cumulative market value. Then the State Tax Commission may add, subtract, or approve the county equalized value to produce the State Equalized Value (SEV). But because Wayne County and state authorities primarily relied upon the City's inaccurate data, the equalization processes were nothing more than smoke and mirrors. Accountability was an illusion. Illegally inflated property tax assessments and bills continued unabated.

Based on the 2012 auditor general's report and investigative reporting that also found profound problems, in the fall of 2013, Doug Roberts — the chairman of the three-member State Tax Commission charged with supervising property tax administration in Michigan — began investigating the overassessments in Detroit.[41] The commission hired a consulting firm that works with local governments throughout the United States to improve property tax administration.[42] The firm's primary finding was that illegally inflated property tax assessments were rampant because the Office of the Assessor's property data were in disarray. The firm thus recommended that the City start afresh by completing a parcel-by-parcel reassessment of each property in its jurisdiction, which Detroit's chief assessor, Alvin Horhn, believed had not been done since the mid-1960s.[43]

With its investigation completed, in April 2014, the State Tax Commission intervened by taking control of Detroit's property tax assessment roll.[44] "No one paid as much attention as we should have," Doug Roberts admitted. "We should have [intervened] sooner."[45] So just as state officials put the City of Detroit under emergency management in 2013, the state also placed Detroit's Office of the Assessor under its mandatory oversight in 2014. The state required the Office of the Assessor to enter a corrective action plan that mandated a reappraisal, costing about $5.85 million.[46] According to Alvin Horhn, the reappraisal is something his division long ago knew needed to happen, but without the 2013 bankruptcy and the weight authorities involved gave to restoring property tax collection, this costly overhaul might never have occurred.

In 2014, as the citywide reassessment got off the ground, Mike Duggan became Detroit's seventy-fifth mayor. Even though he was a write-in candidate, he miraculously won, becoming the city's only white mayor since Coleman Young — the city's celebrated first Black mayor — assumed office in 1974.[47] "The entire revenue collection process for the city of Detroit is broken,"[48] Duggan said during his campaign. "And we need to get a fair property tax system in this state and in the city in particular. I don't have any confidence in the caliber of the assessments. There's an unfair patchwork system that has to be restructured."[49] Upon taking office, Mayor Duggan reiterated his promise. "As I said when I was campaigning, I felt like the assessments in this city were higher than the actual sales price that people could sell their house for." He added, "We made a commitment to have honest assessments."[50]

Knowing that the reassessment would take years to complete, Mayor Duggan wanted to find an immediate way to make good on his campaign promise to institute fair property taxes, so in 2014 and 2015, he ordered across-the-board assessment reductions, ranging between 5 and 20 percent for select districts.[51] But this was the same strategy Linda Bade had implemented years earlier, and the result was "some property owners got cuts they did not deserve, and others did not get enough," Alvin Horhn said. "Linda knew it was wrong." Nevertheless, in the name of political expediency, Mayor Duggan moved forward with the cuts.

It is, therefore, no surprise that the across-the-board cuts left the vast majority of lower-priced properties overvalued — with an average assessment ratio of 3.29, about six times the constitutional limit of 0.5 — while the average ratio for higher-priced properties reduced to 0.29, substantially lower than the constitutional limit.[52] Predictably, Mayor Duggan's fix did not work. A smarter and fairer policy would have called for a drastic reduction for lower-valued homes and an increase or no action for higher-valued homes.

But just like Linda Bade, Mayor Duggan and his administration did not have the data required for this surgical intervention. "I think the rates should have come down sooner," Mayor Duggan said. "But I dealt with what we had and moved as quickly as we could."[53] Detroit property owners had been crushed by property tax injustice for years, and while it seemed that Mayor Duggan was finally lifting the press, data reveal that he was not. Nevertheless, he continues to claim that his across-the-board cuts fixed the problem.

Studies show that — even after the City completed its parcel-by-parcel reassessment of each residential property in 2017, freeing itself from State oversight — the overvaluation problem abated, but it did not disappear. Specifically, the University of Chicago's Center for Municipal Finance found that, while the City did begin assessing properties priced at the average in accordance with the Michigan Constitution, the City continued to illegally inflate the assessed values for its lowest-priced homes.[54] That is, before the reappraisal, the City assessed the lowest-valued homes at a rate that was three times higher than for the highest-valued homes, and after the appraisal, the rate was four times higher. Consequently, even after two attempted fixes — one mandated by Mayor Duggan and the other by the State Tax Commission — illegally inflated property taxes continue in Detroit today for the lowest-valued homes.

To make matters worse, even though he admits that at one time property tax bills were not "honest," Mayor Duggan does not believe that the City has a duty to compensate homeowners for their overtaxation or the resulting foreclosures. "Folks had a process by which they could appeal it. Those years are closed," Mayor Duggan said. "I don't know any lawful way to go back and say to all the taxpayers of the city who did follow the process, 'We're going to raise your taxes to pay the taxes for people who didn't.'"[55] Instead of focusing on the systematically inflated property tax assessments, in the blame boomerang, taxpayers' failure to appeal is a matter of personal irresponsibility, denying them deserved relief.

While Mayor Duggan presents his reluctance to address the City's systematic overassessments as a question of fairness to taxpayers who "did follow the process," this belies the fact that the appeal system, as designed, could never remedy the City's routine over-taxation of homes. Gary Evanko, Detroit's chief assessor from 2013 to 2016, admitted that if every overassessed homeowner had appealed their property taxes, the City could not have handled the volume.[56] That is, the system functioned only because most homeowners could not access it and did not understand it. "The tax bill is, to be honest, confusing," one lifelong Detroit resident who lost her home to tax foreclosure said. "You just kind of just pay what they say and do not look at how it is put together."

Most Detroit homeowners do not have the wherewithal to file an appeal, but for those who do, the first step was the Board of Assessors. Although there was no form to guide taxpayers, the appeal, at minimum, had to contain the property address or parcel number, the reason for the appeal, and some form of evidence. According to a city ordinance, if Detroit homeowners did not submit this information by mail or in person between February 1 and February 15, then they forfeited their right to approach subsequent appellate bodies. Most importantly, the Board of Assessors was an extra mandatory step in Michigan's appeal process that only homeowners in Detroit had to take,[57] giving them about three to four weeks less to appeal than other Michigan homeowners.

The second mandatory step in the appeal process for Detroit homeowners — but the first step for all other Michiganders — was to submit a standardized appeal form by mail or in person to the Board of Review by the second Monday in March.[58] In 2024, activists successfully fought for a law change to ensure that the Assessor Review is no longer mandatory, making the Board of Review the first step in the process for all Michiganders. The board holds a hearing, and most Detroit homeowners show up without representation. They do not have the requisite comparable sales data to prove that the assessor's valuation was wrong. Instead, they come prepared only to tell their stories, leading to poor appeal outcomes.

If Detroit homeowners are not satisfied with the decision they receive at the Board of Review, they can appeal to the Michigan Tax Tribunal by July 31. The filing fee is between $250 and $600, depending on the property's value.[59] But owners of commercial and industrial properties can appeal directly to the tribunal without going through the two preceding steps,[60] which makes the process far less onerous for these well-heeled owners. After the tribunal come the Michigan Court of Appeals and then the State Supreme Court, but these courts can only hear the appeals of property owners who successfully claim that the tax tribunal committed "fraud, error of law or adoption of wrong principles."[61]

Although this legal framework for contesting property tax assessments may seem straightforward, numerous barriers make it difficult for Detroit homeowners who cannot hire a lawyer or real estate professional to file their appeal. First, taxpayers must know that a process exists to protest the local government's valuation of their home. Then, amid their caretaking responsibilities and job demands, busy taxpayers, like Myrisha, must find time to file a property tax appeal. Taxpayers must also understand how the City calculates their property tax bill. Specifically, although it is not stated anywhere on the assessment notice or tax bill, they must somehow know that the home's assessed value multiplied by 2 produces the home's purported market value.[62] Taxpayers must then understand how to estimate their home's market value through recent sales of comparable properties. Next, if taxpayers are not satisfied with one appeal body's decision, then they must know that there are multiple opportunities to further appeal. And finally, taxpayers must also have the time and resources to pursue these additional appeals.

Research shows that because they can afford to hire representatives who are expert at navigating this complex process, middle- and upper-class owners are more likely both to file an appeal and have more success than low-income owners.[63] Also, the two prevailing business models in the property tax appeal industry — the contingency and flat-fee models — make it almost impossible for low-income homeowners to secure representation. In the contingency model, instead of charging an up-front fee, the firm takes a fixed percentage of whatever it saves the taxpayer in the first year. If there are no or low savings, then the firm receives nothing or nominal profits. As a result of this risk structure, firms aggressively court the owners of higher-valued homes, leaving owners of lower-valued homes without access to professional property tax appeal services.

In the flat-fee model, the firm charges a fixed fee plus out-of-pocket expenses such as appraisal and filing fees. But even if the appeal is unsuccessful, homeowners must pay in full. For Detroit residential properties, this is the most common model, and fees can range from about $660 to $1,200. Additionally, professional home appraisals in Michigan cost, on average, between $225 and $355.[64] The math does not work out for lower-valued homes even if their assessments are, in fact, illegally inflated because the monies saved often do not cover the up-front costs. Consequently, the flat-fee model also leaves these homeowners without access to professional property tax appeal services. Without representation, "they don't stand a chance," one property tax appeal entrepreneur exclaimed. "It's a rigged game."

To get to the bottom of this rigged game, it is important to know who exactly is benefiting financially from Detroit's illegally inflated property taxes and the resulting property tax foreclosure crisis. The City of Detroit is certainly not profiting. In fact, compared to other cities, property tax revenues comprise a modest percentage of Detroit's total revenue. Between 2007 and 2016, property tax revenue accounted for, on average, 14 percent of Detroit's total revenues, which is low relative to other Michigan cities, such as Ann Arbor (56.31 percent) and Lansing (25.44 percent), as well as other major cities nationwide, such as Houston (36.7 percent), New York City (25.2 percent), Omaha (23 percent), and Baltimore (37.9 percent).[65] While other cities collect revenue only from income tax and/or property tax, Detroit has four other major sources of tax revenue: charges for services (20.92 percent), state shared taxes (14.22 percent), municipal income (16.32 percent), and wagering/gambling (11.53 percent).[66] As such, Detroit's reliance on property taxes is limited.

Not only does the City of Detroit not earn a significant portion of its revenue from property taxes, but on the other side of the ledger, illegally inflated property taxes and the resulting foreclosures impose several prohibitive costs that the City cannot afford. First, homes emptied by tax foreclosure attract blight and crime, lowering the market value of surrounding properties.[67] One study found that for every property within 500 feet that is vacant or tax delinquent, a neighboring home's selling price reduced by 1 to 2 percent.[68] Also, in certain markets, a recent tax foreclosure can decrease sale prices of nearby homes by 4 to 8 percent.[69]

Second, after tax foreclosure, the prior owners leave, and the homes often become unoccupied and neglected, re-entering the property tax foreclosure auction multiple times.[70] Each new owner who purchases one of these decaying homes abandons it because they soon realize that the cost of rehabilitation is more than the property is worth. So the homes further decay and eventually end up on the City's demolition list, where the City pays for tearing down neglected homes that have become a public health hazard.[71] In fact, using $265 million in federal Hardest Hit Fund dollars, the City of Detroit has razed more than fifteen thousand houses,[72] a sizable investment that could have been used to stabilize the city in other ways.

Third, a comprehensive review of the empirical literature on the effects of foreclosure finds that it adversely impacts the physical and mental health of individuals and communities, prompting increased stress, shame, alcohol abuse, depression, suicide, psychological distress, and anxiety.[73] Additionally, public health scholars have linked property tax foreclosure, more specifically, to preterm birth and elevated blood lead levels in children.[74]

Fourth, Mindy Fullilove finds that when forces like foreclosure cause massive displacement, what occurs is a phenomenon with intergenerational impact that she calls root shock — "the traumatic stress reaction to the destruction of all or part of one's emotional ecosystem" — which causes weakened communities more vulnerable to negative forces, chronic illness, and even death.[75]

Given the detrimental economic, social, and psychological effects of the property tax foreclosure crisis on Detroit and its residents, the city has more to lose than to gain. Then, if not the city, who stands to gain? In Part III, *Plundered* follows the money, and finds that a diverse set of characters have profited from property tax delinquency and foreclosure in Detroit.

PART III:

BUSINESSES THAT PROFIT FROM RACIST POLICIES

Buying Stolen Homes

10

SOUNDS LIKE A STEAL

The wave of mortgage foreclosures in 2007 was followed closely by a wave of property tax foreclosures, which inundated and collapsed Detroit's housing market. When individuals and corporations walked away from their foreclosed properties, the properties eventually came into public ownership. Detroit, therefore, was awash in publicly owned properties, which instead of generating tax revenue required an outlay of money for regular maintenance. To transform the flood of public properties from liabilities into assets, in 2009 officials created the Detroit Land Bank Authority (also known as the Land Bank), which has the ability to acquire, manage, renovate, assemble, sell, and clear title to publicly owned property.[1]

The Land Bank had a daunting job to do: The federally commissioned Detroit Blight Removal Task Force reported that blight marred 94 percent of the 25,666 publicly owned residential properties it had surveyed in 2014.[2] The City of Detroit began transferring its properties to its land bank in 2014,[3] and by January 2015, the City had transferred about 48,000 properties. The total grew to 96,000 by the next year. Overwhelmed by the high number of properties suddenly in its inventory, the Land Bank left most unattended, allowing grass to grow untamed, trash to accumulate, and structures to deteriorate. Blight remained a problem.

In response, the City instituted a series of seemingly well-intentioned measures. A 2016 analysis from the city council's Legislative Policy Division highlights several public interventions, including a fifteen-month project to eliminate blight from four thousand to six thousand publicly owned properties, using $52 million in state funds funneled down from the federal Hardest Hit Fund; a nonprofit-run pilot program to reduce blight in two specific Detroit neighborhoods; and commercial property demolition, using $12 million in repurposed funds from the federal Department of Housing and Urban Development (HUD). There was, however, one eyebrow-raising intervention: "Hantz Woodlands' urban farming project, in connection with which a 150-acre, 1,500-parcel tract of land on the City's lower east side has been acquired by a private party and is being cleared of blight and maintained."[4]

John Hantz is the CEO of Hantz Farms, also doing business as Hantz Woodlands, and its financial services parent company, the Hantz Group. He is a decades-long Detroit resident who can be spotted walking down the tree-lined streets of his Indian Village neighborhood, which is a historic district where the Ford and Dodge families lived at the city's zenith. John has dark hair and often wears dark suits, both of which accentuate his pale white skin.

He is a serial entrepreneur who, at different points in time, has owned a range of companies dealing in diverse businesses like lemonade, golf clubs, bowling equipment, trucking services, computer technology, and charter flights.[5] He had even owned a stock car racing company. John had, however, never before been in the business of removing blight. But as it steadily pummeled the city, he spied an opportunity to halt the onslaught while turning a substantial profit.

In 2014, public agencies owned one in two vacant lots,[6] and John planned to do what neither the City nor its land bank could: remediate these blighted lots by removing trash, cutting the grass, and boarding up or demolishing homes. In exchange, he would receive ownership. More specifically, his investment strategy was to acquire and hold vacant lots all in one contiguous square mile on Detroit's east side so that when the city emerged from its financial turmoil, he could sell them, making bountiful profits. Since Detroit's anticipated comeback could take decades to materialize, the key was to use the empty lots in a way that city residents and politicians could endorse. And so the idea for Hantz Farms was born.

John Hantz was inspired by his childhood memories of Romeo, Michigan, where he grew up alongside the town's apple orchards. But he knew nothing about farms. He, therefore, called the agricultural experts at Michigan State University (MSU) to assess whether creating an urban farm would be feasible. This was when John met the man he would appoint as president of Hantz Farms, Mike Score, an agronomist who worked in MSU's Extension Office in Washtenaw County, specializing in agricultural entrepreneurship.

With his unmanicured gray beard and white skin tanned from hours working outside in the sun, Mike is more comfortable in the fields than behind a desk and prefers cargo pants to suit pants. Mike was born in Detroit, but in 1963, his working-class family was able to decamp to a nearby suburb called Warren, where the houses were bigger and less expensive. "That was before the riots. It wasn't just a Black-white thing," Mike offered, trying to explain why his family participated in the white flight that he knew had impoverished Detroit. "My mom and dad moved there because they wound up having five children, and the house that they had in Detroit was too small. They were building these new suburbs, and we bought the first house on the block that was finished." Even though the Score family was of modest means — his father was an electrician and his mother a housewife — the thriving tax base in Warren gave their children access to first-rate primary and secondary schools, which opened many opportunities not available to even more affluent African American families trapped in Detroit's downward economic spiral.

When he finished high school, Mike left the suburbs to attend MSU, where he studied agriculture. He had first fallen in love with farm life at age eight when he began attending family reunions on his mother's cousin's farm. As a teenager, he would remain on the farm every summer after the reunions to work in his family's crop and livestock business, learning to drive at age twelve on a farm tractor. After graduating from MSU, Mike had several jobs, including as a Mennonite missionary in the Democratic Republic of the Congo (then named Zaire), and also as a faculty member at the University of Kentucky, working with Appalachian communities on mining reclamation, forestry, cattle and fruit production, and public conflict mediation.

After a long career, Mike returned in 1997 to MSU to work at its Extension Office. Then, in 2009, during the Great Recession and at the start of the ensuing mortgage and tax foreclosure crises, Mike witnessed Detroit's housing market collapse, and wanted to participate in its revival. Therefore, in the same year, he officially joined forces with John Hantz, and they set out to acquire all city-owned vacant lots in one square mile bounded by four streets: Mack Avenue, Van Dyke Street, Jefferson Street, and St. Jean Street. The challenge was convincing the City to sell.

John told a reporter from the *Atlantic* that at first the plan was to build the largest urban farm in the world, using technology-intensive growing techniques such as hydroponics and aeroponics and ultimately generating fresh produce along with much-needed jobs.[7] Then, Mike said, the plan changed to a large-scale you-pick orchard that would bring tourism and employment to the city by selling apples, donuts, cider, and a fun family experience. Neighbors, however, did not support these ideas because they worried that commercial-scale food production would bring rats and pesticide pollution to the neighborhood. So it was back to the drawing board. John and Mike finally settled on planting straight rows of hardwood trees in the empty lots. If they coupled this with the promise to remove debris, regularly cut the grass, and prune the trees, could they sell this plan to the City?

Since most publicly owned properties were blighted, which in turn tanked the property values of surrounding private properties, the City was desperate for a solution and ready to parley. "From 2008 to 2012 we worked with an attorney to negotiate with the City, and the City had a thousand reasons for saying no," Mike remembered. "And so, over time, we had to walk through all of their issues and concerns and discuss them until they were resolved." He added, "I think our first million dollars was spent on legal fees just negotiating with the City."

Just as the extended negotiation process seemed to be concluding, another roadblock appeared. The City Planning Commission warned that residential areas were not zoned for commercial agriculture, so the new enterprise would be able to grow trees, but would not be able to sell them. "Well, we actually don't need to sell the trees," Mike remembered telling the commission. "We're just interested in growing them, and growing trees on residential property is a use by right." So the final proposal entailed a "farm" that could not sell trees or anything else grown on the land, and would not yield the tourism and jobs initially promised.

A farm makes money from what is produced on the land, while a land speculation deal makes money from future sale of the land. Through a slow and steady disrobing, the deal, once intended to be an urban farm, began to look more like the land speculation operation that it actually was. "It's definitely a land grab," John haughtily declares, answering opponents who grill him in the opening scene of a documentary that he funded. "You can't farm without land." There was, however, no farming.

One ardent opponent of Hantz Farms was Malik Yakini, the founder of the Detroit Black Community Food Security Network and one of the nation's most celebrated urban farmers. With his long locs, salt-and-pepper beard, spectacles, dashikis, and skin toasted dark brown, Malik is regal and commands respect. He is a life-long Detroit resident, an educator who served for over two decades as the principal of an African-centered elementary school, and he has recently started the Detroit People's Food Co-op, the city's first community-owned grocery.

"I had breakfast with Mike. We knew each other when we worked at Michigan State University," Malik said. "He has legitimate knowledge about agriculture. I think he is a decent guy. I also think he is on the wrong team. It is speculation, whatever he wants to call it."

Malik and other community leaders fought for the City not to transfer the land to Hantz Farms, arguing that the City had better alternatives. "I am in favor of community land trusts that put affected people at the center of the solution. Those folks should be the ones who determine what happens, rather than a wealthy man making the decisions," Malik explained. "It is easier to aggregate all the land in one sale, but this also aggregates power. Another way to do it is smaller bundles of land that are more affordable and accessible to churches and community organizations. It is a question of equity versus efficiency."

Despite Malik's arguments, Mike continued trying to win the City's approval by making a few arguments of his own: "You would collect tax revenue on every parcel. Your overhead costs of these properties would go to zero. And then, if we don't manage them, you could give us blight tickets. You can't lose putting this property back on the tax rolls." Malik disagreed with this position and made it known. "Finding a wealthy person to buy the land and get it back on tax rolls seems like a quick fix," he warned. "But this is accessible only to people with lots of cash, and this means that the city can be owned by a few people." He added, "Wealthy white men having too much ownership of land, that is the big picture."

Despite the clear and cogent alternative vision laid out by Malik and other opponents, on December 11, 2012, Hantz Farms successfully convinced the bankrupt City that the faux farm was a good idea. "We got a five-to-four yes vote," Mike said. City Council members JoAnn Watson, Kwame Kenyatta, Brenda Jones, and Andre Spivey voted no. "My perception was they believed in collective ownership and equal distribution of wealth," Mike said, explaining the four no votes. "And it's not a pejorative statement to say that they were interested in more of a communist approach to economics than a capitalist approach. And our venture is primarily a capitalist approach. And so they were opposed to it for political and economic reasons."

A few months later, on March 25, 2013, the decision withstood another round of scrutiny when Detroit's emergency manager, Kevyn Orr, took control from the city council, nullifying its five-to-four vote. While Orr now had to approve all contracts, he needed the state treasurer's approval to sell assets valued at more than $50,000.[8] Hantz Farms' proposition to return properties to the tax roll, eliminate maintenance costs, and erase blight was highly attractive to the state authorities tasked with balancing Detroit's budget. So in the fall of 2013, Orr and Governor Snyder signed off on the Hantz Farms deal. In exchange for the promise to plant fifteen thousand hardwood trees and conifers, mow every three weeks during the growing season, promptly remove illegally dumped debris, demolish at least fifty blighted structures, and secure empty buildings it elected not to demolish, Hantz Farms acquired 1,558 City-owned lots on Detroit's east side for the very low price of $520,000.[9] That is, for about $350 per parcel, or 8.3 cents per square foot, the company acquired 143.8 acres of land — the equivalent of over 100 football fields — in one of America's most important urban centers.[10]

This sounds like a steal, but John Hantz bristles at this word. "It's a nice buzzword, but it's a lie when people talk about three hundred dollars per acre," he said, lashing back at his critics. "Trash doesn't pick itself up. Grass doesn't get retamed when it's this high cheaply. Rotted trees don't get shredded by themselves. Quality-of-life issues cost money."[11] He added, "Just keeping the lots cleaned and mowed, it's somewhere between a hundred thousand and two hundred thousand dollars per year. It took me five years and one million dollars to get the right to mow the lawns that hadn't been mowed in fifteen years."[12]

Since the law requires every single Detroit homeowner to maintain their lot — which includes mowing the lawn, tending to the property's trees, and picking up trash — one community member drew from the wisdom of a Chris Rock comedy skit where Chris talks about how some people want credit for things that they are supposed to do, pompously bragging about things that others do without fanfare. Like Chris Rock, this resident wanted to tell John, "That's what the f*#k you're suppose to do, you low expectation having mother-f$#cker! Do you want a cookie?" Colorful language aside, John was, indeed, seeking credit for doing things he was legally required to do, but this is partly because other large land speculators did not complete their legal duties.

For example, Michael G. Kelly — one of the largest landowners and slumlords in Detroit, who lives in a high-end Detroit suburb called Grosse Pointe Woods[13] — has purchased thousands of properties from the property tax foreclosure auction, using over forty LLCs.[14] He has not spent the money necessary to demolish decrepit structures and maintain his auction properties as required by law, resulting in numerous blight tickets. Kelly's designation as a predatory landowner does not just emerge from his failure to follow the law, it also arises from his boorish manipulation of the law.

In an unflattering photo on the front page of the *Detroit News*, Kelly is shown cruising through a Detroit neighborhood, unshaven, sporting a baseball cap that accentuates his pale white skin, bushy eyebrows, and thin lips.[15] While he appears sloppy in the photo, Kelly is actually extremely detail oriented. In 2006, he noticed that a narrow piece of land outside a strip club's front door had come to the property tax foreclosure auction, and he purchased it for $1,100. The land, owned by a neighboring business, went into property tax foreclosure after the owner, who had given the strip club permission to use the land, died.

Kelly wanted $35,000 for the land, and when the club owner refused to pay, Kelly bulldozed the thin strip of land and filled the guard booth on the property with manure. Instead of excitement, strip club customers got excrement. They stopped coming. To save the strip club, after spending $30,000 in legal fees, the owners finally paid Kelly $19,000 for the strategically located sliver of land. "He makes his living preying like a damn leech on other people," Jimmy Way, general manager of the Pretty Woman Lounge strip club, said.[16]

In a similar scenario, Kelly noticed that a small parcel in the middle of the Bridgewater Interiors manufacturing facility had gone to the property tax foreclosure auction for unpaid taxes, purchased it for $95,000, and offered to sell it right back to Bridgewater for $2 million. When the company would not pay, Kelly initiated eviction proceedings. This fiasco came to an end when Bridgewater sued Kelly and got its property back, successfully arguing that the County had sold it mistakenly in the first place.[17]

Hantz Farms, in contrast, was paying its property taxes and maintaining its properties, and the company has never engaged in the vulgar law-bending antics for which Kelly has become infamous. In accordance with its contract, Hantz Farms planted fifteen thousand trees and demolished fifty buildings. The tree-planting costs, however, were minimal because on May 17, 2014, about a thousand volunteers planted fifteen thousand oak tree saplings on twenty acres of Hantz's land.[18]

But the agreement's mandate to demolish fifty homes did, indeed, provide a significant benefit to the City. According to Detroit's auditor general, on average, it cost the City $17,198 to demolish a blighted structure, but this number jumped to $27,756 with indirect and administrative costs included.[19] Using this measure, Hantz Farms' demolitions saved the City up to $1.39 million.

Ultimately, Hantz Farms successfully complied with all contract terms,[20] and the City of Detroit issued a certificate of completion in December 2014. "When we came along, these were lots that were all overgrown with mulberry trees and cottonwood trees and tall weeds and, in a lot of cases, abandoned houses. So they attracted wild dogs, they attracted rodents, they attracted illegal dumping. You couldn't see through these properties, so drug dealing was more common then because you could sell drugs here and nobody could do any surveillance," Mike recalled. "And now, with all the brush removed and all the garbage hauled away and more and more vacant houses being rehabbed and occupied or demolished, it's a different landscape. It's a better place to live."

After the City issued its completion certificate, Mike met several times with Maurice Cox, who was then Detroit's Planning and Development Department director. "He told me that in other neighborhoods where the City wanted to orchestrate revitalization, they didn't sell the property like they did to us," Mike said. "They retained the property, but they cleared all their lots from curb to alley, they planted trees, they tore down dangerous structures that couldn't be rehabbed, and they invested in rehab where that was feasible." With an exuberant smile, he added, "It's exactly what we were doing." Mike commended Cox and the City for undertaking these efforts instead of outsourcing this job, and no longer seemed to believe that this was a form of communism.

Though critics like Malik would strongly disagree, it is plausible that in 2013, while the City was in the midst of the largest municipal bankruptcy in U.S. history and hence did not have the capacity to manage or dispose of City-owned properties, allowing Hantz Farms to step in made sense. According to this narrative, once the financial storm subsided and the City's land bank was fully operational, the City could reassert itself and finally take control of the properties it owned. The 2019 sale of additional property to Hantz Farms, at the 2013 fire sale price of $0.0833 per square foot, upended this narrative, revealing unequivocally that Hantz Farm's priority was profit rather than mutual benefit.

Even though the City's financial emergency had long since ended, there was an expansion provision in the original agreement, which allowed Hantz Farms to purchase more property under the same favorable terms: "So long as Hantz Woodlands is not in default under terms of the Agreement, for a period of 5 years from and after the closing date, the City grants to Hantz an exclusive right of first refusal, on substantially the same terms and conditions, to purchase any land acquired by the City within the development zone after the date of the Agreement."

Explaining this provision, Mike said, "This is common in development agreements to include a provision that we wouldn't be punished in an expansion phase for the fact that we brought about higher values." Several city council members thought these expansion terms were unfair, but they believed the City was legally obligated to honor the original agreement, even though the harrowing circumstances that had initially facilitated the deal no longer existed.

The reality is that Hantz Farms forced public officials to honor the agreement. The City needed 3.7 acres of the land it transferred through the first deal for a new development deal with Chrysler Automotive to expand its Jefferson North Assembly Plant. Hantz Farms agreed to a land swap. But the two development deals were bundled, meaning city council members who opposed the Hantz Farms expansion would have to vote no on the Chrysler deal as well. In a six-to-three vote, the city council approved the second deal. So for 3.7 acres (or about 30 properties) plus $160,000, Hantz Farms would receive 366 additional vacant lots and up to 80 structures that it had to renovate within two years.[21] Since there was no demolition requirement increasing acquisition costs this time around, Hantz Farms received another 40 to 45 acres at bona fide bake sale prices.[22]

Time proved that, by facilitating speculation, the City had ultimately shot itself in the foot. Now, whenever the City wants to assemble land for a real estate project that it believes will benefit Detroit residents, like the Chrysler deal, it often has to negotiate with large land speculators who own these properties and sell them back to the City for a substantial profit. Hantz Farms now owns approximately 2,400 parcels in its designated square mile, and the company can demand a handsome profit in any real estate development deal that the City or any other entity would like to complete in the area. According to one investigative report, a decade after the initial purchases, Hantz has sold just a fraction of them for more than $9.5 million in revenue.[23]

While John Hantz, Michael Kelly, and other large land speculators are profiting from property tax injustice in Detroit, they are not the only ones. Small-scale investors, like Dwayne and Ms. Hazel, whom we will meet in the next chapter, are also profiting. These entrepreneurial Detroit natives refused to abandon their beloved city even in its worst moments, so, paradoxically, property tax injustice diminished their cherished communities while also fattening their pockets.

11

PREDATOR AND PREY

Between 2015 and 2020, Dwayne Davis, a Detroit native, acquired about thirty-five residential properties in the city, primarily through the Detroit Land Bank Authority and Wayne County's property tax foreclosure auctions, building a modest but reliable real estate business to provide for himself and his family. With his onyx skin, full lips, and crisp fade, Dwayne is a self-described man's man. His ostentatious diamond stud earrings send a clear signal to others that he is no longer poor. Dwayne's journey from living in poverty to becoming an accomplished businessman was hard, replete with steep hills, seemingly insurmountable roadblocks, and icy roads.

Dwayne was born in 1990, the second of Carrie Johnson's four sons. Carrie, a Detroit native with mahogany-colored skin and a bright smile, worked as a slot attendant at the MotorCity Casino. She did not earn much money, and her economic precarity led to evictions, forcing Carrie and her sons to move constantly, shoving them from house to house, making uncertainty the only certainty.

As Matthew Desmond notes in his book *Evicted,* "Residential stability begets a kind of psychological stability. It begets school stability, which increases the chances that children will excel and graduate. And it begets community stability, which encourages neighbors to form strong bonds and take care of their block. But poor families enjoy little of that because they are evicted at such high rates."[1] One study found that over 25 percent of Black children live in rentals that have received an eviction filing,[2] and Dwayne was one of these children. According to him, the stress of constant evictions converted his mom into a "Bible thumper." Since she was not able to protect her four heartbeats from the violence of poverty, she trusted God to step into the gap and do what she could not.

The good news is that no matter how much his family moved around the city, Dwayne did not lose track of his neighborhood buddies. Ms. Hazel Thompson, his friend's mother, simply would not allow it. Ms. Hazel has lived in her home, which she inherited from her parents, since 1972. She has always been the North Star of her community, preventing neighbors, both young and old, from losing their way. Noted for her high cheekbones, long wavy hair, petite frame, stylish spectacles, and caramel-colored skin, Ms. Hazel has been a mother figure to all the children in her community. She is also a church mother who attends worship services every single Sunday, most often wearing an elaborate hat paired with a freshly pressed skirt suit or dress, never pants.

"Everybody calls her Mom because that was the house to go to," Dwayne explained. Even today, when speaking to Ms. Hazel, Dwayne calls her Mama, and when talking to strangers, he refers to her as his stepmom. Ms. Hazel also considers Dwayne to be a son because he grew up with her own son, grandson, and godson, playing basketball, riding mopeds, and skateboarding together. "The boys would just come in," Ms. Hazel remembered. "I kept cases of pop. I kept bags of potato chips. So the kids would come in and grab stuff to eat, and grill hamburgers or scramble eggs, whatever was in the refrigerator. They'd come in and cook and help themselves."

Compared to others in the neighborhood, Ms. Hazel was a woman of means. Her parents had fled racial terrorism in Mississippi and Tennessee. Using money her mother saved as an accountant and her father amassed from work as a Pullman porter, the couple eventually purchased several properties in Detroit. Ms. Hazel followed suit, buying her first investment property at age twenty and accumulating a sizable real estate portfolio during her lifetime.

In addition to Ms. Hazel and his mother, Dwayne's maternal grandmother was a major figure in his life. Grandma Mattie, born in Mississippi, was the pillar of his family, preventing them from collapsing under the weight of poverty. To give them a break from Detroit's cruel streets, Mattie took her grandsons down South every summer to visit the part of their family that had made the complicated decision not to migrate North. In Mississippi's red-clay dirt, the boys met many family members for the first time and developed unforgettable memories.

"My cousin, her name is Brown Sugar," Dwayne said, chuckling at the nickname his family pinned on her. "She use to always look past the fact that we were family and wanted to be my girlfriend." Snickering while shaking his head in disbelief, Dwayne added, "I guess she did not understand the meaning of what family was."

Dwayne adored his grandmother and valued the time he spent with her both in Mississippi and Detroit. "Her spirit is unmatched," Dwayne declared with pointed conviction. "She had that Southern love. She could cuss at you, yell at you, put you in your place, and love you all in the same breath." As his smile reached his eyes, Dwayne continued, "When she cooked, not only did she cook for her household, she cooked for the whole neighborhood. When my grandma cooked, the whole neighborhood stopped playing and came and sat down to eat." Mattie's love filled the hearts and bellies of her family and community.

Even with help from her mom, Mattie, and Ms. Hazel, Carrie found that, given the violence plaguing Detroit during the 1990s, raising four Black boys was extremely difficult.[3] "I never had a relationship with my father," Dwayne said, reflecting on the missing piece in his childhood puzzle. "He's been in and out of incarceration five times for a total of seventeen years." Dwayne Sr.'s criminal record included offenses such as selling narcotics, larceny, and assault with a deadly weapon, and Carrie prayed fervently that Dwayne would not end up like his father. God, however, did not immediately answer Carrie's prayers.

Dwayne vividly remembers when his encounters with law enforcement began. "I had just lost my grandmother and I was just numb," he said in a solemn tone. "I didn't know how to express emotion. I always tried to bottle up and conceal pain, but the pain always came out as anger." After Grandma Mattie died, Dwayne started hanging out in the hallway instead of attending his classes, and then he stopped going to school altogether.

The police first arrested Dwayne at age sixteen for stealing his mother's car and driving without a license, and at age seventeen, he graduated to assault and battery of a police officer, which landed him in jail for forty-five days plus probation. His first experience behind bars did not sufficiently rattle him, so upon exiting, he continued stealing his mother's car and racked up three additional joyriding offenses. "My emotions was all over the place," Dwayne confessed.

At age eighteen, Dwayne went to prison. "Right when I was supposed to get off probation, I caught a felony home invasion first degree," Dwayne said, shaking his head. "And that's what sat me down for six years." Spending six years in the penitentiary was one of the most difficult things Dwayne has ever had to endure. But having grown up in the Black church, Dwayne knew that the Book of Psalms promised that, even at his darkest hour, God was ordering his steps, turning him around, and putting his feet back on solid ground.

Being locked up "shut me down and gave me an eye-opener," Dwayne said. "I realized that I'm way better than the environment I'm placed in momentarily." After a short contemplative pause, he continued, "When I really think about it, it was a blessing because I could still be going down the troublesome path and I would not be here to tell my story."

In prison, Dwayne worked to obtain his GED (a high school equivalency degree) and vowed that once released, he would never come back. After six long years, in 2013, he completed his prison sentence and was ready to start fighting for his dreams. He, however, soon discovered that although he had served his time, his punishment was not over. It was, in fact, just the beginning of a brutal re-acclimatization process that American society forces formerly incarcerated people to endure.

Some forty-five thousand federal and state laws limit the lives of formerly incarcerated people, restricting their political participation and regulating their employment, housing, and family rights.[4] Michigan has nine hundred and three collateral consequences of incarceration, ranging from counties filing civil actions for reimbursement of confinement costs to the ineligibility to become a volunteer conservation officer.[5] In his book *Halfway Home,* Professor Reuben Miller concludes that "the prison is like a ghost, preceding them into the unemployment line and into the welfare office and into their lovers' arms. It meets them at the table when they share meals with their families, exerting an influence on almost every encounter they'll have. It will do this for a lifetime."[6]

Miller eloquently sums up Dwayne's post-prison experience, which began with worry and stress about where he would live upon release. "When I got home, I went back to my mother's house. That was the only option I had," Dwayne remembered. "I had sent her the little money I scraped together within a year working in the prison because I didn't know what I was coming home to." With a look of defeat, he added, "Shortly after that, maybe like a month or two, we ended up getting evicted."

Shortly before the eviction, Dwayne had found a short-term job through a temp agency, and it was there that he met Kiara, who eventually became his girlfriend. "I had nowhere to go and Kiara's father sat me down and talked to me. He said, 'Stay with us,'" Dwayne recalled. "He said that because he didn't want his daughter out in the streets trying to chase behind me and I didn't have nowhere to live."

Now that Dwayne had stable housing, it was time to find stable employment. "The job selection wasn't very great for a fella," Dwayne said in a joking tone that helped to blunt this sharp, painful truth. In the first year after his release from prison, Dwayne did stints at four different minimum-wage jobs, which ranged from quality-checking sun visors and other auto parts to working at Uncle Ray's potato chip factory alongside migrant workers.

With his deep distaste for idleness, whenever Dwayne was between his temporary job assignments, he worked at Kiara's father's lawn care company and also took classes. "Immediately after I got out, I was in and out of Detroit Training Center just struggling, trying to find something that works and fits me," Dwayne said. "I was just interested in any and every avenue. I wanted to try truck driving, hi-lo. I wanted to do carpentry. I also wanted to do electrical. Whatever would pay me good." He added, "I have a felony, so you're taking a felon. At the end of the day, if you took me, you are going to get one hundred and ten percent out of me. I just wanted to feel they wanted me."

Although he was a hard worker who was eagerly building his skill sets, it took a year for Dwayne to find permanent work. In 2014, an automotive company named Bridgewater finally gave him a chance (and yes, this is the same company that Kelly, the land speculator, tried to exploit after the County mistakenly auctioned a portion of the land where its manufacturing facility sits). Founded in 1998, Bridgewater Interiors gave Dwayne a full-time, unionized job, working on the assembly line that produced seats for the Ford F-150.

"Bridgewater gave me my first opportunity. They paid me sixteen dollars and fifty cents with benefits," Dwayne said, his voice suffused with gratitude. "The other jobs I was working at I was making like eight fifteen, no overtime so where I couldn't provide for a family and barely myself." The work was physically taxing, but always in constant motion, Dwayne never got bored and absolutely loved his job. "It felt just really like home. It didn't feel like work," he said, grinning. "It felt like you was in a barbershop getting a haircut when you look at all the conversation we had."

While things were good at work, his domestic situation was also happily humming along. Dwayne continued living with his girl-friend and her father for about a year while the couple saved money to secure their own space. When they finally located a suitable house, Kiara's father, their indefatigable supporter, gave the couple all his old furniture and bought brand-new furniture for himself. As they settled into their new place, Dwayne and Kiara found out that they were pregnant with Dwayne's first child. He was both excited and scared. Determined to be the provider that his father had failed to be, Dwayne started working significant overtime, stacking his money, and searching for investment opportunities.

"I met a Realtor and we got pretty cool. We actually became buddies, hanging out and barbecuing," Dwayne said. "In the midst of getting ready to go out, he said he had a house he wanted me to take a look at. We go down the block, I'd seen it, we went into it, and I'm like, 'Man, I love this!'" With the memory making him giddy, Dwayne continued, "I just realized it at that moment, I was tired of renting, so I bought it." Dwayne purchased the house for $7,000 and was determined to transform the structure from nothing to a bona fide home where anyone would be proud to raise a family.

Although the home was originally intended for his growing fam-ily, after a seven-month renovation process with a dishonest con-tractor, which unexpectedly cost $42,000, Dwayne could no longer afford for them to move in. Kiara was not pleased but understood. Thankfully, with the home's new carpets, doors, and windows, as well as its decadent Jacuzzi tub in the upstairs bathroom, it did not take Dwayne long to find renters, salving his financial wounds with $925 per month in rental income. The experience, however, depleted his limited capital and tempered his enthusiasm for real estate. But it did not destroy it. "That first house definitely taught me a lesson," Dwayne said soberly.

In 2016, Dwayne's son was born and everything changed. Dwayne no longer wanted to live from paycheck to paycheck. He wanted to build a legacy that he could leave to his son, but he did not know how. Then Dwayne went to dinner with one of his mentors and his mentor's friend, and they conversed with joyful abandon about buying and renovating houses. "They was going back and forth. They weren't paying me any mind. But I was just sitting there listening and soaking up the game," Dwayne recalled. "And I could not remember the name they said, and it finally dawned on me, Detroit Land Bank. And I finally looked it up and voilà, it was there."

The Detroit Land Bank's primary goal is to "make vacant and residential public property available for sale in order to promote homeownership, neighborhood revitalization, urban agriculture and economic growth in the City of Detroit."[7] As of April 2016, the Land Bank held title to 95,954 parcels: 29,572 residential structures, 66,125 vacant parcels, and 257 commercial and industrial structures.[8] "At that time, the Land Bank houses were a thousand dollars, twenty-five hundred dollars, five thousand dollars, and they weren't in bad neighborhoods. They were in neighborhoods aspiring to make a comeback," Dwayne noted. "After I seen a few of the houses, I hit the go button."

In 2016, Dwayne paid $1,000 for his first Land Bank home, put about $26,000 into its renovation, rented it for $825, and used the profits to purchase his second Land Bank home. After rehabbing his second one, Dwayne sold it so that he could purchase two more. He was able to acquire and renovate Land Bank homes at record speed because he found a reliable crew of Mexican contractors. "Them Mexicans. I love them damn Mexicans," he declared. "They will go out drinking all night long and still arrive to the job on time ready to work."[9]

To date, Dwayne has flipped about seven houses, selling them for a modest profit to a group of investors that Ms. Hazel found. But Dwayne's primary business strategy is to buy and hold. "I like flipping. I like the money, but I'm into real estate for the long haul. I want them to be left for my kids when I'm gone," he said, referring to his son and stepdaughter. "I want to leave them everything that I know, everything that I worked so hard for because the only thing I inherited from my parents is a headache."

Once Dwayne began purchasing properties from the Land Bank, he never looked back, and he has purchased twenty-one of his thirty-five properties from either the Land Bank's Own It Now program or its auction, paying between $1,000 and $32,000 to acquire them. Both programs require purchasers to rehabilitate the home in the span of six months, and only after this happens can purchasers receive a marketable title. A Land Bank inspector monitors the purchaser's progress, allowing them to exceed the contractual time period so long as there is evidence of progress, like new paint, windows, or doors.[10] "I've been in violation, and no, they did not come after me," Dwayne stated. "They were patient. They worked with me. The lady that I spoke to said that the compliance officers don't want to take my home. They just want to make sure I was doing my part."

The difference between the Land Bank's Own It Now program and its auction program is that for the auction properties, the Land Bank empties, cleans, and boards up the houses, and also manicures the lawn so that it can take the best possible pictures and get the best possible price at the auction. The auction begins at 9 a.m. with a starting bid of $1,000. The bidding is public and stops at 5 p.m. In contrast, the Land Bank sells the Own It Now properties as is, and offers the properties online for seventy-two hours, during which time bidders can make a concealed bid. Once the bidding period closes, the Land Bank announces who made the highest bid and hence won the property.[11]

Beyond the Own It Now and the auction programs, the Land Bank has three additional programs. The Side Lots program allows owner-occupiers to purchase vacant parcels that are adjacent to their own for $100.[12] The Buy Back program gives people living in Land Bank–owned houses an opportunity to purchase these homes for $1,000 so long as they attend a free financial management course before they receive title to the home and four free workshops within a year afterward.[13] In the Rehabbed & Ready program, "they go in and they rehab the property from top to bottom," Dwayne reported. "They do a phenomenal job but charge a ridiculous amount for the property." Dwayne has never purchased from this program because he can do the renovations himself more cost-effectively.

Because Dwayne has partnered repeatedly with the Land Bank in its mission to return habitable homes to the property tax rolls, he has received its Trusted Buyer status, which allows investors to close on one Land Bank property per month for a total of nine properties in a single calendar year.[14] As a Trusted Buyer, Dwayne has a unique vantage point into the Land Bank's institutional strengths and weaknesses. He believes that the Land Bank's marquee achievement is that it has given Detroit residents a reason to stay by offering a 50 percent discount on its auctioned homes to full-time Detroit school employees, City employees, City retirees, their immediate family members, and trade union members who participate in Detroit's Skilled Trades Employment Program.[15] Consequently, in 2021, about 71 percent of purchasers were Detroit residents.[16]

"So many people just up and left. We've seen a lot of money leave the city," Dwayne observed. "So a way to keep Detroiters here was to allow them an easy and affordable way to buy the land and save it." His voice lifting to falsetto, he added, "And want to raise a family here!"

Dwayne believes that the Land Bank's biggest problem is its failure to properly communicate the extensive damage its homes have suffered at the hands of strippers. Not the ones at the Pretty Woman

Lounge who twirl on poles with panache and flair, but the ones who remove everything of value from vacant homes, including hot water tanks, pipes, electrical lines, doors, and windows. The problem is so extensive that in 2014, the City-owned lighting and electrical distribution grid was losing between $500,000 and $1 million per year worth of copper infrastructure to theft, or about $1,350 to $2,700 per day on average.[17] Dwayne estimates that only three of the thirty-five homes he currently owns have *not* been stripped. So, given the poor shape of most vacant homes in Detroit, renovating them is a tall order best left to those with extensive experience.

"Their approach with marketing tells you that you could be an owner for a thousand dollars and you've got to just rehab the house," Dwayne noted. "A lot of people with the average job just don't have the knowledge of the business and would take one thousand to two thousand dollars, maybe ten thousand dollars, and put it into one of these homes, and don't understand that that's not the finish line. You still have a long way to go." According to Dwayne, just like him when he purchased his first Land Bank home in 2016 and overpaid for renovations, most Land Bank purchasers are in over their heads.

By 2018, Dwayne had used his Bridgewater paychecks to purchase several Land Bank homes, so his real estate side gig was thriving, his family was flourishing, and life was better than it had ever been. Then he got fired. After discovering that Dwayne had served time in prison, a temporary worker on the assembly line began taunting him, claiming that Dwayne was a victim of prison rape. Like a Rottweiler, the man would not stop his attack, humiliating Dwayne in front of co-workers he had grown to love and respect.

"He had an entourage around, looking to gain attention," Dwayne recalled. "And me being me, I laughed at it. I joked until I just didn't feel comfortable anymore." Dwayne lost control, squared up, and punched the man dead in his face. As his tormentor fell to the floor bloodied, so did Dwayne's cherished job.

Only a few months after his termination by Bridgewater, Dwayne obtained an assembly-line job at General Motors (GM), where he was a hi-lo driver charged with loading and unloading the trucks. The classes Dwayne had taken at the Detroit Training Center upon exiting prison paid off. Just like at Bridgewater, with GM, Dwayne worked overtime every time he had the opportunity.

After a long shift, Dwayne would sleep only for a short while so he could spend every waking hour rehabilitating his newly acquired homes and building his burgeoning real estate business. "That baby was broken, spending all his time fixing those houses up and punching that clock," Ms. Hazel said, love lilting in her voice. "Sometime I had to tell Dwayne, 'You need to go home and get some rest.' He was losing weight and I said, 'You're not taking care of yourself.'"

Dwayne was excited to work at GM, but there was one problem. "I had to drive to Flint, and that's an hour and twenty every day on top of working ten hours. I found myself sleeping in rest stops on the road," he explained. "It was around the time they were doing construction on Seventy-Five, and you just never knew what you'd run into. So I had to leave almost two hours in advance and sometimes that wasn't even enough." Eventually, the long commute and sleep deprivation caught up with him, and at the end of 2018, GM terminated him after only about nine months on the job.

At this point, Dwayne decided the time had come to work his real estate business full-time. "I had like twenty grand saved up, and I just kept the last of my money and bet it on myself," he said. "I was just tired of paying people to fix all the houses, and two months later I've got to call you back for the same issue. I had watched them so many times do things wrong that I knew what the right way looked like. I just got fed up." With a smug smile, he added, "Now I'm more in control. I'm the boss. I control my own destiny." When Dwayne struck out on his own, he made several boss moves, including purchasing a "raggedy" truck to haul his drywall, shingles, and other materials so that he would not have to pay others to do it for him. In time, he would own several trucks; train and employ young Detroiters with criminal records that poison other job opportunities; and take part in the movement to restore Detroit one house at a time.

Once Dwayne started building his real estate business full-time, he had increased capacity and needed more homes to purchase and renovate. This was when the property tax foreclosure auction came on his radar. Dwayne's uncle had just rented a home that his landlord had purchased in the tax auction, and one day when Dwayne came through to visit, the landlord came by. They all started to chat. She explained that she had purchased the home for $10,000 and only had to invest about $5,000 to make it habitable.

"I'm like, 'Wow, ten, fifteen altogether?'" Dwayne exclaimed. "And here it is, I'm spending twenty-six and thirty-two for these Land Bank houses, in total, with rehab." This encounter with his uncle's landlord piqued Dwayne's interest in the property tax auction, so he sought advice from Ms. Hazel, who had started buying homes from the tax auction in 2002 and to date has purchased about fifty.

"So Dwayne sat down with me and my husband and we showed him the ropes. He was just so gung ho!" Ms. Hazel exclaimed. "Now, my own son won't listen. Don't wanna listen! I think he's deaf or something." After being momentarily crippled by her own laughter, she continued, "But Dwayne is not like that. He really listens and he takes notes."

In 2017, Dwayne, Ms. Hazel, her husband, and her grandson all sat at the kitchen table, brought out a computer, pulled up the property tax auction website, identified about ten properties, and then jumped in the car to view five of them. "Oh, these are not bad," Dwayne thought to himself. A few days later, Dwayne came back to Ms. Hazel's kitchen table for the auction where he was monitoring the bidding on the properties he had scoped out, but did not buy anything because "the funds just wasn't there."

The next year, in 2018, Dwayne saved up and came back to the kitchen table to bid. "It's like Thanksgiving dinner," he said about auction day at Ms. Hazel's kitchen table. "It's something we always did together." This time Dwayne purchased four houses, but he had to return one. "I got so cocky that I'm just driving past it. The front of this house looked so amazing. The block wasn't all that great, but it wasn't extremely horrible, either," he remembered. "I'm like, 'We can't go wrong with this. We could probably do a flip and make seventy thousand dollars.'"

Since there were about six bidders vying for the house, Dwayne and his friend decided to get aggressive and put in a bid for $42,000. They won. "We thought we had a gold mine," Dwayne remembered. "But we didn't even have a diamond in the rough. The entire back of the house was caved in and half gone. I could not believe what I saw. A tree fell on it," he said, throwing his hands in the air in a gesture of incredulity. Rather than losing all their properties, Dwayne and his friend paid a penalty for reneging on the one house. "Drinking the Kool-Aid and we definitely paid for that. That was a special drink of Kool-Aid."

In 2019, Dwayne was back at Ms. Hazel's kitchen table and purchased an additional seven houses. Because of COVID-19, between 2020 and 2022, Wayne County canceled the tax auction, but neither Ms. Hazel nor Dwayne intended to participate again "because people were finding out about the auction, and they were driving the prices up," Ms. Hazel said with deep annoyance. "People were coming from out of town to come to Detroit specifically for the auction because, unlike Chicago and New York, no one else was having these high number of homes in the auction like Detroit." With eyes wide, she continued, "The foreigners, even they were coming from Dubai and international countries, coming in buying these houses up."

Dwayne had had a good run with the property tax foreclosure auction, almost doubling his existing real estate portfolio and slowly yet steadily building his real estate empire. There were two specific reasons that he much preferred the property tax foreclosure auction homes to Land Bank homes. First, the tax auction is for people "who just lost their house at the end of the day, so they take care of it. If it was not for the taxes, they'd probably still be there," Dwayne said. "The Land Bank is fine, but just know you're going to spend a lot of money because they need everything. Whoa, Lord Jesus, those homes need everything! They need Jesus and them Mexicans."

Dwayne also preferred tax auction homes "because I can buy, wait, be patient, and eventually fix it up," he said. Unlike the Land Bank, Wayne County does not contractually require auction purchasers to rehabilitate the homes *before* receiving marketable title. "A lot of people are buying these houses and putting the bare minimum in," Dwayne complained. He, in contrast, has fully rehabbed all of his tax auction properties, renting them for between $700 and $900, mostly to Detroit's long-standing African American residents, but also to a smattering of recently arrived whites.

Three of the six properties Dwayne acquired from the tax auction had occupants. One was a tenant who found out that her landlord was not paying his property taxes when Wayne County nailed the infamous yellow bag to her porch, giving notice that the home was slated for tax foreclosure the following year. At that point, she stopped paying rent and remained in the home for about a year, uncertain about whether her family would have a roof over their heads in the coming months. After acquiring the home through the tax auction, Dwayne informed her that he was the new owner and was willing to take her on as a tenant if she was willing to sign a lease.

The problem was that, like a sand castle built on the seashore, her dilapidated home was crumbling. So long as Dwayne agreed to make repairs, she was amenable to becoming his tenant. "I still couldn't believe someone stayed there because the kitchen — there was no kitchen. The bathroom is right above the kitchen and it was leaking. It was nasty," Dwayne recalled with a mix of disgust and disbelief. "But I went in and made that repair. I gave her a new kitchen. I gave her a new bathroom and two security doors." With pride, he added, "She's still there to this day."

There was, however, no happy ending with the other two occupants. "The other two were squatters and they were just a horrible situation," Dwayne said. They were "very nasty, living in horrible and poor conditions." Not only did the squatters refuse to leave, but they also scoffed at Dwayne's demands for rent. To get them out of his newly purchased house, Dwayne initiated eviction proceedings in the 36th District Court.

"The way the law is set up, you can't just go in and throw them out," Dwayne complained. "They feel like they got squatters' rights. And if you called the police to come in and assist you, it's true." With several investment homes but very little cash, Dwayne acted as his own lawyer and eventually evicted the squatters.

Over time, Dwayne has gradually become a one-man full-service real estate company, cutting out the middleman by becoming his own lawyer, property management company, contractor, handyman, and lawn care service. "The middleman was draining me," Dwayne said. "But now, life is a lot more simpler. You can give me only four brick walls and a door, and I'm still going to build a house."

Dwayne obtained the necessary construction skills through a combination of reading books, watching YouTube DIY videos, taking a variety of classes offered by the Detroit Training Center, and enrolling in an HVAC (heating, ventilation, and air-conditioning) program at Northwestern Tech. Dwayne learned skills like floor installation, plumbing, and drywall by working alongside the skilled laborers he hired. He is now taking a course to become a real estate agent so he can further cut out the middleman by finding new investment properties himself on a multiple listing service (MLS).

For Dwayne, the most difficult part of his business is not the renovation, it is dealing with tenants. "Just anything you could think of or imagine, I've been through it," he said, resentment lining his forehead. "I've had guns pulled on me. I've had to fight a tenant. I went to court and got the bailiff to evict someone, and then her brother and cousins came back and they wanted to vandalize the house."

With rents ranging from $700 to $900, Dwayne is servicing Detroit's working poor, which comes with its challenges. For instance, since this population very often has poor credit scores, he cannot rely on a credit check to assess whether they will be responsible renters. Instead, he will "pop up" on prospective tenants to see firsthand their current home's level of cleanliness and order. His theory is that if your current home is tidy, you are more likely to take care of his property, physically and financially. Given his profitable portfolio of thirty-five homes, Dwayne's unconventional strategies seem to be working.

Dwayne's success has opened lots of doors, but perhaps the most important is that it has allowed him to belatedly forge a strong relationship with his father, Dwayne Sr. "I was never able to get any emotional companionship out of him," Dwayne said of his father. "But I had a heavy workload last summer and he just kind of came in. He took the light work. I took the heavy work and he's been with me ever since, building houses, buying them, reconstructing them." He added, "I'm teaching him." Dwayne's son is in love with his grand-dad, who is now part of his daily life. As his tide rose, Dwayne lifted his family as well.

"He dug his heels in like his life depended on it," Ms. Hazel boasted. "He has accepted every challenge and faced it and overcame it." She added, "I am so proud of him, I can just break-dance."

There is, however, one crack in Dwayne's rags-to-riches story: the provenance of homes he has purchased through the Land Bank and the property tax foreclosure auctions. Dwayne first heard about Detroit's illegally inflated property taxes when local news channels began covering the *Detroit News*'s blockbuster exposé, revealing that between 2010 and 2016, the City of Detroit had overtaxed its homeowners by at least $600 million.[18]

"For starters, if I go rob a bank, you going to make me pay restitution. I would like some of my money back," Dwayne said in response to the exposé. "You robbing the poor. We already poor and you sitting up here taking more. Come on now!" He added, "I've never seen a person go rob a bank and say, oh, they sorry, and get no time, yet people rob Detroiters and nothing has happened to any of those politicians other than Kwame."

When asked about the connection between the $600 million overcharge and the profits he derived by purchasing tax-foreclosed homes from the Wayne County tax auctions and the Detroit Land Bank, Dwayne said, "One had nothing to do with the other." Yet one study shows that between 2011 and 2015, 10 percent of all Detroit homes — and 25 percent of the lowest-valued ones — would not have gone into tax foreclosure if not for the illegally inflated property tax assessments.[19] Dwayne, nevertheless, could not (or would not) consider the fact that his real estate empire was erected because people could not afford to pay their illegally inflated property taxes. Instead, he insisted that the unprecedented tax foreclosure rates happened because Detroiters were not "saving up their money for taxes and being responsible." Again, the personal irresponsibility narrative does heavy work, masking predatory systems and giving moral cover to the heterogeneous groups of people who profit from them.

A review of Dwayne's real estate portfolio reveals that he is not only a predator but also prey. Like most owners of lower-valued homes, the City of Detroit is currently inflating the estimated market value of his investment properties in violation of the Michigan Constitution, which is in turn inflating his property tax bills. The only thing he can do to stop this is to file a property tax appeal. When asked whether he has ever filed an appeal, Dwayne responded, "No, I did not know about that."

12

SUPPORT SMALL BUSINESS?

In addition to Dwayne Davis and John Hantz, who both live in the city of Detroit, other investors from outside the city have also benefited from illegally inflated property taxes and historic levels of tax foreclosure in Detroit. One such example is Piper and Seamus O'Grady, a middle-aged white couple, who purchased tax-foreclosed homes in Wayne County's annual auctions, becoming landlords of Detroit properties while living in a Detroit suburb.

The couple is not, however, new to Detroit. Piper comes from a long line of Detroit landlords, her legacy commencing with her great-grandmother, who was born in Poland and immigrated to Detroit in the 1920s. "My great-grandmother was a landlord back when there were streetcars," Piper said, citing the stories recounted throughout her childhood. "And she was the very kindest landlord, I heard."

Profits from her family's successful stationery business allowed Piper's great-grandmother to purchase property in the city of Detroit, which she rented to African Americans. Because racial hatred and racially restrictive covenants herded Blacks into a few congested, dilapidated communities, the supply of housing for Blacks was low, while the demand was high. As a consequence, African Americans paid more rent than whites for lower-quality housing. As late as 1960, the median monthly rent in Detroit was $76 per month for Blacks but 16 percent lower for whites.[1] Even landlords as kind as Piper's great-grandmother were reputed to be were profiting from racist policies that infected housing markets.

Piper's grandmother grew up in Detroit but left after marrying an Irishman whose family labored in the woolen mills of Eaton Rapids. The newlyweds decided to build a life in this small farm town abutting Michigan's Grand River, about a hundred miles from Detroit. With money she inherited from her maternal uncle in the 1970s, Piper's grandmother purchased a duplex in Eaton Rapids and rented its one-bedroom apartment to two women.

As children, Piper and her brother thought their grandmother's tenants were odd. "I remember saying to my grandma, 'Grandma, it's two women and they're in the same bed,'" Piper said. She thought her grandmother was naive and was trying to help her connect the dots. Her grandmother, however, needed no such assistance. "They're wonderful ladies, and they pay their rent," her grandma replied with all the authority she could muster, making it painfully clear that this was not a topic open for discussion.

Piper's mom continued the tradition of her family's matriarchs when she inherited her mother's Eaton Rapids duplex along with a cottage in northern Michigan, where the family vacationed every summer. According to Piper, there was one story in particular that shows that Piper's mom, too, was a "kind" landlord who treated all people as equals, despite their race, class, gender, or sexual orientation. When Piper got older, she worked as a court reporter in Detroit, where she became good friends with one of the secretaries. Piper attended her wedding and wanted to give her a weekend at the family cabin as a wedding gift. Piper's mother agreed.

"But when my dad's mom found out that these newlyweds were Black, she told my mom, 'You better tell the neighbors that somebody Black will be staying at your cabin so they don't think that something untoward is happening,'" Piper recalled. "And my mom absolutely refused to tell the neighbors, saying, 'There was no reason to tell the neighbors, it's irrelevant.'" Piper's mother insisted on being race-blind even though the world she lived in was unequivocally not.

Piper — who shares the sandy hair, light eyes, high cheekbones, and pale skin of her forebears — brought her family's tradition full circle when she, like her great-grandmother, became a Detroit land-lord. Piper's journey to close the circle began in the 1990s when she married Seamus — a burly man from a working-class Irish family — and left Eaton Rapids. Although Seamus was born in Detroit, the newlyweds did not move to the city. Instead, like most whites, they chose to move to one of the city's suburbs, Royal Oak.

In 1954, Royal Oak's chamber of commerce published a pamphlet proudly proclaiming that "the population is virtually 100% white,"[2] and when the couple moved there in the 1990s, the situation had not significantly altered. The population was over 95 percent white.[3] Piper and Seamus chose Royal Oak not for its racial composition, but because they wanted to build a family in a safe community with well-ranked schools. As a result of redlining, block-busting, urban renewal, and other racist policies, Detroit did not fit the bill.

Once settled in Royal Oak, the newlyweds started a floor-covering business. Seamus had spent much of his time during and after high school working for a flooring business and was eager to start an operation of his own. Six days a week the couple installed, bought, and sold all types of floor coverings, including carpet, vinyl, and hardwood. Seamus did the installations while Piper handled sales and administrative matters. Although the business was never lucrative, it was sufficient to sustain their lifestyle and pay the mortgage on their Royal Oak home, which gave their three daughters access to the suburbs' excellent schools and other valuable amenities.

Then, in December 2007, came the Great Recession, which sent the couple's floor-covering business into the doldrums, forcing them to explore ways to generate side income. "In 2007, when the market was crashing, we thought it would be really fun to get in on buying houses in Detroit because the prices were so low," Piper remembered. "My husband is super handy and he loved the idea of renovating a house and having a rental portfolio. Also, he has a love of Detroit, and it's awful to see your city deteriorate."

With a business plan in hand, the couple approached Seamus's uncle Wolfgang, who owned factories worldwide and lived in the wealthy Detroit suburb of Grosse Pointe. "He appreciated that we came to him with a business plan versus a family problem because most people go to the rich uncle with their problems," Piper said. They asked him for a loan to buy properties so they could jump-start their new side business. Uncle Wolfgang happily agreed.

He initially set the interest rate at 8 percent but eventually dropped it to 3 percent. Without Uncle Wolfgang's below-market loan, their business plan would have failed because it is almost impossible to secure traditional bank financing to purchase distressed homes in need of substantial repair. Residential mortgage providers, like the federal Fair Housing Administration, require two things: an appraisal to determine the property's market value and hence the maximum loan amount, and an inspection to ensure that the property meets minimum health and safety standards.[4] By definition, distressed homes do not meet the minimum standards, and they also appraise for a low amount, often insufficient to pay for all the needed renovations.

Consequently, short-term "hard-money" loans secured by the property are the only alternative. Interest rates for these loans typically range between 8 and 12 percent nationally,[5] but reach up to 25 percent in Detroit. Private lenders provide these hard-money loans, which borrowers use to acquire and renovate homes and then pay back the lender after they either sell the home or rehabilitate it and then secure a traditional mortgage at a lower interest rate. Thanks to Uncle Wolfgang, Piper and Seamus had access to affordable capital, allowing them to avoid these high-interest hard-money loans as they started their real estate experiment by purchasing thirteen Detroit houses.

One of the first houses they purchased was a four-bedroom brick home in East English Village, on Kensington Avenue, the very street Seamus grew up on. The Kensington home is gorgeous and abounds in character, with leaded stained-glass windows, a regal fireplace in the living room, original wood trim, a grand front porch, a formal dining room, a spacious backyard, a two-car garage, and an artistically tiled entrance. "We'll probably end up retiring there, but we're renting it now because I've got my last one in high school here," Piper remarked. "I eventually want to move because now I live in a bungalow in Royal Oak, and it's ugly and it's flimsy. I don't have a garage. I don't have a front porch."

The couple found it profitable to buy homes in one particular neighborhood within a five-mile radius of East English Village — Regent Park. This up-and-coming Detroit neighborhood was "hot" because it shares a border with two suburbs, Harper Woods and Eastpointe. These suburbs, however, have long kept Blacks out through exclusionary practices. For example, a 2000 *Detroit Free Press* exposé revealed that the Harper Woods police department kept African Americans out through racial profiling, with Officer Bob Bensinger — the department's top ticket-giver, who accounted for 20 percent of its six thousand yearly tickets — giving African Americans 54 percent of the tickets he issued. Although the suburb's population was only 10 percent Black, the department's other top five ticket-givers ticketed African Americans at rates ranging from 25 to 47 percent.[6]

Detroiters like Regent Park and other sections of the city that share a border with Harper Woods and Eastpointe because these areas place them near the valuable amenities found in these hostile suburbs. For instance, Regent Park is close to a diverse array of shops, including a Home Depot, a Lowe's, and a Kroger supermarket in Harper Woods and another large supermarket, ALDI, in Eastpointe.

Additionally, homes in Regent Park are easy to rent because tenants with children like the nearby charter schools.

For each of their thirteen houses in and around Regent Park and East English Village, Piper and Seamus tried to finish the renovation within a year of acquisition. After considerable trial and error, the couple assembled a dependable team that made this possible. "We've worked with a lot of ex-cons," Piper said as a point of pride. "Our crew that works for us and one of our first house-sitters." She paused to explain, "We figured out we needed to have house-sitters to keep our houses from getting robbed while we were waiting to renovate them or between tenants."

During the renovation process, Uncle Wolfgang often rode two miles on his bike from Grosse Pointe to Regent Park to ensure that everything was progressing as planned. "He's one of those people that looked like a homeless man on a bike," Piper said with a mixture of fondness and exasperation. "And we'd be like, 'Uncle Wolfgang, why are you biking here, you can't do this.' He's like 'What, why, that's ridiculous. I grew up around here. This is stupid. I'll go anywhere I want.'" Under Uncle Wolfgang's vigilant eye, the couple would eventually renovate all thirteen homes, and the rental income they collected buttressed their flailing floor-covering business.

Since Detroit is the biggest small town in America, word of their success promptly began to circulate. In 2009, only two years after they had started buying houses with Uncle Wolfgang's money, several out-of-town investors approached the couple. Because Uncle Wolfgang was tightfisted — demanding to see every receipt and then demanding a justification for every cent spent — recruiting new investors was an opportunity for Piper and Seamus to escape their benefactor's well-meaning yet suffocating grasp. Things, however, did not work out as planned.

"It was a complete nightmare. We hated working with them," Piper said with disgust, referring to the various investors they burned through. "Even though it was going really well for us, they always wanted to rewrite the model. We had specific kinds of houses that we bought in specific areas." Piper and Seamus preferred to buy three-bedroom brick bungalows, the prototypical Detroit home built in the Craftsman architectural style because they could renovate these at a fraction of the time and cost that it took for larger homes. Bigger homes also contained more tenants and thus underwent more wear and tear, increasing maintenance costs. Nevertheless, the investors insisted on purchasing all types of homes.

Additionally, instead of focusing on Regent Park and other neighborhoods near East English Village, the investors wanted to gobble up as much property in Detroit as possible. Since the investors did not live in or around Detroit, they did not realize that "you can go from a beautiful street to a war zone within two streets," Piper said. "They did not listen." To make matters worse, the investors were also routinely rude to contractors, underpaying them, burning bridges at every turn, and endangering the valuable business relationships the couple had built. With Piper in earshot, one investor even insulted her, calling her a "bitch," in a conversation with his son.

Most problematically, to minimize their cash outlay and maximize profits, these investors rented homes without doing the basic work necessary to make them legally compliant with existing housing codes. "They just wouldn't do things the right way. They would do things the cheap way, and we have ethics and we weren't going to be slumlords for anyone," Piper said. "So we fired a couple investors that we were working with even though it was to our financial detriment to end the relationship." After rehabbing about fifteen homes, the couple stopped doing business with these investors, whom they found to be morally compromised.

In 2015, the couple sold two homes to pay Uncle Wolfgang in full, and at the same time, swore off partnerships with out-of-town investors. Shortly after, James, an investor from California, contacted Piper because he had come across her glowing real estate reviews online, assumed Piper did property management, and wanted to hire her. Piper told him she was not a property manager; she did not want to work for him; and she was done with out-of-town investors. James was unmoved.

"I told him no for months," Piper recalled. "I told him why: that they wouldn't let me choose the neighborhood. But he kept calling me and asking me." James relentlessly pursued Piper and Seamus, promising to let them choose the neighborhood, tenants, and type of house. The couple finally acquiesced.

Understandably, James wanted to meet his partners in person before putting money into a joint bank account, but the couple could not afford to step away from their floor-covering business even for one day to entertain him. James did not get his wish but still moved forward. "I asked, 'Aren't you worried that I'm going to go to Fiji or something?' He laughed. He's like, 'No, I can tell already you can't afford to do anything like that. You wouldn't be able to live.'" After an awkwardly loud laugh, Piper added, "He was right!"

Only once the first four homes were almost completely renovated did the couple give James a tour of Detroit. Piper and Seamus's seemingly quaint lifestyle and quotidian challenges amused James, who did not have close contact with many working-class families. "I think that was a nice cultural experience for him," Piper said, reflecting on James's first trip to Detroit. "You know, like a middle-American family, middle class, lower middle class, I don't know what we are, but for him to have that kind of exposure to us, I think he was like, 'Wow, these are nice people.'"

But the time they spent touring James around town was time that Seamus was not installing floors, so the couple lost money. Consequently, they almost got their power shut off. "It's always been paycheck to paycheck," Piper said, explaining their precarious financial situation. After taking a long reflective pause, she added, "Money was very, very tight."

When the couple finished the first batch of homes, James encouraged them to ditch their marginally profitable floor-covering business and begin doing property management and renovation full-time. Under James's mentorship and with his financial backing, this is exactly what happened. Real estate became their full-time occupation and the floor-covering business took a back seat, becoming their side gig.

"I didn't know how to answer questions about ROI [return on investment] and stuff like that. He taught me how to do all that," Piper said. Having retired from a successful business career, James wanted to mentor others. "He felt like my husband and I were quite the duo," Piper said. "Between me with a real estate license and sales skills and my husband being handy, and then his financial and business experience, between the three of us, we could really do something." James officially replaced Uncle Wolfgang, and they were off to the races.

Now that James had committed to a more serious investment of his time and money, he insisted that the couple and their daughters come to California and meet his wife. "That was really expensive. We did not have the money to do that, but we did. For Thanksgiving, we flew out there with our three kids and got to stay in their beautiful home," Piper said. "It was funny, I learned why he probably likes working with me when I saw how other people interact with him. They're kind of subservient to him. Whereas I'm like, 'No, I don't want to work with you. I'm not doing it. I don't trust investors.' So it was probably really refreshing for him." But perhaps it was refreshingly familiar because, although there was initial resistance, the couple ultimately acquiesced to all of James's wishes just like everyone else.

With James's financial backing, Piper and Seamus have purchased about one hundred forty Detroit houses. Most of the properties, the couple rents to working-class native Detroiters. But they also sell some to a diverse national and international clientele. Piper, for example, discovered that wealthy Argentines — like the ones who purchased Myrisha's home — are now investing in Detroit. She hired a translator to help her facilitate these international deals, and now even the translator wants to invest.

Piper has cultivated a robust social media presence to attract even more out-of-town investors. The couple's advertisements claimed that while Detroit's real estate industry was filled with "scammers," they were a trustworthy one-stop shop with Seamus as the builder, Piper as the real estate agent, and their floor-covering side business giving them an additional edge. For out-of-town investors who demonstrated that they were serious, the couple offered a package that included an airport pickup, a walk-through of their recently renovated homes, and a tour spanning from downtown Detroit to Grosse Pointe. Now their business has grown to the point where they have people lined up to purchase their properties. Also, their social media boasts that since 2015, their investors have earned a 9 to 15 percent return on investment.

Since Piper, Seamus, and James purchased 62 of their 140 houses from the Wayne County property tax foreclosure auction, their story provides a sight line into property tax injustice in Detroit from the unique vantage point of suburban and out-of-state investors. When the couple met James in 2015, they had almost ten years in the real estate business under their belts, so they had heard the "buzz" about the tax foreclosure auction for some time. They, however, very consciously decided not to participate.

"We heard horror stories about buying at auction because you can't get in the house and you never know what you're getting," Piper said. "But James pushed us to do research on it. We had biweekly meetings with him and he was like, 'Well, what did you learn? Did you look at this? Did you try that? Did you find somebody who's done it? Ask questions!'"

In 2016, at James's behest, the trio made their first incursion into the property tax auction. Since no local government in America had taken more homes through property tax foreclosure than Wayne County, its lists were the longest in the nation. In 2015 alone, there were 28,200 tax foreclosures,[7] or approximately 3,500 property tax foreclosures per 100,000 people, which was drastically higher than other cities and counties like New York City (52), San Francisco (48), LA County (4), Erie County, New York (62), and St. Louis County, Missouri (197).[8] In the years following, property tax foreclosure rates remained dire in Wayne County: 2016 (13,684), 2017 (7,268), and 2018 (4,178).[9]

Each year, the couple used Wayne County's long list of tax foreclosed properties to construct a short list of target properties. Then they drove by each one, evaluating the neighborhood and glancing over the home's facade to assess its condition. The couple was looking for several features, including blocks where the majority of homes were occupied and neighbors routinely mowed their grass in the summer and shoveled their snow in the winter. They also targeted neighborhoods the City had not abandoned, as evidenced by newly built public parks or repaved sidewalks. "We would see other people doing the exact same thing," Piper said. "They would be looking at the exact same houses, especially in Regent Park."

Through this process, each year, the couple identified over a hundred homes that the trio could bid on. And each year, competition sharply increased because the number of tax-foreclosed homes was dropping as the popularity of the tax auction (and hence the number of bidders) was increasing. "We tried to buy houses in Regent Park, but as the years went on, they were overpriced," Piper griped. "We got outbid."

As the contest for homes intensified, the couple responded by expanding their list of targeted properties in hopes of sustaining their yield. In an auction-induced frenzy, Piper and Seamus did not stick to their business model of purchasing only three-bedroom bungalows in their desired geographic radius. Instead, they got "a little too flexible," succumbing to competitive pressures.

Competition was fiercest for higher-valued homes, homes in choice neighborhoods, and homes requiring less costly renovations.

Bidders for these premium homes came to the first property tax auction held in September, where the starting bid is the total of taxes and fees owed. All homes that no one bid on in the first auction went to the second auction, held in October, where the starting bid is $500. Piper and Seamus, who primarily participated in the first auction, won fifteen bids in 2016, twenty-five in 2017, and twenty-two in 2018. By the 2019 tax auction, "the bidding was just insane" and the trio won only three bids.

Each year, after the auction closed, Piper and Seamus would visit their newly acquired homes, entering each one for the very first time to assess the time and money necessary to rehabilitate it. If a home was empty, then Seamus would examine the interior, calculate the renovation costs, and devise the work plan. To prevent the house from being stripped, they would place a house-sitter in the home until construction began.

If, however, a home was occupied, the couple would start eviction proceedings and offer the occupant $300 to leave within the month. This cash-for-keys deal avoided court costs and reduced the likelihood of retaliatory property damage, and according to Piper, it was "more dignified." There were, however, not many takers, so they increased the amount to $500, but this did not work, either. "I think only maybe two or three people did take the money. They wouldn't just leave," Piper said with a perplexed look. "It's a real head-scratcher. It's maybe distrust?" Since the couple had already initiated eviction proceedings before even coming to the door with the cash-for-keys offer, the distrust was not surprising.

Once the homes they acquired through the tax auction were empty, Piper and Seamus renovated and sold them, receiving a $7,000 flat management fee for each one, with James absorbing the remaining profit or loss. "It was always so hard to live paycheck to paycheck that it was attractive to me to know my bills were getting paid because I could always count on that seven thousand dollars,"

Piper said, explaining the profit arrangement. "I mean, why would he share it with us? It was his money he put up."

The trio enthusiastically participated in the tax auction, profiting steadily from this game of ownership roulette. But, as the next chapter will show, the gamble dizzied or destroyed the occupants of the trio's newly acquired homes.

13

THIS IS MY HOUSE

When Piper and Seamus found that some of the homes they purchased from the property tax foreclosure auction were vacant, they did not consider that the homes nevertheless had a history. One of these "empty" homes was owned by Lily, a woman with brown skin and a gentle voice. She wears her kinky black hair in a bun so tight that it elongates her eyes. Although Lily has lived in the city of Detroit her entire life, she is a self-proclaimed "animal nut" whose long-term goal is to one day own a large farm where she can grow herbs and plants, allow her dogs to run wild, and operate an animal rescue where people can drop off their dogs, horses, or any other animal they no longer want.

Since Lily's father was an autoworker and her mother a nurse, Lily and her sister grew up as part of Detroit's middle class, residing near Six Mile and Dequindre. As a child, Lily dreamed of owning a home like the one she grew up in, but later, when she became a single mother who earned only about $30,000 working as a bank teller, this was not likely. In 2007, however, her dream came true. Just before the housing market crashed, Lily purchased her very first home for $54,000, hoping to provide stability for both her two sons and her canine children.

"I remember when I first saw it, I'm like, 'I can't afford this house,' because it was too nice and it was too big," Lily said. It was listed as a two-bedroom, one-and-a-half-bath home because the prior owners had only renovated the bottom floor. They had left the upstairs bathroom without plumbing and the upstairs walls without insulation, making the entire second floor uninhabitable because it was too hot in the summer and too cold in the winter.

Lily purchased this unfinished home through a program at a local bank, which provided her with a Realtor to locate a home and a no-money-down mortgage to purchase it. Her mortgage had a variable interest rate that started at around 6.5 percent, making the monthly mortgage payments affordable. But as with most high-cost, subprime loans, the rate soon escalated dramatically, spurring Lily to refinance.

Lily was not alone. In 2010, about 16.1 percent of mortgages issued in Detroit metro-area neighborhoods with minority populations of 80 percent or more were high cost. In contrast, in neighborhoods with white populations of 90 percent or more, only about 5.7 percent of mortgages issued were high cost.[1] Nevertheless, when asked if she knew what a subprime loan was, Lily replied, "I've never heard of that before."

Despite her subprime mortgage loan, Lily loved her new home and neighborhood. Conant Gardens was quiet, safe, and rich with history. By 1950, Conant Gardens had the highest median income of all the Black neighborhoods in Detroit because—located on land once owned by Shubael Conant, the founder of the Detroit Anti-Slavery Society—the community never had racially restrictive covenants that banned Blacks.[2] Filled with senior citizens who had lived in the community during its heyday, Lily's new community was stable and peaceful.

Then, one Christmas Day, an unattended heater ignited a fire in the house across from Lily's. Although a group of neighbors furiously threw snow into the inferno, trying to contain it while waiting for the fire department to arrive, the home and everything inside burned to the ground, along with the peace that had pervaded her new neighborhood. No people were harmed. But the fire burned that family's two dogs alive. "That hurt," Lily said, hand to heart. "It did, it did, it did."

As time progressed, Lily's dream home gradually transformed into her worst nightmare, each malfunction provoking several others. "It was just a lot of things that just kept going wrong with the house. It was always a water issue," she recalled. "And the house just basically just started falling apart." Plumbers had to dig up pipes in the backyard to fix the plumbing; a pipe in the attic burst twice; during heavy rains, the basement would routinely flood even after she had the pipes replaced; the plumbing problems in the downstairs bathroom caused mold to grow in the walls; and every winter there was an issue with the boiler, so Lily had to completely turn off one radiator because it was spewing water.

"I couldn't get anybody I can afford to come out and actually look at it and fix it all," Lily said, the memories causing discontent to well up in her voice. "Like, there was no bathroom upstairs. I got somebody who started it, but they wouldn't come back out and finish it. And if I tried going through a company, their prices were so high, I couldn't afford it." To get by, Lily made makeshift repairs herself whenever she could. For instance, the concrete porch steps were crumbling, so she covered them with fake grass to hold them together until she could find money and a contractor to replace the steps.

Despite the poor condition of Lily's home, in 2011, she paid about $1,500 in property taxes because the City of Detroit estimated that her home was worth about $38,000.[3] But the City's own data on comparable properties recently sold indicates that the home's market value had plummeted from $54,000 in 2007 to less than $10,000 in 2011. Again, Lily was not alone. Conservative estimates show that in 2011, the City was illegally inflating the assessed value of about 53 percent of residential properties citywide,[4] and in 2012 this number jumped to 73 percent.

While Lily had no idea that the City had illegally inflated the property tax assessments of most of its residential properties in violation of the Michigan Constitution, she was fully aware that many of her friends, family members, and neighbors were losing their homes to property tax foreclosure. In fact, the entire neighborhood was crestfallen when Wayne County sold the home of a neighborhood hero, Ms. Fannie, at its property tax foreclosure auction. The new owners ejected her.

Ms. Fannie, a senior citizen beloved by all neighbors, lived across the street from Lily in a house she had occupied for decades. Lily thought Ms. Fannie had lost her home because she had failed to follow the rules and pay her taxes. Lily did not know that in Detroit, 10 percent of all homes and 25 percent of the lowest-valued homes, like Ms. Fannie's, would not have gone into tax foreclosure but for the illegally inflated property tax assessments.[5]

The predatory loan and illegally inflated property taxes combined drove Lily to her breaking point. "Trying to maintain the mortgage on it, trying to maintain taxes on it, trying to maintain insurance, and just all of that together, I just could not do it," she said in defeat. "I ended up talking to an attorney and they told me just to walk away, and so that's what I did." In 2015, Lily stopped paying her mortgage.

But her house was now worth so little that even the bank did not want it back. According to a report by the federal Government Accountability Office, more banks walked away from homes in Detroit, not even bothering to foreclose, than in any other large American city.[6] As a result, Lily lived in the house free of rent and mortgage payments. Additionally, since a property tax debt must be at least three years old before it triggers property tax foreclosure, she could even have lived in the home for a stretch without paying property taxes.

Nevertheless, because the cost of living in Detroit was too high, after her sons graduated from high school, she moved to the nearest suburb, Warren. The boundary street between Detroit and Warren is Eight Mile Road, and Lily now lives only one short block from this border. "As soon as I crossed Eight Mile, my water bill went down, my gas bill went down, my electric went down, insurance went down," she said. "Until my kids started driving all the time, I used to be one of those who didn't pay my car insurance because it's so high. You can't really afford it other than to just get it long enough to get your registration done."

The average annual premium for car insurance in Detroit is $5,414, which is 18 percent of the median household income for the city. In other Midwestern cities, such as Cleveland, St. Louis, and Chicago, car insurance accounts for just 2 percent to 4 percent of pre-tax income.[7] As a consequence, an estimated 60 percent of Detroit drivers are uninsured, a rate that is four times higher than the national average.[8] Lily, together with her two sons, paid about $875 per month for car insurance in Detroit, but when they moved one block into Warren, the price immediately dropped to $430.

Warren residents not only paid lower car insurance rates than Detroit residents, but they also paid lower property tax rates: between 2007 and 2020, Warren's effective property tax rate was 2.63 percent, while Detroit had an effective rate of 14.92 percent.[9] "Property taxes in Warren was never as high as the ones in Detroit," Lily noted. "And yet they get their streets plowed during the winter. The roads get fixed when they get potholes. The police are always in the community. They have programs. You can see where that money is going." But in Detroit it is a different story, she said. "You have potholes in streets, you have houses that are vacant and need to be torn down, you have streetlights that don't work, you have all these other issues with having enough police officers that they can't come to anything other than homicide."

Lily's new home in one of Warren's mobile home parks has three bedrooms, two bathrooms, and a small, well-manicured lawn. Manufactured housing is the largest source of unsubsidized affordable housing in America,[10] but with the dearth of mobile homes and other affordable housing units in the Detroit metro area, there was a waiting list at the mobile home park. But because the primary leasing agent called in sick and the gentleman covering her shift mistakenly accepted Lily's deposit, she secured the unit ahead of others on the list. Lily believes it was "divine intervention."

After two years of renting, in 2017, she purchased the mobile home for $38,000. She was, again, a homeowner, gladly turning over a new leaf and forgetting about her entire home-buying fiasco in Detroit. That is, until one day a woman named Piper called her and left a voicemail message. Piper explained that she had acquired Lily's Detroit home in the property tax foreclosure auction, and in order to secure title insurance, Piper needed Lily to sign a document. If not, Piper's lawyer would have to bring a legal action to clear the title.

"She sounded really nice and polite," Lily recalled. "But at that time I didn't want anything to do with the house. I walked away and I was done. And then I got a letter from them asking again." With a devious chuckle, she admitted, "And again, I just ignored it." Lily would have continued ignoring the messages if Piper's lawyer had not filed the legal action, which listed Lily as the defendant. Upon receiving the complaint, Lily talked to her lawyer, who advised her to sign Piper's paperwork. So she did.

This was when Lily discovered that while she had purchased the home for $54,000 in 2007, Piper and Seamus had purchased the home in the 2017 tax auction for only $8,100. Lily was shocked. "It always broke my heart when I saw what we bought the house for, and then I looked on public record and saw what the last owner paid for it," Piper said. "I cringed every time."

Another vacant home that Piper and Seamus purchased from the tax auction was previously owned by Ebony, an executive who wears stilettos with her suits. Ebony's people on her father's side hailed from Alabama, with her grandfather finding work in construction and her grandmother as a cleaner. Eventually, they purchased a home in a safe and stable neighborhood called Cadillac Heights, where they raised their four children, including Ebony's father, TJ, and his brother, Amir.

Ebony has endearing memories of the Cadillac Heights home and the time she spent with her grandparents there. Most of all, she remembers how her grandparents always encouraged her to focus on school and to build a successful career. So at a very young age, Ebony began seriously thinking about what she wanted to do when she grew up. She figured it out in sixth grade when she was scheduled to attend a science, technology, engineering, and math (STEM) program. Due to funding cuts, however, the organizers canceled the program, but not before it planted an idea in Ebony's mind — she was going to be an engineer.

Ebony was an exceptionally bright child and dreamed of attending Detroit's premier public high school — Cass Technical. Upon taking the highly competitive entrance exam, like Myrisha, she gained admission. At Cass, Ebony finally had an opportunity to attend a STEM program, hosted by the Ford Motor Company, which lasted six Saturdays and introduced students to computer-aided design. Ebony was enraptured. She went on to earn an engineering degree from Michigan State University in 2009 and immediately secured a job with Nestlé, where she worked in different states, including Wisconsin and Arkansas.

After three years, Ebony came back to Detroit and found work with a local automotive company so she could care for her ailing father, TJ, who was battling kidney failure. Like his father, TJ worked in construction, and he also ran his own asphalt operation.

But since this is seasonal work, he teetered at poverty's edge his entire working life.

Nevertheless, once Detroit housing prices plummeted, TJ was able to purchase his first home in 2011 for around $4,500. It was in Cadillac Heights, where, after fifty years, his mom still lived. At the same time, TJ's brother, Amir, purchased a home three blocks down the street for $2,000. Ebony also purchased two homes in the old neighborhood: hers for $8,000 and her mother's for $3,000.

Cadillac Heights, however, is no longer the stable and safe neighborhood that it was when Ebony was growing up. "The neighborhood is terrible," Ebony reported. "There's literally maybe five viable houses on my grandmother's block today. That's what just saddens me the most because as a kid, and even as a teenager, I can remember it being such a vibrant neighborhood." She added, "My grandmother will be eighty-seven this year, and so we're trying to get her to stay with one of us or go to a seniors' home, but she doesn't want to leave her home." Most of the longtime residents in the neighborhood are senior citizens who likewise refuse to abandon the place they have called home for decades.

Not long after the family returned to Cadillac Heights, in 2012, Ebony's father died at age fifty. "He only enjoyed the house for a year before he transitioned," Ebony said in a whisper. "That's why it was so devastating. He had just got his first home." Before he died, however, TJ transferred his home to Ebony through a quit claim deed, and she did the paperwork to become the owner of record.

"From an emotional standpoint, I couldn't do anything with the home. I was just an emotional wreck. I was just thinking about burying my father," Ebony said. So "I let my cousin literally move in the night my father passed because, living in the inner city of Detroit, we didn't want people to break in, take piping, electrical, and things like that." Ebony's cousin did not have to pay rent and was only responsible for paying the property taxes and maintaining the home, which he managed to do for the first year or two. "My cousin doesn't have a job, he is a street hustler, so a street guy with no consistent income," Ebony explained. Once he got behind on the property taxes, it was almost impossible to catch up because of the statutory 18 percent interest penalty and fees the County added on.

Beset with grief and juggling the demands of her fast-paced engineering job with the needs of her kindergarten-age daughter, Ebony did not have the bandwidth to deal with the impending property tax foreclosure. So she called on her uncle, Amir, to take over. After Ebony transferred the property to Amir with a quit claim deed, he initiated legal proceedings to evict his nephew, who refused to leave the home.

Once his nephew was out, Amir got on a payment plan to pay the delinquent property taxes. But because he was not an owner-occupant, Amir did not qualify for the payment plan that reduces accumulated interest from 18 to 6 percent, and thus the required payments were unaffordable and unsustainable. And so, in 2018, the Wayne County treasurer foreclosed upon the home and sold it at auction to Piper and Seamus.

To the new owners, the property was just one of dozens of investment properties they intended to rent out or flip. When they came to inspect their newly acquired house, they saw potential profits, and not a place that was teeming with history, including a family's dream to reclaim their old neighborhood. Piper and Seamus also did not see the racist policies that had made their purchase possible.

Piper believed she was able to acquire this particular home because, evidently, its prior owners "failed to do what they were supposed to do." But an analysis of the home's property tax records reveals a different story. In 2012, when TJ registered the home in his name, the Detroit Office of the Assessor taxed the home as if it were worth about $37,000. This was in spite of the fact that TJ had purchased it for $4,500 on the open market and the median sale price for homes in the neighborhood was $4,000. Of course, TJ was far from the only Detroiter saddled with an unfair tax burden that year. In 2012, the City of Detroit illegally inflated the property tax assessments of about 73 percent of all residential properties.[11]

"I'm very educated, but I've never really stepped back and realized like, 'Damn, my taxes are substantially high compared to what I paid for the home,'" Ebony said. "What we go through has just become so normalized that I've never stepped back until lately, when this has come to the forefront about the taxes being overpriced in the city of Detroit," referring to the work the Coalition for Property Tax Justice and investigative reporters at the *Detroit News* have been doing to raise awareness of illegally inflated property taxes in Detroit. "But now I'm more aware," Ebony declared. "I get the whole picture now."

Fed up with all the injustice that Detroit dishes out, Ebony is preparing to leave. "I never wanted to turn my back on my city, but I got to show my daughter something different," she explained. "When you hear a gunshot, it's the norm for me, but I don't want that to be the norm for my daughter." Although she believes that the suburb of Livonia is "one of the most racist cities there is," Ebony is considering relocating there because it is close to her job.

While in the process of packing up and selling her home, which was near her father's old house, Ebony discovered something unexpected. "This is where the story gets really creepy," she warned. "So a Realtor comes to my house and he's like, 'Yeah, you know, this is a nice home. You done kept it up, did some work. I will show you homes in the area that have just sold within the last six months.' And the first house he shows me is my father's house." Covering her mouth with both hands, she hissed, "That put me on my back."

After it went through tax foreclosure, Ebony did not know what had happened to her father's home. She had no idea that Piper and Seamus had acquired it at the tax auction for only about $6,000;

renovated the kitchen and bathroom and made a few other improvements; and sold it one year later for $45,000, profiting from Ebony's family's misfortune.

But even Ebony does not have clean hands. She also profited from someone else's misfortune. According to the neighbors, before Ebony moved into her own home in Cadillac Heights, an older African American woman had lived there for decades, and when she died, her heirs could not keep up with the reverse mortgage payments, so the bank reclaimed their legacy. The mortgage foreclosure was what allowed Ebony to purchase her own home for the low price of $8,000, and she recently found a buyer who agreed to pay $45,000 for it, promising a sizable profit. Homeowners in Detroit are playing an extremely destructive game of musical chairs, some willfully and others not. Tragically, it has left the city and its longtime inhabitants bruised and scarred in the fight for that last chair.

In addition to "empty" homes, Piper and Seamus have also purchased occupied homes from the property tax foreclosure auction. Many auction buyers favored occupied properties marked by toys on the porch, a car in the driveway, grass cut in the summer, and in the winter, snow shoveled or furnace smoke twirling in frigid air. Unlike vacant homes, occupied homes are not prey to the scavengers who wreak havoc on Detroit's housing stock. Also, occupied homes gave auction buyers several options: they could either obtain an immediate income stream by renting the home to its existing occupants; evict the existing occupants and find new tenants; sell the home to another investor with the paying tenant increasing the transaction's appeal; sell the home to its occupants on a land contract; or evict the tenant to renovate and resell the home.

Because flipping a property with a paying tenant brings a higher price, when Seamus and Piper encountered occupants in their properties, the couple always gave them the opportunity to stay if they were willing to live in the property during the renovation and pay the proposed rent. For instance, there was one tenant named Tanika who lived in one of their Regent Park homes and had not paid rent for about two years because the landlord had disappeared. "I have to have my kids in these schools. I have to stay here," Tanika told Piper during their first encounter.

Tanika agreed to pay $800 in rent and stayed in the home during its renovation so her children could remain in a nearby, well-ranked charter school. Although the initial uncertainty and construction caused a great deal of stress, Tanika believed the new situation turned out to be a blessing, so she was grateful. But when the rent Piper and Seamus demanded was more than other existing occupants could afford, the couple had to evict them, becoming a curse rather than a blessing.

The eviction of one homeowner in particular will haunt Piper and Seamus as long as they live. It involves Karl Johnson, a senior citizen and veteran of the Vietnam War, who inherited his home from his mother. Like a volcano, his home was overflowing with generations of stuff, making it impossible to walk around. Poverty had pummeled Mr. Karl, and he could not afford his water bill. Consequently, as per its policy, the Detroit Water and Sewerage Department sprayed bright blue paint on the sidewalk in front of his home, indicating that service at the property had been or soon would be disconnected.[12] Without running water, Mr. Karl had no option but to relieve himself in a garbage can, an indignity that no homeowner should have to endure.

Data show that the City of Detroit had also illegally overtaxed Mr. Karl's home every year since at least 2009. For example, despite the poor condition of Mr. Karl's home, in 2013, the City of Detroit assessed its value at about $34,000, but conservative estimates suggest it was actually worth around $10,900, which was the neighborhood's median sale price in 2013. The City of Detroit illegally inflated the value of almost 80 percent of the homes neighboring Mr. Karl's, leading to several tax foreclosures.

Although Mr. Karl's poverty exempted him altogether from paying these illegally inflated property taxes, like many others, he never applied because he did not know about the exemption. Further complicating the situation, Mr. Karl's fragile mental health made filling out the paperwork required each year to receive the exemption virtually impossible. So, in 2016, the Wayne County treasurer foreclosed on Mr. Karl's legacy for failure to pay his illegally inflated property tax debt, which he should not have owed in the first place. Mr. Karl's loss was Piper and Seamus's gain. They purchased his home at auction for about $12,000.

When Seamus came to the home for the first time and knocked on the door, Mr. Karl answered. Seamus began explaining that he was the new owner of the home. Mr. Karl was shocked, repeatedly telling him, "No, it's my house." And Seamus, now accustomed to the unpleasant task of informing homeowners that their houses were no longer their own, kept explaining, "But I'm so sorry, it's not anymore, because you didn't pay the taxes." Mr. Karl objected ferociously. Given that they were at a stalemate, Seamus left.

Because Mr. Karl was a veteran, Piper and Seamus were willing to sell the home back to him for the price they had paid at auction, but unsurprisingly, Mr. Karl did not have the money. Trying a different approach, Piper asked Mr. Karl to pay rent, but he never did. In fact, Mr. Karl had no intention of leaving, buying back the home, or paying rent. With no alternative, after nearly a year of negotiations, the couple initiated eviction proceedings to remove Mr. Karl from the home.

At the eviction court, the situation escalated, transforming into a telenovela-style drama. "When we finally went to court, he was irate," Piper said in despair, supporting her head with her hand. "He wouldn't let the judge talk. He kept interrupting her when she was explaining to him, 'It's not your house. These people were very generous with you. I'm here to tell you, it's not your house. You have to leave.' He was yelling at her and it was nonsensical what he was saying, so she kicked him out."

The sad spectacle did not end there. When the judge adjourned the case, Piper left the courtroom with her lawyer. Mr. Karl, supported by a walker and wearing a veterans' baseball cap, spotted Piper in the hallway and began hollering at full volume. "He was pounding his walker on the floor and he was yelling across the hallway with all these tenants, 'That white woman is kicking me out of my house. You see that white woman? She's kicking me out of my house.' He was ranting that he was a veteran," Piper said, her face ashen. "Everyone's looking at me because I was the only Caucasian person there." After a pensive pause, she added, "I was very scared because there was a movie that had just aired the weekend before about the riots in Detroit, so it was stirring up the hatred, and that's what was going in my head. I'm like, 'Oh my gosh, I bet everyone just saw that movie, too.'"

The drama unfolded in three acts. Act 1: the City and County kicked Mr. Karl out of his home for failure to pay illegally inflated property taxes that he was exempt from paying in the first place. Act 2: Piper and Seamus legitimately purchased his home at the tax auction. Act 3: Mr. Karl and the couple faced off in eviction court. The problem is that by Act 3, Act 2 was hypervisible, but complex processes, procedures, and calculations made Act 1 invisible. Mr. Karl did not have the words to expose the malfeasance that occurred in Act 1. Instead, he could only wail again and again, "This is my house!" His plaintive cries, however, fell on deaf ears. Despite Mr. Karl's righteous obstinacy, he now had no option but to leave.

Kris, the court officer Piper and Seamus had hired to conduct most of their evictions, arrived with a moving crew to eject Mr. Karl but quickly realized there were not enough dumpsters to contain everything in his crowded home. Kris, therefore, canceled the eviction that day. Before leaving, Kris had a long chat with Mr. Karl and discovered he was a veteran who likely had some mental illness. Although Kris conducts hundreds of evictions each year, Mr. Karl's situation tugged at her conscience, so she called Veterans Affairs and found him temporary housing so that when the movers came back, he would not be homeless. While most court officers would not have gone out of their way to lend a helping hand, Kris was uniquely empathetic.

When Kris and her crew returned, she implored Mr. Karl to remove his most valuable belongings from the home before they got to work, but he could not. As the eviction team emptied his life into the dumpsters, Mr. Karl stood immobilized, pleading to the wind, "But this is my house."

"Seven dumpsters of generations of stuff in that house. Yeah, it was something else," Piper said with disgust. "It wasn't worth anything, sadly." Piper was able to see Mr. Karl's belongings only as junk, rather than objects infused with memories. Piper commented on Mr. Karl's incessant pleas by saying, "There probably was some mental illness or just very low IQ. I don't know. He didn't get it."

Since Mr. Karl, Lily, and Ebony were not the only Detroit homeowners who did not pay their property taxes and lost their homes, what was going on? "You know, we speculated a lot about that," Piper responded. "I don't think it's that deep. I think we've all been irresponsible at times in our lives where you just don't take care of business. I hate opening my mail every day. I don't want to look at my bills. I don't want to face it. I have to make myself do it. And my life's not that hard. My life is nowhere near as hard as anybody's is in Detroit."

As a white working-class couple who has lived paycheck to paycheck, Piper and Seamus have struggled financially, and have often been unable to pay their bills. But the couple attributes their recent success to their hard work. And just as their success was a product of their personal responsibility, they believe that the massive dispossession in Detroit was a result of its homeowners' widespread irresponsibility. This personal irresponsibility narrative marks the property tax foreclosure auction as legitimate and masks its predatory aspects, allowing "good people" to participate in it without a vexed conscience.

If Piper acknowledged that Detroit improperly inflated its property taxes, this would change the moral calculus of participating in the tax auction. As a result, Piper ignored this reality, even though she knew it was true from personal experience. Initially, Piper and Seamus did not know much about property taxes. Like most homeowners with a mortgage, their bank created an escrow account for the property taxes and bundled them with the mortgage payment, making the property taxes less salient.[13] But when the couple began purchasing homes without a mortgage, they started paying attention to the property tax bill. Piper knew that a $5,000 tax bill on a property they had purchased for $10,000 was outrageous, so she decided to fight back, filing a property tax assessment appeal. Although in later years, Piper had the resources to pay someone $750 per house to appeal her property tax assessments, receiving a 50 percent reduction for each one, in 2011, she filed the appeal without professional help.

Between February 1 and February 15,[14] she duly submitted paperwork to the Assessor Review, but she did not get a large reduction, so she went to the next step in the appeal process, the March Board of Review, which involves a scheduled hearing. To prove that the City's market valuation is incorrect, homeowners must bring evidence such as sales comparisons, cost of repair records, and photographs showing structural damage. But like most unrepresented homeowners, Piper had no idea what to expect at the hearing, so she did not come prepared with the required evidence. Instead, she came with tons of questions, looking for an opportunity to tell her story and feel heard.

"I went through the process and it was very, very difficult," Piper said, jaw clenched. "I had to appear in front of a whole board of people that could not have been more condescending. They talked over me. I didn't know what they were saying. They used language I didn't understand. I asked for clarification and I got mocked. They were laughing the whole time. I was sitting there telling them, 'But how does that make sense? I don't understand. That would mean this house was worth a hundred thousand dollars and I only paid ten for it.' They said, 'Well, that's not our fault.'" Using every last bit of strength she had to hold her head high and restrain the tears of embarrassment and humiliation, Piper walked out of the March Board of Review hearing, feeling hurt instead of heard.

As she left, a representative from the Office of the Assessor told her that if she was not happy with the board's decision, she could appeal to the Michigan Tax Tribunal by July 31. Piper did just that. She filed her appeal and then waited for her day in court to arrive. When it did, she got to court early and had an opportunity to chat with the magistrate, discovering that the magistrate had been brought in from Canada to help with the tribunal's significant backlog of cases. In 2007, there was a backlog of more than 10,500 cases, with an additional 8,000 filed annually,[15] so the backlog eventually grew to 40,000 appeals, which the tribunal did not eliminate until 2014.[16] Once the magistrate heard the price Piper had paid for the property at the tax auction and compared it with sales of comparable properties in the area, she ruled in Piper's favor and reduced her property tax assessment by about half.

According to a *Detroit News* analysis of over four thousand tribunal decisions filed by Wayne County property owners between 2010 and 2013, the tribunal reduced Detroit property values nearly 50 percent more than the County average. Additionally, owner-occupiers accounted for only 15 percent of the Detroit decisions, although they accounted for more than 50 percent of the city's residential properties.[17] Consequently, well-heeled landlords and businesses were more likely to get substantial relief by making it to the tribunal, the last step in the complicated appeal process. For example, the tribunal reduced the property tax assessments of two well-known Detroit business families, the Morouns and the Ilitches, by 57 percent and 40 percent, respectively, amounting to a $970,000 and a $1.8 million property tax savings per year.

Given that Piper had been through the onerous appeals process and knew firsthand about the illegally inflated property taxes in Detroit, how could she insist that the owners of the homes she purchased from tax auction lost them because of their individual irresponsibility? This is because, despite significant data to the contrary, Mayor Mike Duggan asserts that he fixed the systematic overassessments plaguing Detroit when he authorized across-the-board cuts in property tax assessments in 2014 and 2015.[18] Even though several studies show that this is not true,[19] Mayor Duggan ignores the data and continues to claim that his administration fixed the illegally inflated property taxes in Detroit. Most importantly, Piper, Seamus, and others believe him.

"Property taxes used to be insane, but when Duggan came in, he fixed them and they're fair now, as far as I know. But they used to be really, really high," Piper emphasized. "So I get it. If people are losing their houses to taxes and if it started back then before Duggan made them fair again, that was criminal what the City did." She believed that Mayor Kwame Kilpatrick, whom she referred to as the "most corrupt mayor," was singularly responsible for property tax injustice in Detroit.

But even after Piper discovered that Duggan did not, in fact, fix the illegally inflated property taxes in Detroit, she nevertheless planned to participate in the Wayne County property tax auction as soon as the COVID-19 moratorium ended. "I don't ever want to hurt people," Piper explained. "These houses were for sale. I'm not the one that put them for sale. I don't think that I'm the one that hurt the people by buying them. I don't have control over what the City did. I came into a bad situation and did my best to do right in any way that I could, and I was able to provide a lot of housing for a lot of needy people in a city that's full of slumlords." Shrugging her shoulders in a sign of surrender, she added, "I'm in a financially tough position, and if there's a chance to make my family better and still do good?" After a long pause, she continued, "I don't know, that's really hard."

Piper and Seamus did not break the rules to extract profit. They legally purchased Detroit homes and invested significant time and money to improve them, thereby providing affordable, safe housing in a city where it is scarce yet sorely needed. Despite all the good they have done, Piper and Seamus acquired each of their auction homes at substantial discount, profiting from the misery of others. Participating in a predatory system predicated on racist policies converts even well-meaning participants into predators.

14

SLUMLORDS

By renovating all the homes they purchased through the property tax foreclosure auction, Piper and Seamus not only fulfilled the auction contract, they also increased the supply of safe and affordable rental housing in Detroit. There were, however, many legally noncompliant investors, or slumlords, participating in the tax auction as well. Some became legally noncompliant by not improving the homes and paying their property taxes, as mandated by the auction contract. After three years of unpaid property tax debt, they allowed the treasurer to foreclose and auction the property once again. Since tax foreclosure clears properties of all prior debts, they then repurchased the property debt-free using a new LLC.

Employing a random sample of two hundred Detroit properties auctioned in 2002 and 2003, one study finds that 20 percent of auction buyers did not pay their property taxes and were again in tax foreclosure by 2007. The same study finds that 48 percent of auction buyers did not redevelop the homes.[1] These legally noncompliant investors were only interested in turning a quick profit, and the best way to do that was to sell the foreclosed home to its current occupants through a land contract, which, as described in earlier chapters, is a seller-financed loan that the buyer repays with a down payment and monthly installments similar to rent.

Michael G. Kelly—the land speculator who, in an earlier chapter, placed manure in front of a strip club—often sells homes he purchases at the auction on land contract to low-income residents, most of whom end up foreclosed or evicted. One study found that of the properties that Detroit Leasing, a company Kelly is affiliated with, purchased in 2002 and 2003, one-third went into tax foreclosure by 2007.[2] Also, between 2009 and 2016, Kelly filed 1,160 evictions, which is about 2.5 each day, the highest eviction rate of any known contract seller in Detroit.[3] The saga on Junction Avenue highlights how land contract sales beget tax foreclosures and evictions.

Denise Dussell, a no-nonsense woman whose parents immigrated from Ireland, inherited a quaint three-bedroom, two-bathroom, two-story wood-frame bungalow on Junction Avenue in southwest Detroit, which her family had acquired in 1907. Ms. Denise grew up in the home, and once married, she lived in the home with her husband, who worked as a chauffeur for Henry Ford, and their two children. In 1898, when Ms. Denise was born, Detroit was about 99 percent white, and when she died in 1987 it was about 75 percent African American.[4] Most whites, including her son and daughter, fled to the suburbs, but Ms. Denise remained in her house on Junction Avenue because, after serving as a Detroit public-school teacher for forty-two years, she was deeply connected to her neighborhood and her students.

When she died, Ms. Denise bequeathed the house on Junction Avenue to her daughter Mary and only two of her great-grandchildren, Jack and Matt Baskin. Ms. Denise intentionally left out her granddaughter, Susan, and her four other children because she did not want anything to do with Susan and their father, whom Ms. Denise called an "uncouth hillbilly" every chance she got. Robert, the "hillbilly," was a professional junk dealer who earned a living by collecting scrap metal. Making reference to a popular 1970s sitcom starring Redd Foxx, Jack said, "We were the white version of *Sanford and Son.*"

Robert earned Ms. Denise's scorn not because of his humble profession, but by mercilessly beating his two stepsons, Jack and Matt, forcing child welfare authorities to remove them from the home for a stint. Susan's own struggles with drugs and alcohol prevented her from shielding her sons. "My mom lived a wild life," Jack recalled. "She drank and liked to take pills. She would be out at the bars nine, ten hours a day."

Out of pity, soon after Ms. Denise died, Mary, Jack, and Matt upended her wishes by transferring the home to Susan and allowing her entire family to move in, including the "uncouth hillbilly" whom Ms. Denise had so despised. "My great-grandma was probably turning over in her grave," Jack said, regretting his divided loyalties.

In the early nineties, Jack's mother and stepfather left Detroit and moved to a trailer park in Robert's hometown of London, Kentucky. Jack and Matt, who were then adults, stayed in Detroit. They, therefore, were not there when Robert became a meth addict and Susan's hard life and multiple ailments led to the amputation of her right leg just above the knee. Ultimately, Susan succumbed to her many maladies, dying in 2008. Because she had no will, all six of her children inherited the house on Junction Avenue. They, however, signed it over to Jack, who was the eldest and the only one still living in the home.

At the time, Jack was forty-one years old. He did not have a high school diploma, and his primary job was working at a local grocery store, where, over his twenty-six years of employment, he went from making $3.15 per hour to making $10 per hour. "I was working at a grocery store on Vernor Highway where I did everything from sweep the floor to pack fish and chicken parts, stocking, bagging, security. I pretty much did everything," Jack said, pride swelling his voice. "My boss was Chaldean from Iraq and thought there would be retribution from racists and ignorant people during the Iraq War, so I would stay ten hours a night, guarding the store." With deep disappointment, he added, "I made only three hundred dollars in overtime for that."

Despite Jack's loyalty, his boss fired him in 2007 because droves of Iraqi immigrants, who would work for much less than $10 per hour, began arriving in the Detroit metro area following the war. This was when Jack's property tax troubles began in earnest. He, however, should not have been paying property taxes in the first place because he qualified for the poverty tax exemption. But, like so many others, he did not know about this entitlement, and even if he had, the City of Detroit erected several barriers to receiving the exemption.

In addition, the City overvalued Jack's home for years, leading to illegally inflated property taxes that he could not afford to pay. In 2011, for instance, Jack's property tax bill was about $1,800 because the City of Detroit estimated the value of his home at about $21,000. But sales data show that at this time, the home's true market value was between $3,500 and $11,200, and the City overvalued 70 percent of the neighboring properties that sold. Although Jack tried to keep up with the bloated payments, he could not. He fell behind.

On top of this, in 2011, after doctors diagnosed Jack's brother, Matt, with terminal cancer, he moved back to Junction Avenue. "He did not want hospice," Jack remembered with a shaky voice. "He only wanted me to take care of him. He wanted to die in our home." In addition to Jack being Matt's primary caretaker, Jack's own health was failing because his long-undiagnosed diabetes caused extensive nerve damage in his hands, feet, legs, and eyes. Jack was also clinically depressed.

Although he found a new job at another grocery store, Jack could only work part-time because of his ailments, earning the minimum wage of $7.40. Jack maintained the entire household with his paycheck—which after taxes was $150 per week—and his brother's paltry disability check. The brothers barely had enough money for food, but they nevertheless had to pay their overinflated property tax bills, which were worsened by the State of Michigan's statutorily mandated 18 percent interest penalty on delinquent property tax debt. As a result, Jack's property tax debt ballooned to about $5,000.

Without the money to pay the debt and save his home from tax foreclosure, Jack sank deeper into depression. And then later that year, the day after Thanksgiving, Matt's cancer killed him. Jack was devastated and spiraling downward, but he took comfort in the fact that his little brother had gotten his dying wish. Like his dear great-grandmother, Ms. Denise, Matt lived his last days in the house on Junction Avenue.

In March 2012, Wayne County confiscated title to Jack's family home because he had failed to pay his illegally inflated property taxes. The house had been in Jack's family since 1907, providing shelter and stability for five generations. "It is ridiculous what they do to people who cannot afford to live as it is," Jack lamented. "You can never win against the government." Wayne County sold the home at its September auction for $600 to Suburban Renaissance V LLC, a Dearborn-based company owned by Mr. Michael Hamade and his family.

Because Jack knew that the tax foreclosure had happened in March, a simple knock at the door evoked anxiety and desperation as he waited for the new owners to appear. He could only hope that after listening to his story, the new owners would understand why he could not leave. In the fall of 2012, representatives from Suburban Renaissance finally showed up and politely asked to enter the home so they could see its interior for the very first time. What they saw left them aghast.

"The original cedar shake under the asphalt on the roof got rotted out and there were half a dozen holes in the roof the size of basketballs. I could see daylight if I looked up through the ceiling, as bad as it had gotten. I was only able to live in two rooms," Jack said. "I could not get any loans to fix the roof, so there was water damage everywhere from years of the roof leaking, and everything else was collateral damage from this. Like there were holes in the wall where the plaster fell off. The floor was collapsing into the subbasement. My mom's room downstairs (which was my great-grandmother's room) got so bad the upstairs floor collapsed into that room. We could not use the upstairs bathroom because the ceiling fell in. There was mold throughout the house."

Jack paused, the pain of the memories written on his face. "There was no electricity. A neighbor let me use an extension cord from his house to run my microwave and TV. It got overwhelming when I lost my job and could not pay my bills and so they shut the electricity off, same as the water. I used to fill up gallons of water at my friend's house and bring it home every couple of days and take a shower and wash clothes at her house."

Suburban Renaissance quickly realized that Jack was living in abject poverty and his beloved home was literally collapsing all around him, threatening to bury him alive. Renting the home back to Jack was out of the question because it did not meet the minimum legal standard of habitability. Some investors who walk into dire situations like this sell the home back to the occupant, recovering only the money paid at auction. But not Suburban Renaissance. This company was not interested in charity. They were only interested in turning a profit.

Knowing that Jack had a sentimental connection to his uninhabitable home and hence was willing to keep it at all costs, the company sold it back to him on a land contract for $4,000, paid in monthly installments of $300. "When I was in their office to make my monthly payment, I saw other people coming in and they were all similar. I believe they make sure the properties they buy are occupied," Jack conjectured. "I was living off of one-dollar packs of bologna and one-dollar bags of bread just so I could make the payments."

In 2014, Jack finally started receiving a disability check for his long-standing ailments and used the extra income to finish off his land contract installment payments. After making over 500 percent profit, Suburban Renaissance transferred the house on Junction Avenue back to Jack. He got his legacy back. Although victorious, Jack still could not afford to renovate, and the City of Detroit was still illegally inflating his property taxes and making the exemption difficult to access.

Unsurprisingly, in 2016 Wayne County, once again, confiscated the house on Junction Avenue when Jack defaulted on his property tax debt from 2013. The total tax debt had mushroomed to over $8,000. Records show that a Mr. Ortiz purchased the home at the auction for $15,000. The auction purchase price had increased from $600 in 2012 to $15,000 in 2016 for two reasons. With time, there were fewer homes and more bidders at the property tax foreclosure auction, spiking competition and thus prices. Also, southwest Detroit began to gentrify, multiplying the demand for homes on Junction Avenue and the surrounding area.

"He first told me to go to a homeless shelter," Jack said, describing the rancorous conversation he had with Ortiz's representative when he first arrived at the door. "Then he was going to let me stay there if I agreed to work for him and clean out the houses he bought. When I went to see one house, it had so much junk that I could not climb up the stairs. I am already in pain all the time and cannot lift heavy things, so I told him I would not be able to do it. So he said his boss wants me out." With tears rolling down his cheeks, Jack continued, "I said I would be out in a week and moved in with my friends around the block." Jack moved in with the same friend who had allowed him to shower and do laundry at her house when the City disconnected his water.

After two and a half years of construction, Ortiz completed a gut renovation, refurbishing the entire home. "They say it's really nice in the inside now. The upstairs bathroom even has a Jacuzzi tub. They rented it out, and I think they are paying eleven hundred dollars rent," Jack said. "I still want the house till this day, but I could not afford it."

Jack's family's drama is not unique. From a sample of two hundred homes sold via land contract in 2016, *Bridge Michigan* found that, on average, one in three sellers purchased the homes from the tax foreclosure auction for $10,000 and sold them for $45,000.[5] This was only possible because, while tax-delinquent homeowners could not cobble together the thousands of dollars required to pay their debts and save their homes from tax foreclosure, they could afford the land contract payments, which often involved a $500 down payment and a $200 to $500 monthly payment.

Land contracts are the favored tool of legally noncompliant investors because they do not provide buyers with the traditional protections afforded to mortgage holders or renters, giving sellers outsized power. For instance, although the monthly payments are similar to rent, land contracts are not subject to common law protections reserved for renters, such as the warranty of habitability, which protects consumers from housing unfit for human habitation. Instead, under a land contract, owners assume responsibility for all repairs. Also, mortgage holders who default are entitled to their equity, which is the difference between the value of the home and the amount owed. In contrast, with land contracts, the property title most often remains with the seller until the loan is paid in full, so if the buyer defaults, the seller can retake the home even if payments are almost complete. The buyer loses the down payment and monthly installments already rendered as if they were rental payments rather than equity.

Most detrimentally, Michigan exempts land contract sellers from disclosing debts or liens on the property.[6] As a result, only after completing their monthly installments do many low-information, first-time home buyers discover that the property has delinquent property tax debt, water department liens, recorded blight tickets, and a slew of other title impairments that the law forces sellers to disclose to mortgage holders. *Bridge Michigan* found that, of two hundred homes sold on land contract in 2015, one in five went into tax foreclosure in 2017, meaning the homes were already two years delinquent upon sale. This could not happen with traditional bank financing because in order to secure a mortgage, the owner must first clear all liens and debts.[7]

Despite these pronounced inequities, land contracts are the only option for most Black home buyers in and around Detroit. Because Michigan law does not require land contract sellers or buyers to publicly file these contracts, data are limited, but after scraping together the data that do exist, Professors Joshua Akers and Eric Seymour found that between 2011 and 2015, 65 percent of land contracts in the Detroit metro area were located in majority-Black census tracts, while these neighborhoods accounted for only 27 percent of other home sales.[8] By 2016, the number of land contracts outpaced the number of mortgages in Detroit.[9]

African Americans are disproportionately confined to land contracts because, in a modern form of redlining, mainstream banks typically do not provide mortgages for homes selling for less than $50,000. Although race neutral on its face, this mortgage limitation has dire racial consequences. Between 2011 and 2017, only 14 percent of mortgages issued in Detroit were for less than $50,000, while about 79 percent of single-family homes sold for this amount.[10] Analyzing Wayne County's other two majority-Black cities, the data shows a similar trend: between 2007 and 2017, the average price of a home was about $25,000 in both Highland Park and Inkster.[11]

Redlining—both modern and historic—has curbed access to mortgages, home repair loans, and other investments in Detroit and other majority-Black cities. And white people, like Jack's family, who live in these Black spaces are also adversely affected. Most importantly, these racist policies transform vulnerable homeowners into prey for legally noncompliant investors like Hamade.

To fight back against Hamade and other legally noncompliant investors, the City of Detroit has launched three principal lines of attack. First, it aggressively issues blight tickets for violations of the

Detroit Property Maintenance Code,[12] which include infractions such as excessive weed or plant growth and failure to remove animal waste or maintain vacant buildings. Records show that the City has issued about 264 blight tickets on properties owned by the various LLCs registered to Hamade and his family, half of which the City dismissed and the other half of which required payment.[13] If Hamade and others fail to pay these blight tickets, then the City can secure the monies owed by garnishing their wages, attaching their assets, and placing a lien on their property.[14] Between January 2004 and April 2021, blight violators paid the City, on average, $1.85 million per year in fines and fees.[15]

In addition to increasing blight tickets, the City of Detroit also began its nuisance abatement program, which brings lawsuits against properties it has designated as a nuisance. Under Michigan common law, a public nuisance is any act that causes "unreasonable interference" with a common right enjoyed by the general public, which includes conduct that is illegal or significantly interferes with people's health and safety.[16] Additionally, under statutes enacted by the State of Michigan and the City of Detroit, nuisance includes everything from failing to keep up a property to neglecting to register a vacant building, as required by law.[17] Consequently, like a sprawling fishing net, nuisance captures a wide range of activities and conditions, giving the nuisance abatement lawsuits an expansive reach and allowing the City to remediate 1,745 properties between 2014 and 2024.[18]

In its written complaints, the City uses the broken windows theory to argue that nuisance produces despair, encourages others to break the law, and adversely affects neighboring properties by opening the door to gang activity, prostitution, arson, drug activity, sexual assaults, fire hazards, vandalism, and rodent infestation.[19] To prove that neglected properties contribute to the blight that is gnawing the city from the inside out, city lawyers pointed to empirical evidence, including a study showing that between 2014 and 2016, there was an 11 percent decline in homicides and serious injuries caused by firearms in the surrounding areas after the demolition of multiple blighted homes.[20] Likewise, City lawyers cite a 2015 study finding that each demolition of a vacant, blighted home within Detroit's Hardest Hit Fund zones increased the value of occupied single-family homes within 500 feet by 4.2 percent.[21]

If the City is successful and the court declares that a property is a nuisance, the owner can retain it only if they sign an agreement, promising to abate the nuisance within six months. If an owner fails to make repairs, the City usurps ownership and transfers the home to the Detroit Land Bank Authority, which sells the property. All Land Bank purchasers contractually agree to rehabilitate the property within six months, thereby mending the nuisance.

Taking title, however, is not the customary remedy for nuisance. Courts can grant damages as well as an injunction or warrant to stop or prevent the nuisance.[22] But the City of Detroit argues that these traditional remedies are inadequate because even after several blight tickets, most owners remain unresponsive, failing to abate the nuisance, which is evidence that they never will. Therefore, a declaration of constructive forfeiture is necessary. The courts have agreed, allowing this extraordinary remedy.

Between 2014 and 2024, the City filed more than 215 nuisance lawsuits relating to over four thousand properties, and just over 35 percent received default judgments because owners did not attend their court dates.[23] This systemic unresponsiveness is connected to Detroit's poor property record keeping, which makes it difficult to identify and locate property owners. The problem is that homebuyers regularly fail to record their ownership by filing a Property Transfer Affidavit (PTA) upon purchase. Some buyers don't do it because they do not know they have to, while for others it is strategic behavior: the maximum fine for late filing is $250, which is a small price to pay if investors want to take advantage of the owner-occupancy status and attendant lower tax liability of the prior owner.

Some commentators believe that the city's nuisance abatement program is illegal because it circumvents state constitutional amendments designed to curb the use of eminent domain to cure blight by increasing the local government's burden of proof.[24] Other legal commentators argue that the program is legal. While the legality of the nuisance abatement program is not clear, what is clear is that it has successfully held legally noncompliant owners accountable, effectively communicating to owners that their property rights come with certain unavoidable duties.

Lastly, to further impede legally noncompliant investors, in 2017, the City of Detroit contracted a law firm called Motor City Law to pursue buyers who, after purchasing their properties from the property tax foreclosure auction, did not bother to pay their property taxes. These buyers breached two agreements — the auction contract and deed covenants — and the City initiated lawsuits to hold these scofflaws accountable. "My hope is that people have confidence that the big landlords, the big auction purchasers, eventually have to pay their taxes just like everybody else," one Motor City Law firm partner said.

In its first set of lawsuits, Motor City Law held the taxpayers of record personally liable for failing to pay property taxes, as mandated by the deed covenants. For these lawsuits, the Wayne County treasurer must have taken the property through tax foreclosure and sold it at auction with a resulting deficiency, which means the proceeds were insufficient to pay the uncollected taxes, fees, interest, penalties, and costs. After the auction, Wayne County has no further authority to collect taxes and charges cities for any deficiencies it was unable to collect. Detroit, in turn, sued the taxpayer of record for these deficiencies.

In 2017, the City sued for a total of $30 million, and a city spokesperson announced, "We're going to continue to file these every year after the foreclosure auction, because as much as this is about recovering money that's due to the City, it's also about disrupting the business model where property owners invest in property, don't pay their taxes and think they can get away with that."[25] Through a memorandum of understanding with other taxing authorities such as the Detroit Zoo and the school district, the City collects monies that the litigation captures on their behalf.

To start the second set of lawsuits, based on the auction contract, Motor City Law first asked Wayne County officials if they would like to undertake this litigation. Wayne County said no. These officials wanted to encourage as many investors as possible to participate in the County's annual property tax auctions, driving the bids and its profits ever higher, so suing investors for failure to abide by the auction contract was contrary to the County's financial interest. Undeterred, Motor City Law successfully convinced the City of Detroit that it had the power to sue as a third-party beneficiary of the auction contract between Wayne County and investors. So, in 2017, the law firm began this line of litigation.

Often a person bids on a property and then transfers the deed of the property it wins to an LLC. Whether or not a bidder becomes the actual owner of the property, they are contractually responsible for the year-of-auction taxes. Additionally, because the deed covenant is included in the auction contract, the deed recipient is contractually responsible for the year-of-auction taxes plus two additional years. Even if they transfer the property to a third party within the three-year period, the deed recipient is still liable for all the taxes, unless the third party contractually assumes this liability.

Each year, Wayne County has only reluctantly provided the data required for these lawsuits. "By the end of the first week of February, the City was unable to get any response from the County of Wayne giving us the data that we needed," one Motor City Law partner noted with frustration. "I don't know why they were holding up the data, but they did it every year. They don't like the lawsuit." By securing the data from other sources, the law firm was able to push forward despite Wayne County's obstructive tactics.

About 80 percent of defendants do not appear in court, entitling the City to default judgments in its favor. But even when defendants do show up, battling the City can be like trying to slay a dragon with a butter knife. "To get it all sorted out, it would have cost so much just to try to defend myself. So the best course of action just turned out to be me making an agreement and taking the settlement," said a defendant who bid on several auction properties on behalf of a company but was never a deed holder. "Nobody wanted to go up against them."

Even though arguably heavy-handed, the lawsuits were holding legally noncompliant investors accountable. "Well, I can tell you that we've chased a whole bunch of people out of the auction process that just abused the hell out of it," a Motor City Law partner said with pride. "People that used to buy three hundred or four hundred properties that are no longer showing up to bid because of the potential liability." One person who is no longer participating in the auction is Mr. Hamade, the owner of Suburban Renaissance, who profited from the poverty and desperation of Jack Baskin and hundreds of other Detroit homeowners.

According to the lawsuit, from 2010 to 2016, Mr. Hamade and his family purchased over 550 properties from the property tax foreclosure auction under about 80 different LLCs, prompting the City to call Hamade "the poster boy for bulk buyers and landlords who have abused the WCT's [Wayne County treasurer's] auction process." The City added that "Hamade has made millions doing so while the properties he purchased and subsequently forfeited continue to deteriorate and re-cycle through the auction process."[26]

Although Michigan law prohibits individuals and companies who fail to pay their property taxes from participating in the tax auction, investors routinely dissolve one LLC and participate in the auction under a new one. This is the ruse Hamade adopted. Consequently, in its written briefs, the City argued that Hamade "set up new limited liability companies to avoid being barred from the 2012

Auction because his previous entities failed to pay tax obligations. Defendant Hamade was able to outbid honest bidders because his business plan did not include paying taxes. These actions reduced the City's tax receipts and its ability to fund its schools, police and fire departments, and other public services to improve the lives of Detroit's residents."[27]

In a 2018 settlement, Hamade paid the City $240,000 for properties he personally bid on and won in the 2011 tax auction and subsequently failed to pay the property taxes on.[28] The City also won $300,000 in judgments against LLCs Hamade admitted to controlling or solely owning.[29] But once the lawsuits are filed six years later, it is almost impossible to collect from LLCs that hold deeds because owners usually have dissolved these entities. Michigan has only a two-year statute of limitations for unlawful distributions to LLC members.

Nonetheless, Motor City Law remained optimistic about collecting the $300,000 from Hamade's LLCs, as well as monies due from other LLCs. "I'm pretty good at piercing the veil of limited liability," one partner said confidently. "I spent thirty-plus years litigating those kinds of cases." In Michigan, to hold an individual personally liable for the actions of an LLC (that is, to pierce the corporate veil), the LLC must be a mere instrumentality of the individual, and the LLC must have been used to commit a wrong or fraud that caused unjust injury or loss.[30] Despite the firm's confidence, this is a tall order. Success will be difficult to achieve.

In addition to his 2011 purchases, the City is also suing Hamade for 205 properties he purchased at the 2012 tax auction for a total of $523,008 and sold for $913,465.[31] The City is claiming damages of $442,377 for unpaid taxes, fees, and costs. The City also added demolition costs because in addition to agreeing to pay taxes, the auction contract requires owners to "improve, maintain, or demolish their auction purchases."[32] According to the complaint: "The City had to demolish 3 Auction Property structures. When 18 Auction

Properties were re-auctioned in 2015 and 2016, they received no bids and ended up in the Detroit Land Bank Authority's inventory. When re-auctioned in 2015 and 2016, 26 Auction Properties sold for $30,241 less than they were sold to Defendant Hamade at the 2012 Auction. These results can all be attributed to the deterioration of the properties' condition during the time of Defendant Hamade's control."

Each year, the City has continued suing Mr. Hamade and other auction buyers who have failed to pay their property taxes. Because it gets paid a percentage of the monies collected, Motor City Law litigates aggressively. "Our up-front cost to get this program kicked off in 2017 was, I don't know, a million bucks that we came out of pocket," a partner said. Although it is impossible to collect all monies due, the lawsuits have been lucrative for both the City and the law firm. And as the case of Michael G. Kelly demonstrates, the lawsuits have given the City other economic advantages.

Kelly has purchased over a thousand Detroit properties from the property tax foreclosure auction. He personally bid on several properties and hence was contractually liable to pay the year-of-auction taxes. The City needed certain properties he owned in and around a Detroit neighborhood called Eastern Market and near the new Chrysler plant, on the city's east side, for a development project. Kelly, knowing that the City desperately needed his properties, began making outrageous demands.

But the City used to its advantage the fact that it was suing him for unpaid blight tickets and his failure to pay the year-of-auction taxes, as required by the contract. In October 2018, Kelly gave the City thirty-eight properties near the Chrysler plant and twenty-three properties in Eastern Market. In exchange, the City forgave several blight tickets and canceled pending lawsuits on seventy-five properties,[33] all debts released totaling more than $2 million.[34] Then, in May 2019, the City gave Kelly fourteen of its properties in exchange for five of his.[35] While many commentators believed that the City was taken for a fool in these two deals, one Motor City Law partner was, nevertheless, pleased. He said, "We were able to leverage these third-party lawsuits to achieve objectives that the City thought were important."

Although these auction lawsuits have successfully reined in several legally noncompliant investors, they are not without their flaws. While the lawsuits are meant to punish errant landlords whose business model is based on not paying their property taxes, distressed homeowners sometimes become collateral damage. To minimize the chances of this happening, "we have to show that an individual owns more than two properties in Wayne County," one Motor City Law partner said. "But if you're an LLC, a corporation, or a partnership, I don't have to prove that you own more than two properties."

Since the law firm earns a percentage of all monies it secures, to recoup the initial investment and turn a profit, it is in the firm's interest to cast a wide net, and vulnerable Detroit homeowners, such as Charles Biggams, have gotten caught in the imbroglio. Charles worked as a building engineer for the Detroit Public Schools for over thirty years. In 2007, he purchased an east side home via a land contract for $80,000. After about three years of monthly installments, he paid down $20,000, but the Great Recession hit, tanking home values. "Now the houses on that street are worth five thousand dollars, so there's no way I was going to pay sixty thousand dollars when all the homes are selling for four thousand dollars, five thousand dollars," Charles said. "So I called the owner up and told him that I was going to move, and so that's what I did. I gave him the house back and I moved."

Going through a very similar situation, Charles's friend allowed the bank to reclaim her home, and since she had already moved out, Charles moved in temporarily. "While I was staying there, I was on vacation at the time, so I just went out to the restaurant, got some breakfast. I was gone four hours," Charles recalled. "When I got back to the house, somebody had broke in and stole everything I own. I left everything packed because I wasn't gonna stay there long." Exasperated, he added, "Man, it was horrible." Robbers pulled up to the home with a U-Haul and carried away all of his belongings, even his bulky washer and dryer. They got away because the neighbors assumed Charles had hired a moving crew.

With no clothes or furniture, Charles moved into a one-story, 720-square-foot bungalow on Grandville Avenue. This wood-paneled home sat on a spacious corner lot, its doors and windows clad with wrought iron security bars. Although records show that in 2004, the home carried a mortgage of about $92,000 — before the 2008 Great Recession eviscerated home values in Detroit — Charles purchased it for only $6,500 in 2009. Astonishingly, his property tax bill was approximately $3,000, almost half the property's purchase price. Charles did not appeal because, at the time, he did not know he could.

"I thought it was high," Charles said. "I just assumed it's high because it was a corner house. I said, 'They must be trying to get me to pay because it's on two streets.'" In addition to the City's overinflated valuation of his home, his property tax bill was high because, in order to avoid Detroit's astronomical car insurance rates, his driver's license listed an empty lot he owned in the nearby suburb as his home address. Consequently, Charles did not qualify for the homestead exemption, which reduces the tax liability of owner-occupiers.

In 2011, Detroit's embattled public-school authority implemented severe budget cuts, which terminated Charles's long-held employment and commenced a financially turbulent period in his life. "I just couldn't keep the payments up because the taxes was high," Charles lamented. Records show that, as with so many other struggling Detroit homeowners, his property taxes were not just high, they violated the Michigan Constitution. In 2011, the City of Detroit estimated the market value of Charles's property at $46,876 and taxed him accordingly, although the City's own sales data shows that the home was actually worth closer to $4,500, about ten times less.

When Charles could not afford to pay the illegally inflated property taxes, the County attached the statutory 18 percent interest penalty to his delinquent bills, making it even more difficult for him to catch up on his payments. The County allowed him to enter a payment plan, but it did not help because, while it gave him more time to pay, it did not reduce his illegally inflated property tax bill. Consequently, in 2013, Charles was no longer able to pay his property tax bill, which he reports had swelled to over $9,000. So Wayne County foreclosed on his home and sold it at auction.

Charles was, however, able to buy his home back at auction a few months later for $5,600 because the law prohibiting owners from repurchasing their homes at auction did not come into force until 2017. Even though Charles recovered his beloved home, there was no happy ending. The City continued to overassess his property, leading to illegally inflated property tax bills that he still could not afford to pay. Although Charles repurchased his home for $5,600 and comparable homes in his area sold for this amount or lower, his property tax bill was about $2,100 in 2013, $1,400 in 2014, $1,300 in 2015, and $1,200 in 2016. In 2016, the City's sales data reveals that his home was worth about $4,000, but the City assessed it as if it were worth about $23,000, about five times more than its true value.

Charles was not alone. Between 2010 and 2017, thirty of the fifty-eight homes on Charles's city block alone completed the property tax foreclosure process after the City illegally inflated their property tax assessments. As a result, homes stood empty, blight took hold, and the neighborhood rapidly began to deteriorate. Things got so bad that when he left his home one day, audacious thieves stole one of his cars from his driveway in broad daylight. Since the security gate that surrounded his house was chained closed, the robbers hooked it to a tow truck, yanked it down, stormed into his driveway, and carried his car off with the tow truck, all in a blink of an eye.

More interestingly, Charles never reported the car stolen because downtown — the location of both the main police station and the office where Detroiters must protest property taxes — is an unfriendly and difficult environment to navigate. "I went to the police station near downtown and there wasn't too many places to park, so I kind of pulled over where I could put my vehicle, and I got out," Charles said. "And then the police started snapping at me. Just real nasty. So I'm like, 'Man, forget it.' I just got in my car and left."

In addition, several security cameras fastened to the wall of the church across the street caught another burglary, on a different day, from beginning to end. The footage showed a robber removing an air-conditioning unit from Charles's neighbor's window, breaking into her house, and stealing her purse. Upon exiting the house, the burglar peeked into Charles's car but decided to keep moving. The camera showed the robbers entering a house five doors down and never coming out, apparently returning home. Neighbors were robbing neighbors. On yet another occasion, a thief tried to break into Charles's home by ripping the wrought iron security door from his home's side entrance. They were, however, unable to enter because the door was nailed shut from the inside.

As if all this were not bad enough, gunfire in Charles's neighborhood went from occasional to commonplace. One night, "I was laying in bed. I heard something go bang. And I'm like, 'Damn, who's that?' They out here shooting," Charles said, distress rocketing his voice up two octaves. "So I said, 'Oh well.' I just stayed in bed. So when I woke up that morning, I said, 'What's all this dust?' And I looked up in the ceiling, and it was a big gouge in the ceiling. Then I looked over by the window, next to the window, just above it, it was a hole in the wall. And the bullet was laying on the floor in the house." Shaking his head, he added, "I could have possibly got hit if I was walking up the stairs at that time."

In yet another episode of violence, a group of young people moved into the neighborhood and invited their friends to squat in a vacant home next door. "A car drove down the street, a guy popped up out the sunroof, and shot up the house where the squatters was," Charles reported. "And I'm like, 'I can't deal with all this shooting.'" Fed up with the theft and gun violence in his neighborhood, Charles fled to Southfield, a nearby suburb, and never again returned to his home on Grandville Avenue. Since moving, he has never heard a single gunshot or been robbed.

Unable to pay both his rent in Southfield and his Detroit property taxes, Charles allowed his home on Grandville Avenue to go into tax foreclosure once again because he said, "I just didn't feel comfortable being there anymore." In 2018, Wayne County sold his home at its tax auction for $9,200, and just about a year later, the auction buyer flipped the house, selling it for $40,000.

In January 2021, the City of Detroit sued Charles for $7,500 because he had failed to pay the 2013, 2014, and 2015 property taxes after reacquiring his home through the tax auction in 2013. According to the City's written complaint, while the unpaid taxes amounted to $3,920, the penalty, fees, and costs tacked on amounted to another $3,647. Struggling to understand why the City would sue him for $7,500, Charles concluded, "I guess they need money. Just being greedy. They just throwing stuff against the wall to see what sticks."

Charles is on several medications to control his heart problems, and the stress of the lawsuit is compounding his ailments. He is working with a lawyer, who charges $250 per hour, to defend himself, hoping the City will dismiss the suit before the legal bill upends the new life he was able to build in Southfield. All of Charles's stress and legal bills could have been avoided if the City had instructed its lawyers not to sue individuals who owned fewer than five homes in Wayne County, which would ensure that it was going after only the worst offenders rather than vulnerable homeowners like Charles who abandoned his home because, as he said, "I can't live like this."

The auction lawsuits, along with the city's other two mechanisms for holding slumlords accountable — the blight tickets and nuisance abatement lawsuits — are all blunt instruments that embroil bad actors along with others. Moving forward, the City must act with much more precision, ensuring that its nets catch slumlords, like Hamade and Kelly, without also entangling homeowners, like Charles, who are only searching for peace and safety.

PART IV:

GOVERNMENT ENTITIES THAT PROFIT FROM RACIST POLICIES

The Grandson's Plan

15

THE INFAMOUS TURNAROUND PLAN

When Robert Ficano was a child, his grandpa Bucci, a UAW diehard, would take him to the Local 182's annual Christmas party without fail. "They had great gifts. I had the first camera I ever had. It was plastic," Robert said fondly. "They lined us all up and Santa Claus came in." For a kid in the 1960s, receiving a plastic camera was as exhilarating as receiving one of Willy Wonka's golden tickets, so the union earned unmitigated reverence from all the children in attendance, especially little Bobby. As he grew older, Robert's union loyalty also grew because, over the years, Grandpa Bucci faithfully took his grandson to UAW events and activities.

Robert would one day hold the highest office in Wayne County, and his journey to this post began at these UAW Christmas parties and activities, which piqued his interest in unions and politics. His political journey took further shape in 1972 when, as an undergraduate at Michigan State University, he won his first election. Robert defeated "an old-timer" for the post of precinct delegate, representing the Livonia and Redford areas in the Democratic Party's state convention. At this point, it became clear to Grandpa Bucci that his grandson's interest in politics was not fleeting, so in Robert's senior year at Michigan State, as he considered whether or not to attend law school, Grandpa Bucci offered some sage advice.

"Grandpa, it's twelve years straight of K through twelve, then four straight years at the university, so I'm thinking of just taking a break," Robert told his grandfather. "Or you know what? Instead of law school, why don't I maybe do labor relations? I might have an interest. They have a master's program up here."

"Wait a minute!" Grandpa Bucci replied, his tone urgent. "Look, you have a strong interest in politics. But if you really ever get into politics for a living, you've got to have a 'tell them to go to hell' degree."

"What in God's name are you talking about?" Robert asked, mouth agape.

"If you are ever in a political office and somebody comes to you and they want you to do something that's unethical or that you're not comfortable with or whatever it is, you can tell 'em to go to hell because you've got another profession," Grandpa Bucci explained with a certitude hard-won through decades of struggle. "I want you to go straight through to law school. Right now."

Robert did just what Grandpa Bucci commanded. Upon receiving his bachelor's degree in 1974, Robert enrolled in law school at the University of Detroit Mercy, graduated in 1977, and later that year passed the Michigan bar exam. Little Bobby successfully executed the plan born that long-ago day when he bounced into Grandpa Bucci's lap and discovered that he could not follow in his grandfather's footsteps and become a factory worker.

With a law license in hand, it was time for Robert to start a family of his own. In 1979, he married Rosemarie, whom he first met when they were both students at Michigan State, working in the Michigan Parks and Recreation Division one summer. They served Grandpa Bucci's potent homemade wine at the wedding, and all the guests left feeling very good. Nobody, however, left feeling better than Grandpa Bucci because he knew his only grandson would be able to return home each night to his family without oil-stained hands.

Robert practiced law as an associate at Wilson, Deremo & Raymond and then at Bokos, Jones & Plakas. Since Grandpa Bucci had instilled in him the importance of unions, Robert most enjoyed his work negotiating labor relations between the City of Westland and their fire and police departments. Because Robert's political aspirations never faded, while practicing law, he served as the chair of the Democratic Party's Second District in Wayne County.

Then, in 1979, a state representative covering Westland and Livonia, Robert Law, resigned, so there was a special election, and after knocking on practically every door in the district, Robert won the Democratic primary. "Oddly enough, the woman who won the Republican primary was my old den mother from Cub Scouts," Robert remembered with a smile. "Crazy, I know." Although he won the primary, Robert lost the general election by about a hundred votes, a crushing disappointment made bearable only by the fact that his opponent, Sylvia Scarelle, was always "very polite, very nice" to little Bobby from her Cub Scout troop, who had grown into an honorable man.

Robert did not allow this defeat to extinguish his fire for politics, policy, and government service. He eventually left the practice of law altogether to become the deputy to Wayne County's clerk, James Killeen. This positioned Robert for his big break in 1982, when Sheriff Bill Lucas successfully ran for the newly created office of Wayne County executive, leaving his office vacant. The county clerk, chief judge of probate, and county prosecutor had the power to appoint the sheriff's successor, but they could not agree.

As Robert remembers it, all the suggested successors "had one vote. Nobody had two votes out of the three. So I was the compromise." Robert continued, "What really gave me the edge was there was a huge labor dispute with the deputies' unions. I had a lot of experience from Westland dealing with labor unions." The trio appointed Robert, and without even a day of law enforcement experience, he officially became the Wayne County sheriff in 1983.[1] In the next scheduled election, Robert ran as the incumbent and won by a sizable margin, and he went on to win many more elections, serving almost twenty years as the Wayne County sheriff.

While Robert enjoyed being sheriff, his political ambitions swelled beyond the office. In fact, before the chief judge of probate, Joseph Pernick, cast his vote to appoint Robert to his post, he spoke frankly.

"You know what?" Joseph asked.

"What?" Robert replied with anxious anticipation.

"I'm going to vote for you," Joseph announced. "But you have got to promise me something."

"What's that?" Robert replied, eyebrows instinctively rising.

"You can't stay in that job," Joseph said, much to Robert's surprise. "You've got too much talent to stay there. The sheriff's a comfortable job. You probably could get re-elected a hundred times once you're in there and you got the system down. But you have got to do other things." Robert took Joseph's advice to heart and ran for Wayne County executive in 2002. He won and remained in that office until 2014.

While Robert was county executive, his team penned the infamous 2014 Turnaround Plan, which is the key to understanding how Wayne County reaped the greatest profits from property tax delinquency and foreclosure in Detroit, even more than John Hantz, Dwayne Davis, Piper and Seamus O'Grady, Michael Hamade, and other buyers in its property tax auctions.

It all started when Detroit went through its bankruptcy in 2013. Wayne County watched apprehensively because it, too, had severe budget shortfalls and was heading toward a financial emergency. In 2012, the County overestimated revenues by $12.5 million and underestimated expenditures by $23.7 million. Likewise, in 2013, the County overestimated revenues by $26.5 million and underestimated expenditures by $16.7 million.[2] The County's budget deficit reached $154.4 million.[3] In 2014, the County had only 45 percent of the funds required to pay its pension obligations in full, and less than 1 percent of the monies to pay its healthcare–related obligations.[4] As a consequence, by 2015, investors began to question the County's financial future.[5] Moody's and Fitch credit rating agencies downgraded Wayne County to a noninvestment grade (or junk) rating, while Standard & Poor's placed the County on its CreditWatch, alerting investors that a negative rating action in the next ninety days was likely.[6] Wayne County was teetering on the brink of financial disaster.

But how did Wayne County end up in financial turmoil when, in 2008, the County had an operating surplus of $18 million?[7] The Great Recession and the ensuing mortgage foreclosure crisis caused home values to decline precipitously, and consequently so did property tax revenues, which from 2006 to 2009 constituted around 20 percent of Wayne County's budget.[8] Between 2007 and 2014, the taxable value of all properties in Wayne County dropped by a total of 36 percent, declining from $132 billion to $85 billion.[9] Accordingly, between 2007 and 2015, property tax revenues fell by approximately 24 percent.[10]

Additionally, unwise decisions made by Wayne County's leadership contributed to its financial mayhem, with the failed jail construction being their most conspicuous and politically explosive debacle. Since Governor John Engler shut down most of Michigan's mental health facilities in the 1990s, the Wayne County Jail has replaced them, functioning as one of the state's largest mental health facilities.[11] Inmates abounded.

As the former Wayne County sheriff in charge of the jails, Robert knew that the County's three detention facilities were desperately overcrowded. "Quite frankly, the jails were a disaster," Robert said. "Something had to be done to build them. We had a huge shovel-ready grant from the Obama administration available that made the bonds easier." In 2011, two years before Detroit's bankruptcy, the County's leadership approved $300 million in bonds to finance a new jail.[12]

The jail build was an unequivocal disaster "that just exacerbated the whole financial crisis," Robert admitted. "What had happened was there was a general contractor who was supposed to make sure that they're all doing what they're supposed to do under a budget and the company that was supposed to do it got bought out, and so they didn't have a team that actually watched it for about two months or three months. They came back and said, 'Oh, it's gonna be over budget.' I said, 'You're giving me a report that said everything was okay.' And so at that point they said, 'Oh, don't worry, government's always over budget on these kind of projects.' I said, 'No, stop, we're gonna sue,' which politically cost me tremendously."

Facing anywhere between $42 million and $91 million in estimated cost overruns,[13] Wayne County authorities suspended further construction and then filed a lawsuit against the contractor and project manager. Although Wayne County suspended construction, they could not suspend the $14.3 million in bond debt service due annually. The County had borrowed money to pay for the jail, and the creditors demanded their money; the construction crews needed their money; and the lawyers suing the project manager would not be denied their money. The County, however, was out of money.

With millions spent and absolutely nothing to show for it, voters resented these payments and questioned the need for a new jail in the first place. That skepticism was confirmed years later when, within three months after the onset of the coronavirus pandemic in 2020, the County was able to reduce its prison occupancy by about 40 percent through administrative release programs like tethers and bond reductions.[14] Wayne County unnecessarily condemned its citizens to jail cells while also financially imprisoning itself.

As a result of the financial turmoil, in 2013, after the State of Michigan appointed Kevyn Orr as Detroit's emergency manager, many assumed it was just a matter of time until Wayne County also declared bankruptcy, unwillingly received an emergency manager, or both. According to Robert, "Governor Snyder and the Treasury

Department really pushed for an emergency manager of some type," but County officials fought like wildcats to avoid this outcome. Robert recoiled at even the thought of an emergency manager because "in essence you're setting a czar," he said. "It wasn't representative government."

Robert's reference to a czar is not wildly off the mark. Imagine for a moment a situation in medieval Europe, where one of the czar's noblemen has positioned his castle and crops on the most fertile lands adjacent to the river's source. Then, one day, the nobleman decides to construct a dam to redirect even more water toward his crops, depriving his serfs downstream of the water necessary for their crops to flourish. When the serfs' lands become unproductive and they thus can no longer pay their tributes and taxes, the nobleman condemns them for poor management of their resources, takes over their farms, and implements draconian cost-cutting measures. The serfs can only regain control of their farms once the nobleman determines that they can, once again, responsibly manage them. Everyone in the empire ignores the damage done by the nobleman's decision to erect the dam, and instead they focus on the serfs and their personal irresponsibility.

The czar was Governor Rick Snyder and the noblemen were his executive administrators. The dam erected was the 2012 Economic Vitality Incentive Program (EVIP), which reduced discretionary revenue-sharing payments to localities by about one-third.[15] But once the State's budgetary problems subsided, revenue-sharing payments never returned to their pre-EVIP levels,[16] leaving Wayne County and many other localities in the economic bind from which they were struggling to emerge. Instead of acknowledging its role in producing the financial chaos, the State threatened to appoint an emergency manager to take control from irresponsible officials and balance the budget.

In Michigan, emergency managers are controversial. For some period between 2008 and 2013, 51 percent of Michigan's Black population was living under emergency management, and for every 10 percent increase in the local Black population, the odds that the State of Michigan will assign an emergency manager increases 50 percent.[17] White flight and the racialized disinvestment that followed have predisposed majority-Black cities to fiscal distress.[18] So although, on its face, the emergency management law is race neutral, it has had racialized consequences.

Nevertheless, in 2011, the state legislature enacted Public Act 4 (PA 4), drastically expanding emergency managers' powers by allowing them to take actions like temporarily preempting collective bargaining laws and modifying city ordinances.[19] In response to this unprecedented assignment of power, Michigan voters placed a referendum on the ballot to repeal the new law, and won a hotly contested election by 52 percent to 48 percent.[20] One month after this victory, however, the Michigan legislature introduced PA 436, which made no changes to the recently defeated emergency management law other than including an appropriations measure to pay emergency managers' salaries because Article II, section 9 of the Michigan Constitution states that the power of referendum "does not extend to acts making appropriations for state institutions or to meet deficiencies in state funds."[21] On January 24, 2013, Snyder signed the very slightly revised version of the emergency manager law that voters had rejected in the referendum. Through a nakedly anti-democratic process, these unelected emergency managers, whom voters had expressly rejected in a statewide referendum, were again positioned to overrule democratically elected leaders and dictate policy, most heavily affecting Michigan's Black cities.

Today, emergency managers in Michigan can receive and disburse all federal, state, and local funds; modify or terminate existing contracts or collective bargaining agreements; remove or replace trustees of the local pension board; eliminate local government departments; sell or transfer local government assets; reduce employment and cut wages; and take over any local government entity.[22] Most commonly, emergency managers have used their escalated powers to "gut the employees," Robert said. "I did not want this, so we fought it." He continued, "Yeah, they would have balanced the budget, but it would have been a lot of people that worked [for the County] for years suddenly losing everything. I just didn't want a legacy that we were going to succumb because this seems to be the easy way to do it." To avoid the appointment of an emergency manager, Robert and his team implemented a series of measures.

Most notably, his administration fought against the unions, which likely caused Grandpa Bucci to turn over in his grave. Even though benefits constituted 70 percent of the County's long-term liabilities,[23] collective bargaining units fought hard to prevent reductions. As a compromise, Robert implemented a 10 percent across-the-board cut in salaries, which he believed was necessary to avoid the more drastic cuts that would inevitably come with emergency management. After the cuts were finalized, Robert was at a UAW event, and a union executive made a beeline for him, intent on asking him just one question: "Did you take the ten percent cut, too?" When Robert replied, "Yes," the UAW rep said, "Then I have no problem with this." This short exchange made Robert feel as though he had done right by Grandpa Bucci.

After the pay cut, Robert's administration had only one strong play left — the turnaround plan, a budgeting strategy outlined in a document dated February 11, 2014, from Robert Ficano to the Wayne County Commission.[24] Between 2015 and 2019, the Turnaround Plan relied upon $286 million in revenue from the Delinquent Tax Revolving Fund (also known as the revolving fund) to cover the County's budget deficit. Consequently, understanding the revolving fund is key to grasping how Wayne County fled from emergency management and bankruptcy on the backs of Detroit homeowners and the illegally inflated property taxes and resulting foreclosures that they endured.

Prior to the year 2000, Michigan had in place a property tax lien system, which enlists private investors to collect delinquent property taxes. With twenty-eight states using the lien system, this is the most common property tax debt collection system in the U.S.[25] In Michigan, if in any given year a homeowner failed to pay their full property tax bill, on December 1, the city placed a lien on the property for the unpaid amount.

After three years, counties sold the liens to investors through their annual auction at a price equivalent to the overdue tax, fees, and interest owed.[26] The investor who bid the smallest ownership interest (if tax foreclosure occurred and they therefore acquired ownership rights) won the lien at auction. If owners failed to repay the debt, then investors had a right to foreclose on their homes to collect the debt. Investors profited by charging owners 15 percent annual interest,[27] and an additional penalty equivalent to 50 percent of the unpaid debt.[28] If foreclosure occurred, investors also made a profit through their ownership interest.[29]

There were numerous problems with this system: interest and legal fees quickly mushroomed the original debt; investors failed to provide legally required notices, making ownership transfers legally questionable; non-competitive bidding occurred at the auction; and lien holders often foreclosed and sold homes for minuscule debts, all because vulnerable homeowners did not understand the complex system. These problems with the tax lien system were not unique to Michigan. The U.S. Department of Justice has, for instance, prosecuted entities for rigging tax lien sale auctions in several states, including New Jersey and Maryland.[30]

Michigan moved away from its ineffective and predatory tax lien system in 1999 and established a new property tax debt collection system, which is centered upon the Delinquent Tax Revolving Fund. The revolving fund is designed to counter volatile local government revenues caused by tax delinquency, thereby securing the monies necessary to provide public services such as schools, libraries, and parks without interruption.[31] When a property owner fails to pay their property taxes for one whole year, the city sends the debt to the county on March 1. If the county does not have sufficient funds to assume the debt,[32] it issues bonds purchased by private banks. With these funds, the county will advance the unpaid taxes to localities so that their immediate ability to provide services is not impaired.

The county then becomes the debt collector entitled to the base tax, the statutorily mandated 18 percent interest rate, fines, costs, and revenues from property tax foreclosure sales. Most importantly, the law mandates that counties deposit all monies received from property tax delinquencies into the revolving fund, which includes both surplus and profit. *Surplus* is the amount remaining after counties advance money to their cities, while *profit* is the surplus minus bond interest rates, administration fees, and other transaction costs.

Michigan's current property tax debt collection system is, indeed, complicated. But when we focus on Myrisha's individual experience, this convoluted system becomes more understandable. Once Grandma Brown died in 2008 and Myrisha inherited the Baylis home, she took over the property tax payments. The City of Detroit billed Myrisha on July 1 and December 1 of each year. When she did not pay the bill on time, the City levied a 0.5 percent interest rate on the past due amount each month.[33] On March 1, 2009, the 2008 property taxes officially became delinquent and the County assumed the unpaid debt and increased the interest to 18 percent, applied retroactively to the date when the taxes were first due.[34]

In addition to interest penalties, as Myrisha's legacy slid into tax foreclosure, a slew of additional costs accumulated, including an administration fee (4 percent), an annual fee for providing notice of delinquency ($1 to $5), a per-parcel fee ($15), a title search fee ($175), a forfeiture certificate filing fee ($9), a redemption certificate recording fee ($9), a mailing and publication fee ($40), and a posting fee ($100). Wayne County deposited all interest, penalties, fees, and costs collected from Myrisha and others into the revolving fund. As shown in

Figure 6, from 2008 to 2012, Wayne County's surplus amounted to over one-third of what Myrisha owed.

Figure 6: Myrisha's Property Tax Bill

	Base tax	Fees/int. paid	Total paid	% surplus
2008	1,083.33	1,088.08	2,171.41	50
2009	1,049.03	871.64	1,920.67	45
2010	1,065.28	767.05	1,832.33	42
2011	1,421.05	592.58	2,013.63	29
2012	1,333.57	93.35	1,426.92	7
Total	5,952.26	3,412.70	9,364.96	36

In 2016, Wayne County anticipated $7.9 million in revenue from interest, fees, and fines from property tax delinquency and forfeiture.[35] In 2017, it anticipated around $8.9 million.[36] Between 2009 and 2016, Loveland Technologies (now doing business as Regrid) estimates that the revolving fund's various streams of revenue brought in from $399,923,489 in 2009 to $230,842,267 in 2016, and its surplus was $60,457,170 in 2013, and $29,342,843 in 2015.[37]

For a financially ailing county, the surplus, earned from Myrisha and others struggling to pay their property taxes, was desperately needed to cover its structural deficit. But were transfers from the revolving fund to the County's general fund to cover fiscal shortfalls even legal? At first glance, it appears that these transfers did not comport with the revolving fund's singular purpose, which was to obtain "funds to pay to all taxing units within the county the total amount of delinquent real property taxes, which have not been collected by the due date."[38] But the statute also specifically provides that "any surplus in the fund may be transferred to the county general fund by appropriate action of the county board of commissioners."

Who exactly had the power to declare a surplus and transfer it to the general fund? Was it Robert, who was the county executive? Was it the county commissioners? Or the county treasurer, Raymond Wojtowicz, who served in the position from 1976 to 2015? Customarily, it had been the treasurer, but Robert argued that this was wrong. A document signed by Robert's chief and deputy financial officers argued that, although the General Property Tax Act designates the treasurer as the fund's agent and hence the power to transfer the surplus historically has resided with the treasurer,[39] this was wrong because "the statute refers to 'any surplus' in the fund, not 'any surplus as determined in the discretion' of any particular party."[40]

Robert lost this political fight. In the end, so long as he did not commingle revolving fund monies with other funds in his custody,[41] the treasurer maintained almost complete control over the revolving fund. So every year, Robert had to fight with the treasurer to get the funds he desperately needed for the County's budget. "He would give some money, but it was always like hat in hand going over and trying to get it. He gave us slight amounts. We never anticipated getting it because the treasurer never would let loose of it." This is because — while the county executive and commission had an incentive to maximize transfers from the revolving fund to the general fund — Treasurer Wojtowicz had a personal financial incentive to stockpile the money.

Under Michigan's Public Act 206, beginning in 1976, county treasurers could receive a bonus of up to 20 percent of their salary for managing the revolving fund.[42] While most Michigan county treasurers had this bonus incorporated into their salaries, Wayne County did not do this. In an interview conducted before he died in January 2020 at age ninety, Raymond Wojtowicz explained how he had profited from the revolving fund. "There was a legitimate point of compensation for county treasurers who had a revolving fund and was agent of the fund. There was an agency fee that was paid proportionally. Most of my colleagues throughout the state of Michigan, when the law was enacted years ago, had that agency fee incorporated into their regular salary, whatever it was. Mine was not." As wrinkles of regret showed through his time-worn skin, Treasurer Wojtowicz continued, "I was very disappointed that mine wasn't included right up front at the beginning like the others." Treasurer Wojtowicz, instead, received an agency fee.

In 2012, Robert picked what would turn out to be the costliest fight of his political career — he crossed Treasurer Wojtowicz by lobbying to eliminate his agency fee.[43] "We stepped up on that to try to stop it and that caused a lot of ill will because Wojtowicz didn't want it to stop," Robert remembered, wagging his head from side to side. "But, morally, we just felt no public official should personally benefit from hardships on others."

The treasurer was furious with Robert for messing with his money. Cautiously selecting his words, Treasurer Wojtowicz said, "I also feel very bad and sorrowful a particular legislator had the law amended, allowing the agency fee to be repealed, and I did not then qualify for it." In an increasingly dispirited tone, he continued, "And I lost that kind of compensation for a job that was really very, very important."

Like a bear extracting honey from a busy hive, Robert's decision to go after the treasurer was dangerous. Without sullying his reputation for professionalism, Treasurer Wojtowicz would eventually exact a stinging revenge. That day came in 2014, when the electorate was fuming because financial chaos had overtaken Wayne County on Robert's watch. If Robert did not fix the situation, voters were going to boot him out of office and end his political career, so he urgently needed access to the revolving fund surplus in order to balance the budget and make things right. "Therefore, we recommend the unrestricted fund balance of the Delinquent Tax Revolving Fund which at September 30, 2013 amounted to $81 million, be used to reduce the accumulated deficit,"[44] Robert's team wrote in a memo.

Since Treasurer Wojtowicz controlled these funds, he could ignore Robert's recommendation and hold back the money. So Robert did what any other dignified politician in this situation would do. He began to beg. "Look, if you're going to collect the money, put it into the general fund because we need it at this point," Robert pleaded with the treasurer. "We're bleeding right now."

Nevertheless, with Robert's political career hanging in the balance, Treasurer Wojtowicz denied his request. That is, the treasurer would not allow Robert to use funds derived principally from property tax delinquency and foreclosure in Detroit to balance Wayne County's budget. Robert fought like a bear to balance the budget and prevent the state from taking over Wayne County, but in the 2014 election, dissatisfied voters sent him into hibernation because of the yawning deficit.

"When I left office, we probably would have had about one hundred million or about eighty million dollars to finish the deficit," Robert said, referring to the revolving fund surplus. "Politically, he held it back until the new exec came in and then, voilà, the budget had 'balanced' on it."[45] Revenge is a dish best served cold.

Robert secured only 6 percent of the vote in the Democratic primary,[46] which is an astonishingly low number for an incumbent. "I'd been in office a long time," he explained. "And I think people were very frustrated because the economy was so down, and then you had this jail debt service expense that was coming up." Warren Evans emerged from the general election as Wayne County's new executive after receiving about 70 percent of the vote.[47] Conjecturing about why he trounced Robert, Warren concluded, "I think it was as much him self-destructing as it was me winning."

On January 1, 2015, Warren Evans became Wayne County's fifth executive. The pressing question became: With an African American who was born and raised in Detroit now at the helm, would the County stop transferring monies from the revolving fund to the general budget, thereby allowing the majority-white County to profit from property tax delinquency and foreclosure in Detroit, the majority-Black city?

16

BLOOD MONEY

Born in Tennessee on May 15, 1883, Warren Evans's maternal grand-father, Albert Buford Cleage Sr., was the son of a slave. He defied the expectations and restrictions of his time to become a medical doctor.[1] He studied at Knoxville College, a historically Black educational institution, and then went on to Indiana University School of Medicine, where he graduated second in his class. In 1916, as the Great Migration swelled Detroit's African American population, Warren's grandfather established a medical practice in the city, providing treatment for Blacks when white doctors and institutions would not. In 1918, he cofounded Dunbar Hospital, the first hospital for Detroit's Black residents.[2]

Warren's paternal grandfather came from Alabama to work at Ford Motor Company when his father was still just a boy. "My grandfather went to Ford Motor Company every day without missing a day for over thirty years," Warren boasted. "And during that time, they put my father through medical school, so my father was also a medical doctor." Warren's mother — with her bachelor's degree in education from Wayne State University — had solid middle-class employment as an art teacher in the Detroit public school system. Despite the racial discrimination that daily beleaguered Blacks in

Detroit, Warren's family managed to rise above it, safely landing in the upper echelons of the Black community.

Like many middle-class Blacks in Detroit, Warren and his family spent their summers at Idlewild, a northwestern Michigan resort town established in 1912 that allowed African Americans to vacation and purchase property when other resort towns did not.[3] The famous Madam C. J. Walker and W. E. B. Du Bois also owned property in Idlewild, where the day's top entertainers, professionals, and fun-seekers came together every summer to dance, camp, boat, fish, hunt, roller-skate, swim, and ride horses.

Idlewild had "a good blend of Black folks who made it to the top however they had to do it, the doctors on the one side, and the numbers men on the other," Evans remembered. "But there were also people that came and stayed at the local hotels that weren't well-heeled." By the 1950s, Idlewild would draw twenty-five thousand visitors in a given weekend.

Idlewild was where Warren, at age twelve, met a retired buffalo soldier, which is the moniker given to African American soldiers who fought in America's westward expansion and the Great War. "He had seen me peeking over the fence every morning bright and early while he was out taking care of the horses," Evans said. "And we just kind of hit it off." The retiree taught Warren many things, including how to ride horses, a pastime Warren and all of his grandchildren enthusiastically partake in even today.

On December 12, 1970, Warren, the Black cowboy, became a Wayne County sheriff's deputy, and his long climb to become the county executive officially began. Even though Warren chose his vocation on a whim, he would go on to have a thirty-five-year career in law enforcement. He remained in the profession for so long because it presented him with a variety of exciting opportunities, such as working in the jails, on patrol, in the crime lab, and in the narcotics and organized crime divisions.

In one of his many jobs, Warren was in charge of the Identification Bureau, which deals with fingerprints and photographs. As he was purging some old information, he discovered that his maternal grandfather's brother, Jake, was one of the first African Americans to become a deputy detective in the Wayne County Sheriff's Department. Warren had had no idea that his accidental profession was, in fact, his legacy.

While employed as a police officer, Warren earned his bachelor's degree from Madonna University and a master's degree in criminal justice from the University of Detroit Mercy. As he advanced his education, Warren was also getting job promotions at record-breaking speed. "I think I still have the record for the youngest police sergeant and police lieutenant," Warren speculated. "And so there were only a few promotions to go and a lot of years to go to retire, so that motivated me to go to law school." Warren graduated from the Detroit College of Law, which later became Michigan State University Law School.

In 1981, Warren took a leave of absence from the sheriff's office to work for Detroit's first African American mayor, Coleman Young, as his administrative coordinator for the Detroit Water and Sewerage Department. Coleman Young "was always a nice guy, you always knew he had your back. You knew you were supported, but he'd cuss you out in a heartbeat," Evans recalled. "He was very, very concerned that the federal government was attempting to investigate him and try to charge him with something. And let me just say, all the time I was there, I think that's the furthest thing from the truth that he was doing anything criminal, but Black folks somehow get held to a different standard."

Warren continued, "A couple of times, I remember, he called me to the mayor's residence, which was known as the Manoogian Mansion, and he'd want to meet with me, straight, aboveboard business meeting, but we'd sit in his study, and he had four televisions on, with the volume up on all of them because he had concerns about the office being bugged. He would always say, 'People think I'm paranoid, but that doesn't mean I'm wrong.' And history showed he was absolutely right."

Because Robert Ficano offered him a high-level job as the director of jails, a few years later, Warren left the Young administration and returned to the sheriff's department. Soon after, a retirement left the number two position in the sheriff's office, the undersheriff, vacant. Robert "offered me the job as undersheriff and I jumped at it," Warren said. "The undersheriff traditionally is the guy who runs the day-to-day operations. He's not the one who kisses the babies and goes to the spaghetti dinner, which is what politicians wind up having to do. And so in an ideal situation, I probably would have stayed there and retired as undersheriff because I really enjoyed the work."

The situation, however, was not ideal. "The only problem with being number two is you've got to be able to get along with number one," Warren lamented. "It didn't work out in the sheriff's office. We didn't see the world the same way. I was a career police officer. He'd never been one."

Even though several people encouraged him to run against Robert for sheriff, Warren, who said he did not want to "muddy the waters," refused and instead took a job with the County Commission. "If I had run against him, my sense is no other African American would have got the opportunity to be number two," Warren surmised. "Now, I can't prove that, but my sense is I would have been poisoning the well for other people in the future, and I refused to do that."

After only six months, Warren grew tired of the work in the County Commission and went to work with the second Wayne County executive, Edward McNamara, serving as his assistant county executive from 1990 to 1997. Then, in 2000, Warren went to work for the county prosecutor's office as the chief of special operations, working under Prosecutor Duggan, who is now Detroit's

mayor. The position "involved a hodgepodge of different departments that I ran, but the one that I hired in to begin and to run was
the police shooting team. At that time, Detroit was having a significant rash of police-involved shootings, and I asked for permission
to and was granted permission to put together a prosecutorial team
that would respond to the scenes of these police shootings and not to
interfere, but to watch what was going on."

Warren explained, "What I know is the minority community
was very suspicious, and I wanted to make sure that I could say with
some certainty when we were making charging decisions and inves-
tigations on these shootings, that scenes had not been modified or
altered."

During Warren Evans's stint in the McNamara administration,
Robert Ficano ran for Wayne County executive and won, leaving the
sheriff post vacant. Accordingly, the county clerk, the chief judge of
probate, and the county prosecutor, again, had the power to appoint
the sheriff's interim successor. They unanimously chose Warren. He
subsequently ran as the incumbent and won with ease, serving as
county sheriff from 2003 to 2009.

During his time as sheriff, Hurricane Katrina hit New Orleans
and wiped out entire neighborhoods. "I can remember now sitting
there watching people standing on the roofs of houses those first
couple of days and knowing that the response to it was really, really
weak, and that people were suffering through it," Warren said. He,
therefore, jumped to action. According to the *New York Times*:

> On Aug. 31, Sheriff Edmund M. Sexton, Sr., of Tuscaloosa
> County, Ala., and president of the National Sheriffs' Asso-
> ciation, sent out an alert urging members to pitch in. "Folks
> were held up two, three days while they were working on the
> paperwork," he said. Some sheriffs refused to wait. In Wayne
> County, Mich., which includes Detroit, Sheriff Warren C.
> Evans got a call from Mr. Sexton on Sept. 1. The next day, he

led a convoy of six tractor-trailers, three rental trucks and 33 deputies, despite public pleas from Gov. Jennifer M. Granholm to wait for formal requests. "I could look at CNN and see people dying, and I couldn't in good conscience wait for a coordinated response," he said. He dropped off food, water and medical supplies in Mobile and Gonzales, La., where a sheriffs' task force directed him to the French Quarter. By Saturday, Sept. 3, the Michigan team was conducting search and rescue missions.[4]

When reflecting on the decisions he made during Hurricane Katrina, Warren was proud. "I know it was the right thing to do," he said. "Based on what I was seeing, it was really the only thing to do."

As sheriff, Warren again made headlines during the mortgage foreclosure crisis, which hit Wayne County hard. "People were buying houses that they couldn't afford, but they didn't know that. Clearly predatory lending," Warren said. "And so I saw many of these people as victims. But on top of them being victimized by the predatory lending practices, all of their neighbors were also victimized by the abandoned houses, the scavengers, and the crime rate that often ensued."

Since the sheriff and his office are charged with executing evictions, the 32 percent increase in mortgage foreclosures— which happened between 2006 and 2007 when the housing bubble burst — drastically increased their workload.[5] To many onlookers, this was merely a shocking statistic, but for Warren and his deputies, it was an evil they could touch, smell, and see firsthand as they escorted many families out of their homes. Like an indelible scar that forms after a wound, Warren can never forget the day he had to evict a grandmother and her grandchildren from the home their family had owned for over sixty years.

While waiting for the federal government to craft a solution, Warren decided that something had to be done in the interim. The carnage of the mortgage foreclosures was terrorizing both the evicted and the evictors. In 2009, Warren enjoyed another brief moment of national celebrity when he sent a letter to Michigan governor Jennifer Granholm, asking her to declare a state of emergency and a six-month moratorium on mortgage foreclosures in Wayne County. He wrote, "Not only is Wayne County experiencing a time of great public crisis, disaster, and catastrophe, public safety is imperiled by the number of foreclosed citizens living on the street or committing crimes with the actual intent of being jailed."[6] The governor responded, claiming that this issue was outside her purview. Warren felt that this left him with no other choice but to deliberately exceed the bounds of his authority as sheriff to place a temporary moratorium on all mortgage foreclosures.[7]

"We didn't have a substantive role in the foreclosure process, but we did have a ministerial role that would stop everything if we stopped doing it," Warren said. "And so the idea of all of these people losing their home before some federal relief came along just weighed at me, so I just had our people shut down processing the foreclosure documents. I knew this was something that wasn't going to last so long, but it seemed to me that it really needed to be done." Warren encouraged all other Michigan sheriffs to join his defiance of the status quo. But when the *Detroit Free Press* spoke to the sheriffs of the two neighboring counties, they said that while they were sympathetic, they would not change their foreclosure procedures without state authorization.[8]

Without a strong legal basis to stop the evictions, Warren suspected that businesses and law firms would come for him, but so long as he could buy folks some time to catch up on their mortgage payments, the inevitable legal flogging he would endure was worth it. "Many of them did catch up and thank me to this day for them still being in their house," he said. "One of the things that makes me feel really good even today is I could be out in a public gathering and someone will come and you can see the teardrops in their eyes."

With more than a hint of irritation, Warren continued, "It's very interesting, my former boss, Robert Ficano, was totally unsupportive of the issues. He was then county executive and I certainly got no support." Like his mentor from Idlewild, in the turbulence of the mortgage foreclosure crisis, Warren transformed into a modern-day buffalo soldier — controversial, courageous, and insistent on defying all odds.

The risks Warren took created a reservoir of goodwill with the people of Wayne County, which proved essential when it became clear that the unbalanced budget would soon end Robert's stint as the Wayne County executive, leaving that seat open. Although Warren refused to run against Robert for sheriff, he eagerly ran against him for Wayne County executive because the circumstances were different.

There were several candidates with better name recognition and bigger election purses in the race, but Warren could nevertheless prevail if he thrashed his opponents in Detroit, the county seat and the place where his family had lived for five generations. He also needed to make a decent showing outside of Detroit, relying on the fact that, as a sheriff's deputy, he had been patrolling their neighborhoods and getting to know these people since the 1970s. In the end, Warren emerged victorious. With the win, he was following in the capacious footsteps of one of his heroes, Bill Lucas, Wayne County's first Black sheriff and its first county executive.

But when Warren stepped into office, he walked into chaos. "The attempt to build a new jail was a real mess that cost the County a ton of money, and a ton of litigation that we had to resolve before we could figure out how to move forward," he said. "We had an accumulated deficit in the County of about a hundred and twenty million dollars, and a structural deficit of about fifty-two million." Warren's greatest fear was that the financial chaos would drive the County to bankruptcy or emergency management. Accordingly, he believes his greatest achievement was preventing this seemingly inevitable fate.

"Sometimes people get selective amnesia through time, but the truth of the matter is Detroit was just coming out of bankruptcy, and there wasn't a pundit or media person or anybody else that didn't figure we were going into bankruptcy. The only question was timing," Warren remembered. "And my position was, if there's any way for us to get out of it without bankruptcy, that's the way I want to go. Not just because of my ego, but because when you get caught in bankruptcy there are collective bargaining agreements, retirements, a bunch of things they get out of your hands to be able to try to control, and your employees can really take a haircut that they didn't necessarily deserve. Of course a ton of money then goes to pay for the bankruptcy court and attorneys."

Alongside the County Commission, Warren Evans made his first monumental move as the new Wayne County executive on June 17, 2015. They asked the State of Michigan to officially declare that Wayne County was in a financial emergency because — under the emergency management law that was put in place despite voters' expressly rejecting it — this declaration gave Wayne County four options: consent agreement, Chapter 9 bankruptcy, mediation, or emergency management.[9] On August 6, 2015, Warren and the County Commission selected the consent agreement option, placing the County under state oversight. The consent agreement also mandated that officials improve the County's liquidity, ensure funding for future pension obligations, and erase the County's $52 million structural deficit.[10]

The consent agreement was ideal because it avoided both emergency management and bankruptcy proceedings. In addition, the agreement not only allowed the County's leadership to retain most of its decision-making power, but it also gave Warren certain extraordinary powers usually reserved for an emergency manager.[11] "I don't see any way in the world we would have come to terms with our bargaining units that we needed to come to terms with without the leverage that we were able to get from the consent agreement,"

Warren said. "I just don't think there was any other way that could have happened."[12]

Under the consent agreement, Warren relied on two primary measures to generate resources and eliminate the structural deficit. The first was to sell the County's underutilized real estate holdings. "We had a ton of County assets that we didn't need like buildings that were forty percent occupied," Warren reported. "Where selling those assets not only brought needed cash into the County, but also took the liabilities off of us, like maintenance, for example. You'd have the buildings division complain that they needed another eight or ten skilled tradespeople to take care of the County facilities, but we didn't need all the facilities."

The second measure was the most controversial — hefty transfers from the revolving fund to the general fund first contemplated in Robert Ficano's infamous Turnaround Plan. Although Robert and his team created the Turnaround Plan before their electoral defeat, Warren and his administration were the ones to actually implement it. "He who's in the chair gets the credit," Robert grumbled. "That's the political way it works. Whether it's fair or not, that's the way it works." He paused, then continued. "I think [Warren's administration] helped implement parts of it. There's no doubt about that," Robert conceded, while also giving credit to many people on his own team.

Regardless of who deserves credit (or blame) for the Turnaround Plan, all involved parties — the county executive, county treasurer, County Commission, and state treasurer — knew that the revolving fund surplus was Wayne County's only way to avoid bankruptcy and emergency management. As a result, the consent decree explicitly protected it by prohibiting the County Commission and executive from taking actions or failing to take actions that would impede payments from the fund, deposits into the fund, or debt servicing payments on the bonds that financed the fund.[13] In other words, the consent decree acknowledged and protected the County's diabolical saving grace — the revolving fund.

Robert's complaints about receiving only crumbs from the

revolving fund to balance his budget were correct. From 2002 to 2013, Treasurer Wojtowicz and the fifteen-member County Commission authorized only relatively modest transfers from the revolving fund to the general fund: 2002 ($0), 2003 ($10 million), 2004 ($25.5 million), 2005 ($21 million), 2006 ($8 million), 2007 ($14.5 million), 2008 ($5 million), 2009 ($0), 2010 ($0), 2011 ($4 million), 2012 ($15 million), 2013 ($23 million).[14] The Turnaround Plan, however, required the County to break from this custom and take these morally questionable transfers to the next level. Upon his taking office in 2015, Warren's administration transferred $160,975,779 from the revolving fund to the general fund, shifting over six times more than any sum transferred before. That is, in one year, the transfers exceeded the combined total of the previous twelve years by more than $30 million. Then, in 2015, Wayne County's leadership transferred another record-breaking amount, $161,222,041, to the general fund.

Although there was not much that Warren and Robert agreed upon, they were in total agreement that the revolving fund transfers

Figure 7:

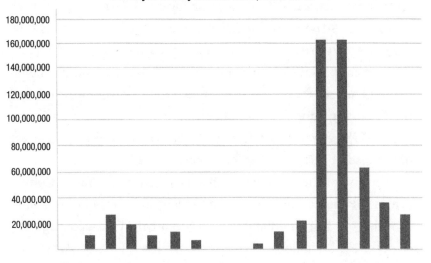

Transfers from the Delinquent Tax Revolving Fund (DTRF) to the Wayne County General Fund, 2002–2018

were morally dirty, and yet the County could not forgo them. "So nobody, I think, was comfortable with the way it was coming in," Robert said, forehead taut. "But once it's in the system, use it for Wayne County at that point versus just hoarding it and hanging on to it."

Warren emphatically agreed. "I mean, I'll use the money if it's there. What administrator with the revenue source wouldn't use it?" he asked rhetorically. "The money has already been taken from people, their homes have already been seized, so why in the hell wouldn't you use it to get the County on a decent footing so that we can provide better services rather than have it hoarded in an account in the treasurer's office that he's profiting from?" Warren added, "But on the other hand, if I was able to trade it away, in other words, not have foreclosures and forgo the money, I'd do it in a heartbeat. I'd much rather people be in their homes and not having them foreclosed upon because I really think that the revenue generated from people in their houses and small businesses and having vibrant communities and a vibrant society is the ticket to a strong county, not bleeding it to death through foreclosures and the delinquent tax process."

The Wayne County Commission did not share Robert and Warren's compunctions about the revolving fund surplus. "As a local government striving to work its way out of the hole occasioned by the recession of 2008–2009, with many thousands of tax delinquencies and foreclosures during the past few years, the county should not be penalized for achieving revenue through foreclosure sales and the Revolving Fund process," the commission wrote in a 2015 document. "These transfers certainly compensate for cash flow distress occasioned in part from unpaid property taxes."[15]

Because of the revolving fund surplus, in 2016, Wayne County concluded the consent decree and emerged from State oversight, convalescing financially but broken morally.[16] "I'm operating with eighty-five million dollars less a year than the county was operating in '08, and we've balanced the budget and have a rainy-day fund,"

Warren bragged. Taking a jab at Robert, his longtime rival, Warren continued, "Like, excuse my French, but what in the hell were they doing? We changed significantly the way we managed and prepared legitimate, honest budgets. I think the history speaks for itself, seven years, seven balanced budgets. Most years we had surpluses, and really in the last few years, we've been in a position to give employees raises again, which is something they haven't had for at least ten years prior to me taking office."

Warren is, indeed, running a tight ship, and Wayne County's economic resurgence has been nothing less than remarkable. The moral cost of this triumph, however, has been formidable. Speaking about the revolving fund surplus, Warren admitted, "The reality to me is it's blood money, and our county and society would be a lot better if you didn't have that money because we would have stable neighborhoods." Robert agreed with the term *blood money* to describe the revolving fund surplus because "it preys on the misery of people. I don't know how else to describe it. I think it's a horrible practice. It's an inhumane practice."

There are four explicit racist policies that make the revolving fund's surplus predatory, justifying its characterization as blood money. *First* are the routinely overstated property tax assessments and the subsequent property tax foreclosures when homeowners like Myrisha could not afford to pay their illegally inflated property tax bills. Conservative estimates show that 10 percent of Detroit's residential properties willingly sold between 2009 and 2013 would not have gone through tax foreclosure if it were not for the illegally inflated property tax assessments.[17] Additionally, since Detroit's Office of the Assessor overassessed lower-priced homes at a greater frequency and magnitude than higher-priced homes, 25 percent of the lowest-valued homes would not have gone into tax foreclosure if it were not for unconstitutional property tax assessments.

Second, the revolving fund surplus is predatory because many homeowners who contributed — through interest, fees, and auction sales resulting from delinquent property tax payments — were not even supposed to be paying property taxes in the first place. "What's exacerbating [the tax foreclosures] is most people don't know about the poverty exemption," Robert said. "Okay, if you have the where-withal and you don't pay your taxes, okay, foreclosure is part of what happens. But you should have the right to use all of the exemptions that you can to keep your home."

Over 30 percent of Detroit residents live below the federal poverty threshold, and hence those who were homeowners qualified for the poverty tax exemption.[18] Most qualified homeowners did not receive the exemption because the City of Detroit made the application process unduly onerous and nearly impossible for poor people — like the Vietman veteran Mr. Karl — to traverse. "The people weren't aware of the poverty exemption that could have saved them from [tax foreclosure]. And it's unfair that suddenly it's like a gotcha move. You didn't do it, so now I'm gonna be able to foreclose on it," Robert said, disgruntled. "Too many people are losing their homes that shouldn't be losing them."

Third, the revolving fund surplus is predatory because after counties sold a tax-delinquent property at auction, a Michigan law allowed them to keep all the proceeds, even if the money gained far exceeded the amount owed. The Michigan Supreme Court addressed this suspect practice in *Rafaeli, LLC v. Oakland County*.[19] After inadvertently underpaying, Uri Rafaeli owed a tax debt of $8.41 on a rental property, and Oakland County foreclosed on his home to collect it. The home sold for $24,500 at the tax foreclosure auction and Oakland County pocketed the surplus. Another plaintiff, Andre Ohanessian, owed a $6,000 tax debt, and the county sold his home at auction for $82,000 and commandeered the windfall.

Myrisha, although not a claimant in the *Rafaeli* lawsuit, experi-enced the same injustice. Wayne County foreclosed on her Baylis home and sold it in its 2016 auction for $7,212. At the time of fore-closure, Myrisha owed $3,417.41 in total, so the auction sale brought

Wayne County a $3,800 surplus. This is "fundamentally wrong. It's ass backwards. It's asinine. It shouldn't work like that," Robert insisted.

In 2020, the Michigan Supreme Court agreed with Robert, ruling this practice illegal. Then, in a 2023 case, *Tyler v. Hennepin County*, the United States Supreme Court followed the Michigan Supreme Court's lead, ruling that the Fifth Amendment Takings Clause prohibits local tax authorities from keeping monies collected in excess of the tax debt. While the courts have outlawed this plunder, it is unclear whether all past victims will get their money back.

Fourth, the revolving fund surplus is predatory because its largest tributary is the state's statutorily mandated 18 percent interest penalty on delinquent property debt.[20] The question is, why would Michigan lawmakers stipulate this excessive penalty? Michigan's Washtenaw County treasurer, Catherine McClary, shed light on this mystery. "I am shocked by the number of business people and LLCs whose business model is to pay at the last minute. The eighteen percent was designed as a deterrent," she explained. "Eighteen percent in today's interest rates, it does sound, and it is, exorbitant," but legislators enacted the statutory interest rate in 1999 when "we were a decade away from the 1980s where interest rates routinely on bank accounts and CDs was eighteen, nineteen, twenty percent."[21]

The statutory 18 percent interest penalty is predicated upon the assumption that property owners have the money to pay their property taxes but don't want to. When, however, homeowners are indigent and do not have the ability to pay, the 18 percent interest penalty only makes the situation worse. It becomes a punishment for being poor. "It should've never been turned into a punishment, and that's what it has become," Robert explained. "It has turned into a yoke and punishment on everybody."

Although both Warren and Robert agree that the transfers from the revolving fund to the general fund are "blood money," they continued even after Treasurer Wojtowicz ended his thirty-nine-year career as Wayne County treasurer in 2016, and his deputy, Eric

Sabree, replaced him: 2016 ($62,047,215), 2017 ($35,153,226), 2018 ($26,050,724).[22] Unlike Wojtowicz, Treasurer Sabree never had a personal financial incentive to keep the money in the revolving fund. "Wojtowicz was the last treasurer that actually got the bonus from the revolving fund," Robert noted. "They grandfathered in some of the older treasurers, but Sabree can't get it now."

Without a financial incentive to do otherwise, Treasurer Sabree has transferred substantial amounts out of the revolving fund, and the fact that the financial emergency has ended is inconsequential. The treasurer is, however, transferring the money every year because Warren continues to request it, despite his deep reservations. This time, the transfers, according to Warren, are not to cover a budget deficit, but instead to "enhance the budget."

"If the treasurer says, 'I've got seven million dollars for you that I can send over from the Delinquent Tax Revolving Fund,' I'm sure my response will be, 'Treasurer, can you give me fourteen?' and we may cut the baby in the middle," Warren explained. "I mean, I'm gonna beg because I got a budget that I'm doing, too. But it's a gentleman's begging. We both would rather not even be talking about this fund." He continued, "If there was two million dollars, that's two million dollars that could be used in the general fund for salary increases, for any of a number of things, I have no clue as to why the treasurer would want to hold it forever. It's county taxpayers' money. The rational place for it to go would be into the county budget, I think!"

Robert criticized both Treasurer Sabree and Warren for the ongoing revolving fund transfers. "Now it's transferred, from what I understand, pretty heftily. They took it to the nth degree of doing it," Robert said disapprovingly. "For a temporary fix, it works, but it's horrible. It's not a permanent fix. You shouldn't run government with it." Warren knew that Robert's words were true, but they irritated him nonetheless. "But the only thing that Robert Ficano doesn't note is, in his time as county executive when this is going on, not one of those issues did he do a damn thing about," Warren said, annoyed by

Robert's newfound righteousness. "I think it's kind of easy to sit back afterwards and point back and talk about all the things that should occur, and to me, the first question is, 'And you did what to deal with that?'"

Given that even the two rivals, Robert and Warren, who do not agree on much, agree that the revolving fund surplus transfers are blood money, the bold "buffalo soldier" move would be for Warren to lead a campaign, demanding that Treasurer Sabree return the ill-gotten gains to the rightful owners. But this is where the difference between Warren the sheriff and Warren the county executive is striking. As sheriff, even when the governor's office tried to discourage him, Warren and his crew of officers went to New Orleans in the aftermath of Hurricane Katrina because, according to him, "based on what I was seeing, it was really the only thing to do." Likewise, Warren decided that the mortgage foreclosure crisis was morally repugnant and instituted a temporary moratorium, exceeding the bounds of his authority to do what he thought was just, decent, and necessary. But Warren the county executive is standing by as the County forecloses on many homeowners who, both scholars and politicians have acknowledged, overpaid at best, and at worst were not even supposed to be paying the property taxes that triggered the foreclosure in the first place.

When confronted with this tension between his actions as the sheriff versus those as the county executive, Warren replied, "If the City of Detroit has done a number of things that have created that inequity and hurt people, then I think they are the ones that ought to be held liable to deal with it." In a more somber tone, he then added, "I'm certainly not blind to the fact that the County has used that money that was received in the past to support County functions, so would I be willing to contribute and help in a fund to try to get as close to equity and common sense as we can get? Absolutely, I would." Like the historic buffalo soldiers who fought wars against Native Americans but also served as the first national park rangers and leveraged military service to secure equal rights, Warren is also a complicated hero.[23]

The Great Recession was a shipwreck, and Wayne County stayed afloat by desperately clinging to the debris left by property tax delinquencies and foreclosures, occurring primarily in Detroit to people like Myrisha. When, under Warren, the County began to use the revolving fund even after the storm was over, it converted this debris into a pirate's ship. Most detrimentally, these morally questionable practices have contributed to the Detroit metro area's long-standing racial divide.

CONCLUSION

IN SEARCH OF JUSTICE

Over the last century, whites left Detroit for cheaper, more spacious homes in newly constructed suburbs with superior public amenities, but racially restrictive covenants and racial animus prevented African Americans, like Grandpa Brown, from following suit. Consequently, white suburbanites thrived while Blacks — relegated to a city with deteriorating infrastructure, an emaciated tax base, and concentrated poverty — did not. More importantly, after inheriting homes in the declining city, Myrisha Brown and other Blacks have been unable to build wealth, while the suburban homes of Robert Ficano and other whites became their primary source of intergenerational wealth. When the County used the revolving fund surplus to cover its structural deficit — saving itself from bankruptcy and emergency management by using funds from property tax delinquency and foreclosure, coming primarily from Detroit — it exacerbated the already existing racial and wealth divide between the majority-white suburbs and the majority-Black city.

Robert understood that this was flat-out wrong, yet he was a key architect of the plan that facilitated the entire fiasco. "As an administrator, you're trying to do the best you can to hold it together," he explained. "I never regret anything. I just look forward. I did the best I could with what tools we had." After a long silence punctuated by a nervous chuckle, he continued, "And do I wish it would've turned out better? Of course I do."

While Wayne County itself made the most profits from property tax delinquency and foreclosure in Detroit, a diverse array of investors also profited by purchasing homes discounted due to property tax foreclosure. This includes large-scale land speculators like John Hantz and Michael G. Kelly; non–Detroit-based investors like Piper and Seamus O'Grady, and Beatriz Hernandez; and Detroit-based entrepreneurs like Dwayne Davis and Ms. Hazel Thompson. Some investors made profits while remaining legally compliant, duly paying their property taxes, and improving their purchased homes as required by the auction contract.

Many auction purchasers' business models were, however, predicated on legal noncompliance. Hence, in the name of profits, they failed to pay their property taxes and invest in their purchased properties, furthering neighborhood deterioration. Through blight tickets, nuisance abatement lawsuits, and property tax auction lawsuits, the City of Detroit tried to rein in legally noncompliant investors. The results were mixed.

Whether legally compliant or legally noncompliant, all participants in the property tax foreclosure auction were part of a predatory system enabled by policies or processes that produce or sustain racial inequity, otherwise known as racist policies. The story of Lily — the bank teller who bought a home to serve as a sanctuary for herself, her sons, and her fur babies — shows these racist policies at work. Historic and present-day redlining, which made affordable credit inaccessible, left Lily with no option other than a predatory mortgage loan to purchase her home, and denied her access to home repair funds. Redlined car insurance rates further drained Lily's bank account, leaving her and her sons financially vulnerable. Then the statutory 18 percent interest penalty compounded her illegally inflated property tax bill. When she could no longer afford to pay her mortgage and property taxes, foreclosure resulted. Only when Lily moved her family a few blocks over into a majority-white suburb did they circumvent the effects of redlining and get their property taxes properly calculated, finally securing relief from the racist policies that dog Detroit and many other majority-Black cities.

Despite their disastrous effects on Lily and so many other home-owners' lives, these racist policies were almost entirely invisible. Society could only see the personal irresponsibility of homeowners who failed to pay their property taxes. This is what Piper and Seamus chose to see. This is what even Dwayne — a Detroit native punished by the racist policies that he also profited from — chose to see. This is exactly what makes racist policies so dangerous: their ability to hide in plain sight.

While the Black Lives Matter movement has spotlighted police violence unjustly perpetrated against Black bodies, there has been no movement to spotlight the predatory governance enacted by other public officials and private actors. Cell phone videos and police body cameras have captured state violence and galvanized the public into long-overdue demands for change. But there is no easy way to con-vey the devastation that occurs when public officials replenish public accounts through racist policies. And yet predatory governance sys-tematically cripples Black people like Mr. Karl, the Vietnam veteran who lost his family home for failure to pay property taxes that he should not have owed in the first place.

As Piper and Seamus evicted Mr. Karl, he pleaded, "But this is my house. This is my house." No one heard him. *Plundered* amplifies the plaintive cries of Mr. Karl and others like him who daily experi-ence the ruinous impacts of predatory governance. They, too, deserve to be heard. They also deserve justice.

Although people like Myrisha, Mr. Karl, and Lily lost their homes to property tax foreclosure, the sequel to this book will delve deeply into the grassroots movement that eventually brought about property tax justice for other Detroit homeowners, preventing them from losing their homes because of illegally inflated property taxes.

Somewhat unexpectedly, it was research that ignited this movement. Reliable empirical evidence showing that property tax assessments systematically violated the Michigan Constitution, producing illegally inflated property taxes, proved to be an immensely powerful lever for change.

The well-documented illegality ignited a critical class action lawsuit in 2016, *Morningside v. Sabree.* The ACLU of Michigan, the NAACP Legal Defense and Educational Fund, and the law firm of Covington & Burling brought suit against the City of Detroit and Wayne County in state court.[1] The case against Wayne County was based on the Fair Housing Act, claiming that the policies that caused unconstitutional property tax assessments and foreclosures had a disparate impact on Wayne County's African American homeowners. The lower court ruled that the case should have been brought to the Michigan Tax Tribunal,[2] and the appellate court agreed,[3] so the case against Wayne County died for three reasons.

First, the tribunal is not a court, it is an administrative agency. It, therefore, has no class action facility and can only deal with individualized harms. It could not redress the systemic violations central to *Morningside.* Additionally, since the tribunal is not a court, it does not have injunctive power and hence could not deliver the primary remedy requested in *Morningside:* an injunction ordering Wayne County both to stop the scheduled tax sales of owner-occupied homes and to change the policies that caused the unjust foreclosures to abound. Lastly, while the Fair Housing Act gives plaintiffs two years to bring a case, under the tribunal, Detroit homeowners had only fifteen days because they had to file an appeal between February 1 and February 15 at the city's Assessor Review in order to access the tribunal.[4]

Although the Michigan Constitution is clear — no property shall be assessed at more than 50 percent of its market value — *Morningside* revealed that there is no remedy for systemic violations of this constitutional mandate in Michigan courts. There is only a remedy for individualized harms. Unfortunately, the legal team also could not bring their case before federal courts because of the Tax Injunction Act, which does not allow federal courts to "enjoin, suspend or restrain the assessment, levy or collection of any tax under State law where a plain, speedy and efficient remedy may be had in the courts of such State."[5] Unable to secure justice in state and federal courts, Detroit homeowners had no other choice but to work outside the courts. A grassroots power-building movement was necessary.

In 2017, galvanized by the research laid out in this book, community groups united under the capacious and righteous umbrella of eradicating illegality, and the Coalition to End Unconstitutional Tax Foreclosures was born. This collective of over a dozen Detroit grassroots organizations used research, legal interventions, and community organizing to upend the racist policies undergirding the predatory governance in Detroit. In 2018, the group changed its name to the Coalition for Property Tax Justice, redefining itself based on what it demanded rather than what it was against. Despite the name change, since its inception, the Coalition has had the same three goals.

The *first* goal is to end unconstitutional property tax assessments and the resulting illegally inflated property tax bills in Detroit. Even in 2024, the data show that Detroit's Office of the Assessor is still systematically overassessing lower-valued homes.[6] Therefore, since its start in 2019, the Coalition's Property Tax Appeal Project (PTAP) has aggressively fought back, using community members and law students to file over eight hundred appeals at no cost to these homeowners. Additionally, PTAP has connected more than three thousand homeowners to its partner community organization, the Wayne Metropolitan Community Action Agency (Wayne Metro), to receive wraparound services such as utility assistance, weatherization, and connection to the various Michigan State Housing Development Authority programs that pay delinquent property taxes and other debts. Until the empirical evidence shows that the City of Detroit is systematically valuing all properties in accordance with the Michigan Constitution, PTAP will stand in the gap.

In addition to ensuring that the City is taxing individual homeowners the correct amount, the Coalition has also drafted a property tax reform ordinance to effectuate the structural changes necessary. Among other things, the ordinance redesigns the property tax assessment notice to ensure that it is understandable to the average resident; makes various types of data readily available to improve transparency; and provides the city council with a mechanism to identify and correct property tax assessments that systematically violate the Michigan Constitution. As a result of the Coalition's grassroots organizing campaign, Detroit's city council passed the ordinance in November 2023, ensuring that unconstitutional property tax assessments will become a thing of the past.

The Coalition's *second* goal is to stop property tax foreclosure of owner-occupied homes in Detroit. It is one thing to lose your home because you failed to pay your property taxes, but it is a whole other thing to lose your home because you could not pay the illegally inflated property taxes that you should have been exempt from paying in the first place. Here, the second portion of the *Morningside* lawsuit, the case against the City of Detroit for obstructive administration of the poverty tax exemption, was key.

As part of the lawsuit's settlement agreement, homeowners who qualified for the exemption but did not receive it could remove their homes from the tax foreclosure auction by paying $1,000 or the amount of taxes owed, whichever was less. Among other things, the settlement also required the City to: redesign the exemption application, making it more user-friendly; reduce the amount of paperwork required to receive the exemption; provide training for all city officials who interacted with constituents in the exemption process; mail a letter that supplied clear reasons for any exemption denials within ten days of the Board of Review's close; advertise the exemption widely; make the exemption application freely available at City

Hall, online, and at public meeting places; and stop stamping the exemption application with artificial deadlines.

Since the *Morningside* settlement lasted only three years, in 2018 the Coalition worked with Council member Mary Sheffield to create a city ordinance that made the described changes permanent. Then, in 2020, Governor Gretchen Whitmer signed into law Public Act 253, which created a new standardized statewide exemption application that extends many of the *Morningside* settlement wins to homeowners across the entire state of Michigan.[7] Although the Duggan administration stubbornly insisted on retaining its burdensome and unnecessary notarization requirement throughout the lawsuit and ordinance negotiations, the statewide law successfully repealed this, making the exemption application more accessible.

Like the other provisions of the *Morningside* settlement, the one allowing homeowners who qualified for the exemption to pull their homes out of tax foreclosure by paying $1,000 or the amount of taxes owed also expired after three years.[8] But, in 2020, the State of Michigan passed the Pay As You Stay (PAYS) program, which reduces the delinquent taxes owed for owner-occupiers who qualify for the exemption, expanding the *Morningside* win to all Michigan homeowners.[9] Then the Rocket Community Fund and the Gilbert Family Foundation created the Detroit Tax Relief Fund, which paid any remaining balance owed for Detroit homeowners, ensuring that never again would those who qualified for the exemption face tax foreclosure.[10]

Our favorite senior citizen from Devine Street, Ms. Mae, was one of the many low-income Detroit homeowners who had her sizable property tax debt erased by a combination of the PAYS program and the Detroit Tax Relief Fund. "I felt good because I did not have to pay all of that money that I have been paying," Ms. Mae said. "I really don't like it though because you've got to fill out all that paperwork every year, but they already know I'm poor because I get food stamps and I've got to fill out a whole lot of paperwork for that."

With an imperfect yet robust solution in place for Ms. Mae and other homeowners who live below the poverty line, the Coalition began its campaign to ensure that other owner-occupiers avoided property tax foreclosure. Because of the COVID-19 pandemic, the Coalition was able to negotiate with the Wayne County treasurer for a moratorium on tax foreclosures in 2020 and 2021.[11] In 2022 and 2023, the Coalition successfully negotiated for another moratorium on owner-occupied homes, arguing that homeowners on the brink of tax foreclosure could pay their past-due balances using monies the U.S. Department of the Treasury gave Michigan under the American Rescue Plan Act of 2021 to combat pandemic-related hardships.

With over $242 million to spend, in February 2022, the Michigan Homeowner Assistance Fund (MIHAF) began, providing households with up to $25,000 to pay debts — including property tax, mortgage, and utility bills — directly related to COVID-19. To be eligible, Michigan homeowners had to own and occupy their home as their primary residence, and make no more than $99,450 for a one-person family and no more than $187,550 for an eight-person family.[12] Initially, the State of Michigan only allowed MIHAF funds to apply to property tax debts incurred after January 21, 2020, even though the federal Treasury placed no such restriction on the funding. The Coalition successfully spearheaded a campaign that compelled the State of Michigan to allow payment of property tax debts incurred prior to the COVID-19 pandemic but payable during it.

The Coalition's *third* and final goal is to compensate homeowners for the illegally inflated property taxes and the resulting foreclosures. Through its research and advocacy, the Coalition laid the groundwork for an independent compensation fund called the Dignity Restoration Project (DRP), which mobilizes resources from foundations, corporations, government, and individuals to compensate the hardest-hit Detroit homeowners: those who lost their homes through tax foreclosure, although they were exempt from paying property taxes. Dignity restoration is a specific legal remedy that places dispossessed individuals and communities in the driver's seat and allows them to determine how they are made whole. The DRP, therefore, centers autonomy by providing eligible beneficiaries with a menu of compensatory options. Although it is impossible to fully compensate homeowners for all of the material and nonmaterial harms suffered, the DRP seeks to provide symbolic compensation that will restore assets and autonomy.

Through research, legal actions, and power-building campaigns, the Coalition is slowly unwinding the racist policies upholding the predatory governance in Detroit. But Detroit is not the only place where public officials replenish public coffers through racist policies. Predatory governance is an American problem. In Ferguson, Missouri, racially targeted ticketing and fines have bolstered public accounts; in Washington D.C., abuses of civil forfeiture have augmented law enforcement budgets; in New Orleans, local courts have inappropriately jailed defendants to collect court debts that finance its operations; and inequitable property taxation is improperly transferring money from the pockets of African American and Hispanic homeowners throughout the nation to local governments.

Most commonly, narratives of personal irresponsibility—such as the idea that people just need to pay their tickets, fines, court debts, and property taxes—have allowed these racist policies to hide in plain sight. Detroit, a city that is most often associated with urban dysfunction rather than one that has been dogged by racist policies for decades, offers a shining example of how to discern and dismantle the predatory governance that flies below the radar in towns and cities across the United States. Citizens from Maine to California can use and adapt the strategies that Detroit activists deployed to upend these narratives of personal irresponsibility and expose the underlying structural injustices. Until this happens, racist policies will continue to silently drive the racial wealth divide in America.

ABOUT THIS PROJECT

I am a socio-legal scholar whose work focuses on land stolen from Black people. My first ethnographic project, which I began in 2008, dealt with land stolen during colonialism and apartheid in South Africa, and the post-apartheid government's attempt to provide a remedy in accordance with Section 25 of its constitution. To understand the social, political, and psychological impacts of redress, I conducted over 150 interviews with dispossessed individuals and families in two of the nation's provinces, and I spent nine months embedded in the South African Land Restitution Commission, working alongside its officials, who are charged with providing compensation for past land theft. From this treasure trove of qualitative data, I produced several articles and a book entitled *We Want What's Ours: Learning from South Africa's Land Restitution Program*. In 2014, at the book's official launch in Johannesburg, the deputy land claims commissioner publicly announced that his commission would adopt 90 percent of the book's recommendations.

This project, although wildly successful, was very uncomfortable for me in that it examined Black people as victims. Hence, for my next ethnographic project, I wanted to flip the script and study Black agency. Because squatting is an instance where vulnerable populations take land instead of being stolen from, I decided that this would be my focus. In the 1990s, one of America's most significant instances of urban squatting occurred on New York's Lower East Side.[1] But because of Detroit's severe depopulation—which led, in 2015, to vacancy in about 22 percent of the city's properties—squatting in Detroit far surpassed what had transpired in New York.[2] According to city data, in 2015, around five thousand publicly owned buildings in Detroit were occupied by squatters,[3] in addition to a sizable but unknown number occupying privately owned properties.

I, therefore, decided Detroit would be my next research site. It took months to design a rigorous study, but in 2016, all the hard work paid off when I won a prestigious National Science Foundation grant to fund my research. I moved to Detroit in January 2017 to complete my fieldwork.

A squatter is someone who occupies a property without the permission of the owner of record. There are two types of squatters—takeovers and holdovers—and I interviewed both for my sample. Takeovers are people who occupy a property with which they have no prior legal relationship. Holdovers are people who have had a legal relationship to the property (as an owner or tenant, for instance), but when the relationship ends, they stay without permission. When I began interviewing the holdovers, one person after another told me that they lost ownership of their home through property tax foreclosure, but stayed, waiting for the new owners to appear.

I knew a lot about mortgage foreclosure, but less about property tax foreclosure, so I began doing my homework. I soon discovered that between 2011 and 2015, the local government had confiscated one in four Detroit homes for failure to pay the property taxes,[4] which is the highest number of property tax foreclosures in American history since the Great Depression. Since my new neighbors were losing their homes in droves, I could not ignore the gravity of the situation, and thus switched my research focus from squatting to property tax foreclosure.

Before I began my own property tax research, there were several academic articles written about property tax assessment inequity in

Detroit and also about the city's high property tax rates. No scholar had, however, examined whether Detroit's property tax calculations comported with the Michigan Constitution, which states that localities cannot assess a property at more than 50 percent of its market value. This was, therefore, where I decided to begin. After receiving ethics clearance from the institutional review board at my university, I wrote three quantitative articles.

In my first article, my co-author and I found that between 2009 and 2015, the City of Detroit assessed 53 to 84 percent of its homes in violation of the Michigan Constitution. This illegality was both more pronounced and habitual for lower-valued properties.[5] In the next paper, I dealt with race directly. Of Wayne County's 43 municipalities, 33 have a population that is 70 percent or more white and 3 have a population that is 70 percent or more African American: Detroit, Inkster, and Highland Park. I found that, while cities with a supermajority of African American residents experienced high rates of illegally inflated property tax assessments and tax foreclosure, the white ones did not.[6] In my third and final quantitative article, my co-author and I found that, if not for the illegally inflated property tax assessments, 10 percent of all homes would not have gone through tax foreclosure between 2011 and 2015.[7] Because Detroit's assessor overvalued lower-priced homes more often than higher-priced homes, conservative estimates suggest that 25 percent of the lowest-valued homes would not have gone into property tax foreclosure but for the rampant illegality.

While using quantitative methods to describe and measure the problem was ideal, I switched to qualitative methods when I began trying to explain why the problem occurred. More specifically, I used semi-structured interviews, participant observation, government records, and secondary sources to more deeply understand Detroit's property tax foreclosure crisis and how it related to the challenges of Black homeownership nationwide. I personally conducted over two hundred semi-structured interviews with various populations, including overtaxed homeowners who either had lost their homes to tax foreclosure or were on the verge of losing their homes; public officials in Detroit and Wayne County charged with property tax administration; individuals who purchased tax-foreclosed homes from the Wayne County property tax auction or the Detroit Land Bank; and activists fighting on behalf of overtaxed homeowners. The interviews lasted from 30 to 120 minutes, and each respondent received a $20 Subway gift certificate in gratitude for their time. I stopped interviewing each group of people when I reached the point of data saturation, which is when new interviews do not produce new themes, ideas, or patterns.

My interview style focuses on educing both factual details and the emotional landscapes surrounding them. As a result, the stories in this book are weighty and emotionally rich. To ensure that I captured each of the main characters' stories correctly, after I wrote a story up, I scheduled an additional interview to read it back to the person, stopping after each paragraph to get their approval or adjustments. This not only helped to ensure the accuracy of the stories, but as the readback sparked additional memories, it also elicited more compelling information. Most importantly, this technique gave my respondents a notable degree of agency in crafting their stories.

When given the profound responsibility of telling other people's stories, deciding what to leave out and what to include is tricky. The storyteller's goal should be to use each person's virtues as well as their imperfections to make their humanity shine. There is, however, a well-intentioned "respectability politics,"[8] which guards against the routine dehumanization of Black people by writing flat stories that hide their flaws and accentuate their strengths. I roundly reject this approach. I, instead, consider it my job to present people in their full complexity. Anything else is, in fact, dehumanizing.

Because I am a socio-legal scholar and not a journalist, the manner in which I must secure permission for my interviews is highly regulated and controlled by the university's institutional review board. I used an approved consent script for public servants and public figures that did not guarantee anonymity, and a different consent script for everyone else that did. To honor the agreement with people who were not public servants or figures — including Myrisha, Mona, Frederick, Ms. Mae, Piper, Dwayne, Ms. Hazel, Beatriz, Jerry, Lily, Ebony, Kris, Jack, and Charles — I have changed minor identifying details and used a pseudonym for each of these people as well as anyone they mentioned.

Of the hundreds of interviews I completed, I selected the particular stories that appear in *Plundered* because they best captured the themes and patterns I found across my qualitative data. But every story that I had the privilege of hearing was important, even if I did not single it out for a detailed examination in this book. To ensure equal dignity, I refer to the characters in this book by their first names, even the politicians. I do, however, make an exception for community elders — like Ms. Mae, Ms. Hazel, Ms. Denise, and Mr. Karl — whom I would never call by their first names because I was raised by a Black mama. I, therefore, know better.

I have a story for how I met each person featured in this book. Most of the homeowners who had experienced property tax foreclosure I met through the United Community Housing Coalition (UCHC). In 2017, a UCHC volunteer randomly selected and called clients who had lost their homes to tax foreclosure between 2014 and 2016, asking if they would be willing to participate in my study. About a hundred clients expressed interest, including Myrisha and also Jack, who lost the home his family had lived in since 1907 to tax foreclosure. My research team called each interested person to schedule an interview with me.

Myrisha was among the first few people that I interviewed. We met in one of UCHC's stuffy meeting rooms cluttered with books and papers. Despite the disorder, once we settled into the cushy brown chairs, both Myrisha and I were extremely comfortable in each other's presence. While some interviewees need prompts, Myrisha did not. She came prepared and eager to tell her story. She spoke while I listened with my ears and my body, nodding often to provide assurance that I was with her.

At several points in her story, Myrisha burst into tears, and being the empath that I am, I joined her, sobbing. I then tore up the already disheveled room trying to locate Kleenex. After I had heard two hours of her riveting story, time was running short. My next appointment was waiting in the lobby. Even though Myrisha was far from done, I had to officially end the interview and stop the recording. We wiped our faces one last time, clearing the tear stains so no one could detect that we had been weeping. I promised her we would soon pick up where we had left off.

"Man! That was unexpected. This was ther-a-peu-tic," Myrisha said as she got up to leave, singing every syllable of the word therapeutic. "Thank you. Thank you for listening to my story. Thank you for listening to li'l ole me," she said with a nervous chuckle. "It was not until now, when I had to tell you everything, that I realized just how much I have gone through." After another nervous chuckle, she said, "I been through a lot."

"Yes, my love, you have been through a lot," I replied. "And I thank *you* for sharing your story with me. You are so very powerful. Your story is so very powerful. And I am blessed to have met you."

"I pray my story will make a difference," Myrisha said as she walked toward the door.

"It already has," I responded, following behind her. "It already has." Through several follow-up interviews over the course of many years, Myrisha got to finish telling her story, and I had the privilege and honor of chronicling it.

Myrisha introduced me to her father, Frederick, and her mother, Mona, who added invaluable layers to the story of her stolen legacy. I found Beatriz by looking up the LLC that purchased Myrisha's inheritance, identifying the owners, finding their phone numbers, and then contacting them. Surprisingly, Beatriz was excited to tell her story and provided lots of vital information about the Baylis home's acquisition that even Myrisha did not know. After the pandemic ended, I tried to do another follow-up interview with Beatriz, but she declined.

"I got burned over there in Detroit," she said. "I would just prefer to leave all that in the past and move on with my life."

"I totally understand," I replied. "Best of luck to you."

To better understand the perspective of people, like Beatriz, who purchased homes through the property tax foreclosure auction, I used public records to identify individuals and LLCs that had purchased several properties, and then contacted and interviewed those investors. This is how I met Piper and Dwayne. Dwayne's story allowed me to communicate the typical challenges and advantages that I was hearing from the investors hailing from the city of Detroit. Dwayne introduced me to Ms. Hazel, who added an important sight line into his story.

Likewise, Piper's story allowed me to relay the trends I identified among investors who did not reside in Detroit. To locate the prior owners of the homes that Piper and her partners had purchased from the property tax foreclosure auction, my research team used public records to locate them, and then scheduled interviews with as many as we could, including Lily and Ebony. I tried to find Mr. Karl, but it appeared that he had already passed away, so his story relies on the memories of both Piper and Kris, the court officer who performed his eviction.

In addition to the interviews, my qualitative data included participant observation, which is when the researcher is immersed for an extended period in the cultural environment and daily activities of the people she is studying. For eight years, I lived on Detroit's east side to understand the city's property tax foreclosure crisis from the perspective of those I lived beside. More specifically, I lived in the city's 48214 zip code, where 85.4 percent of the population is African American; 37.5 percent live below the poverty level; and 19 percent of the properties completed the tax foreclosure process between 2002 and 2013. Additionally, I joined a church whose explicit mission is to minister in the 48214 zip code, attended block club and community meetings, and patronized local establishments.[9]

In addition to embedding myself on the east side, I was also the principal convener of the Coalition for Property Tax Justice, which is a group of over one dozen grassroots organizations that I began to accomplish three goals: to stop unconstitutional property tax assessments; to suspend property tax foreclosures until authorities can confirm that the City has not unconstitutionally assessed delinquent taxpayers; and to compensate Detroit residents who have already lost their homes through illegally inflated property tax bills they could not afford to pay. Using research, law, and community organizing, the Coalition is a major player in remedying the property tax foreclosure crisis in Detroit.

With my students serving as the movement's worker bees, the Coalition has had several wins since its founding in 2017. We have filed over 1,000 property tax appeals for Detroit homeowners; hosted a People's Forum to discuss compensation with over 700 Detroit residents in attendance; secured $6 million from the City of Detroit to compensate overtaxed homeowners; generated over 100 press hits, changing the narrative about the crisis's origin from one of personal irresponsibility to one predicated upon unconstitutional property tax assessments; led successful campaigns to place a moratorium on property tax foreclosures in 2020 through 2024, preventing over 13,000 homes from going to the tax auction; helped over 1,000 Detroiters sign up for $4.4 million in federal funding to pay their delinquent property taxes; and generated a lawsuit, which is ongoing, to challenge the City of Detroit's failure to provide homeowners with an adequate opportunity to appeal their property tax assessments in 2017. In the sequel to *Plundered,* I will tell the story of the Coalition's zigzag journey toward justice.

My intricate involvement with the Coalition has provided extraordinary access to community members, policymakers, government bureaucrats, activists, and social service organizations. I, for instance, met our spicy senior citizen from Devine Street, Ms. Mae, through the Coalition's work, signing homeowners up for the poverty tax exemption. Also, through my work with the Coalition, I met Charles, the homeowner whom the City sued after he decided to desert his crime-ridden neighborhood.

Most importantly, my involvement with the Coalition provided important information that I could not otherwise have obtained. When, for instance, the Coalition drafted and passed its poverty tax exemption ordinance in 2018 and its property tax reform ordinance in 2023, I was constantly in meetings with the public servants in charge of property tax administration. In addition to having a front-row seat to these legislative wins, I also used the time before and after meetings to verify facts, ask questions, and test newly forming hypotheses.

My level of engagement was, however, unusual. Being a disengaged observer is the more common approach among academics. I do things differently because I find the academy's protocols for collecting stories from poor Black people and other vulnerable populations to be unnecessarily extractive. Usually, researchers enter a community with research questions that they have created without community input. If circumstances indicate that there are other, more pressing questions to prioritize, many are unwilling to abandon their initial research questions and design.

Even worse, when, in exchange for modest research incentives, people tell their stories, most researchers do not even bother to send the resulting findings to their respondents. This is largely because universities do not provide academics who do the hard and time-consuming work of communicating their findings to the communities studied — through things like op-eds, community teach-ins, and presentations — with reduced teaching or service loads. Academics must do this crucial work on their own time and often at high personal cost.

My deep involvement with overtaxed homeowners was meant to impact them, changing my role from a more traditional observer who records events to a changemaker who catalyzes them. Many of my colleagues worry that my deep engagement erased my neutrality. But neutrality is a farce. Disengaged outsiders may not be compromised by their deep affinity for the population under study, and they may not impact the phenomenon under study, but their "neutrality" is compromised by other things like their race, class, age, profession, and gender. The way to effectively deal with bias, which is perennially present, is for researchers to be honest about how their positionality affects their data collection. Clinging to uncritical and barren notions of neutrality is futile.

In my case, because Detroit is an 80 percent Black city, being an African American woman helped me to gain trust and develop deep bonds with the people I interviewed, and also with those I joined in the justice work. Our common racial identity produced an intimacy that allowed people to open up and share things that they might not otherwise have shared. My interviews were, therefore, full of priceless details and raw emotion, which enliven this book.

Similarly, my role as a Coalition leader engendered trust. Over the years, Detroit has been flush with researchers who come to study "urban dysfunction." Very few, however, take the time to address the problems that their research surfaces. Because I did, this set me apart. I could be trusted because I was not the typical extractive academic, and this trust was an absolute asset to the research.

My position as a law professor also generated trust. People like Myrisha signed up for an interview with me because it was both a surprise and an honor that an accomplished law professor thought that they were important and wanted to hear their story.

My profession also helped in the fight for property tax justice. Unfortunately, authorities routinely dismissed homeowners' complaints about their property taxes being too high, but when I produced uncontested data, showing that property tax assessments in Detroit were in violation of the Michigan Constitution, no one could ignore me.

While the intimate bonds of trust I formed propelled the research, this also had its costs. Namely, as an empath, I carry people's sorrows and pain as if they are my own, so when people open up to me, this is both a blessing and a burden. Too often researchers — who hear traumatic stories one after another — ignore the emotional and psychological impact that this has on them. I thus had to be very intentional about self-care during the duration of this research project. I encourage others to do the same.

While my position as a Black female law professor, who was one of the Coalition for Property Tax Justice's leaders, generated trust with overtaxed homeowners and their allies, it also had its downsides. Namely, it prevented me from investigating certain facets of Detroit's property tax foreclosure crisis. I, for instance, am not well positioned to tell this story from the perspective of the city's mayor and other public officials. While these are important perspectives, my justice work has created a tense relationship with these individuals. I, therefore, leave this worthwhile research for other scholars to complete.

As with all other researchers, my methods are not perfect. But they are exceptionally defendable. Most importantly, through the quantitative and qualitative data that my research has generated, I was able to develop the concept of predatory governance, which is when local governments intentionally or unintentionally raise public dollars through racist policies. This is what connects the property tax injustice in Detroit to the loss of wealth happening in other majority-Black communities. As explained earlier, predatory governance is what has happened in Ferguson, Missouri; Washington D.C.; and New Orleans. It may well also be happening in your own community. Although it most often hides in plain sight, people committed to racial justice must learn to recognize predatory governance, call it out, and put a stop to it. Vulnerable individuals and families are counting on us.

INSTITUTE FOR LAW AND ORGANIZING

To learn more about how you can join the movement to eradicate racialized property tax administration in America, visit www.lawandorganizing.org.

NOTES

Introduction – This House Means Everything to Me

1. Bernadette Atuahene and Timothy R. Hodge, "Stategraft," *Southern California Law Review* 91, no. 2 (2018): 286.

2. Christine MacDonald, "Detroit Homeowners Overtaxed $600 Million," *Detroit News*, January 11, 2020, accessed January 20, 2023, https://eu.detroitnews.com /story/news/local/detroit-city/housing/2020/01/09/detroit-homeowners-overtaxed -600-million/2698518001/ [https://perma.cc/V38N-QAN7].

3. Mike Wilkinson, "Whites Get Half of Mortgages in Detroit, Nation's Largest Majority Black City," *Bridge Michigan*, June 13, 2019, accessed August 8, 2024, https://www .bridgemi.com/urban-affairs/whites-get-half-mortgages-detroit-nations-largest -majority-black-city [https://perma.cc/3C9C-D9X5].

4. Aditya Aladangady, Andrew C. Chang, and Jacob Krimmel, "Greater Wealth, Greater Uncertainty: Changes in Racial Inequality in the Survey of Consumer Finances," Federal Reserve System, October 18, 2023, accessed August 8, 2024, https://www.federalreserve.gov/econres/notes/feds-notes/greater-wealth-greater -uncertainty-changes-in-racial-inequality-in-the-survey-of-consumer-finances -20231018.html#fig1.

5. Sherrilyn A. Ifill, "Creating a Truth and Reconciliation Commission for Lynching," *Minnesota Journal of Law & Inequality* 21, no. 2 (December 2003): 264.

6. Michael Wagner and Tom Walsh, "Slain Tycoon Left Hostility Behind," *Detroit Free Press*, June 19, 1983.

7. Michael Wagner and Tom Walsh, "Mystery Meeting Called Key to Oakland Tycoon's Murder," *Detroit Free Press*, June 15, 1983.

8. Michael Wagner and Tom Walsh, "Did David Auer's business dealings catch up with him?" *Detroit Free Press*, June 19, 1983.

9. "Home Value and Purchase Price," U.S. Census Bureau, accessed April 12, 2024, https://data.census.gov/table/ACSDT5Y2020.B25075?q=Housing%20Value %20and%20Purchase%20Price&g=160XX00US2621000,2622000,2635480 ,2649000,2684000.

10. Ibram X. Kendi, *How to Be an Antiracist*, 1st ed. (New York: One World, 2019).

11. See U.S. Department of Justice, Civil Rights Division, *Investigation of the Ferguson Police Department* (2015), 3, 15, 42, accessed August 8, 2024, https://www.justice.gov /sites/default/files/opa/press-releases/attachments/2015/03/04/ferguson_police _department_report.pdf [https://perma.cc/HF22-7D4D].

12. Pamela Huber, "Policing for Profit: When Your Property Does the Time," *AWOL*, December 12, 2013, accessed August 8, 2024, https://awolau.org/847 /uncategorized/policing-for-profit-when-your-property-does-the-time [https://perma .cc/EPG2-Q64R].

13. Authorities can only jail debtors if they have the ability to pay and are not willing to do so. See *Bearden v. Georgia*, 461 U.S. 660 (1983); *Tate v. Short*, 401 U.S. 395, 398 (1971); *Williams v. Illinois*, 399 U.S. 235, 240–41 (1970).

14. Jason Grotto, "The Tax Divide: An Unfair Burden," *Chicago Tribune*, June 10, 2017, apps.chicagotribune.com/news/watchdog/cook-county-property-tax-divide /assessments.html.
15. Cook County, Il, Code of Ord., § 74-64.
16. Carlos F. Avenancio-León et al., "The Assessment Gap: Racial Inequalities in Property Taxation," *Quarterly Journal of Economics* 137, no. 3 (August 2022): 1431.

1 – The Rise of Two Sharecroppers

1. Edward E. Royce, *The Origins of Southern Sharecropping* (Philadelphia: Temple University Press, 1993), 219.
2. Royce, *Southern Sharecropping*, 211–19.
3. "The Carolina of To-Day! Views of a Gentleman of the Old School," *The Charles Daily News*, May 31, 1871, accessed July 2, 2024, https://chroniclingamerica.loc .gov/lccn/sn84026994/1871-05-31/ed-1/seq-1/#date1=1870&sort=date&rows=20& words=lazy+negroes&searchType=basic&sequence=0&index=19&state=&date2 =1950&proxtext=negro+lazy&y=8&x=16&dateFilterType=yearRange&page=2
4. Vann Newkirk, *Lynching in North Carolina: A History, 1865–1941* (Jefferson, NC: McFarland & Company, 2009), 167–169.
5. "Lynching Statistics by Year," University of Missouri Kansas City, accessed April 11, 2024, http://law2.umkc.edu/faculty/projects/ftrials/shipp/lynchingyear.html.
6. Deborah Davis, *Guest of Honor: Booker T. Washington, Theodore Roosevelt, and the White House Dinner That Shocked a Nation* (New York: Atria Books, 2012).
7. Dewey W. Grantham Jr., "Dinner at the White House: Theodore Roosevelt, Booker T. Washington, and the South," *Tennessee Historical Quarterly* 17, no. 2 (June 1958): 116, https://www.jstor.org/stable/42621372.
8. Grantham Jr., "Dinner at the White House," 117.
9. Laurie Lanzen Harris, *The Great Migration North, 1910–1970 (Defining Moments)*, 1st ed. (Detroit, MI: Omnigraphics, Inc., 2011), 4, 32, 52.
10. Matt Anderson, "Ford's Five-Dollar Day," The Henry Ford, January 3, 2014, https://www.thehenryford.org/explore/blog/fords-five-dollar-day/.
11. Isabel Wilkerson, *The Warmth of Other Suns: The Epic Story of America's Great Migration*, Reprint (New York: Vintage, 2011), 36–204.
12. Joyce Shaw Peterson, "Black Automobile Workers in Detroit, 1910–1930," *Journal of Negro History* 64, no. 3 (July 1979): 177.
13. Peterson, "Black Automobile Workers," 178.
14. David I. Kertzer, "European Peasant Household Structure: Some Implications from a Nineteenth Century Italian Community," *Journal of Family History* 2, no. 4 (December 1977): 334.
15. Annalisa Luporini et al., "Multi-Task Sharecropping Contracts: The Italian Mezzadria," *Economica* 63, no. 251 (August 1996): 446.
16. "World War II and Post-War Monetary Stabilization," Banca d'Italia, Eurosistema, accessed November 6, 2023, https://www.bancaditalia.it/chi-siamo/storia/seconda -guerra-mondiale/index.html?com.dotmarketing.htmlpage.language=1.
17. Fabio Degli Esposti, "Post-War Economics (Italy)," *International Encyclopedia of the First World War 1914–1918 Online*, accessed November 19, 2023, https:// encyclopedia.1914-1918-online.net/article/post-war_economies_italy.
18. Bertrand Blancheton and Jerome Scarabello, "Italian Immigration in France (1870–1913)," *Cahiers du GREThA* (2010): 2, accessed July 12, 2024, https://ideas .repec.org/p/grt/wpegrt/2010-13.html.

19. Marie-Claude Blanc-Chaléard, "Old and New Migrants in France: Italians and Algerians," in *Paths of Integration: Migrants in Western Europe (1880–2004)*, ed. by David Feldman et al. (Amsterdam: Amsterdam University Press, 2006), 47.

20. "Industrial Revolution: Working Conditions," Norwood Secondary College Library, accessed January 5, 2024, https://library.norwood.vic.edu.au/c.php?g=944311&p=6839744.

21. Thomas J. Sugrue, *The Origins of the Urban Crisis: Race and Inequality in Postwar Detroit* (New Jersey: Princeton University Press, 2005), 17; "Ford Rouge Factory Tour: History and Timeline," The Henry Ford, accessed June 30, 2024. https://www.thehenryford.org/visit/ford-rouge-factory-tour/history-and-timeline/timeline.

22. Charles Denby, *Indignant Heart: A Black Worker's Journal* (Boston: South End Press, 1978), 30–31.

23. Elizabeth Esch, *The Color Line and the Assembly Line: Managing Race in the Ford Empire* (Berkeley: University of California Press, 2018), 97.

24. Peterson, "Black Automobile Workers," 179.

25. Sugrue, *The Origins of the Urban Crisis*, 25; Kuniko Fujita, "Black Worker's Struggles in Detroit's Auto Industry, 1935–1975," MSU Libraries Digital Collections: Electronic Theses & Dissertations (1977): 24, https://d.lib.msu.edu/etd/42696.

26. Sugrue, *The Origins of the Urban Crisis*, 99.

27. Frank B. Woodford and Arthur M. Woodford, *All Our Yesterdays: A Brief History of Detroit* (Detroit: Wayne State University Press, 2017), 312.

28. David Littmann, "The 5 Greatest Economic Downturns in Michigan," *DBusiness Magazine*, July 2, 2014, accessed April 11, 2024, https://www.dbusiness.com/business-features/the-5-greatest-economic-downturns-in-michigan/ [https://perma.cc/8JC6-WHWU].

29. "1930 Census: Volume 1. Unemployment Returns by Classes for States and Counties, for Urban and Rural Areas, and for Cities with a Population of 10,000 or More," U.S. Census Bureau, last modified October 8, 2021, https://www.census.gov/library/publications/1931/dec/1930c-vol-01-labor.html.

30. Stephen H. Norwood, *Strikebreaking and Intimidation: Mercenaries and Masculinity in Twentieth-Century America* (Chapel Hill: University of North Carolina Press, 2002), 184; "Union Recruiting Poster, 'Unionism Not Fordism, Now Is the Time to Organize!,' 1935–1936," The Henry Ford, accessed January 19, 2023, https://www.thehenryford.org/collections-and-research/digital-collections/artifact/97069/.

31. Norwood, *Strikebreaking and Intimidation*, 184.

32. "Ford Signs First Contract with Autoworkers' Union," *HISTORY*, last updated June 17, 2021, https://www.history.com/this-day-in-history/ford-signs-first-contract-with-autoworkers-union.

33. Donald R. Deskins Jr., "Race, Residence, and Workplace in Detroit, 1880 to 1965," *Economic Geography*, 48, no. 1 (January 1972): 91. ("There was a wide white-Negro income differential which was nearly twice as favorable for white workers engaged in jobs similar to those performed by Negroes.")

34. Fujita, "Black Worker's Struggles," 15; Donald R. Deskins Jr., "Race, Residence, and Workplace in Detroit, 1880 to 1965," *Economic Geography*, 48, no. 1 (January 1972): 91. ("There was a wide white-Negro income differential which was nearly twice as favorable for white workers engaged in jobs similar to those performed by Negroes."); Harris, Cheryl, I. "Whiteness as Property." *Harvard Law Review* 106, no. 8 (1993): 1736.

35. Sugrue, *The Origins of the Urban Crisis*, 19.

36. Sugrue, *The Origins of the Urban Crisis*, 28–29.

37. Charlie Fater, "1943 Packard Race Strikes," ArcGIS StoryMaps, May 4, 2020, https://storymaps.arcgis.com/stories/375d58df595c4003ad6ad42d9c9e41d8.

38. Harvard Sitkoff, *Toward Freedom Land: The Long Struggle for Racial Equality in America* (Lexington: University Press of Kentucky, 2010), 46–52.

39. "Race Riot of 1943," Detroit Historical Society, accessed November 6, 2022, https://detroithistorical.org/learn/encyclopedia-of-detroit/race-riot-1943.

40. Fujita, "Black Worker's Struggles," 10.

41. Thomas J. Sugrue, "'Forget about Your Inalienable Right to Work': Deindustrialization and Its Discontents at Ford, 1950–1953," *International Labor and Working-Class History* 48 Fall (1995): 120.

42. Sugrue, *The Origins of the Urban Crisis*, 97, Table 4.1.

43. Beth Tompkins Bates, *The Making of Black Detroit in the Age of Henry Ford* (Chapel Hill: University of North Carolina Press, 2012), 66.

44. Reynolds Farley, "The Bankruptcy of Detroit: What Role Did Race Play?," *City & Community* 14, no. 2 (2015): 124, https://deepblue.lib.umich.edu/bitstream /handle/2027.42/112014/cico12106.pdf?sequence=1.

45. "1950 Census of Population: Volume 2. Characteristics of the Population. Michigan, Detailed Characteristics Table 76-94," U.S. Census Bureau, Table 87. https:// www2.census.gov/library/publications/decennial/1950/population-volume-2 /37779850v2p22ch5.pdf; "1950 Census of Population: Volume 2. Characteristics of the Population. United States Summary, Detailed Characteristics Table 1-141," U.S. Census Bureau, Table 137, https://www2.census.gov/library/publications /decennial/1950/population-volume-2/21983999v2p1ch4.pdf.

2 – The American Nightmare

1. Jeremy Williams, *Detroit: The Black Bottom Community* (Charleston, SC: Arcadia Publishing, 2009), 46.

2. Peterson, "Black Automobile Workers," 182.

3. Werner Troesken et al., "Collective Action, White Flight, and the Origins of Racial Zoning Laws," *Journal of Law, Economics, and Organization* 35, no. 2 (July 2019): 289.

4. *Buchanan v. Warley*, 245 U.S. 60, 82 (1917). Many cities ignored Buchanan, including Atlanta, Indianapolis, New Orleans, Richmond, Kansas City, St. Louis, and Austin; Christopher Silver, "The Racial Origins of Zoning in American Cities," in *Urban Planning and the African American Community: In the Shadows*, eds. June Manning Thomas and Marsha Ritzdorf (Thousand Oaks, CA: Sage Publications, 1996), 7.

5. Ta-Nehisi Coates, "The Other Detroit," *Atlantic Monthly*, April 2011, https://www .theatlantic.com/magazine/archive/2011/04/the-other-detroit/308403/.

6. Richard Brooks and Carol Rose, *Saving the Neighborhood: Racially Restrictive Covenants, Law, and Social Norms* (Cambridge: Harvard University Press, 2013), 106.

7. *Parmalee v. Morris*, 188 N.W. 330, 331 (Mich. Ct. App. 1922); Harris, Cheryl, I. "Whiteness as Property." *Harvard Law Review* 106, no. 8 (1993): 1731.

8. Richard Rothstein, *The Color of Law: A Forgotten History of How Our Government Segregated America* (New York: Liveright Publishing, 2017), 84.

9. Rothstein, *The Color of Law*, 85.

10. Peterson, "Black Automobile Workers," 183–84.

11. Reynolds Farley, "Detroit Fifty Years After the Kerner Report: What Has Changed, What Has Not, and Why?," *RSF: The Russell Sage Foundation Journal of the Social Sciences* 4, no. 6 (September 2018): 208.

12. Sugrue, *The Origins of the Urban Crisis,* 44.
13. Jeffrey D. Gonda, *Unjust Deeds: The Restrictive Covenant Cases and the Making of the Civil Rights Movement* (Chapel Hill: University of North Carolina Press, 2015), 26.
14. Sugrue, *The Origins of the Urban Crisis,* 37.
15. "Mapping Inequality: Redlining in New Deal America," Digital Scholarship Lab, accessed July 4, 2024, https://dsl.richmond.edu/panorama/redlining/map/MI /Detroit/context#loc=10/42.3479/-83.1366.
16. Sugrue, *The Origins of the Urban Crisis,* 37.
17. Bud Goodman, "City's 'Rat Belt' Residents Fight Losing Battle," *Detroit Free Press,* August 23, 1953.
18. Goodman, "City's 'Rat Belt.'"
19. Detroit (Mich.). City Plan Commission, *The People of Detroit.* (Detroit: The Commission, 1946), 33.
20. Sugrue, *The Origins of the Urban Crisis,* 42.
21. Sugrue, *The Origins of the Urban Crisis,* 43.
22. Sugrue, *The Origins of the Urban Crisis,* 54.
23. Reynolds Farley et al., "Stereotypes and Segregation: Neighborhoods in the Detroit Area," *American Journal of Sociology* 100, no. 3 (November 1994): 75.
24. Dominic J. Capeci, *Race Relations in Wartime Detroit: The Sojourner Truth Housing Controversy of 1942* (Philadelphia: Temple University Press, 1984); Dominic Capeci and Martha Francis Wilkerson, *Layered Violence: The Detroit Rioters of 1943,* 1st ed. (Jackson: University Press of Mississippi, 1991).
25. Rothstein, *The Color of Law,* 146.
26. Fujita, "Black Worker's Struggles," 24.
27. "Prelude to 1967: Detroit's Racial Clashes of 1942–43," *Detroit News,* July 10, 2017, https://eu.detroitnews.com/story/news/local/michigan-history/2017/07/07 /detroit-riots-1942-43/103482496/.
28. Sugrue, *The Origins of the Urban Crisis,* 82–83; Capeci, *Race Relations in Wartime Detroit; Shelley v. Kraemer,* 334 U.S. 1 (1948).
29. Sugrue, *The Origins of the Urban Crisis,* 183.
30. Reynolds Farley et al., "Continued Racial Residential Segregation in Detroit: 'Chocolate City, Vanilla Suburbs' Revisited," *Journal of Housing Research* 4, no. 1 (1993): 8.
31. David Good, *Orvie: The Dictator of Dearborn: The Rise and Reign of Orville L. Hubbard,* 1st ed. (Detroit: Wayne State University Press, 1989), 264–65.
32. Shawn G. Kennedy, "Orville L. Hubbard of Dearborn; Ex-Mayor a Foe of Integration," *New York Times,* Dec. 17, 1982, https://www.nytimes.com/1982/12 /17/obituaries/orville-l-hubbard-of-dearborn-ex-mayor-a-foe-of-integration .html.
33. "Hubbard, Orville," Detroit Historical Society, accessed April 15, 2024, https:// detroithistorical.org/learn/encyclopedia-of-detroit/hubbard-orville.
34. Reynolds Farley, "Population Trends and School Segregation in the Detroit Metropolitan Area," *Wayne State Law Review* 21, no. 3 (1975): 893.
35. Chris Perkins, "How Detroit Assembly Lines Changed Music Forever," *Road & Track,* October 29, 2020, accessed April 12, 2024, https://www.roadandtrack.com /car-culture/a34518490/motown-assembly-line-berry-gordy/.
36. Farley, "Detroit Fifty Years After," 225.

3 – The American Dream

1. Arthur M. Woodford, *This Is Detroit, 1701–2001* (Detroit: Wayne State University Press, 2001), 186–91.

2. Woodford, *This Is Detroit,* 186–91.

3. Ben Hopper, "The Great Depression in Michigan," *MLPP,* December 14, 2021, mlpp.org/announcement/the-great-depression-in-michigan/.

4. Gregory Sumner, "Michigan History: State Was Home to 6,000 POWs during WWII," *Detroit Free Press,* March 3, 2019, accessed August 10, 2024, https://eu.freep.com/story /opinion/contributors/2019/03/03/michigan-history-pows-wwii/1941032002/; Kevin T. Hall. "The Befriended Enemy: German Prisoners of War in Michigan," *Michigan Historical Review* 41, no. 1 (2015): 57, https://doi.org/10.5342/michhistrevi.41.1.0057.

5. "St. Rita Catholic School," Detroiturbex.com, accessed January 19, 2024, http: //www.detroiturbex.com/content/schools/stritaschool/index.html; "St. Rita Catholic Church," Detroiturbex.com, accessed July 4, 2024, https://detroiturbex.com/content /churches/strita/index.html.

6. "1950 United States Census of Population," U.S. Department of Commerce, 1952, accessed July 1, 2024, https://www2.census.gov/prod2/decennial/documents /41557421v3p2ch02.pdf.

7. Thomas W. Hanchett, "The Other 'Subsidized Housing': Federal Aid to Suburbanization 1940s–1960s," in *From Tenements to the Taylor Homes: In Search of an Urban Housing Policy in Twentieth Century America,* eds. John F. Bauman, Roger Biles, and Kristin M. Szylvian (University Park: Pennsylvania State University Press, 2000), 163–179.

8. *Sipes v. McGhee,* 25 N.W.2d 638 (Mich. Ct. App. 1947).

9. Brief for Ardmore Ass'n, Inc. et al. as *Amici Curiae* Supporting Respondent at 14, *Sipes v. McGhee,* 25 N.W.2d 638 (Mich. Ct. App. 1947).

10. Brief for Ardmore Ass'n, Inc. et al. as *Amici Curiae* Supporting Respondent at 14, *Sipes v. McGhee,* 25 N.W.2d 638 (Mich. Ct. App. 1947).

11. Brief for Ardmore Ass'n, Inc. et al. as *Amici Curiae* Supporting Respondent at 14, *Sipes v. McGhee,* 25 N.W.2d 638 (Mich. Ct. App. 1947).

12. Sugrue, *The Origins of the Urban Crisis,* 50.

13. "Urban Renewal, Family Displacements, and Race 1950–1966," Digital Scholarship Lab, accessed April 11, 2024, https://dsl.richmond.edu/panorama /renewal/.

14. "Urban Renewal, 1950–1966."

15. Rothstein, *The Color of Law.*

16. Roger Biles, "Expressways before the Interstates: The Case of Detroit, 1945–1956," *Journal of Urban History* 40, no. 5 (May 2014): 850.

17. Farrell Evans, "How Interstate Highways Gutted Communities—and Reinforced Segregation," *History,* last updated September 21, 2023, accessed August 8, 2024, https://www.history.com/news/interstate-highway-system-infrastructure -construction-segregation.

18. Mindy Thompson Fullilove, *Root Shock: How Tearing Up City Neighborhoods Hurts America, and What We Can Do About It* (New York: New Village Press, 2016), 11.

19. Fullilove, *Root Shock,* 14; Susan Saegert et al., "Mortgage Foreclosure and Health Disparities: Serial Displacement as Asset Extraction in African American Populations," *Journal of Urban Health* 88, no. 3 (June 2011): 397.

20. "About," South Redford School District, accessed January 25, 2024, https://www
    .southredford.org/apps/pages/index.jsp?uREC_ID=1194299&type=d&pREC
    _ID=1436427.
21. South Redford School District Office of Curriculum and Instruction, *Elementary
    and Secondary Curriculum 1968–69*, xviii–xix.
22. "History," City of Livonia, accessed July 4, 2024, www.livonia.gov/1418/History.
23. "'Wonderland' Is Started," *Detroit Free Press*, November 7, 1958.
24. "Census of Housing, 1950: Volume I, General Characteristics, Michigan," U.S.
    Census Bureau, https://www2.census.gov/library/publications/decennial/1950
    /housing-volume-1/36965082v1p4ch01.pdf.
25. Reynolds Farley, "The Bankruptcy of Detroit: What Role Did Race Play?," *City
    & Community* 14, no. 2 (2015): 126, https://deepblue.lib.umich.edu/bitstream
    /handle/2027.42/112014/cico12106.pdf?sequence=1; "Table 23. Michigan—Race
    and Hispanic Origin for Selected Large Cities and Other Places: Earliest Census
    to 1990," U.S. Census Bureau, 1990, accessed February 6, 2023, https://www2
    .census.gov/library/working-papers/2005/demo/pop-twps0076/mitab.xls.
26. "St. Rita Catholic School / Helen Field Learning Academy," Detroiturbex.com,
    n.d., http://www.detroiturbex.com/content/schools/stritaschool/index.html.

4 – The Color of Suburbia

1. Branden Hunter, "MLK First Had a Dream in Detroit in 1963," *Michigan
   Chronicle*, April 4, 2018, https://michiganchronicle.com/mlk-first-had-a-dream
   -in-detroit-in-1963/.
2. "Walk for Freedom," *Detroit Under Fire: Police Violence, Crime Politics, and
   the Struggle for Racial Justice in the Civil Rights Era*, accessed April 15, 2024,
   https://policing.umhistorylabs.lsa.umich.edu/s/detroitunderfire/page/walk-for
   -freedom#:~:text=On%20June%2023%2C%201963%2C%20Detroit,Rights
   %20leaders%20read%20the%20 march.
3. Farley, "Detroit Fifty Years After," 206.
4. "The 43 Casualties of 1967," *Hour Detroit*, April 25, 2017, accessed April 15, 2024,
   https://www.hourdetroit.com/community/the-43-casualties-of-1967/.
5. Lorraine Boissoneault, "Understanding Detroit's 1967 Upheaval 50 Years Later,"
   Smithsonian Magazine, July 26, 2017, https://www.smithsonianmag.com/history
   /understanding-detroits-1967-upheaval-50-years-later-180964212/; "Uprising of
   1967," Detroit Historical Society, accessed April 12, 2024, https://detroithistorical
   .org/learn/encyclopedia-of-detroit/uprising-1967.
6. Carter A. Wilson, "Restructuring and the Growth of Concentrated Poverty in
   Detroit," *Urban Affairs Review* 28, no. 2 (December 1992): 188; John F. McDonald,
   "What Happened to and in Detroit?," *Urban Studies* 51, no. 16 (January 2014):
   3320.
7. Joe T. Darden and Sameh M. Kamel, "Black Residential Segregation in the City
   and Suburbs of Detroit: Does Socioeconomic Status Matter?," *Journal of Urban
   Affairs* 22, no. 1 (March 2000): 4.
8. Joe T. Darden, Joshua G. Bagaka's, and Shun-Jie Ji, "Racial Residential Segregation
   and the Concentration of Low- and High-Income Households in the 45 Largest
   U.S. Metropolitan Areas," *Journal of Developing Societies* 13, no. 2 (December
   1997): 183–84.

9. Farley et al., "'Chocolate City, Vanilla Suburbs' Revisited," 2.
10. Angela G. Kelly, "Letter to the editor," *Washington Post, Times Herald*, July 30, 1967.
11. Sugrue, *The Origins of the Urban Crisis*, 128.
12. Sugrue, *The Origins of the Urban Crisis*, 128.
13. Sugrue, "'Forget about Your Inalienable Right to Work,'" 117.
14. Sophia Crisafulli, "The Cost of Gasoline the Year You Started Driving," *Stacker*, September 20, 2022, https://stacker.com/business-economy/cost-gasoline-year -you-started-driving.
15. Sugrue, *The Origins of the Urban Crisis*, 28.
16. Farley, "The Bankruptcy of Detroit," 121.
17. Farley, "The Bankruptcy of Detroit," 134.
18. Farley, "Detroit Fifty Years After," 209.
19. Sugrue, *The Origins of the Urban Crisis*, 44.
20. Sugrue, *The Origins of the Urban Crisis*, 221.
21. Melvin L. Oliver and Thomas M. Shapiro, *Black Wealth/White Wealth: A New Perspective on Racial Inequality* (New York: Routledge, 1996), 148; Farley, "Detroit Fifty Years After," 213. ("Segregation in the suburban ring peaked in 1970 with a score of 92, but then declined, especially after 1990, as middle-class blacks migrated to the suburbs. By 2016, the suburban segregation score declined to 57. Douglas Massey and Nancy Denton describe scores of lower than 60 as indicating moderate segregation. Detroit's suburban ring has gone from hyper to moderate segregation in the decades since the Kerner report.")
22. Farley et al., "'Chocolate City, Vanilla Suburbs' Revisited," 20.
23. George Galster, "Racial Steering in Urban Housing Markets: A Review of the Audit Evidence," *Review of Black Political Economy* 18, no. 3 (January 1990): 105-129; George Galster, "Racial Steering by Real Estate Agents: Mechanisms and Motives," *Review of Black Political Economy* 19, no. 1 (June 1990): 39–63; George Galster and Erin Godfrey, "By Words and Deeds: Racial Steering by Real Estate Agents in the U.S. in 2000," *Journal of the American Planning Association* 71, no. 3 (September 2005): 251–68.
24. U.S. Department of Housing and Urban Development, "HUD Charges Facebook with Housing Discrimination Over Company's Targeted Advertising Practices," March 28, 2019, accessed January 18, 2023, https://archives.hud.gov/news/2019/ pr19-035.cfm; Brakkton Booker, "Housing Department Slaps Facebook with Discrimination Charge," *NPR*, March 28, 2019, https://www.npr.org/2019/03/28 /707614254/hud-slaps-facebook-with-housing-discrimination-charge.
25. U.S. Attorney's Office, Southern District of New York, "United States Attorney Resolves Groundbreaking Suit Against Meta Platforms, Inc., Formerly Known as Facebook, to Address Discriminatory Advertising for Housing," June 21, 2022, accessed August 11, 2024, https://www.justice.gov/usao-sdny/pr/united-states -attorney-resolves-groundbreaking-suit-against-meta-platforms-inc-formerly.
26. Tim Bates and David Fasenfest, "Enforcement Mechanisms Discouraging Black-American Presence in Suburban Detroit," *International Journal of Urban and Regional Research* 29, no. 4 (December 2005): 960–71.
27. Bates et al., "Enforcement Mechanisms," 960.
28. Bates et al., "Enforcement Mechanisms," 969.
29. Maria Krysan and Michael Bader, "Perceiving the Metropolis: Seeing the City Through a Prism of Race," *Social Forces* 86, no. 2 (December 2007): 702.

30. Krysan et al., "Perceiving the Metropolis," 702.
31. "Table B25077: Median Value (Dollars)," Census Reporter, accessed January 19, 2023, https://censusreporter.org/tables/B25077/.
32. Jeremy Ney, "School Segregation Thrives in America's Most Liberal Cities," American Inequality, June 21, 2023, https://americaninequality.substack.com/p /school-segregation-and-inequality.
33. William L. Taylor, "Desegregating Urban School Systems after Milliken v. Bradley—The Supreme Court and Urban Reality: A Tactical Analysis of Milliken v. Bradley," Wayne Law Review 21, no. 3 (March 1974): 752.
34. "Grades 3-8 State Testing (Includes PSAT Data) Proficiency," Michigan School Data, accessed July 4, 2024 https://www.mischooldata.org/grades-3-8-state -testing-includes-psat-data-proficiency/.
35. Reynolds Farley, Sheldon Danziger, and Harry Holzer, Detroit Divided (Multi-City Study of Urban Inequality) (New York: Russell Sage Foundation, 2002), 65.
36. Michael A. Stoll et al., "Within Cities and Suburbs: Racial Residential Concentration and the Spatial Distribution of Employment Opportunities across Sub-Metropolitan Areas," Journal of Policy Analysis and Management 19, no. 2 (January 2000): 213. ("Regardless of how low-skill jobs are defined, at least 65 percent of them are located in white suburbs.")
37. Ted Mouw, "Job Relocation and the Racial Gap in Unemployment in Detroit and Chicago, 1980 to 1990," American Sociological Review 65, no. 5 (October 2000): 747.
38. Stoll et al., "Within Cities and Suburbs," 213.
39. "American Community Survey Dashboard, 1-Year Data," Detroit Data Center, accessed January 19, 2023, https://detroitdatacenter.org/acs-dashboard.
40. David Sands, "How Detroit's Inequitable Transit Costs Black Detroiters More— and What We Can Do to Change It," Metromode, December 21, 2021, https://www .secondwavemedia.com/metromode/features/economic-equity-in-detroit-2 .aspx; Ryan Felton, "How Detroit Ended up with the Worst Public Transit," Detroit Metro Times, March 11, 2014, https://www.metrotimes.com/news/how-detroit -ended-up-with-the-worst-public-transit-2143889
41. "Livonia," History and Social Justice, accessed April 11, 2024, https://justice .tougaloo.edu/sundowntown/livonia-mi/; "QuickFacts: Livonia City, Michigan," U.S. Census Bureau, accessed January 14, 2023.
42. William Serrin, "Mayor Hubbard Gives Dearborn What It Wants—And Then Some," New York Times, January 12, 1969.
43. "1970 Census of Population, Volume 1, Characteristics of the Population, Michigan," U.S. Dept. of Commerce (March 1973), accessed April 15, 2024, https: //www2.census.gov/prod2/decennial/documents/1970a_mi-01.pdf; "1970 Census of Population, General Housing Characteristics, Michigan," U.S. Census Bureau, accessed July 4, 2024, https://www2.census.gov/library/publications/decennial /1970/housing-volume-1/38133711v1p24ch1.pdf.
44. Robert Reinhold, "Pressure to Admit Blacks Worries Michigan Town," New York Times, July 4, 1977, www.nytimes.com/1977/07/04/archives/pressure-to-admit -blacks-worries-michigan-town.html.
45. Reinhold, "Pressure to Admit Blacks."
46. Susan Vela, "Livonia Mayor, Police Chief React to 'Driving While Black' Warning Billboard," Hometownlife.com, July 6, 2020, https://eu.hometownlife.com/story /news/local/livonia/legal-notices/2020/07/06/livonia-mayor-police-chief-react -driving-while-black-billboard/5387742002/.

47. Andrew Wright, "Newly Released Statistics Confirm Racism in Metro Detroit Policing," *People's World*, September 15, 2021, https://www.peoplesworld.org /article/newly-released-statistics-reveal-racism-in-metro-detroit-policing/.

48. Andrew Kaczynski, Nathan McDermott and Christopher Massie, "GOP Congressman Said Blacks Have 'Entitlement Mentality' and View Themselves as Victims," CNN, July 20, 2018, https://www.cnn.com/2018/07/20/politics /kfile-jason-lewis-racial-comments/index.html.

5 – Black Wealth, White Wealth

1. "Bloomfield Hills City, Michigan," U.S. Census Bureau, accessed April 15, 2024, https://data.census.gov/profile/Bloomfield_Hills_city,_Michigan?g=160XX00 US2609180.

2. "About Bloomfield Hills," City of Bloomfield Hills, accessed April 15, 2024, https://www.bloomfieldhillsmi.net/278/About-Bloomfield-Hills.

3. "Bloomfield Hills City, Michigan. 2020: ACS 5-Year Estimates Subject Tables," U.S. Census Bureau, accessed July 2, 2024, https://data.census .gov/all?q=income%20 in%20bloomfield%20hills%20in%202020; "Michigan. 2020: ACS 5-Year Estimates Subject Tables," U.S. Census Bureau, accessed July 2, 2024, https://data.census .gov/all?q=income%20in%20michigan%20in %202020.

4. Eric Langowski, "Mortgages Analysis," accessed July 4, 2024, https://app.box.com/s /epza6swhntnqzrel0g12wmyyfpel4v6j. This report uses Consumer Financial Protection Bureau Home Mortgage Disclosure Act data from [2007–2017] (https://www .consumerfinance.gov/data-research/hmda/historic-data/?geo=mi &records=first-lien -owner-occupied-1-4-family-records&field_descriptions =labels). Mortgages for first-lien, owner-occupied, 1- to 4-family homes were used. Data was gathered for all of Michigan, but only Wayne County data is presented here.

5. Melvin L. Oliver and Thomas M. Shapiro, *Black Wealth/White Wealth: A New Perspective on Racial Inequality* (New York: Routledge, 1996), 148; Rowan Arundel, "Equity Inequity, Inter and Intra-Generational Divergences, and the Rise of Private Landlordism," *Housing, Theory and Society* 34, no. 2 (February 2017): 179; Lindsay Appleyard and Karen Rowlingson, *Homeownership and the Distribution of Personal Wealth* (York, UK: Joseph Rowntree Foundation, 2010); Karen Rowlingson and Stephen McKay, *Wealth and the Wealthy: Exploring and Tackling Inequalities Between Rich and Poor* (Bristol, UK: Policy Press, 2012).

6. "1970 Census: Housing, Volume I. Housing Characteristics for States, Cities, and Counties," U.S. Census Bureau, fig. 10, accessed April 15, 2024, https://www2.census .gov/library/publications/decennial/1970/housing-volume-1/13276827v1p1ch01.pdf; "Census of Housing: 1980, HC80-1-A24," U.S. Census Bureau, 108, Table 20, digitized for HathiTrust, accessed April 15, 2024, https://babel.hathitrust.org/cgi /pt?id=mdp.39015031742193&seq=108. Note: The median values are for condo units; "Census of Housing: 1990, CH-1-24," U.S. Census Bureau, Table 60, digitized for HathiTrust; "Decennial Data Summary File 3, 2000 H076 Median Value Dollars for Specified Owner-Occupied Units," U.S. Census Bureau; "Table B25077: Median Value (Dollars)," Census Reporter, accessed January 19, 2023, https://censusreporter .org/tables/B25077/.

7. Christopher Berry, "An Evaluation of Property Tax Regressivity in Wayne County, Michigan," University of Chicago, Center for Municipal Finance, accessed

July 4, 2024, https://s3.us-east-2.amazonaws.com/propertytaxdata.uchicago.edu
/nationwide_reports/desktop/Wayne%20County_Michigan.pdf.

8. Bernadette Atuahene, "'Our Taxes Are Too Damn High': Institutional Racism,
    Property Tax Assessments, and the Fair Housing Act," *Northwestern University
    Law Review* 112, no. 6 (2018): 1557–61.

6 – Burdens of Caretaking

1. City of Detroit Open Data Portal: https://data.detroitmi.gov/, Analysis of homes
    between Puritan/Hamilton/Lawton up to Detroit Golf Club on the North.
2. William M. Doerner et al., "The Role of Representative Agents in the Property
    Tax Appeals Process," *National Tax Journal* 68, no. 1 (2015): 59 (discussing the
    compensation model for tax appeal representatives, and the incentives for them
    to "target affluent neighborhoods in making their solicitations"); William M.
    Doerner et al., "An Empirical Analysis of the Property Tax Appeals Process,"
    Property Tax Assessment & Administration 11, no. 4 (2014): 5 (discussing the fact
    that richer property holders have disproportionately more success with appeals
    than do poorer and minority populations); Robert Ross, "The Impact of Property
    Tax Appeals on Vertical Equity in Cook County," University of Chicago, Center
    for Municipal Finance, Working Paper (May 2017), accessed April 5, 2024, http://
    harris.uchicago.edu/files/ross-vertical_equity_in_cook_county_0.pdf; Rachel N.
    Weber et al., "Ask and Ye Shall Receive? Predicting the Successful Appeal of Property
    Tax Assessments," *Public Finance Review* 38, no. 1 (2010).
3. Steven Shavell, "The Appeals Process as a Means of Error Correction," *Journal of
    Legal Studies* 24 no. 2 (June 1995): 372; Chad M. Oldfather, "Error Corrections,"
    Indiana Law Journal 85 no. 1 (2010): 49–85.
4. Atuahene et al., "Stategraft," 286.
5. Mike Duggan, "Question and Answer with Mike Duggan, Detroit Mayor, at
    Mayoral Press Conference at City Hall" (January 23, 2017), accessed July 4,
    2024, https://www.youtube.com/watch?v=subLTFdk_C4; Bernadette Atuahene,
    "Detroit's Homeowners Deserve Better," *Detroit News,* January 31, 2017, http://www
    .detroitnews.com/story/opinion/2017/01/31/property-assessments/97304442/ [https:
    //perma.cc/4XU5-QEWX].
6. "Law Reducing Interest Rates on Delinquent Property Taxes Extended," Michigan
    Public, July 1, 2019, accessed July 14, 2024, https://www.michiganpublic.org/law
    /2019-07-01/law-reducing-interest-rates-on-delinquent-property-taxes-extended.
7. Ruqaiijah Yearby, "Racial Disparities in Health Status and Access to Healthcare:
    The Continuation of Inequality in the United States Due to Structural Racism,"
    American Journal of Economics and Sociology 77, no. 3–4 (May 2018): 1121, https:
    //doi.org/10.1111/ajes.12230; Brietta R. Clark, "Hospital Flight from Minority
    Communities: How Our Existing Civil Rights Framework Fosters Racial Inequality in
    Healthcare," *DePaul University Journal of Health Law* 9, no. 2 (2005): 1023.
8. Lin Cui et al., "Foreclosure, Vacancy and Crime," *Journal of Urban Economics* 87
    (2015): 72, https://doi.org/10.1016/j.jue.2015.01.001.
9. *C.A.F. Inv. Co. v. Michigan State Tax Comm'n,* 221 N.W.2d 588, 592 (Mich. 1974);
    see also *Great Lakes Div. of Nat'l Steel Corp. v. City of Ecorse,* 576 N.W.2d 667, 672
    (Mich. Ct. App. 1998). ("True cash value is synonymous with fair market value.")
10. Nancy Kaffer, "By any measure, there are too many fires in Detroit," *Detroit
    Free Press,* September 4, 2015, https://www.freep.com/story/opinion/columnists
    /nancy-kaffer/2015/09/04/any-measure-there-too-many-fires-detroit/71654806/.

11. "Foreclosure Statistics," Charter County of Wayne, Michigan, accessed October 8, 2023, https://www.waynecounty.com/elected/treasurer/foreclosure-statistics.aspx; Loveland Technologies, "After the Fire: Assessing the Impact of Fires in Detroit, January 1st to July 1st, 2015," *Regrid,* accessed April 5, 2023, https://app.regrid .com/reports/fire.

7 – The Yellow Bag

1. "Hardest Hit Fund (HHF)," U.S. Department of the Treasury, accessed April 1, 2024, https://home.treasury.gov/data/troubled-assets-relief-program/housing/hhf; "Hardest Hit Foreclosure Initiative," NCHSA, accessed April 5, 2024, https://www .ncsha.org/advocacy-issues/hardest-hit-foreclosure-initiative/#:~:text=On %20February%2019%2C%202010%2C%20President,by%20unemployment %20and%20foreclosure%20to.

2. Nushrat Rahman, "Michigan Pandemic Housing Aid Program Will Stop Taking Applications in December," *BridgeDetroit,* November 22, 2023, accessed July 14, 2024, https://www.bridgedetroit.com/michigan-pandemic-housing-aid-program -will-stop-taking-applications-in-december/.

3. "A Report on Nationwide Property Tax Regressivity," University of Chicago, Center for Municipal Finance, accessed April 5, 2024, https://s3.us-east-2.amazonaws .com/propertytaxdata.uchicago.edu/core_logic_nationwide.html.

4. For those approved from July 2010 to December 2017, the qualifying hardship was: Death (3%), Underemployment (20%), Unemployment (29%), Divorce (2%), Medical condition (21%), Other (24%).

5. John Gallaher and Edward Lynch, "Buying In: Opportunities for Increasing Homeownership in Detroit Through Mortgage Lending," Detroit Future City's Center for Equity, Engagement, and Research, March 2022, 28, https: //detroitfuturecity.com/wp-content/uploads/2022/03/Buying-In-Report.pdf.

6. Joshua Akers and Eric Seymour, "Instrumental Exploitation: Predatory Property Relations at City's End," *Geoforum* 91 (May 2018): 131–32, https://doi.org/10.1016/j .geoforum.2018.02.022. (Akers and Seymour's work tracks land contracts over time, showing that they exceeded mortgage lending in 2008.)

7. "Regrid," Wayne County, accessed April 10, 2024, https://app.regrid.com/us/mi /wayne#.

8. City of Detroit, Mayor's Office, "Avoid Property Tax Foreclosure," accessed July 2, 2024, https://detroitmi.gov/Portals/0/docs/Neighborhoods/AvoidPropertyTax Foreclosure.pdf.

9. Wayne County Treasurer Media, "Yellow Bag Notice," 1:00, Dec. 20, 2017, https: //www.youtube.com/watch?v=JCu0jd7CgCI&ab_channel=TreasurerMedia.

10. Diana Hernandez, "Understanding 'Energy Insecurity' and Why It Matters to Health," *Social Science & Medicine,* 167 (October 2016): 1, https://doi.org/10.1016/j .socscimed.2016.08.029.

11. Nancy Kaffer, "Wealthy Donors and Poor Homeowners," *Detroit Free Press,* February 6, 2015, https://www.freep.com/story/opinion/columnists/nancy-kaffer /2015/02/06/jeb-bush-detroit/22950057/.

12. Christine MacDonald, "Effort to Stave Off Detroit Foreclosures Leaves Many Deeper in Debt," *Detroit News,* December 5, 2019, https://www.detroitnews.com /story/news/local/detroit-housing-crisis/2019/12/05/detroit-foreclosures-effort -wayne-county-treasurer-puts-many-residents-into-deeper-debt/1770381001/.

13. "Annual Meeting 2016," United Community Housing Coalition, November 9, 2016, https://static.wixstatic.com/ugd/a98955_8380961860454476aa98c670792cdad5 .pdf; "Annual Dinner 2017," United Community Housing Coalition, November 16, 2017, https://static.wixstatic.com/ugd/6da088_22e3baac4ce04b75a27117a0926f9914.pdf; "Annual Dinner 2018," United Community Housing Coalition, November 15, 2018, https://static.wixstatic.com/ugd/a98955_636b7b904e854a14ad13a35581f78eca.pdf; "Annual Dinner 2019," United Community Housing Coalition, November 7, 2019, https://static.wixstatic.com/ugd/6c8a1f_e8d7e0c5630a469eaf4e6041c7a2a51e.pdf.

14. Frank Witsil, "As Property Tax Deadline Approaches, Thousands Scramble," *Detroit Free Press,* June 30, 2016, https://www.freep.com/story/money/business /michigan/2016/06/30/wayne-county-treasurer-taxes/86561128/.

15. Witsil, "As Property Tax Deadline Approaches."

16. Pat Batcheller, "Wayne County Starts Foreclosure Hearings, WDET 101.9 FM, January 9, 2017, https://wdet.org/posts/2017/01/09/84467-wayne-county-starts -foreclosure-hearings-video/.

17. FOIA of 2016 foreclosure data of Wayne County.

18. "Who We Are," United Community Housing Coalition, accessed July 2, 2024, https://www.uchcdetroit.org/who-we-are.

8 – Stolen Legacy

1. "School Closings: Metro Detroit Schools Close Thursday as Snow Is Cleaned Up," *WXYZ 7 Action News Detroit,* December 13, 2017, https://www.wxyz.com /news/school-closings-metro-detroit-schools-close-ahead-of-wednesday-snow -storm; "December 14, 2017 Historical Weather at Detroit Metropolitan Wayne County Airport," Weather Spark, December 14, 2017, https://weatherspark .com/h/d/146721/2017/12/14/Historical-Weather-on-Thursday-December-14 -2017 -at-Detroit-Metropolitan-Wayne-County-Airport-Michigan-United-States #Figures-Temperature.

2. "Quickfacts," U.S. Census Bureau, accessed April 8, 2024, https://www.census .gov/quickfacts/. Type in each city and select "Housing," then compare median rents.

3. "Who Is Eligible for Detroit Promise?" Detroit Promise, accessed April 8, 2024, http://detpromise.wpengine.com/do-i-qualify/.

4. Kat Stafford, "Detroit Aims to Target Thousands of Noncompliant Landlords," *Detroit Free Press,* May 24, 2017, https://www.freep.com/story/news/local /michigan/detroit/2017/05/24/detroit-landlords/343220001/; Detroit, Mich., City Code § Sec. 8-15-81 (2022), https://tinyurl.com/yp3hkryc.

5. MacDonald, "Persistent Evictions."

6. MacDonald, "Persistent Evictions."

7. MacDonald, "Persistent Evictions."

8. Detroit, Mich., City Code § Sec. 8-15-34 (2021); Detroit, Mich., City Code § Sec. 8-15-35 (2021); Detroit, Mich., City Code § Sec. 8-15-36 (2017).

9. "Detroit Rental Ordinance: How to Operate a Rental Property in the City of Detroit," City of Detroit, 21, https://detroitmi.gov/sites/detroitmi.localhost/files /2021-08/Landlord%20Guide.pdf.

10. "Detroit Rental Ordinance: How to Operate a Rental Property in the City of Detroit," City of Detroit, 27, https://detroitmi.gov/sites/detroitmi.localhost/files /2021-08/Landlord%20Guide.pdf.

11. Mich. Comp. Laws, § 333.5475a (2002).

12. Detroit, Mich., City Code § 8-17-12 (n.d.)
13. MacDonald, "Persistent Evictions."
14. "Rental Housing Registration," Baltimore County Government, accessed April 12, 2014, https://www.baltimorecountymd.gov/departments/pai/rental-registration/; "Landlord Registration for Non Owner-Occupied Buildings," City of Jersey City, accessed April 12, 2024, https://www.jerseycitynj.gov/cityhall/Clerk/landlordregistration; "Rent Registry," Los Angeles County Consumer and Business Affairs, accessed April 12, 2024, https://dcba.lacounty.gov/rentregistry/; "Ordinance 265-20," City and County of San Francisco, accessed April 12, 2024, https://sfgov.legistar.com/View.ashx?GU ID=79C40690-896E-43CD-9855-77B3AC909AEF&ID=9024120&M=F; "Rental Housing Business," DC Department of Licensing and Consumer Protection, accessed April 12, 2024, https://dlcp.dc.gov/node/1618681.
15. Sarah Alvarez, "Detroit to make changes to its rental registry ordinance due to limited compliance," *Curbed,* November 8, 2019, https://detroit.curbed.com/2019 /11/8/20955085/detroit-rental-registry-ordinance-changes-renter-landlord.
16. Detroit, Mich. City Code, § 8-15-82(d), *Rodgers v. Rosman,* 19-002064-AV (3rd Cir. Ct. App. Sept. 12, 2019), https://tinyurl.com/bdheww75.
17. "If you are a landlord, or the agent for a landlord, who is commencing a summary proceeding to recover possession of premises from a person in possession, you will be asked to provide a copy of your City of Detroit issued Certificate of Compliance pursuant to Detroit City Code Section 8-15-82. Failure to provide the Certificate of Compliance could negatively impact your case." "Landlord-Tenant/Summary Proceedings: Starting a Landlord-Tenant Case," 36th District Court, accessed February 21, 2023, https://tinyurl.com/5n8t8snc.
18. Alexa Eisenberg et al., "Reinforcing Low-Income Homeownership Through Home Repair: Evaluation of the Make It Home Repair Program," *Poverty Solutions* (University of Michigan, February 2021), 10, accessed February 21, 2023, https: //tinyurl.com/2p8xvaj3.
19. Aaron Mondry, "The Perils and Pitfalls of Renting in Detroit," *Outlier Media,* December 7, 2022, https://outliermedia.org/perils-pitfalls-renting-detroit -evictions-affordable/.
20. Frank Witsil, "Detroit Among Top Metro Areas for Flipping Houses, Report Says," *Detroit Free Press,* May 26, 2015, https://www.freep.com/story/money /business/michigan/2015/05/26/home-flipping-detroit-michigan/27949669/.
21. Alexa Eisenberg and Katlin Brantley, "Crisis Before the Emergency: Evictions in Detroit Before and After the Onset of Covid-19," June 2022, *Poverty Solutions,* 11, accessed July 4, 2024, https://tinyurl.com/bdz39k3p.
22. Detroit, Mich., City Code § Sec. 42-2-93 (2017): "Owner or Operator Responsible for Removal of Solid Waste; Nuisance; Placement in Large Movable Container on Private Area of Owner or Operator's Property Only, for Eviction; Tenant's Personal Property to Be Disposed of in Large Movable Container Only; Removal of Large Movable Container Required within 48 Hours; Owner, Operator, or Other Person Who Fails to Use a Large Movable Container for the Disposal of Tenant's Personal Property Is Subject to Immediate Issuance of a Blight Violation Notice."
23. Alexa Eisenberg and Katlin Brantley, "A Public Health Crisis, Not a Property Dispute: Learning from Covid-19 Eviction Response Measures in Detroit," *Poverty Solutions,* November 2022, accessed April 9, 2024, https://sites.fordschool .umich.edu/poverty2021/files/2022/11/PovertySolutions-Learning-from-COVID -19-Eviction-Response-Measures-in-Detroit-policybrief-111122.pdf.
24. American Community Survey 1-Year Data 2005-2022, "U.S. Census Bureau,"

accessed April 11, 2024, https://www.census.gov/data/developers/data-sets
/acs-1year.html. (In 2010, 47 percent of all households were renter occupied in
Detroit and 27 percent in Michigan, but in 2019, 52 percent of all households were
renter occupied in Detroit and 28 percent in Michigan.)

9 – Rigged Game

1. Atuahene, "'Our Taxes Are Too Damn High:' Institutional Racism, Property Tax
Assessments, and the Fair Housing Act," *Northwestern University Law Review*
112, no. 6 (2018): 1501.
2. Jenny R. Yang and Jane Liu, "Strengthening Accountability for Discrimination:
Confronting Fundamental Power Imbalances in the Employment Relationship,"
Economic Policy Institute, January 19, 2021, 1, https://www.epi.org/unequalpower
/publications/strengthening-accountability-for-discrimination-confronting
-fundamental-power-imbalances-in-the-employment-relationship/.
3. Sidita Kushi and Ian P. McManus, "Gender, crisis and the welfare state: Female
labor market outcomes across OECD countries," *Comparative European Politics*
16, no. 3 (2018): 434–63. https://doi.org/10.1057/cep.2016.21.
4. See, e.g., Dianne Feeley, "A Hurricane Without Water: Detroit's Foreclosure
Disaster," *Black Agenda Report* (June 3, 2015), https://blackagendareport.com
/detroit_foreclosure-disaster.
5. "Former Detroit Police Chief Convicted of Embezzlement," *New York Times,*
May 8, 1992, https://www.nytimes.com/1992/05/08/us/former-detroit-police-chief
-convicted-of-embezzlement.html; Reynolds Farley, "The bankruptcy of Detroit:
What role did race play?" *City & Community* 14, no. 2 (2015): 123, https://doi-org
.libproxy2.usc.edu/10.1111/cico.12106.
6. "Former Detroit City Treasurer Sentenced to Eleven Years in Prison for Taking
Bribes in Exchange for Tens of Millions in Detroit Pension Investments," United
States Attorney's Office, September 21, 2015, https://www.justice.gov/usao-edmi
/pr/former-detroit-city-treasurer-sentenced-eleven-years-prison-taking-bribes
-exchange-tens.
7. "Driven by Greed: A Database of Corruption in Detroit," *Detroit News,* accessed
April 9, 2024, https://content-static.detroitnews.com/projects/driven-by-greed
-corruption-database/index.htm.
8. Andrew W. Kahrl, "The Power to Destroy: Discriminatory Property Assessments
and the Struggle for Tax Justice in Mississippi," *Journal of Southern History* 82,
no. 3 (August 1, 2016): 580–81, https://doi.org/10.1353/soh.2016.0165; Andrew
W. Kahrl, *The Black Tax: 150 Years of Theft, Exploitation, and Dispossession in
America* (Chicago: University of Chicago Press, 2024).
9. Jacob S. Rugh and Douglas S. Massey, "Racial Segregation and the American
Foreclosure Crisis," *American Sociological Review* 75, no. 5 (October 1, 2010): 646,
https://doi.org/10.1177/0003122410380868. ("About 40 percent of all 2004 to 2006
loans were subprime in the Detroit-Livonia-Dearborn, MI Metro division.")
10. "Save the Dream: Michigan Foreclosure Data," Michigan State Housing
Development Authority, accessed July 4, 2024, https://perma.cc/P7EC-6H5X.
11. "Detroit Home Values," Zillow, accessed April 12, 2024, https://www.zillow.com
/home-values/17762/detroit-mi/.
12. For 2007, the SEV for only real property was $12,466,718,586, but when including
personal property it was $14 billion, as indicated. "County Equalization," Charter
County of Wayne Michigan: 3–4, https://www.waynecounty.com/departments/mb
/equalization/county-equalization.aspx.

13. 2013's total real property SEV was actually $7.12 billion. "County Equalization" Charter County of Wayne Michigan, 10, https://www.waynecounty.com /departments/mb/equalization/county-equalization.aspx.

14. Atuahene et al., "Stategraft," 286.

15. Peter S. Goodman, "Unemployment Rate Rises to 10.2%, Offering Little Reassurance to Job Seekers," New York Times, November 7, 2009, https://www.nytimes .com/2009/11/07/business/economy/07jobs.html; Cassidy Johncox, "Data: Detroit Unemployment Rate Drops to Lowest Point in 23 Years," ClickOnDetroit, May 3, 2023, https://www.clickondetroit.com/news/local/2023 /05/03/data-detroit -unemployment-rate-drops-to-lowest-point-in-23-years/#:~:text=Detroit%27s%20 average%20annual%20unemployment%20rate,in%20the%20city%20since%202000; Andrew Clark, "General Motors Files for Bankruptcy Protection," The Guardian, June 2, 2009, https://www.theguardian.com/business/2009/jun/01/general-motors -bankruptcy-chapter-11; Chris Isidore, "Chrysler Files for Bankruptcy," CNN Money. May 1, 2009, https://money.cnn.com/2009/04/30/news/companies/chrysler _bankruptcy/.

16. Christine MacDonald and Mike Wilkinson, "From the Archives: Half of Detroit Property Owners Don't Pay Taxes," Detroit News, June 14, 2018, https:// www.detroitnews.com/story/news/local/detroit-city/2018/06/13/detroit-property -owners-tax-delinquency/700005002/.

17. Peter Weber, "The Rise and Fall of Detroit," The Week, January 8, 2015, https:// theweek.com/articles/461968/rise-fall-detroit-timeline.

18. John Naglick et al., "'The Grand Bargain': Detroit's Financial Fall to Bankruptcy and Rise to New Possibilities," Essays in Economic and Business History 38, no. 38 (June 30, 2020): 315, https://www.ebhsoc.org/journal/index.php/ebhs/article /view/522.

19. Naglick et al., "'The Grand Bargain'": 317.

20. Weber, "The Rise and Fall of Detroit."

21. "Proposal for Creditors," City of Detroit, June 14, 2013, accessed April 10, 2024, https://detroitmi.gov/sites/detroitmi.localhost/files/2018-05/City%20of%20Detroit% 20Proposal%20for%20Creditors1.pdf.

22. Detroit, "Proposal."

23. Matt Helms, Joe Guillen, John Gallagher, and JC Reindl, "Nine Ways Detroit Is Changing After Bankruptcy," Detroit Free Press, November 9, 2014, https: //eu.freep.com/story/news/local/detroit-bankruptcy/2014/11/09/detroit-city -services-bankruptcy/18716557/.

24. Danielle Kurtzleben, "Everything You Need to Know about the Detroit Bankruptcy," Vox, December 15, 2014, https://www.vox.com/2014/12/15/18073574 /detroit-bankruptcy-pensions-municipal.

25. Jane Slaughter, "Detroit Bankruptcy Takes Aim at Pensions," Labor Notes, July 19, 2013. https://www.labornotes.org/2013/07/detroit-bankruptcy-takes-aim-pensions.

26. Jonathan Oosting, "How Michigan's Revenue Sharing 'Raid' Cost Communities Billions for Local Services," MLIVE, March 30, 2014, accessed April 10, 2024, https://perma.cc/5S89-L2N2.

27. "Revenue Sharing Payments, FY 2000–2001 through FY 2020–2021," Michigan Senate Fiscal Agency, accessed April 10, 2024, http://www.senate.michigan.gov /sfa/Departments /DataCharts/DCrev_RevSharePayType.pdf; Jim Stansell, "Budget Briefing: State Revenue Sharing," House Fiscal Agency, March 2022, accessed July 5, 2024, https://www.house.mi.gov/hfa/PDF/Briefings/State_Tax_Revenue_Sharing _Budget_Briefing_fy22-23.pdf.

28. Anthony Minghine, "The Great Revenue Sharing Heist," Michigan Municipal League, February 2014, accessed April 10, 2024, https://perma.cc/R5L6-LWXH.

29. Chad Livengood, "Unpaid Fines Strand Drivers, Crimp Region's Workforce," *Crain's Detroit Business*, August 6, 2017, accessed April 10, 2024, https://www.crainsdetroit.com/article/20170806/news/635666/unpaidfines-strand-drivers-crimp-regions-workforce; Offense Code Index, Michigan Department of State, accessed April 10, 2024, https://www.michigan.gov/documents/OffenseCode_73877_7.pdf.

30. Kathleen Gray, "Drivers Have Glimmer of Hope to Get Rid of Responsibility Fees," *Detroit Free Press*, October 10, 2017, https://www.freep.com/story/news/politics/2017/10/10/driver-responsibility-fees-amnesty/748282001.

31. Sarah Cwiek, "Five Things to Know About the End of Michigan's Driver Responsibility Fees," *Michigan Radio NPR*, March 6, 2018, https://perma.cc/88SG-SSFT.

32. Brett Theodos, Christina Plerhoples Stacy, and Helen Ho, "Taking Stock of the Community Development Block Grant," Urban Institute, April 2017, accessed March 5, 2023, https://www.urban.org/sites/default/files/publication/89551/cdbg_brief_finalized.pdf.

33. "About Grantees," HUD Exchange, accessed April 10, 2024, https://www.hudexchange.info/grantees. (Under "Find a Grantee Page," select "by State" and select "Michigan"; change "All Grantees" to include both "Wayne County, MI" and "Detroit, MI"; then select "by Program" and select "CDBG: Community Development Block Grant Program"; click search, and under the results pages of "Wayne County, MI" and "Detroit, MI" select "CDBG" on the left-hand side and then select "View More Awards" to view 2004 amounts.)

34. *See* Office of Revenue and Tax Analysis, Michigan Department of Treasury, *School Finance Reform in Michigan: Proposal A Retrospective*, December 2002, accessed April 12, 2024, https://www.michigan.gov/documents/propa_3172_7.pdf.

35. Mark Lockridge, "Performance Audit of the Finance Department Assessment Division, City of Detroit's Office of the Auditor General," City of Detroit, 19, September 10, 2012, https://detroitmi.gov/sites/detroitmi.localhost/files/2018-05/finance_assessment_performance_07-2008_06-2011.pdf.

36. Lockridge, "Performance Audit," 43.

37. Lockridge, "Performance Audit," 9.

38. Lockridge, "Performance Audit," 9.

39. Lockridge, "Performance Audit," 10.

40. State Tax Commission, *Michigan Assessor's Manual, Vol. III*, February 2018, 118, accessed April 10, 2024, https://www.michigan.gov/documents/treasury/Merged_Volume_III_With_All_Edits_051817_575835_7.pdf. ("According to the Michigan Supreme Court, a Board of Review may not make wholesale or across the board adjustments to assessments. A Board of Review must consider each parcel and act upon it individually.")

41. Christine MacDonald, "Michigan's Tax Board to Investigate Whether Detroit is Overtaxing Property Owners," *Detroit News*, April 8, 2013.

42. Christine MacDonald, "Detroit's property tax system plagued by mistakes," *Detroit News*, February 22, 2013, accessed July 2, 2024, https://www.detroitnews.com/story/news/local/detroit-city/2018/06/13/detroits-property-tax-system-plagued-mistakes-waste/700547002/#:~:text=Critics%20said%20Detroit's%20taxes%20are,t%20included%20in%20the%20study.

43. Christine MacDonald, "Detroit tax appeals reveal stark imbalance," *Detroit News*, June 14, 2018, accessed July 13, 2024, https://www.detroitnews.com/story/news/local/detroit-city/2018/06/14/detroit-tax-appeals-reveal-stark-imbalance/703650002/.

44. "City of Detroit Reappraisal," City of Detroit, 2023, accessed July 5, 2024, https://perma.cc/UV5X-6X2T.
45. Christine MacDonald, "Detroit Homeowners Overtaxed $600 Million," *Detroit News*, January 11, 2020, https://www.detroitnews.com/story/news/local/detroit-city/housing/2020/01/09/detroit-homeowners-overtaxed-600-million/2698518001/.
46. MacDonald, "Detroit Homeowners."
47. Sarah Hulett, "In Detroit, A Lopsided Mayor's Race Still Reveals Divisions," *Michigan Public Radio*, November 3, 2017, accessed July 5, 2024, https://www.michiganpublic.org/politics-government/2017-11-03/in-detroit-a-lopsided-mayors-race-still-reveals-divisions; David Jesse, "New Mayor Takes Office in Detroit," *USA Today*, January 1, 2014, accessed July 5, 2024, https://www.usatoday.com/story/news/nation/2014/01/01/new-mayor-takes-office-in-detroit/4279797/.
48. "Land Banks Could Slow City Foreclosures," *Detroit News*, February 22, 2013.
49. "Duggan Runs on Record," *Michigan Citizen*, March 10, 2013.
50. Atuahene et al., "Stategraft", 290–91.
51. Atuahene et al., "Stategraf," 264; Christine MacDonald and Christine Ferretti, "Detroit Assessments to Fall 5–20 Percent," *Detroit News*, January 28, 2015, accessed July 5, 2024, http://detne.ws/2b4hcyz.
52. Atuahene et al., "Stategraft," 288.
53. Christine MacDonald, "Detroit Homeowners Overtaxed by 600 Million," *Detroit News*, January 29, 2015, https://www.detroitnews.com/story/news/local/detroit-city/housing/2020/01/09/detroit-homeowners-overtaxed-600-million/2698518001/.
54. "An Evaluation of Residential Property Tax Assessments in the City of Detroit, 2016–2018," University of Chicago Harris School of Public Policy (February 2020), 9–12, https://harris.uchicago.edu/files/evalrespropertytaxasdetroit20162018.pdf.
55. MacDonald, "Detroit Homeowners."
56. MacDonald, "Detroit Homeowners."
57. Detroit, Mich., City Code § 18-9-3 (September 29, 2017).
58. Detroit, Mich., City Code § 44-4-6 (1982). ("Such appeal shall be filed on or before the second Monday in March and may not be filed thereafter.")
59. "Tax Tribunal Rules," Michigan Tax Tribunal, accessed July 4, 2024, https://www.michigan.gov/taxtrib/entire-tribunal/assets/tax-tribunal-rules#217. (Under R792.10217 Fees, Rule 217, if the property is less than $100,000, fee is $250, for $100,000.01–$500,000, it is $400 and for above $500,000, it is $600.)
60. Mich. Comp. Laws § 205.735(a)(4)(a) (2008). (Property classified as commercial, industrial, or utility can appeal directly to the Michigan Tax Tribunal.)
61. See Mich. Const. art. IV, § 28. ("In the absence of fraud, error of law or the adoption of wrong principles, no appeal may be taken to any court from any final agency provided for the administration of property tax laws from any decision relating to valuation or allocation.")
62. SEV and AV are equal 99 percent of the time. Only if there is a factor applied by the County do these two numbers diverge.
63. William M. Doerner et al., "An empirical analysis of the property tax appeals process," *Journal of Property Tax Assessment & Administration* 11, no. 4 (2014): 5–34 (discussing the fact that richer property holders have disproportionately more success with appeals than do poorer and minority populations).
64. "Michigan Real Estate Appraisal Costs & Prices - ProMatcher Cost Report," ProMatcher Real Estate Appraisal, accessed April 10, 2024, https://appraisers

.promatcher.com/cost/michigan.aspx. (Range for a single-family home or condominium.)

65. "Accounting and Budget," Lansing Michigan, accessed April 10, 2024, https://www .lansingmi.gov/452/Accounting-Budget; "Annual Financial Reports," Houston Controller, accessed April 10, 2024, https://www.houstontx.gov/controller/acfr .html; "FinancialReports," City of Detroit, accessed July 13, 2024, https://detroitmi .gov/node/50766; "Archived Financial Reports," City of Ann Arbor, accessed April 10, 2024, https://www.a2gov.org/departments/finance-admin-services/financial -reporting/Pages/Archived-Financial-Reports.aspx; "Annual Comprehensive Financial Report," New York City Comptroller, accessed April 10, 2024, https: //comptroller.nyc.gov/reports/annual-comprehensive-financial-reports/; "Comprehensive Annual Financial Report 2016," City of Omaha, https://finance.cityofomaha .org/; "Comprehensive Annual Financial Report," Baltimore City, see each year's report at https://finance.baltimorecity.gov/public-info/reports.

66. "Financial Reports," City of Detroit, accessed July 13, 2024, https://detroitmi.gov /node/50766.

67. Loveland, "After the Fires"; Margaret Dewar, "The Effects on Cities of 'Best Practice' in Tax foreclosure: Evidence from Detroit and Flint," Center for Local, State and Urban Policy, accessed April 10, 2024, https://closup.umich.edu /research/working-papers/effects-cities-best-practice-tax-foreclosure-evidence -detroit-and-flint.

68. Stephan D. Whitaker et al., "Deconstructing Distressed-Property Spillovers: The Effects of Vacant, Tax-Delinquent, and Foreclosed Properties in Housing Submarkets," *Journal of Housing Economics* 22, no. 2 (June 1, 2013): 79, https://doi .org/10.1016/j.jhe.2013.04.001.

69. Whitaker, "Deconstructing."

70. Dewar, "The Effects on Cities."

71. Joshua Akers et al., "The Eviction Machine: Neighborhood Instability and Blight in Detroit's Neighborhoods," Working Paper Series No. 5-19, Poverty Solutions at the University of Michigan, 2019 (documenting how properties purchased through tax foreclosure are more likely to end up being demolished at public cost).

72. Bryce Huffman and Kayleigh Lickliter, "Detroiters spent $49M on demolition. Where did the money go?" *BridgeDetroit*, Aug. 19, 2022, accessed 5/30/24, https://www.bridgedetroit.com/detroiters-spent-49m-on-demolition-where-did -the-money-go/.

73. Alexander C. Tsai, "Home foreclosure, health, and mental health: a systematic review of individual, aggregate, and contextual associations," *PLOS One* 10, no. 4 (2015): https://doi.org/10.1371/journal.pone.0123182; Sarah A., Kristin S. Seefeldt, and Sarah Zelner, "Housing Instability and Health: Findings from the Michigan Recession and Recovery Study," *Social Science & Medicine* 75, no. 12 (2012): 2215–24, https://doi.org/10.1016/j.socscimed.2012.08.020; Jason N. Houle et al., "The home foreclosure crisis and rising suicide rates, 2005 to 2010," *American Journal of Public Health* 104, no. 6 (2014): 1073; Kathleen A. Cagney et al., "The onset of depression during the great recession: foreclosure and older adult mental health," *American Journal of Public Health* 104, no. 3 (2014): 498; Karen McCormack, "Comfort and Burden: The Changing Meaning of Home for Owners At-Risk of Foreclosure," *Symbolic Interaction* 35, no. 4 (2012): 421, https://doi.org/10.1002/symb.32.

74. Shawnita Sealy-Jefferson et al., "Neighborhood tax foreclosures, educational attainment, and preterm birth among urban African American women,"

International Journal of Environmental Research and Public Health 16, no. 6 (2019): 904, https://doi.org/10.3390/ijerph16060904 (linking neighborhood tax foreclosures to preterm birth); https://www.ncbi.nlm.nih.gov/pmc/articles /PMC6466185/; Alexa Eisenberg et al., "Toxic structures: Speculation and lead exposure in Detroit's single-family rental market," *Health & Place* 64 (2020): https://doi.org/10.1016/j.healthplace.2020.102390 (showing that children living in investor-owned homes purchased out of the tax foreclosure auction are more likely to experience elevated blood lead levels).

75. Fullilove, *Root Shock*.

Chapter 10 – Sounds Like a Steal

1. Michigan Comp. Laws §§ 124.751, et seq. (2004); "Second Amended and Restated Articles of Incorporation of Detroit Land Bank Authority," Secretary of State, accessed April 11, 2024, https://s3.us-east-2.amazonaws.com/dlba-production -bucket/cms/Articles+-+2nd+Amended.pdf. (The land bank exists to assemble and clear title to property in a coordinated manner, facilitate the use and development of property, and promote economic growth.)

2. "Every Neighborhood Has a Future...And It Doesn't Include Blight: Detroit Blight Removal Task Force Plan," Detroit Blight Removal Task Force, May 2014, 50–51, https://www.dropbox.com/s/d6rcwl8hlaeavc0/Every%20Neighborhood%20Has%20 a%20Future%20-%20Detroit%20Blight%20Taskforce%2005-2014.pdf?e=1&dl=0.

3. Sarah Cwiek, "Detroit City Council Approves Massive Property Transfer to City Land Bank," *Michigan Public*, April 16, 2014, accessed on July 2, 2024, https://www.michiganpublic.org/politics-government/2014-04-16/detroit-city -council-approves-massive-property-transfer-to-city-land-bank.

4. "FY 2016-2017 Budget Analysis by the Legislative Policy Division," City of Detroit, City Council, Legislative Policy Division, February 24, 2016, https://detroitmi .gov/sites/detroitmi.localhost/files/migrated_docs/legislative-policy-reports /Budget%20Analysis%20Reports/2016-2017/Finance%20Dept.pdf.

5. Kirk Pinho, "Hantz Ready for Tree Farm to Take Root: After Years of Red Tape Delays, Hantz Farms Nears Sprouting," *Crain's Detroit Business*, February 15, 2014, https://www.crainsdetroit.com/article/20140216/news/302169981/after-years -of-red-tape-delays-hantz-farms-nears-sprouting.

6. "Detroit Blight Removal Task Force Plan," 52.

7. The Editors, "A New Harvest for Detroit," *The Atlantic*, May 27, 2010, https://www .theatlantic.com/projects/the-future-of-the-city/archive/2010/05/a-new-harvest -for-detroit/57308/.

8. Mich. Comp. Laws § 141.1552(3) (2013); Mich. Comp. Laws § 141.1555(1) (2013). ("Unless the potential sale and value of an asset is included in the emergency manager's financial and operating plan, the emergency manager shall not sell an asset of the local government valued at more than $50,000.00 without the state treasurer's approval.")

9. Diane Bukowski, "CC Agenda 12 11 12," *Voice of Detroit*, December 10, 2012, 62, https://voiceofdetroit.net/2012/12/10/hantz-off-our-land-council-vote-set-for -tues-dec-11-10-am/cc-agenda-12-11-12//; "Press Release: Hantz Woodlands Gets Green Light; State of Michigan Continues Blight Elimination in Detroit," Department of Human Services, October 18, 2013, https://www.michigan .gov/-/media/Project/Websites/mdhhs/Folder2/Folder74/Folder1/Folder174 /pressrelease_Hantz.pdf?rev=64074c5694834edaaa6ada92b77a8f67.

10. Bukowski, "CC Agenda"; Randy Rieland, "Can Planting Gardens and Orchards Really Save Dying Cities?" *Smithsonian Magazine,* November 26, 2013, https://www.smithsonianmag.com/innovation/can-planting-gardens-and-orchards-really-save-dying-cities-180947846/.
11. Pinho, "Hantz Ready for Tree Farm to Take Root."
12. Pinho, "Hantz Ready for Tree Farm to Take Root."
13. Michigan Radio Newsroom, "Gilbert Owns Downtown Detroit, But Who Owns the Most Private Land in the Whole City?," *Michigan Public,* June 20, 2013, https://www.michiganradio.org/economy/2013-06-20/gilbert-owns-downtown-detroit-but-who-owns-the-most-private-land-in-the-whole-city.
14. Josh Akers, "Serial Evictor: Michael Kelly and Detroit Property Exchange," *Urban Praxis,* September 20, 2018, https://urbanpraxis.org/2018/09/20/serial-evictor-michael-kelly-and-detroit-property-exchange/.
15. Charles E. Ramirez, Christine MacDonald, and Candice Williams, "Detroit Erases $1.3M in Debt, Fines in Deal with Controversial Landowner," *Detroit News,* November 7, 2019, https://www.detroitnews.com/story/news/local/detroit-city/2019/11/07/detroit-erases-debt-fines-deal-controversial-landowner-michael-kelly/2510624001/.
16. Christine MacDonald, "Private Landowners Complicate Reshaping of Detroit," *Detroit News,* February 3, 2011, 5A.
17. MacDonald, "Private Landowners Complicate Reshaping."
18. Gus Burns, "1,000-plus Hantz Farms Volunteers Plant Eventual Forest in Previously Blighted Detroit Neighborhood," *MLIVE,* May 17, 2014, https://www.mlive.com/news/detroit/2014/05/1000-plus_hantz_farms_voluntee.html.
19. Office of the Auditor General, "Audit of Demolition Activities Interim Report on Contract Administration for City-Funded Residential Demolitions," November 2019, 13–14, https://detroitmi.gov/sites/detroitmi.localhost/files/2019-11/AuditofDemolitionActivitiesInterimReport_11082019.pdf.
20. DBusiness Daily News, "Hantz Woodlands Fulfills Detroit Blight Removal Project, Adds 15K Trees," *DBusiness Magazine,* December 10, 2014, https://www.dbusiness.com/daily-news/hantz-woodlands-fulfills-detroit-blight-removal-project-adds-15k-trees/.
21. "FCA Project Overview: Mayor's Office and DEGC Presentation to Detroit City Council," City of Detroit Mayor's Office (May 2019): 62, https://s3-prod.crainsdetroit.com/2019-05/FCA-city%20of%20Detroit%20presentation%20May%209.pdf.
22. "FCA Project Overview."
23. Jena Brooker, "Hantz Tree Farm Falls Short on Solving East Side Blight," *Bridge Michigan,* January 26, 2023, https://www.bridgemi.com/business-watch/hantz-tree-farm-falls-short-solving-east-side-blight.

11 – Predator and Prey

1. Matthew Desmond, *Evicted: Poverty and Profit in the American City* (New York: Crown, 2016), 296.
2. Craven, "Eviction Is One of the Biggest Health Risks."
3. "Summary Crime Reported by City Police Departments," FBI Crime Data Explorer, accessed July 12, 2024, https://cde.ucr.cjis.gov/LATEST/webapp/#/pages/explorer/crime/crime-trend. (Average number of reports from 1989 to 1999: Detroit: 25,243; New York: 905.)

4. Cameron Kimble and Ames Grawert, "Collateral Consequences and the Enduring Nature of Punishment," Brennan Center for Justice, June 21, 2021, accessed July 4, 2024, https://www.brennancenter.org/our-work/analysis-opinion/collateral -consequences-and-enduring-nature-punishment.

5. MCLS §801.87; MCLS §324.1607.

6. Reuben Jonathan Miller, *Halfway Home: Race, Punishment, and the Afterlife of Mass Incarceration* (New York: Hachette Book Group, 2021), 144.

7. "Vacant Land Policy," Detroit Land Bank Authority, accessed July 5, 2024, https: //detroitmi.gov/sites/detroitmi.localhost/files/2020-07/DLBA%20-%20Vacant %20Land%20Policy%20202003.pdf.

8. Detroit Land Bank Authority, "Quarterly Report," April 14, 2016, accessed April 15, 2024, https://s3.us-east-2.amazonaws.com/dlba -production-bucket/City_Council _Quarterly_Report/DLBA-City-Council -Report-April-2016-Final.pdf.

9. Several studies provide context for this quote by explaining the many ways in which Mexican workers in America are vulnerable. E.g., Ruth Gomberg-Muñoz, "Willing to Work: Agency and Vulnerability in an Undocumented Immigrant Network," *American Anthropologist* 112, no. 2 (June 2010): 307; https://doi.org/10.1111/j.1548-1433.2010.01227.x; James Quesada et al., "Structural Vulnerability and Health: Latino Migrant Laborers in the United States," *Medical Anthropology* 30, no. 4 (July 2011): 339–62, https://doi.org/10.1080/01459740.2011 .576725.

10. "Compliance," Detroit Land Bank Authority, accessed April 11, 2024, https: //buildingdetroit.org/compliance; Malachi Barrett, "Land bank home renovation program leaves half of buyers with tax debts," *BridgeDetroit*, April 28, 2023, accessed July 14, 2024, https://www.bridgedetroit.com/land-bank-housing-renovation -program-tax-debts/.

11. "Structures," Detroit Land Bank Authority, accessed April 11, 2024, https: //buildingdetroit.org/structures.

12. "Land Reuse Programs," Detroit Land Bank Authority, accessed January 12, 2024, https://buildingdetroit.org/land-reuse-programs.

13. "Buy Back/Occupied," Detroit Land Bank Authority, accessed January 12, 2024, https://buildingdetroit.org/buy-back.

14. "Sales and Programs," Detroit Land Bank Authority, accessed April 11, 2024, https://dlba-production-bucket.s3.us-east-2.amazonaws.com/Building+Blocks /Virtual+Building+Blocks+-+S%26P+Information.pdf.

15. "Discount," Detroit Land Bank Authority, accessed April 11, 2024, https: //buildingdetroit.org/city-of-detroit-discount/; Matt Helms, "Detroit Offers Home Discount to City Workers," *Detroit Free Press*, January 26, 2015, https: //www.freep.com/story/news/local/michigan/detroit/2015/01/26/detroit-land -bank-incentives/22327567/.

16. Detroit City Council, "City Council Quarterly Report FY 2021 Q4," July 15, 2021, 4, accessed April 15, 2024, https://dlba-production-bucket.s3.us-east-2.amazonaws .com/City_Council_Quarterly_Report/Q4+FY2021+CCQR+DRAFT+FINAL.pdf.

17. Chad Halcom, "Scrappers Cost Detroit More Than Money: School Days, Treated Water, Manpower Also Casualties," *Crain's Detroit Business*, March 14, 2014, https://www.crainsdetroit.com/article/20140314/BLOG011/140319906/scrappers -cost-detroit-more-than-money-school-days-treated-water.

18. Christine MacDonald, "Detroit Homeowners Overtaxed $600 Million," *Detroit*

News, January 9, 2020, https://www.detroitnews.com/story/news/local/detroit-city /housing/2020/01/09/detroit-homeowners-overtaxed-600-million/2698518001/.

19. Bernadette Atuahene et al., "Taxed Out: Illegal Property Tax Assessments and the Epidemic of Tax Foreclosures in Detroit," *UC Irvine Law Review* 9, no. 4 (May 1, 2019): 866, https://scholarship.law.uci.edu/ucilr/vol9/iss4/3.

12 – Support Small Business?

1. Sugrue, *The Origins of the Urban Crisis,* 54.
2. David M. P. Freund, *Colored Property: State Policy and White Racial Politics in Suburban America* (Chicago: University of Chicago Press, 2010) https://press .uchicago.edu/ucp/books/book/chicago/C/bo5298959.html (citing Royal Oak Chamber of Commerce, "Royal Oak: Michigan's Most Promising Community," c. 1954, 16, ROHC).
3. 1990: 97.89% white; 2000: 94.80% white. "1990 Census of Population: General Population Characteristics: Michigan," U.S. Department of Commerce, 152, https://www2.census.gov/library/publications/decennial/1990/cp-1/cp-1-24 .pdf; "Michigan: 2000: Summary Population and Housing Characteristics," U.S. Department of Commerce, 128, Nov. 2002, https://www2.census.gov/library /publications/2002/dec/phc-1-24.pdf.
4. Brandon Cornett, "FHA Loan Appraisal Guidelines in 2024: What the Appraiser Looks For," *FHA Handbook,* updated November 2023, accessed April 10, 2024, http://www.fhahandbook.com/appraisal-guidelines.php.
5. Taylor Moore, "Hard Money Loans Basics," *TIME,* January 7, 2021, https://time .com/nextadvisor/mortgages/hard-money-lenders/.
6. "Michigan: 2000: Summary Population and Housing Characteristics," U.S. Department of Commerce, 140 (November 2002), accessed April 25, 2024, https:/ /www2.census.gov/library/publications/2002/dec/phc-1-24.pdf; Amber Arellano, "Officer Seeks Lawbreakers Along Border with Detroit," *Detroit Free Press* June 1, 2000.
7. "State-Wide Real Property Tax Forfeiture and Foreclosure Statistics," Michigan Department of Treasury (2013 Forfeiture through 2019 Foreclosure), accessed April 15, 2024, https://www.waynecounty.com/elected/treasurer/foreclosure -statistics.aspx.
8. Atuahene et al., "Stategraft," 267.
9. "State-Wide Real Property Tax Forfeiture and Foreclosure Statistics," Michigan Department of Treasury (2013 Forfeiture through 2019 Foreclosure), accessed July 15, 2024, https://www.waynecounty.com/elected/treasurer/foreclosure-statistics .aspx.

13 – This Is My House

1. "Diversity Data Project, Housing Opportunities Profile for Detroit-Warren-Livonia, MI," Harvard School of Public Health, http://diversitydata.sph.harvard .edu/Data/Profiles/Show.aspx?loc=420&notes=Tr ue&rgn=None&cat=1, https:// perma.cc/UFA2-YVCX.
2. "Conant Gardens Historic District," Detroit Historical Society, accessed April 10, 2024, https://detroithistorical.org/learn/encyclopedia-of-detroit/conant-gardens -historic-district.

NOTES

3. Both assessed value (AV) and taxable value (TV).
4. Atuahene et al., "Stategraft," 263.
5. Atuahene et al., "Taxed Out," 847.
6. "Mortgage Foreclosures: Additional Mortgage Servicer Actions Could Help Reduce the Frequency and Impact of Abandoned Foreclosures," Government Accountability Office, November 2010, https://www.gao.gov/assets/gao-11-93.pdf.
7. Patrick Cooney et al., "Auto Insurance and Economic Mobility in Michigan: A Cycle of Poverty," University of Michigan Poverty Solutions (March 2019), accessed April 15, 2024, https://poverty.umich.edu/files/2019/05/auto_insurance _and_economic_mobility_in_michigan_2.pdf.
8. "Facts Statistics: Uninsured motorists," Insurance Information Institute, accessed April 15, 2024, https://www.iii.org/fact-statistic/facts-statistics -uninsured-motorists.
9. "An Evaluation of Property Tax Regressivity in Macomb County, Michigan," University of Chicago Harris School of Public Policy, Table 7.5.1, accessed Jan. 27, 2024, https://harris.uchicago.edu/files/evalrespropertytaxasdetroit20162018.pdf; "An Evaluation of Property Tax Regressivity in Wayne County, Michigan," University of Chicago Harris School of Public Policy, Table 7.5.1, accessed July 5, 2024, https: //s3.us-east-2.amazonaws.com/propertytaxdata.uchicago.edu/nationwide_reports /web/Wayne%20County_Michigan.html#:~:text=When%20lower%20value %20homes%20are,highest%20value %20homes%20are%20overassessed.
10. Esther Sullivan, "Dignity takings and trailer trash: The case of Mobile Home Park Mass Evictions," *Chicago-Kent Law Review* 92 (2017): 938–39.
11. Atuahene et al., "Stategraft."
12. "Behind Detroit's Grim Blue Graffiti," Zócalo Public Square, May 28, 2015, accessed April 15, 2024, https://www.zocalopublicsquare.org/2015/05/28/behind -detroits-grim-blue-graffiti/viewings/glimpses/.
13. Andrew T. Hayashi, "The legal salience of taxation," *University of Chicago Law Review* 81 (2014): 1443.
14. Detroit, Mich., Code of Ordinances, § 18-9-3b (December 21, 2016). ("The period for the review by the board of assessors shall be February first [1st] to February fifteenth [15th], inclusive, each year.")
15. "A Summary of House Bills 4433-4437 as Reported from Committee," Michigan Tax Tribunal, accessed April 15, 2024, http://www.legislature.mi.gov /documents/2007-2008/billanalysis/House/htm/2007-HLA-4433-3.htm#_ftn1.
16. "Michigan Tax Tribunal Announces Improvements," *Record Eagle*, February 15, 2014, accessed July 6, 2024, https://www.record-eagle.com/news/state_news /michigan-tax-tribunal-announces-improvements/article_272ee230-901e-5d17 -af1e-4c0cb4c7b3bb.html.
17. Christine MacDonald, "From the Archives: Detroit Tax Appeals Reveal Stark Imbalance," *Detroit News*, accessed April 10, 2024, https://www.detroitnews .com/story/news/local/detroit-city/2018/06/14/detroit-tax-appeals-reveal-stark -imbalance/703650002/.
18. Atuahene, et al., "Stategraft," 290–91. (In 2014, assessments "decreased for District 2 (25%), District 3 (12%), District 7 (20%), District 9 (35%), and District 10 (24%). The remaining districts experienced persistent over-assessment with no correction. In 2015, assessments decreased between 10% and 69% for all districts excluding District 8 (40% increase).")
19. "An Evaluation of Residential Property Tax Assessments in the City of Detroit,

2016–2018," University of Chicago Harris School of Public Policy, accessed April 15, 2024, https://harris.uchicago.edu/files/evalrespropertytaxasdetroit20162018 .pdf; Atuahene et al., "Stategraft," 290–91.

14 – Slumlords

1. Margaret Dewar, "The Effects on Cities of 'Best Practice' in Tax Foreclosure: Evidence from Detroit and Flint," Center for Local, State and Urban Policy (February 2009), 29, accessed April 15, 2024, https://closup.umich.edu/research /working-papers/effects-cities-best-practice-tax-foreclosure-evidence-detroit -and-flint.

2. Margaret Dewar, "Reuse of abandoned property in Detroit and Flint: Impacts of different types of sales," *Journal of Planning Education and Research* 35, no. 3 (2015): 368, https://doi.org/10.1177/0739456X15589815

3. Josh Akers, "Serial Evictor: Michael Kelly and Detroit Property Exchange," *Urban Praxis*, September 20, 2018, https://urbanpraxis.org/2018/09/20/serial-evictor -michael-kelly-and-detroit-property-exchange/.

4. Campbell Gibson and Kay Jung, "Historical Census Statistics on Population Totals by Race, 1790 to 1990, and by Hispanic Origin, 1970 to 1990, for Large Cities and Other Urban Places in the United States," U.S. Census Bureau (February 2005), accessed April 15, 2024, https://www.census.gov/content/dam/Census/library /working-papers/2005/demo/POP-twps0076.pdf.

5. Joel Kurth, "How to Cash In on a Crappy Home. Step One: Find a Sucker to Sign a Land Contract," *Bridge Michigan*, May 18, 2017, accessed April 15, 2024, https:// perma.cc/34K2-AU9T.

6. Joel Kurth, "Loose Regulations Make Land Contracts a Tool to Exploit Low-Income Homeowners," *Crain's Detroit Business*, June 24, 2017, accessed June 17, 2024, https://www.crainsdetroit.com/article/20170521/news/628861/loose -regulations-make-land-contracts-tool-exploit-low-income.

7. Joel Kurth, "How to Cash In on a Crappy Home. Step One: Find a Sucker to Sign a Land Contract," *Bridge Michigan*, May 18, 2017, accessed April 15, 2024, https:// perma.cc/34K2-AU9T.

8. Joshua Akers and Eric Seymour, "The Eviction Machine: Neighborhood Instability and Blight in Detroit's Neighborhoods," Poverty Solutions at the University of Michigan (2019), 14, accessed April 15, 2024, https://poverty.umich .edu/files/2019/07/Akers-et-al-Eviction-Machine-Revised-June-18.pdf.

9. Karen Ann Kling and Evelyn Zwiebach, "In Good Faith: Reimagining the Use of Land Contracts," Poverty Solutions, University of Michigan, May 2021, https://poverty .umich.edu/files/2021/05/PovertySolutions-Land-Contracts-PolicyBrief.pdf; Joel Kurth, "Land Contracts Trip Up Would-Be Homeowners," *Detroit News*, February 29, 2016, https://www.detroitnews.com/story/news/local/detroit-city/2016/02/29 /land-contracts-detroit-tax-foreclosure-joel-kurth/81081186/.

10. Property Sales in Detroit, Detroit Open Data; Eric Langowski, "Mortgage Analysis," https://app.box.com/s/epza6swhntnqzre10g12wmyyfpe14v6j (using Consumer Financial Protection Bureau Home Mortgage Disclosure Act data).

11. Zillow Home Values Index (Average for Inkster – $26,321; average for 48203 zip code in 2017 - $23,341).

12. Detroit, Mich., City Code §8-15-11(a) (1999).

13. "Blight Violations," City of Detroit Open Data Portal, accessed April 15, 2024, https://data.detroitmi.gov/datasets/blight-violations/explore?location=42 .349446%2C-83.117041%2C9.81.

14. "Citizen Guide," City of Detroit, Department of Administrative Hearings, accessed April 15, 2024, https://detroitmi.gov/Portals/0/docs/Brochures/DAH/DAH _Citizen_Guide.pdf.

15. "Blight Violations," City of Detroit Open Data Portal, accessed April 15, 2024, https://data.detroitmi.gov/datasets/blight-violations/explore?location=42.34944 6%2C-83.117041%2C9.81.

16. *Cloverleaf Car Col. v. Phillips Petroleum Co.*, 540 N.W.2d 297 (Mich. Ct. App. 1995).

17. Mich. Comp. Laws, §125.539 (2003) (Dangerous building defined); Mich. Comp. Laws, §333.2455 (1978) (Buildings violating health law according to public health code); Detroit, Mich., City Code, Chapters 8 & 16; Detroit, Mich., City Code §§ 9.1.1, et seq.

18. Detroit Land Bank Authority, "2024 Second Quarter Report," January 2024, accessed June 7, 2024, https://dlba-production-bucket.s3.us-east-2.amazonaws .com/City_Council_Quarterly_Report/01122024+DLBA+Q2+FY24+City+Council +Quarterly+Report+WEB.pdf.

19. William Sousa and George Kelling, "Of 'Broken Windows,' Criminology, and Criminal Justice," *Police Innovation: Contrasting Perspectives,* May 4, 2006, 77–97, https://doi.org/10.1017/CBO9780511489334.004; Wesley G. Skogan, "Broken Windows: Why—and How—We Should Take Them Seriously," *Criminology & Public Policy* 7, no. 2 (May 2008): 195–201, https://doi.org/10 .1111/j.1745-9133.2008.00501.x.

20. Kara Gavin, "Blight-Busting Demolitions Reduced Gun Injuries, Deaths in Detroit Neighborhoods," *Michigan News,* August 1, 2019, accessed July 5, 2024, https:// news.umich.edu/blight-busting-demolitions-reduced-gun-injuries-deaths-in -detroit-neighborhoods/; Jonathan Jay, Luke W. Miratrix, Charles C. Branas, Marc A. Zimmerman, and David Hemenway, "Urban Building Demolitions, Firearm Violence and Drug Crime," *Journal of Behavioral Medicine* 42, no. 4 (August 2019): 626–34. https://doi.org/10.1007/s10865-019-00031-6.

21. "Policy Brief: Detroit Blight Elimination Program Neighborhood Impact," *Detroit Demolition Impact Report,* 2015, accessed July 5, 2024, https://web.archive.org /web/20160410041052/http://www.demolitionimpact.org/#thereport [https://perma .cc/F8AP-VXUN].

22. Mich. Comp. Laws, §600.2940(1)–(3) (1961).

23. "Nuisance Abatement," Detroit Land Bank Authority, accessed April 10, 2024, https://buildingdetroit.org/nuisance-abatement.

24. Mich. Const. art. X, § 2.

25. Christine Ferretti, "Detroit Suits Seek $30 Million in Unpaid Property Taxes, *Detroit News,* September 2, 2017, https://www.detroitnews.com/story/news/local /detroit-city/2017/09/02/detroit-lawsuits-unpaid-property-taxes/105202920/.

26. *City of Detroit v. Murray, et al.*, 19-0002769-CH (Mich. Cir. Ct. July 13, 2021), *Motion for Summary Judgment/Disposition filed by Plaintiff City of Detroit,* p. 24.

27. *City of Detroit v. Murray, et al.*, 19-0002769-CH (Mich. Cir. Ct. July 13, 2021), *Motion for Summary Judgment/Disposition filed by Plaintiff City of Detroit,* p. 23.

28. *City of Detroit v. Murray, et al.*, 19-0002769-CH (Mich. Cir. Ct. July 13, 2021), *Motion for Summary Judgment/Disposition filed by Plaintiff City of Detroit*, p. 14.

29. *City of Detroit v. Murray, et al.*, 19-0002769-CH (Mich. Cir. Ct. July 13, 2021), *Motion for Summary Judgment/Disposition filed by Plaintiff City of Detroit*, p. 14.

30. *Florence Cement Co v. Vittraino*, 807 NW2d 917 (Mich. Ct. App. 2011).

31. *City of Detroit v. Murray, et al.*, 19-0002769-CH (Mich. Cir. Ct. July 13, 2021), *Motion for Summary Judgment/Disposition filed by Plaintiff City of Detroit*, Exh. N and R.

32. *City of Detroit v. Murray, et al.*, 19-0002769-CH (Mich. Cir. Ct. July 13, 2021), *Motion for Summary Judgment/Disposition filed by Plaintiff City of Detroit*, p. 27.

33. Allie Gross and Ross Jones, "A Detroit Landlord Is Being Sued for Failing to Maintain Homes. The City Forgave $1M in Unpaid Property Taxes," WXYZ Detroit, February 1, 2022, accessed July 6, 2024, https://www.wxyz.com/longform /a-detroit-landlord-is-being-sued-for-failing-to-maintain-homes-the-city -forgave-1m-in-unpaid-property-taxes.

34. Allie Gross and Ross Jones, "More than $2M of Debt Has Been Erased for Michael Kelly. Can the City Reign in the Property Owner?," WXYZ Detroit, December 5, 2019, https://www.wxyz.com/news/local-news/investigations/more-than-2m -of-debt-has-been-erased-for-a-detroit-landlord-can-the-city-reign-in-the -property-owner.

35. "FCA Deal with Michael Kelly from City of Detroit," WXYZ Detroit, November 7 2019, accessed June 10 2024, https://www.scribd.com/document /433884330/FCA-deal-with-Michael-Kelly-from-City-of-Detroit?doc_id =433884330&download=true&order=637196022.

15 – The Infamous Turnaround Plan

1. John Wisely, "Scandals derail 30-year political career for Wayne County's Ficano," *Lansing State Journal*, August 6, 2014, accessed July 13, 2024, https:// www.lansingstatejournal.com/story/news/politics/elections/2014/08/06/scandals -derail-30-year-political-career-for-wayne-countys-ficano/13663173/.

2. Wayne County Financial Review Team, "Report of the Wayne County Financial Review Team," State of Michigan, Department of Treasury Lansing, July 21, 2015, 5, https://www.michigan.gov/documents/treasury/Wayne_County_Review_Team _Report_494907_7.pdf.

3. Wayne County, "Report."

4. Consent Agreement between Wayne County and the State Treasurer, August 10, 2015, https://www.michigan.gov/-/media/Project/Websites/treasury/County/Wayne /Wayne_County_Consent_Agreement_2015.pdf?rev=a274ccbbe6.

5. Caitlin Devitt, "Wayne County Exec. Warns of State Takeover, Bankruptcy," *Bond Buyer*, February 9, 2015, https://www.bondbuyer.com/news/wayne-county -exec-warns-of-state-takeover-bankruptcy; Yvette Shields, "Wayne County Loses Last Investment-Grade Rating," *Bond Buyer*, February 17, 2015, https://www .bondbuyer.com/news/wayne-county-loses-last-investment-grade-rating.

6. State of Michigan Department of Treasury, "Final Report - Preliminary Review of Charter County of Wayne," June 30, 2015, https://www.michigan.gov/documents /treasury/Wayne_County_Final_Preliminary_Review_493194_7.pdf.

NOTES

7. Robert A. Ficano, "Charter County of Wayne Deficit Elimination Plan," February 11, 2014, http://media.mlive.com/news/detroit_impact/other/Deficit%20Elimination %20Plan.pdf.

8. Wayne County, "Budget Summary All Funds, FY 2007–2008," https://www .waynecounty.com/departments/mb/reports/fy-2007-2008.aspx; Wayne County, "Budget Summary All Funds, FY 2010–2011," https://www.waynecounty.com /departments/mb/reports/fy-2010-2011.aspx.

9. State of Michigan Department of Treasury, "Final Report - Preliminary Review of Charter County of Wayne," June 30, 2015, https://www.michigan.gov/documents /treasury/Wayne_County_Final_Preliminary_Review_493194_7.pdf.

10. State of Michigan Department of Treasury, "Final Report - Preliminary Review of Charter County of Wayne," June 30, 2015, https://www.michigan.gov/documents /treasury/Wayne_County_Final_Preliminary_Review_493194_7.pdf.

11. Ross Jones, Ann Mullen, and Adam Brewster, "Dumping Ground: The New Home of the Mentally Ill," *WXYZ 7 Action News Detroit*, September 16, 2014, updated April 19, 2017, https://www.wxyz.com/news/local-news/investigations /the-dumping-ground-how-jails-and-prisons-have-become-the-last-hope-for -michigans-mentally-ill.

12. Wayne County Financial Review Team, "Report of the Wayne County Financial Review Team," State of Michigan, Department of Treasury Lansing, July 21, 2015, 14, https://www.michigan.gov/documents/treasury/Wayne_County_Review_Team _Report_494907_7.pdf. ("Approximately $200.0 million in bonds were issued [authorization for the remaining $100.0 million lapsed] and roughly $150.0 million was expended.")

13. "Ficano Tries to Explain Wayne County Jail Debacle," *CBS News Detroit*, August 15, 2013, https://www.cbsnews.com/detroit/news/ficano-tries-to-explain-wayne -county-jail-debacle/.

14. Angie Jackson, "How Nonprofits Are Getting People Out of Metro Detroit Jails During Covid-19 Pandemic," *Detroit Free Press*, June 16, 2020; Nancy Fishman, Stephen Roberts, Alex Roth, Melvin Washington II, Andrew Taylor, and Amy Cross, "Wayne County Jail—Report and Recommendations" (Vera Institute, May 2020), https://www.vera.org/publications/wayne-county-jail-report-and -recommendations.

15. Jonathan Oosting, "How Michigan's Revenue Sharing 'Raid' Cost Communities Billions for Local Services," *Mlive*, March 30, 2014, https://www.mlive.com /lansing-news/2014/03/michigan_revenue_sharing_strug.html, [https://perma.cc /5S89-L2N2].

16. Michigan Senate Fiscal Agency, "Revenue Sharing Payments: Cities, Villages, Townships (CVTs), and Counties," July 20, 2018, http://www.senate.michigan.gov /sfa/Departments/DataCharts/DCrev_RevSharePayType.pdf (showing the total statutorily authorized payments per fiscal year from 2000 to 2017) [https://perma .cc/E8QQ-JRAR]; Jim Stansell, "Budget Briefing: State Revenue Sharing," House Fiscal Agency, March 2022, accessed July 5, 2024, https://www.house.mi.gov/hfa /PDF/Briefings/State_Tax_Revenue_Sharing_Budget_Briefing_fy22-23.pdf.

17. L. Owen Kirkpatrick and Nate Breznau, "The (Non)Politics of Emergency Political Intervention: The Racial Geography of Urban Crisis Management in Michigan," (SSRN) (March 24, 2016), https://doi.org/10.2139/ssrn.2754128.

18. Melissa Heil, "Debtor Spaces: Austerity, Space, and Dispossession in Michigan's Emergency Management System," *Environment and Planning: Economy and Space* 54, no. 5 (December 31, 2021): 974, https://doi.org/10.1177/0308518x211070302.

19. Eric Scorsone, "Frequently Asked Questions: The Suspension of the Emergency Manager Law and its Implications," (MSU Extension Center for Local Government Finance and Policy, Agricultural, Food, and Resource Economics), accessed January 10, 2024, https://www.canr.msu.edu/center_for_local_government_finance_and_policy/uploads/files/MSUE-PA4Suspension_FAQ-9-7-12.pdf; Local Government Fiscal Responsibility Act, 1990 Mich. Pub. Acts 72 (repealed 2012), Local Government Fiscal Responsibility Act, 1988 Mich. Pub. Acts 101 (repealed 1990); Mich. Comp. Laws § 141.1549(2) (2016).

20. Curt Guyette, "How the Capitol Exploded," *Detroit Metro Times*, December 12, 2012, accessed July 5, 2024, https://www.metrotimes.com/news/how-the-capitol-exploded-2147057.

21. Mich. Const. art 2, § 9 (1963).

22. Mich. Comp. Laws §§ 141.1552(1)(a)-(ff).

23. State of Michigan Department of Treasury, "Final Report - Preliminary Review of Charter County of Wayne," June 30, 2015, https://www.michigan.gov/documents/treasury/Wayne_County_Final_Preliminary_Review_493194_7.pdf.

24. Wayne County Executive, "Charter County of Wayne Deficit Elimination Plan," February 11, 2014, http://media.mlive.com/news/detroit_impact/other/Deficit%20Elimination%20Plan.pdf; Wayne County Ord.§118-3; Wayne County Ord.§118-2. (Although the document is entitled "Deficit Elimination Plan," it was widely referred to as the turnaround plan; "Definition. Deficit elimination plan means an internal county plan that sets forth measures that will correct or prevent projected expenditures from exceeding projected revenues for the current fiscal period, which may include, by way of illustration and not elimination; limiting or eliminating the use of overtime; canceling requisitions, contracts or other requests for payment; reduction in personnel or other expenditures.")

25. "What Is Tax Lien Investing?," *Forbes*, October 21, 2022, accessed July 13, 2024, https://www.forbes.com/sites/qai/2022/10/21/what-is-tax-lien-investing/.

26. Kevin T. Smith, "Foreclosure of Real Property Tax Liens Under Michigan's New Foreclosure Process," *Michigan Real Property Review* 4 (2002): 51–62.

27. Owners have until the first Tuesday in May of the year following the tax sale to redeem parcels from the preceding year's tax sale pursuant to Section 74 of the Act by payment of the judgment amount plus interest at 1.25 percent per month or a portion thereof.

28. "Redemption requires payment of the amounts set out above for redemption under Section 131c, plus an additional amount of 50 percent of the taxes for which the property was offered at the tax sale, and a 50 percent fee is deposited in the state delinquent property tax administration fund. The additional 50 percent penalty is not applicable if redemption occurs after the first Tuesday in November, but before the Department of Treasury's sending of the 131e hearing notice." Michigan Department of Treasury, *The Repealed Tax Sale & Tax Lien Process*, accessed October 3, 2024, 3, https://www.michigan.gov/treasury/-/media/Project/Websites/treasury/Property_2/Repealed_Tax_Sale_Process.pdf?rev=63c8344da63c409a8d011b0c3a50eade&hash=F295FE4B8DEADB1B6A4C8AF1DF8325CD.

29. Citizen's Research Council of Michigan, "Changes to the Property Tax Delinquency and Reversion Process in Michigan," CRC Memorandum No. 1052 (January 2000), https://crcmich.org/wp-content/uploads/memo1052.pdf.

30. Department of Justice, "Agent of Tax Lien Business Agrees to Plead Guilty to Rigging Bids at Maryland Tax Lien Auctions" (press release), June 3, 2008, accessed April 14,

NOTES

2024, https://www.justice.gov/archive/atr/public/press_releases/2008/233784.htm;
Department of Justice, "Three New Jersey Investors Plead Guilty to Bid Rigging at
Municipal Tax Lien Auctions," August 24, 2011, accessed March 25, 2024, https://
www.justice.gov/opa/pr/three-new-jersey-investors-plead-guilty-bid-rigging
-municipal-tax-lien-auctions; Department of Justice, "Pennsylvania Corporation
Pleads Guilty to Bid Rigging at Municipal Tax Lien Auctions in New Jersey,"
September 26, 2012, accessed April 15, 2024, https://www.justice.gov/opa/pr
/pennsylvania-corporation-pleads-guilty-bid-rigging-atmunicipal-tax-lien
-auctions-new-jersey.

31. Mich. Comp. Laws § 211.87b.
32. Oakland County, for instance, has not borrowed money to cover the gap. Oakland
    County, MI, "Oakland County Fiscal Scorecard," https://www.oakgov.com
    /community/dashboard/oakland-county-fiscal-scorecard (accessed November
    12, 2023). Go to "Cash Balances."
33. Detroit Code of Ordinances § 18-9-89 (2009).
34. Mich. Comp. Laws § 211.78g(3)(b) (2015).
35. Wayne County Government, "Wayne County Treasurer Adopted Budget FY
    2015-2016 and Projected Budget FY 2016-2017," accessed June 7, 2024, https://www
    .waynecounty.com/departments/mb/reports/fy-2015-2016.aspx (an increase of $170,375
    from the 2014–2015 budget).
36. Wayne County Government, "Wayne County Treasurer Adopted Budget FY
    2017-2018 and Projected Budget FY 2018-2019," accessed June 7, 2024, https://www
    .waynecounty.com/departments/mb/reports/budget.aspx.
37. "Wayne County Delinquent Tax Fund Graph," Loveland Technologies, June 11,
    2018, accessed June 8, 2024, https://perma.cc/S5VU-RPXD.
38. John Axe, "Delinquent Tax Revolving Fund in 2016 and Beyond," Michigan
    Association of County Treasurers, 2016 Summer Conference, Marquette, Michigan,
    August 7, 2016, 6, accessed June 10, 2024, https://perma.cc/MD9F-5GK2. ("[T]he
    county has no right, title or interest in the delinquent tax revolving fund and the
    county treasurer is only a collecting agent.")
39. "(2) If a delinquent tax revolving fund is established, the county treasurer shall
    be the agent for the county, on behalf of the taxing units in the county and this
    state, and, without further action by the county board of commissioners, may
    enter into contracts with other municipalities, this state, or private persons,
    firms, or corporations in connection with any transaction relating to the fund
    or any borrowing made by the county pursuant to section 87c or 87d, including
    all services necessary to complete this borrowing." Mich. Comp. Laws § 211.87b
    (2015).
40. "Charter County of Wayne Deficit Elimination Plan," Wayne County Department
    of Management and Budget, February 11, 2014, accessed April 15, 2024, http:
    //media.mlive.com/news/detroit_impact/other/Deficit%20Elimination%20Plan
    .pdf.
41. Mich. Comp. Laws§ 211.87b (2015). ("Money and other property held in the
    delinquent tax revolving fund shall be kept separate from and shall not be
    commingled with any other money in the custody of the county treasurer.")
42. Mich. Comp. Laws §211.87 (c)(2002), (3) If provided by separate resolution of the
    county board of commissioners for any year in which a county determines to
    borrow for the purposes provided in this section and subject to subsection (15),
    there shall be payable from the surplus in the fund an amount equal to 20% of

the following amount to the county treasurer for services as agent for the county and the remainder of the following amount to the county treasurer's office for delinquent tax administration expenses; Citation for legislative history: Mich. Comp. Laws. Ann § 211.87c (West 2016) (Historical and Statutory Notes).

43. "H.B. 5839, of 2012," Michigan Legislature, accessed April 15, 2024, https://legislature.mi.gov/Home/Document?objectName=2012-HNB-5839.

44. "Charter County of Wayne Deficit Elimination Plan," Wayne County Department of Management and Budget, February 11, 2014, accessed April 15, 2024, http://media.mlive.com/news/detroit_impact/other/Deficit%20Elimination%20Plan.pdf.

45. State of Michigan Department of Treasury, "Final Report - Preliminary Review of Charter County of Wayne," June 30, 2015, https://www.michigan.gov/documents/treasury/Wayne_County_Final_Preliminary_Review_493194_7.pdf.

46. "August 5, 2014 Primary Election Results," Charter County of Wayne, Michigan, accessed April 15, 2024, https://www.waynecounty.com/elected/clerk/august-5-2014-primary.aspx. Go to "Official Summary Primary Results."

47. "November 4, 2014 General Election Results," Charter County of Wayne, Michigan, accessed April 15, 2024, https://www.waynecounty.com/elected/clerk/november-4-2014-general.aspx. Go to "Official General Elections Results."

16 – Blood Money

1. "Dr Albert Buford Cleage Sr.," Find a Grave, accessed April 15, 2024, https://www.findagrave.com/memorial/71848655/albert-buford-cleage.

2. Angela D. Dillard, *Faith in the City: Preaching Radical Social Change in Detroit* (Ann Arbor: University of Michigan Press, 2007), 239.

3. Patrick Dunn, "Michigan's 'Black Eden': A short history of Idlewild," *Second Wave Michigan*, October 10, 2020, accessed April 15, 2024, https://www.secondwavemedia.com/features/Idlewild-mnrtf-series-14.aspx.

4. Eric Lipton, Christopher Drew, and Scott Shane, "Breakdowns Marked Path From Hurricane to Anarchy," *New York Times*, September 11, 2005.

5. Kris Hamel, "Detroit Sheriff Suspends Foreclosure Sales," *Workers World*, February 8, 2009, accessed April 15, 2024, https://www.workers.org/2009/us/detroit_sheriff_0212/.

6. Hamel, "Detroit Sheriff."

7. Hamel, "Detroit Sheriff"; Kelly Curran, "Michigan Sheriff Halts Foreclosure Sales," *HousingWire*, February 4, 2009, accessed April 15, 2024, https://www.housingwire.com/articles/michigan-sheriff-halts-foreclosure-sales/).

8. Curran, "Michigan Sheriff."

9. "Wayne County Executive Evans Asks State to Declare Financial Emergency," *ClickOnDetroit*, June 18, 2015, https://www.clickondetroit.com/news/2015/06/18/wayne-county-executive-evans-asks-state-to-declare-financial-emergency/; "Gov. Snyder Confirms Financial Emergency in Wayne County, Bankruptcy on the Horizon?" CBS News, July 30, 2015, accessed July 4, 2024, https://cbsnews.com/detroit/news/gov-snyder-confirms-financial-emergency-in-wayne-county-bankruptcy-on-the-horizon/.

10. "Consent Agreement," between Wayne County and the State Treasurer (final negotiated agreement as of Aug. 10, 2015), https://www.michigan.gov/documents/treasury/Wayne_County_Consent_Agreement_2015_498140_7.pdf.

11. "In addition to and separate from powers retained by the County Commission

and the County Executive under section l(b), the County Commission and the County Executive are hereby jointly granted the powers prescribed for emergency managers under section 12(1) of Act 436." Consent Agreement between Wayne County and the State Treasurer (final negotiated agreement as of August 10, 2015), https://www.michigan.gov/documents/treasury/Wayne_County_Consent _Agreement_2015_498140_7.pdf.

12. Eric D. Lawrence, "How Wayne County Navigated Its Financial Crisis," *Detroit Free Press*, October 20, 2016, https://www.freep.com/story/news/local/michigan /wayne/2016/10/20/wayne-county-ends-consent-agreement/92469844/ (updated October 21, 2016).

13. Consent Agreement between Wayne County and the State Treasurer (final negotiated agreement as of August 10, 2015), https://www.michigan.gov /documents/treasury/Wayne_County_Consent_Agreement_2015_498140_7.pdf.

14. The treasurer will still be able to transfer any current year net revenues from the revolving fund to the general fund, which has averaged $42 million annually from 2009 through 2013; Atuahene et al., "Predatory Cities," 167.

15. State of Michigan Department of Treasury, "Final Report - Preliminary Review of Charter County of Wayne," June 30, 2015, https://www.michigan.gov/documents /treasury/Wayne_County_Final_Preliminary_Review_493194_7.pdf.

16. "Wayne County Exit Letter," State of Michigan Department of Treasury, October 18, 2016, accessed March 26, 2024, https://www.michigan.gov/documents /treasury/Wayne_County_Exit_Letter_550365_7.pdf. ("Specifically, I find that the county has satisfied the Consent Agreement terms found in Subsections ll(a)(1)-(3) of the Agreement. As a result of this determination, the County has successfully completed and is hereby released from its Consent Agreement.")

17. Atuahene et al., "Taxed Out," 847.

18. "QuickFacts Detroit City, Michigan," U.S. Census Bureau, accessed June 8, 2024, https://www.census.gov/quickfacts/fact/table/detroitcitymichigan/IPE120222; "American Community Survey 2022 1-Year Estimates," U.S. Census Bureau, 2022, accessed June 9, 2024, https://data.census.gov/table/ACSST1Y2022.S1701?q =poverty%20in%20Detroit.

19. *Rafaeli, LLC v. Oakland County*, 952 N.W.2d 434 (Mich. Ct. App. 2020).

20. About 75% of the County's profit on delinquent taxes comes from people PAYING their 18% interest/penalties/fees, not auction sales. Alex Alsup, "The Profit Motive Will Remain," Medium, July 19, 2020, accessed April 15, 2024, https://medium .com/@detroit/the-profit-motive-will-remain-62376269afdd.

21. Alexa Eisenberg, Roshanak Mehdipanah, and Margaret Dewar, "'It's Like They Make It Difficult for You on Purpose': Barriers to Property Tax Relief and Foreclosure Prevention in Detroit, Michigan," *Housing Studies* 35, no. 8 (2020): 1415–41, https://doi.org/10.1080/02673037.2019.1667961.

22. Loveland Technologies FOIA; Sarah Cwiek, "What Is the Delinquent Tax Revolving Fund, and How Does It Work?," *Michigan Public Radio*, January 20, 2020, https://www.michiganpublic.org/economy/2020-01-20/what-is-the-delinquent -tax-revolving-fund-and-how-does-it-work; Beth LeBlanc, "High court: Michigan counties cannot make profit on tax-foreclosed homes," *Detroit News*, July 17, 2020, accessed July 5, 2024, https://www.detroitnews.com/story/news/local/michigan /2020/07/17/court-michigan-counties-cannot-make-profit-tax-foreclosed-homes /5460232002/; Jennifer Dixon, "Wayne County exec blasts county treasurer over real estate dealings," *Detroit Free Press*, March 11, 2019, accessed July 5, 2024,

https://www.freep.com/story/news/local/2019/03/14 /warren-evans-eric-sabree-wayne
-county/3143324002/.

23. "Buffalo Soldiers," National Museum of African American History and Culture,
accessed April 15, 2024, https://nmaahc.si.edu/explore/stories/buffalo-soldiers.

Conclusion: In Search of Justice

1. "Case: Morningside v. Sabree," Legal Defense Fund, 2016, accessed July 10, 2024,
https://www.naacpldf.org/case-issue/morningside-v-sabree/.

2. *Morningside Community Organization v. Wayne County Treasurer,* No. 336430,
2017 WL 4182985, at 2 (Mich. Ct. App. 2017).

3. *Morningside Community Organization v. Wayne County Treasurer,* No. 336430,
2017 WL 4182985, at 4 (Mich. Ct. App. 2017).

4. Atuahene, "'Our Taxes Are Too Damn High,'" 1513.

5. 28 U.S.C. § 1341 (2012).

6. Christopher Berry, "Reassessing the Property Tax," University of Chicago Harris
School of Public Policy, unpublished draft, March 2021, accessed April 15, 2024,
https://drive.google.com/file/d/1ZKp1fA0_3LzwkEq8jcoJ5bl Alnyo0mot/view; "An
Analysis of Property Tax Assessments in Detroit," Center for Municipal Finance,
University of Chicago Harris School of Public Policy, and Mansueto Institute for
Urban Innovation, University of Chicago, March 20, 2024, https://bpb-us-w2
.wpmucdn.com/voices.uchicago.edu/dist/1/1010/files/2024/03/Detroit-Sales
-Ratio-Study-03-20-2024-34400db655df648a.pdf.

7. "Bulletin 22 of 2023: MCL 211.7u Poverty Exemption," State of Michigan
Department of Treasury, December 19, 2023, accessed July 10, 2024, https://www
.michigan.gov/treasury/-/media/Project/Websites/treasury/STC/Bulletins/2023
/Bulletin-22-of-2023---Poverty-Exemption.pdf.

8. Stipulation and Order of Settlement and Dismissal, *Morningside Community
Organization v. Wayne County Treasurer,* No. 16-008807-CH, 10, https://
clearinghouse.net/doc/111351/.

9. "Governor Whitmer Signs 'Pay As You Stay' Legislation to Help Michiganders Stay
in Their Homes," State of Michigan Office of the Governor, March 3, 2020, accessed
July 5, 2024, https://www.michigan.gov/whitmer/news/press-releases/2020/03/03
/governor-whitmer-signs-pay-as-you-stay-legislation-to-help-michiganders-stay
-in-their-homes.

10. Eric Sabree, "Pay As You Stay (PAYS) information," Charter County of Wayne
Michigan, https://www.waynecounty.com/elected/treasurer/pay-as-you-stay-pays
-information.aspx (accessed March 26, 2024); "Gilbert Family Foundation,
Rocket Community Fund Announce $500 Million Philanthropic Investment in
Detroit, First Allocation Will Pay Off Property Tax Debt of 20,000 Low-Income
Detroit Homeowners," Rocket Companies, March 25, 2021, accessed July 5, 2024,
https://www.rocketcompanies.com/press-release/gilbert-family-foundation
-rocket-community-fund-announce-500-million-philanthropic-investm
ent-in-detroit-first-allocation-will-pay-off-property-tax-debt-of-20000-low
-income-detroit-homeowners/.

11. "36th District Court Announces Extension of Eviction Moratorium," 36th District
Court, July 16, 2020, https://www.36thdistrictcourt.org/about-us/announcements
/2020/07/16/36th-district-court-announces-extension-of-eviction-moratorium
(https://perma.cc/4LR9-QMZ2); "Wayne County Tax Foreclosures Postponed
Another Year for Occupied Properties—But Taxes Are Still Due," WDET 101.9

FM, May 11, 2021, https://wdet.org/2021/05/11/wayne-county-tax-foreclosures-postponed-another-year-for-occupied-properties-but-taxes-are-still-due/.

12. U.S. Department of Housing and Urban Development (HUD), Office of Policy Development and Research (PD&R), HUD User, "FY 2023 Homeowner Assistance Fund Income Limits Summary," accessed April 15, 2024, https://www.huduser.gov/portal/datasets/il/il2023/2023sum_haf.odn?inputname=METRO19820M19820*Detroit-Warren-Livonia%2C+MI+HUD+Metro+FMR+Area&area_choice=hmfa&year=2023.

About This Project

1. "Squatters of the Lower East Side," 99% Invisible, May 30, 2017, https://99percentinvisible.org/episode/squatters-lower-east-side/.

2. "USPS Reports Decreased Vacancy Rates in Detroit," Drawing Detroit, April 20, 2021, accessed July 5, 2024. http://www.drawingdetroit.com/tag/detroit-vacancy/.

3. Joel Kurth, "Detroit neighborhood plea: 'We want squatters,'" Detroit News, September 17, 2015, accessed July 14, 2024, https://www.detroitnews.com/story/news/local/detroit-city/2015/09/17/detroit-neighborhood-plea-want-squatters/32558019/.

4. Atuahene et al., "Stategraft"; Atuahene, "Predatory Cities," 107–82.

5. Atuahene et al., "Stategraft."

6. Atuahene, "'Our Taxes Are Too Damn High,'" 1548.

7. Bernadette Atuahene et al., "Taxed Out: Illegal Property Tax Assessments and the Epidemic of Tax Foreclosures in Detroit."

8. Evelyn B. Higginbotham, Righteous Discontent: The Women's Movement in the Black Baptist Church, 1880–1920 (Cambridge, Massachusetts: Harvard University Press, 1994); Boris Heersink and Jeffery A. Jenkins, Republican Party Politics and the American South, 1865–1968 (Cambridge, United Kingdom: Cambridge University Press, 2020).

9. Atuahene, "Predatory Cities."

INDEX

ABOUT THE AUTHOR

Harvard and Yale trained law professor **Bernadette Atuahene** is the Duggan Professor of Law at the University of Southern California Gould School of Law. She is a property law scholar who focuses on land stolen from people in the African diaspora. She has served as a judicial clerk at the Constitutional Court of South Africa, practiced at Cleary Gottlieb, a global law firm, and worked as a consultant for the South African Land Claims Commission. She is the author of *We Want What's Ours: Learning from South Africa's Land Restitution Program*. Atuahene has published extensively in academic journals such as *NYU Law Review* and the *California Law Review*, winning the Law & Society Association's John Hope Franklin Prize for best article on race in 2020 and another prize for the best all-around article in 2024. Her work has appeared in the *New York Times,* the *LA Times,* NPR's *Democracy Now!*, and the *Washington Post,* among others.